PRAISE FOR
BILL MADDEN AND *PRIDE OF OCTOBER*

"A standout....Madden asks the simple question in the title and gets some wonderful answers, which he reports with grace and wit....This one's a keeper."

— *Booklist* (starred review)

"Captivating...truly remarkable....Madden shows the reader the former Yankees not just as ballplayers but as individuals with real human emotions."

— *Abilene Reporter*

"An absorbing story....Yankee fans will enjoy the perspective of what it was like to be young and a Yankee in a number of different eras."

— *Publishers Weekly*

"A nostalgic piece...a New York Yankees version of Lawrence Ritter's classic *The Glory of Their Times.*"

— *Tampa Tribune*

"Delivers superbly....Madden tells stories not written before, and there's a freshness to them....This book is pure Yankee....Get it and enjoy all the tales."

— *New York Daily News*

"Captures the Yankee ethos beautifully."

— *Weekly Standard*

"Intimately portrays the human sides of these seventeen former Yanks."

— *Palm Springs Desert Sun* (CA)

more...

"A rhapsody to a nation's summer game....This is a special book. One you will pick up again and again."

"A volume any baseball fan will treasure."

"A broad-brushed canvas of stories and perceptions about what it's like to be young and playing ball for the greatest franchise in sports history....One of [Madden's] best efforts ever."

"Madden has been in the dugouts. He's had his shoes spit on. He has worked in the rain, wind, and brutal heat. He has a sense of the history of the game, the link from past to present. He has now put his skill, his appreciation, and his astute sense of observation together in this gem of a book....A real classic."

PRIDE OF OCTOBER

What It Was to Be
Young and a Yankee

BILL MADDEN

WARNER BOOKS

NEW YORK   BOSTON

The photograph on page 105 appears courtesy of the San Diego Padres; those on pages 197, 269, 285, 343 and 407 are courtesy of the New York Yankees. The photographs on pages 1, 21, 41, 61, 89, 123, 143, 163, 217, 241, 313 and 373 are from the author's collection.

Warner Books

Time Warner Book Group
1271 Avenue of the Americas, New York, NY 10020
Visit our Web site at www.twbookmark.com.

Printed in the United States of America

Originally published in hardcover by Warner Books

First Trade Printing: April 2004

10 9 8 7 6 5 4 3 2 1

The Library of Congress has cataloged the hardcover edition as follows:

Madden, Bill.
    Pride of October : what it was to be young and a Yankee / Bill Madden.
        p. cm.
    Includes index.
    ISBN 0-446-52932-X
      1. New York Yankees (Baseball Team) – History. 2. New York Yankees (Baseball team) – Biography. I. Title

    GV875.N4 M335 2003
    796.357'64'097471 – dc21   2002191063

ISBN: O-446-69269-7 (pbk.)

Cover design by Andrew Newman Design
Cover photo courtesy of New York Yankees, Inc.
Book design and text composition by Mada Design, Inc.

This book is dedicated to the memory of Charles J. Madden, who weaned me on sports writing and newspapers; and took me to my first major league baseball game—Yankees-Indians, June 27, 1953, Lopat vs. Garcia—and my first World Series game, October 8, 1956.

It is also dedicated to the memory of George McLaughlin, an uncle who was like a second father and who taught me an appreciation for the lore and history of baseball.

Acknowledgments

The author gratefully acknowledges the following people whose considerable contributions (or, in some cases, just plain friendship and support) helped make this book possible:

Moss Klein, valued friend, and collaborator on a previous Yankees/baseball project for Warner, who served as first proofreader and fact-checker.

The Baseball Hall of Fame, particularly Vice President of Communications Jeff Idelson, for fulfilling a myriad of requests, and Bill Francis, in the Hall of Fame library, who researched countless items of information and provided a mountain of newspaper clippings that served as a supplement to all the information contained in this book.

The New York Yankees. In particular, Rick Cerrone, Director of Media Relations and Publicity, for his cooperation and support through the entire process of this project; Mark Mandrake, Director of Publications and Multimedia, and Managing Editor Glenn Slavin, for their assistance in procuring so many of the vital pictures in this book. Also: Vice President of Marketing Deborah Tymon, who assisted in the location of many of the former players interviewed for this book; Senior Advisor Arthur Richman, and media relations assistants Jason Zillo, Joa Martin and Joe Rocchio, for their assistance in procuring newspaper material, other photographs and statistical and team history information from the Yankee archives.

Marty Appel, a pal for a lifetime and Yankee historian, who was always available at all hours of the day and night to provide vital information, insight and counsel.

Art Berke, Vice President of Communications at *Sports Illustrated*, a dear friend and longtime colleague who provided the full resources of his magazine in the compilation of research material.

Frank Dolson, longtime friend and writing colleague, who assisted in the editing and fact-checking.

The Elias Sports Bureau: In particular Seymour Siwoff, Steve Hirdt,

Tom Hirdt, John Labombarda, Chris Thorne, Bob Waterman, Bob Rosen, Sal D'Agostino, Santo Labombarda, Ken Hirdt, Matt Martingale and Todd Betcag, all of whom assisted and provided statistical data essential to this project.

Russ Benedict, Yankee loyalist and early mentor, who provided insight and historical perspective.

Dave Kaplan, director of the Yogi Berra Museum, for his assistance in providing research materials and the museum's other resources for the chapter on Mr. Berra.

Robert Creamer, whose book *Stengel* was a source for materials on Casey Stengel.

Christopher Longinetti, an "adopted son" who assisted in the research of the San Francisco sandlot ballparks.

Barry Halper, collector extraordinaire, who furnished letters and other historical data used in this book.

Scotty Browne, Jimmy Converso, Alan Delaqueriere, Pete Edelman, Ellen Locker, Shirley Wong and Faigi Rosenthal from the *New York Daily News* library, who helped in the research of many of the newspaper accounts used for verification of stories and anecdotes in this book.

Hal Bock and Ronald Blum of the Associated Press, who researched the Jackie Robinson debut coverage.

Fred Chase, one helluva copyeditor and fact-checker.

The late Tom Meany, who once befriended and encouraged an aspiring (very) young sportswriter, and whose '50s historical Yankee profile books, *The Magnificent Yankees* and *The Yankee Story*, served as an early inspiration for this book.

Jack Lang for historical perspective contributions.

The late Dick Young and Milton Richman, Hall of Fame baseball writers and mentors.

Phil Pepe, who thankfully adhered to Dick Young's No. 1 Baseball Writers Commandment: "Always take care of your beat man."

Bob Raissman and Mark Kriegel, comrades-in-arms who supported.

Elaine Kaufman, believer and counselor of writers who touted and promoted from her bully pulpit.

Dom Amore, student of the game, who provided anecdotes over dinner.

Thanks to my compadre Neil Leifer, the official "in-house photographer" for all Madden Book projects, for lending his time and considerable skill in shooting the Monument Park author photo.

Dan Ambrosio, a lifelong Phillies fan who somehow managed to put all that misery aside to contribute mightily to the editing and production process of this book.

Rick Wolff, great editor and baseball man who "got" this book right away and with his faith, enthusiasm and acumen, made it happen.

Rob Wilson, friend for life, agent, editor and believer who saw to it this book made it into the right hands.

Steven and Thomas Madden, the author's support system.

And lastly, Lil, the pride of all my months and seasons.

contents

Prologue

"Today, I consider myself the luckiest man on the face of the earth."
—Lou Gehrig, 1939

"I'd like to thank the Good Lord for making me a Yankee."
—Joe DiMaggio, 1949

"It's great to be young and a Yankee."

—Waite Hoyt, 1927

On a chilly, sun-splashed mid-December afternoon in 2001, almost exactly 100 years from the day American League President Ban Johnson finalized plans to transfer his Baltimore Orioles franchise to New York City, Jason Giambi strode to the microphone at the center of the podium in the Great Moments Room of Yankee Stadium and held aloft the size 50, No. 25 New York Yankees jersey he had just contracted to wear for the next seven seasons. Looking down the dais at his father, John, Giambi was suddenly overcome with emotion and, in a barely audible, choking voice said: "Look, Pop . . . pinstripes."

Although he had grown up in Southern California, John Giambi had been a lifelong Yankee fan and, in particular, a devotee of Mickey Mantle. "During the '50s, the only major league baseball we got was the Saturday afternoon Game of the Week on TV," the elder Giambi explained, "and the Yankees, to us, truly were America's team, playing in the World Series just about every year and playing regularly on that Saturday game. I can remember running to the newspaper stand every day and reading about Mickey and the Yankees. If you liked baseball, that's how you grew up then, watching and reading about the Yankees."

After the press conference concluded, the Giambi family—John, Jason, his mother, Jeanne, and his fiancée Kristian Rice—were escorted down the corridor to the Yankee clubhouse. "This is where Mickey walked," said Jeanne Giambi, and now it was her husband whose eyes began welling up. I later said to him: "From everything you've said, it would seem this is even more of a 'dream come true' day for you than it is for Jason."

"You'll never know how many times I thought about what it must be like to play for the Yankees," John Giambi replied.

I did not tell him I had already begun a journey around the country, seeking out former Yankees from all different eras and, in particular, asking that very question of them. This was the premise of the book I had wanted to write about the Yankees on the occasion of their 100th anniversary. It was given birth by a conversation I'd had at the 1997 World Series between the Florida Marlins and Cleveland Indians, with Charlie Silvera, a seldom-used backup catcher for the Yankees from 1949 to 1956. We were sitting at a poolside table at the World Series gala in Miami and Silvera, who was a scout for the Marlins at the time, was lamenting how much change had come over baseball in the last 40 years with the advent of expansion and free agency.

"Don't get me wrong," Silvera said. "I'm grateful to the Marlins for keeping me in the game and bringing me to this World Series when they didn't have to. But I have a hard time believing there's actually a major league team here in South Florida, playing in the World Series no less. I guess it all goes back to when I was playing. There was a saying then: 'Some guys make the big leagues, and some guys make the Yankees,' and I believe there really was something to that. I know *I'll* always be a Yankee and I suspect anyone you talk to will tell you the same thing."

Love them or hate them—and the legions of baseball fans in both camps are probably about equal in number—no other professional sports franchise has come close to approaching the success of the New York Yankees, winners of 26 World Series and 38 American League championships in the 99 years following their birth as the transplanted Baltimore Orioles in 1903. As George Steinbrenner put it when he bought the Yankees from CBS in 1973 (a time when they were just emerging from one of their lowest ebbs): "I feel like I've bought the *Mona Lisa* of sports franchises." By contrast, some 20 years earlier it was the famous stand-up comic Joe E. Lewis who had said: "Rooting for the Yankees is like rooting for U.S. Steel."

In any case, the Yankees, with their unparalleled success and accompanying gallery of legends, have become a proud and distinct part of Americana. It is then perhaps no surprise that they conceived the annual Old-Timers' Day event in which they invited back so many of their star players of the past (at no small expense to the team) for what amounted to little more than a five- to 10-second curtain call. Yet, as I watched these rituals through the years, the parade of legends being introduced in order of importance from the mere fan favorites, Billy Martin, Hank Bauer, Tommy Henrich, Elston Howard, Moose Skowron, Joe Pepitone, Allie Reynolds, Vic Raschi, Bobby Murcer et al., to the legitimately great Yankees, Whitey Ford, Phil Rizzuto, Yogi Berra, and finally to the supreme baseball deities, Mickey Mantle and Joe DiMaggio, my attention was always directed to the visiting team players standing on the top step of the dugout, watching in silence as the applause from 55,000 fans built to a crescendo. "What must they think of this?" I said to myself. "How could they not be at least *somewhat* awestruck?"

Some guys make the big leagues and some guys make the Yankees.

So after my conversation with Silvera, I determined to explore this proposition. I drew up a list of 18 significant Yankees from all different eras with the idea of having them recount the history of this storied franchise as they saw and helped create it. But more than that, I wanted to know what it meant to them to have been a Yankee and whether they had felt, as Silvera did, they had been part of baseball royalty.

First and foremost, I wanted to talk to Frank Crosetti, who, at 90, was one of the oldest living Yankees and most certainly the one who could provide the most detailed history of their golden era. Crosetti, who lived in Stockton, California, had the distinction of having cashed more World Series checks than any other person in baseball history, as a player for the Yankees from 1932 (the end of Babe Ruth's Yankee time) to 1947, and then as third base coach for all the Casey Stengel– and Ralph Houk–managed championship teams, through 1968. "The Cro," as he was affectionately called, had indeed seen it all, but rarely deemed to talk about it. I knew him casually from seeing him as a visitor to the Yankee clubhouse when the team came into Oakland to play the Athletics over the years. Unfortunately, when I contacted him about sharing his memories of what it was like to be a Yankee and part of all those storied teams of Ruth, Gehrig, Dickey, DiMaggio, Mantle and Berra, he put me off.

"Ahhh, I can't tell you anything about those guys," he said. Later, however, he revealed to me he was hoping to write a book of his own. I wished him good luck and proceeded to move on in my interview process, beginning with the two most prominent "locals"—Berra and Rizzuto—with whom I'd developed a warm relationship, traveling with them through the years in my capacity as a reporter and columnist covering the Yankees for the *New York Daily News*. Both of them lived in New Jersey and were established Yankee legends. Yet, despite having forged Hall of Fame careers, they'd both had their hearts broken by the Yankees, too (in Berra's case twice), and I especially wanted to talk to them about that.

As the months went by and I began traveling around the country— to the Carolinas for Bobby Richardson and Tommy Byrne; to Indiana, where Don Mattingly had gone into self-imposed retreat after his final October disappointment in 1995; to San Francisco to revisit with Silvera and see firsthand those sandlots that had spawned so many talented Yankee players over the first 50 years of this century (DiMaggio, Tony Lazzeri et al.)—I would periodically receive letters from Crosetti inquiring about my progress on the book. At one point, he even provided me with some suggestions as to old-time Yankee players I needed to talk to and what questions I should ask them.

"You really need to see Tommy Henrich up in Prescott, Arizona," Crosetti wrote in August of 2001, "and when you do, ask him about the song 'Too Much Mustard.' This happened at the Book Cadillac Hotel in Detroit." He didn't elaborate, but knowing the customarily effusive Henrich as I did, I figured he'd be able to supply the rest of the story in all its color and detail.

I had intended to visit with Henrich while I was at the 2001 World

Series in Arizona between the Yankees and the Diamondbacks, but was disheartened to learn he had taken ill and been moved to San Francisco by his daughter, who had put out the word that he was temporarily unable to do interviews. I wrote back to Crosetti, informing him of Henrich's deteriorated state of health and got a reply a week later that seemed to have a tone of urgency to it.

"I may not have enough for a book now," Crosetti said, "and I've been thinking of forgetting it. But I've written a lot of stuff down and I'm sure you could get plenty for your chapter on me. You're welcome to have it. Maybe my grandkids can read what I have written someday. Stay healthy, Cro."

I was naturally encouraged by Crosetti's change of heart, but I still wanted to sit down with him in person and listen to his stories. So instead of telling him to go ahead and send me what he'd written, I made a mental note to call him after the New Year and hopefully arrange a visit to Stockton before the start of spring training. By this time, I was getting nearly a letter a month from him in which he would comment on the most recent developments in baseball or offer a thumbnail critique of the latest baseball book he'd read. I wrote him a letter around Christmas, wishing him well for the holidays while offhandedly mentioning that I'd be giving him a call before heading off to spring training. When, by early February, I hadn't heard back from him, I began to be concerned. Then, one afternoon I got a phone call from Rizzuto, who said he'd just gotten word that Crosetti had taken a fall and was in the hospital in critical condition. "I know you've been wanting to get together with him," Rizzuto said. "That's why I'm calling. I don't think it's good."

The next day word came from Stockton that Crosetti had passed away at age 91.

A few weeks later, at spring training in Florida, I finished up the interviews for the book, visiting with octogenarians Ralph Houk at his home in Winter Haven and Marius Russo in Fort Myers, in between sessions with Reggie Jackson and Bobby Murcer at the Yankee camp in

Tampa. Russo, who had inadvertently proved elusive in efforts to locate him, was vital to the book in that he was one of the last remaining links to Gehrig. Meanwhile, I was pleasantly surprised to see how much Houk had mellowed since retiring from the baseball wars and I even detected a trace of remorse (however small) regarding the volcanic and sometimes physical abuse of sportswriters for which he had become notorious.

Murcer, I confirmed, still bears the scars of his unceremonious exile from the Yankees in 1974, but harbors no bitterness at all for the unfair and unrealistic comparisons to Mantle that dogged him throughout his career. Rather—and remarkably—he actually feels honored by them.

In the case of Jackson—who has proclaimed with pride through the years at being "a student of the game" while simultaneously expressing his uncompromising views of race relations in baseball—I was especially curious as to how he viewed himself in the overall context of (mostly white) Yankee history. Humility is not a word generally associated with him, but I nevertheless came away from our time together with a distinct sense of that quality as he began his passage into middle age, comfortable with all he'd achieved.

Upon returning to New York for the final editing process, my thoughts returned to Crosetti. He, after all, had been the link to practically all of them, most notably Ruth. If nothing else, I wished I had taken him up on his offer to send me his writings. Throughout our correspondence, I had tried to convince him how important he was to this project, and in the end he had finally relented. I remembered what he'd said in his last letter about wanting his grandkids to see what he'd written. Through Silvera, I was put in touch with Crosetti's grandson, Jim McCoy.

"I'll see if I can find the stuff," McCoy told me. "Then, after that, it'll be up to my grandmother [Crosetti's widow, Norma] as to whether you can use any of it. But I'll talk to her."

A couple of weeks went by and then, just after the last chapters had been submitted to the publisher, a package arrived in the mail from McCoy. The "Crosetti papers" were a bit disjointed (and, I suspected, a good deal purified), but amid all the banality Cro did manage to dispel one of baseball's longest-enduring myths: Ruth's "called shot" homer against the Chicago Cubs in the 1932 World Series:

"I have been asked this nine million times, if Babe pointed to center field when he hit that home run off Charlie Root. When Mark Koenig was playing shortstop for the Yankees in the '20s, he'd become a good friend of Babe's. The Cubs had bought Mark from the San Francisco Mission Reds of the Pacific Coast League in August of '32 and he helped them win a few games down the stretch with his timely hitting. But the Cubs voted him only a half-share of the World Series money and Babe, outspoken as he was, called them all tightwads—along with a few other choice words. All these remarks got written up in the papers and when Babe came to bat, the Cubs players were all razzing him. Root got two quick strikes on him and now the Cubs players were on the top step of the dugout really giving it to him.

"Babe nonchalantly stepped out of the batter's box. He did not point his finger to center field. Looking at the Chicago dugout, with his bat resting on his shoulder and being held by his left hand, he raised his right arm and shook his index finger in front of his face, meaning he had one more strike. On the next pitch he hit a home run. This shut the Cubs players up. The next day I'm sitting next to him in the dugout and he said: 'If the writers all want to say I pointed to center field, let 'em. I don't care.' That's the story, right from the horse's mouth."

If only we'd have had that sit-down in Stockton for so many more stories. My solace is the letters and our "pen pal" relationship in his final year. There is no chapter on the Cro here, but his grandkids should know he was one very significant Yankee.

Bill Madden, October 1, 2002

PRIDE OF
OCTOBER

A HUCKLEBERRY FRIEND AND THE LOSS OF INNOCENCE

PHIL RIZZUTO

It is no great mystery how the town of Hillside—which Phil Rizzuto has called home since 1942—got its name. Situated in the rolling hills of central New Jersey, many of its residents can actually see the New York skyline on a clear day. Rizzuto, for one, felt a certain pride, not to mention security, on the occasions he'd gaze out his attic window and view the tops of the World Trade Center twin towers off on the distant horizon.

"I can't bear to look out there anymore," he was saying on this day. "They're gone and I feel as empty as my view."

We were drinking coffee in his kitchen on a sunny, crisp early October afternoon, the foliage of the huge trees surrounding his house in full color. Rizzuto's wife, Cora, had also left some cookies on the counter and as we talked, the silver-haired "Scooter," who had celebrated his 84th birthday a few days earlier, would occasionally get up and help himself to one. He was always the smallest guy in the room or on the field, but now, his spine hunched as he walked, he looked even smaller.

"Straighten up!" Cora admonished him, gently slapping his back.

"Ohhhh, she keeps on me," Rizzuto said, obligingly straightening up. "Where were we? Oh, yeah, the attack. I just felt so helpless, so empty after it happened. We were supposed to go on a cruise up to Canada for my birthday, but we canceled out. No way either of us wanted to go anywhere. Then my daughter, Penny, who works for the Albany County crisis intervention team, called me. She had just spent two days down on Pier 94 counseling all the victims' families. 'You've got to go down there, Dad,' she said, and after talking it over for a couple a minutes, Cora and I decided to go. We didn't know what we were supposed to do when we got there, but the families were so happy to see us, it was unbelievable. We wound up spending four and a half hours there. As always, Cora knew right away what to say. I just told my Yankee stories and they seemed so happy to have someone take their minds off their grief and the awful business of waiting for a death certificate or a body part.

"It was rewarding, but so heartbreaking at the same time. I don't think I'll ever get out of my mind the image of all those teddy bears, lining the walls the whole length of the pier. They'd been sent by schoolkids in Oklahoma City, with individual notes on every one of them . . ."

As his voice trailed off upon recalling it, his eyes began to well up and he removed his glasses to wipe them. As with anyone in the New York metropolitan area, the closeness of the tragedy had made it even more overwhelming. He was sure, he said, a day would not go by for the rest of his life when he wouldn't, at some point, feel a flood of emotion over the enduring memory of September 11 and its aftermath.

"Maybe we should get to some Yankee stories now."

"Yeah, good idea," he said. "Where should we start?"

"Why not the beginning? Brooklyn."

According to the baseball encyclopedias, he was born in Brooklyn,

September 25, 1917, except that's not entirely true. He was actually born there a year earlier, but upon filling out the questionnaire the Yankees gave him at his signing with them, he made it 1917.

"The other guys all told me: 'Make yourself a year younger. It'll get you an extra year at the end of your career.' Everybody did it, although, come to think of it, it didn't do me any good in 1956 when the Yankees released me. As far as they were concerned, it didn't matter how old I was. They needed a space on the roster and I was it."

His father was a motorman on the trolley that ran through Brooklyn and Queens. Rizzuto would ride with him every morning, the last stop being 114th Street, which was a 20-minute walk from Richmond Hill High School in Queens where, in spite of his diminutive stature, he developed into a baseball player of citywide renown. This, despite the fact his coach at P.S. 68 in Ridgewood had scoffed at his size and dispatched him to left field, dismissing him as "a cricket—best suited for covering the outfield."

Fortunately, the coach at Richmond Hill, Al Kunitz, had a little more foresight about Rizzuto's size and ability.

"You'll never be an outfielder, kid," Kunitz said. "You're too small. But with a pair of hands and an arm like you've got, what a shortstop you'll be! Rabbit Maranville was a midget, but he got by for 20 years in the big leagues."

That said, Kunitz switched Rizzuto to shortstop and began teaching him the intangibles of the game that would help him more than compensate for his lack of size.

"Kunitz had tried out for the minor leagues as a catcher," Rizzuto said, "and he taught me all the pitfalls of the tryout camps—which served me well after I got rejected by both the Dodgers and Giants."

In each case, Rizzuto got introduced—quite rudely, you could say—to one of the game's legends. Actually, Casey Stengel hadn't come close to attaining his legendary status when, as manager of the second-division Dodgers in 1935, he took one look at the pint-sized Rizzuto standing on line for a tryout at Ebbets Field and huffed: "Go get a shoebox."

"I never let Casey forget that when I wound up playing for him with the Yankees," Rizzuto said. "But Bill Terry was just as bad with the Giants. He wouldn't even let me play when I went to their tryout camp at the Polo Grounds. He looked at me and said: 'You can watch, kid, but you're too small to play.'"

Perhaps most importantly, though, Kunitz taught Rizzuto how to bunt—which became his staple in his 13-year Yankee career. Indeed, for all his accomplishments as a Hall of Fame shortstop—a five-time All-Star, American League MVP in 1950, a pair of fielding titles (to which the Yankees' stalwart right-hander Vic Raschi once remarked: "My best pitch is anything the batter grounds, lines or pops in the direction of Rizzuto")—his defining moment as a player was his ninth-inning, suicide squeeze bunt that scored Joe DiMaggio to beat the Cleveland Indians, September 17, 1951, sending the Yankees off to their third straight pennant.

"Oh yeah," he said, "without question that was it. [Bob] Lemon was so mad he threw his glove up onto the screen afterward. He knew the squeeze was on. He threw the pitch right at my head and I'm sure he couldn't believe I was able to make contact with it. DiMag almost spiked me coming home 'cause he'd left a little too soon. And a lot of people forget, Mickey [Mantle], who was a rookie then, was in the on-deck circle. There he is, in all the pictures, jumping up in the air, as DiMag is racing home."

At least the abrupt rejections from the Dodgers, Giants—and later the Cardinals as well—didn't prompt Rizzuto to pursue other dreams. Rather, with Kunitz's encouragement, he played semipro ball in the summers after the high school season ended and, in doing so, merely confirmed to himself—and others—his ability.

"We played against all the great black teams," Rizzuto said. "I know I'll never forget the day I batted against Satchel Paige. I was a teenager and here I was playing against the great Satchel Paige, who, by then, was probably in his late 30s. With that sidearm whip motion of his, he threw me a fastball inside I couldn't even see. But I managed to get a piece of it. I didn't know where the ball went. It split my bat and rolled down the first base line. Satch, for all his pitching ability, didn't move too well. I'm running with everything I've got to first, not knowing where the ball is, but seeing Satch loping toward the first base line out of the corner of my eye. I beat it out for a base hit.

"It was one of my proudest moments because, by then, Satch was already a legend. Years later, when I faced him in the big leagues, I'd always bunt on him, remembering that hit. I'm glad he was such a good guy and didn't throw the ball right at me. He had every right to, and he'd have killed me, the way he threw.

"We played all kinds of teams those summers—the House of David, those guys with the beards who did all those trick things—and it was a great experience. I guess it was after seeing me in one of those semipro games [Yankee chief scout Paul] Krichell called me and asked me to come to a Yankee tryout. You have to understand, in those days in New York, every kid wanted to be either a Yankee, Joe Louis or go to Notre Dame, so the Dodger and Giant rejections had been long since forgotten. And Krichell was the one guy who didn't say I was too small."

Unlike the other tryouts, which had been conducted in half a day, the Yankee tryout went on for a week while the big club was out of town. Under the observation of Krichell, Yankee coach Johnny Schulte and occasionally even general manager Ed Barrow, there was a workout in the morning, followed by a full game every afternoon.

"Nobody could say they didn't get a fair look," Rizzuto said. "At the end of the week, Krichell came up to me and said: 'We want to sign you. We'll give you $75 a month and we'll send you up to our farm team in Wellsville, New York. That's where we send all our top prospects.' I said: 'Oh jeez, can't I play down South?' I had low blood pressure and I hated playing in the cold weather. So Krichell says, 'Okay, you can go to Bassett, Virginia, but it's for the same money and you report a month earlier.'"

Rizzuto didn't ask for a bonus. The $75 a month was considerably more than most of his friends were making working real jobs in Brooklyn. "Years later," he laughed, "Ed Barrow loved to tell people he signed me for 15 cents—a dime to call me up for the tryout and a nickel for the cup of coffee they gave me when I got to the Stadium."

So in the spring of 1937, Rizzuto boarded a train in New York and left home for the first time for what was then a nearly day-long trip to Virginia. His father had pinned a $20 bill to his undershirt with the warning, "You gotta watch out for the guys on those trains," and the Yankees had made sure to provide him with a nice seat, no sleeper. Along the way, the train made stops at Washington, D.C., and Richmond, where, for dinner, Rizzuto remembered partaking in his first meal of Southern fried chicken.

"They served it with grits," he said. "I found out later they served everything with grits in the South. I didn't know what they were, so I just stuffed 'em in my pocket!"

On any given holiday at the Rizzuto household in Brooklyn there were probably more people around the dinner table than were residing in the entire town of Bassett. Upon getting off the train, Rizzuto looked around in bewilderment at the barren surroundings—a tiny drugstore, a movie theater and a diner, that was it—and wondered aloud whether it was he or the Yankees who had made a terrible mistake. *This was the home of a professional baseball team?*

"I was met at the train by the town sheriff—Sheriff Koontz," he related. "It didn't take me long to discover they talked different down there. I didn't understand them and they didn't understand me!"

Looking back at it now, some 64 years later, the Bassett experience, he said, was in many ways his coming of age. It was only that one year, but two dramatic incidents, entirely separate from the basic conflict of an immigrant's son from Brooklyn suddenly relocated in a rural Southern town, would have a profound effect on him the rest of his life.

He had only been in Bassett a few weeks when, running to first base on an infield grounder, he stepped in a gopher hole and suffered what he thought was a strained muscle in his thigh area. His manager at Bassett, Ray White, also served as the team trainer, and upon a cursory examination of the discolored leg the next day, determined it was merely a charley horse.

"So he wrapped it up with wool and tape," Rizzuto said. "I played on it a couple more days but it got worse and worse. Finally, it got to the point where I couldn't run and this old umpire who lived nearby and worked the games on weekends took a look at me and said to Ray: 'Get this kid to the hospital.' So Ray drove me to Roanoke, which was where the nearest hospital was. On the way, we passed nothing but cows and goats. We got there and they took me in to see this Dr. Johnson, who took one look at the leg and said: 'We've got to operate immediately. Give me your mother's phone number.' Now I'm really scared, but probably not as much as I was the next day when I woke up and Dr. Johnson told me that in another couple of days they would have had to amputate it. My parents drove all the way down from Brooklyn to stay with me and my brother fainted when he saw the leg."

It turned out, not only had Rizzuto torn the muscles in the leg but the blood vessels around them as well, resulting in a gangrenous infection.

"They told me it was something that happened maybe once in a million times," he said. "I just knew it happened to me."

And that wasn't all the bad news. He was told the leg would heal completely with a couple of months stay in the hospital, but, beyond that, he should forget about ever playing ball again.

"That, I couldn't accept. I took my St. Christopher medal—this was way before they demoted him—and wore it around my neck when I got out of the hospital. I went back to playing. It was crazy to do, I guess, but it didn't hurt. I played the rest of the season, hit .310, and went home, satisfied my career was still on track. The only thing was I wasn't quite as fast as I'd been. Before that, I was so fast I'd outrun balls. I can't say I could beat Mickey [Mantle], but I could give him a good race. I was forever grateful to Dr. Johnson, though. I told him: 'If I ever get to the big leagues and we're in the World Series, you've got tickets. I got him tickets to the Series every year for as long as he lived."

The second Bassett incident was even scarier—and never left him—

although, admittedly, he used it to his advantage as part of his broadcast booth shtick years later. On the night of June 27, 1937, Bassett was playing Mayodan. It was hot, muggy and overcast and, as he peered into home plate from his shortstop spot, Rizzuto was vaguely aware of some heat lightning periodically illuminating the rickety old ballpark. Suddenly, he felt a thrust against the back of his legs and, after gathering his senses, looked up to see his catcher, a Cuban named Manuel Cueto, kneeling as if in prayer. An eerie silence had come over the field and, upon turning around, Rizzuto saw the Bassett left fielder, James Taylor, and the center fielder, Charlie Wanny, lying on the ground.

"It was awful," he said. "I felt like I'd been kicked in the back of my legs by a mule. Then I saw Taylor and Wanny lying there. Taylor was a big, strapping kid, a helluva player. I think he might have been leading the team in hitting. I thought lightning had hit him, but it actually hit the flagpole in center field—splintered and disintegrated it! Wanny came to, but they carried Taylor in on a stretcher. I couldn't look. They said he was burned from the top of his spine to his legs. You never get over something like that. At least I didn't. From that day on, lightning always terrified me, although I admit I used it to my advantage all those years in the broadcast booth when I used to duck and hide under the window every time there'd be a lightning flash in the park. It was one of my best excuses for leaving after the seventh inning.

"I guess considering everything else that happened to me that year, the thing Crosswhite pulled on me wasn't much of a big deal."

A twinkle had returned to his eye, foretelling another tale of the childlike innocence that has made him such a favorite foil for antagonists, friendly and otherwise, all his life.

"Oh, that Jack Crosswhite, he was some practical joker. I got my first case of jock itch that year. Crosswhite comes over to me and hands me this bottle and tells me to rub this stuff all over myself down there. It was alcohol. Ohhhh . . . I still feel that sting just talking about it!"

The following year, Ray White was moved up to Class B Norfolk by the Yankees and he took Rizzuto with him, even though Norfolk already had a top-rated shortstop prospect named Claude Corbitt. The Yankees told White he could have only one of them and therefore had to make a decision. Further complicating that decision was the fact that Corbitt was a Norfolk native. Nevertheless, after pitting the two against each other all spring, White risked the wrath of the local fans by keeping Rizzuto, even though Corbitt had led the club in batting all spring. Rizzuto justified the manager's confidence by hitting .336 that season. Just as impressive, though, were the .323 batting average and 73 RBI by Rizzuto's keystone partner, the second baseman Gerry Priddy.

"Priddy," Rizzuto sighed, his eyes casting upward to the kitchen ceiling. "That huckleberry. He was something else. We were close, even though we were opposites in a lot of ways. He was cocky . . . oh he was sure of himself. Me, on the other hand, I was shy and always worried. He took me under his wing, but he loved playing tricks on me, too . . . like nailing my shoes to the floor, ripping up all my fan letters, all those things."

They played alongside each other three straight seasons, Norfolk in '38 and Kansas City in '39 and '40, both of them hitting over .300 and attaining All-Star status all three years. They were the talk of all minor league baseball, this slick-fielding, hard-hitting middle infield duo from opposite ends of the continent; Rizzuto out of the New York Krichell factory; the Los Angeles–born Priddy signed by the Yankees' Southern California scouting chief Bill Essick. And by 1940, they had become the talk of New York, too, as Mel Allen regularly informed Yankee fans on his WABC-860 broadcasts of the exploits of the coming double play combo at Kansas City. In the '20s, the Yankees had also groomed a second baseman–shortstop combo through their system and onto the big club and Tony Lazzeri and Mark Koenig teamed up for three straight pennant winners, 1926–28. "But Priddy and Rizzuto," promised Allen, "are going to be best the Yankees have ever had."

Apparently, Yankee manager Joe McCarthy got the message because when spring training convened in 1941, he announced Rizzuto and Priddy would be his starters in the middle of the infield, replacing the venerable Frank Crosetti at short and the acrobatic two-time All-Star Joe Gordon at second. Crosetti, 31, had hit only .194 in 1940 and was considered to be nearing the end of the line after nine seasons as the Yankees' regular shortstop. But Gordon was only 26 and, after two straight 100-plus RBI seasons in which he hit 28 and 30 homers, loomed as a budding star.

"We don't want to break up Rizzuto and Priddy," McCarthy said, "so my plan is to move Gordon to first base."

For his part, Priddy brashly put his endorsement on McCarthy's experiment by walking up to Gordon in the clubhouse and pronouncing: "I'm the better second baseman. I can make the double play better than you . . . do everything better than you."

But McCarthy's grand experiment didn't last long, doomed, for the most part, by a sluggish Yankee start. They had lost five in a row to fall six and a half games behind in fourth place. On May 18, which had been declared "I Am an American Day," McCarthy made his own declaration. Citing Rizzuto's .248 average and Priddy's .204, he announced Crosetti would be going back to short, Gordon would be returning to second and singles-hitting Johnny Sturm, a defensive specialist, would take over at first.

"Priddy could hit for power and he was as good as Gordon on the double play," Rizzuto said. "For some reason, when he got to the big leagues he just didn't hit the way he had. I didn't either. Then Cro got spiked and I got back in there and started hitting. I wound up at .307 but I've gotta laugh when I think back at spring training that year. I was a scared kid. Crosetti and DiMaggio were my heroes and here I was, suddenly their teammate. I waited for them to talk to me. I felt it was me and 24 other players. The Yankees had a way. They'd all take extra batting practice so as not to let the new kids on the block get any time in the cage. Finally, one day DiMag steps in and says: 'If, as it seems, this kid is going to be our shortstop, we better start letting him get his swings. We're going to need him.' That's all it took.

"And Crosetti was great, too. He was a Yankee all the way. Even though I was taking his job, he'd teach me things. He got hit by more pitches than anybody I'd ever seen. He wore a big blouse, as big as Ruth's, and he'd use that to get hit. He taught me when to shorten up in the field on a hitter, how to position myself. On the very first day of the season that year, we were playing Washington and they had three left-handed hitters, Buddy Myer, Buddy Lewis and Cecil Travis, who all liked to hit the ball the opposite way. Cro told me to shade closer to third, rather than second, and, sure enough, if that wasn't where they all hit the ball all day long."

Maybe if Priddy hadn't been so disrespectful of Gordon, he'd have gotten the same Yankee treatment. Instead, he never got untracked with the bat, never got off the bench and never got any sympathy. He hit .213 in 56 games, filling in at first base for Sturm and third base for Red Rolfe, but never got a call in the World Series against the Dodgers. It was pretty much the same thing the next year and, during the winter of '42–'43, Priddy aired his discontent publicly, stating he was being wasted by the Yankees, and asked to be traded. On January 29, 1943, they obliged him, sending him to the lowly Washington Senators with pitcher Milo Candini in exchange for pitcher Bill Zuber and cash.

With Washington, Priddy found another manager with whom he couldn't get along in Senator icon Ossie Bluege, and after three so-so seasons was traded again to the equally moribund St. Louis Browns. He lasted in the majors until 1953, and after his retirement tried his hand briefly—and unsuccessfully—on the pro golf tour. He never came close to achieving the promise everyone had held for him as Rizzuto's second base sidekick at Norfolk and Kansas City.

"I'll never understand what happened with him, other than bad luck and some injuries," Rizzuto said. "Gerry was a better player than I was. He had more power and he could play the heck out of second base."

Then, on June 6, 1973, Gerry Priddy's life took a truly bizarre turn. He was arrested by the FBI in California and charged with trying to extort $250,000 from a steamship company by threatening to put a bomb aboard one of their vessels, the *Island Princess*. He was later convicted and sentenced to nine months in prison and in 1980 he died of a heart attack at his home in North Hollywood.

"I never could believe that whole extortion thing," Rizzuto said. "That wasn't the Gerry I knew. He was outspoken, and hotheaded, a little like Billy Martin, but outside of baseball he was a regular guy. He knew a lot of prominent businesspeople. It just didn't make sense. He called me when he got out of prison and told me if he'd have had to spend one more day in there he'd have been a hardened criminal."

It was right about the same time McCarthy decided to return Gordon to second base that the most compelling story of the 1941 season began to unfold. On May 15, DiMaggio, in the midst of a desperate slump that had pared nearly 100 points off his average to .306, went 1-for-4 in an otherwise forgettable 13–1 Yankee loss to the Chicago White Sox. Innocuous as it was, that marked the beginning of DiMaggio's 56-game hitting streak, the most unassailable and revered of all baseball records (especially once the regular season home run record, which, in 1998, had stood for 37 years, got inflated by nine and then 12 within the course of four seasons). With the war in Europe expanding by the day, making the U.S. entry into it all the more inevitable, DiMaggio's streak, as it wore on through June and into July, provided a welcome diversion for a worried and wary nation.

When the streak ended in Cleveland on July 16, with Indian third baseman Ken Keltner twice depriving him of potential hits with standout plays, and shortstop Lou Boudreau making another, his Yankee teammates instinctively left him to himself in the clubhouse afterward. Keltner made a backhanded stab of a sizzling grounder past the third base bag in the first and another fine play on a hard-hit grounder in the seventh, while Boudreau sealed DiMaggio's fate by snaring a bad-hop grounder to short in the eighth. It had been a remarkable streak in every way, coinciding with the Yankees taking command of the pennant race and rendering forgotten both their slow start and McCarthy's infield experiment. DiMaggio hit .408 during the streak with 15 homers, 55 RBI and only seven strikeouts.

"The game was over and nobody wanted to say anything to Joe," Rizzuto recalled. "I was dressing at my locker when I looked over at Joe, only to see him wave me over. 'Wait for me until I'm ready to go,' he whispered. I felt so bad for him, but I also felt honored that he wanted me to stay with him. We waited until the stadium was empty. Even the locker room guy had gone home and Joe had forgotten to get his valuables out of the safe. I had $18 on me. We walked out of the ballpark and started up the hill to our hotel. On the left-hand side there was this bar. 'I'm going in there,' Joe said. So I started to follow him. 'No,' he said. 'You go on back to the hotel. I don't have any money, though. Give me what you've got.' So I gave him the $18. I never got it back and over the years I made a career of telling that story about him, on the air and at banquets. People laughed, but I don't think they thought it was really true. Finally, one time at an Old-Timers' Day in the '80s, he said to me: 'I'm tired of you always telling that. Here's the damn $18.' I told him I couldn't take it. It would ruin my story.

"Looking back, I remember the infield was damp from some rain that had fallen and I think that might have slowed down one of those balls to Keltner. I know through the years Joe always said it was Keltner who had stopped him because he was playing deep and daring him to bunt—which he knew Joe would never do. But if you ask me, the toughest one was the bad hop to Boudreau. He really hit that one hard. And then, to think, he hit in 16 more straight after the streak was broken!"

Rizzuto, the rookie who hit .307 in 1941, watched his idol make history all that summer, even palled around with him on the road (as much as Joe would allow), and marveled at how this first Yankee team of his stampeded to the pennant by 17 games over the Red Sox, then whipped the Dodgers four games to one in the World Series. He, above all, had come to know what Waite Hoyt had meant about how great it was to be young and a Yankee. And there was one other off-the-field, DiMaggio-related event that gave the '41 season an almost mystical quality for him.

"I liked movies and Joe liked movies," Rizzuto said, "and so we'd go on off-days and sometimes at night after the games. We always sat in the back row because Joe didn't want anyone to see him. So other than Lefty Gomez—who was the only guy on the team Joe ever went to dinner with—I was as close to him as you could be.

"Shortly after the season and the World Series, Joe was supposed to go to a Communion Breakfast in Newark, only at the last minute he had to cancel because his first wife, Dorothy Arnold, was having their baby and there were some problems. So he asked me to go in his place. You can imagine the disappointment of all those people who were expecting to see Joe and instead they got me, this rookie none of 'em ever heard of. Imagine getting booed at a Communion Breakfast? Actually, there was dead silence, and then people started walking out. I was scared to death. I felt like the enemy. After the breakfast was over, the guy in charge of the entertainment committee, Emil Esselborn, who was a chief in the Newark Fire Department, asked me if I wanted to go over to his house for a cup of coffee. I said sure. Well, in Mr. Esselborn's kitchen I got introduced to his daughter, Cora, this beautiful blonde."

As he related the story he looked around the corner into the living room, but Cora had apparently gone back upstairs.

"Anyway," he said, "I asked her out for a date right there. You know how ballplayers are. A couple of days later we went to the circus at the Garden and, well, I was hooked on this girl. I took her out every day after and, to be closer to her, I moved to a Newark hotel and didn't even go home for two months. There was no hanky-panky, though. Not back then. It was like that scene in *The Godfather*. Cora had relatives all over Newark. We didn't go anywhere they didn't see us."

That winter, the Japanese bombed Pearl Harbor and the world changed. Rizzuto never dreamed it would change just as drastically again in his lifetime. He played the 1942 season, as did DiMaggio, and after winning the American League pennant by nine games over the Red Sox, the Yankees lost the World Series 4–1 to the St. Louis Cardinals. It was the only World Series they would lose in 13 appearances from 1936 to 1953.

After the '43 season, Rizzuto enlisted in the navy even though, as he said, "I got seasick on the ferry." For his boot camp, he was sent to familiar surroundings—Norfolk—and on June 23, 1943, he wed Cora, after which they enjoyed a one-day honeymoon. For the rest of the war, Rizzuto bounced around the Pacific, though without seeing any combat. He served on a supply ship going between Finchhaven, New Guinea, and Manus, then spent nine months in the Philippines. It was upon rejoining the Yankees in 1946, following his discharge from the navy, that Rizzuto unwittingly found himself caught in the middle of a tempest that threatened to rock the foundation of baseball. In the end, the famed "Mexican League raids" were relegated to footnote status in baseball labor history. But upon reflection some 55 years later, Rizzuto remains convinced his wife's stern advice to resist the temptation of riches beyond his imagination saved him from baseball oblivion.

In Mexico, an independent professional baseball league, funded largely by a dynamic multimillionaire businessman named Jorge Pasquel, began making raids on major league clubs, especially on returning service veterans, while paying no heed to existing contracts. Initially, Pasquel had concentrated his recruiting efforts on the National League. On May 23, 1946, he induced three prominent members of the Cardinals, pitchers Max Lanier and Fred Martin and infielder Lou Klein, to jump the team during a series in New York and go to play south of the border. Not long after, Pasquel hit the Brooklyn Dodgers, luring catcher Mickey Owen upon his discharge from the navy, as well as outfielder Luis Olmo, the sixth-leading hitter in the NL in '45. The New York Giants suffered the heaviest losses of the Mexican raids, losing pitchers Sal Maglie, Adrian Zabala, Ace Adams and Harry Feldman, first baseman Roy Zimmerman, second baseman George Hausmann, third baseman Napoleon Reyes and outfielder Danny Gardella.

"Danny Gardella's brother, Al, had been a teammate of mine in Bassett," Rizzuto recalled. "One day, during the '46 season, Al came into our clubhouse and said to me: 'There's some people from Mexico outside who want to talk to you and [second baseman George] Stirnweiss.' So I went with him. They were waiting in this big Cadillac and we drove around the stadium under the bridge that goes over the Harlem River. 'If you leave right now and go to Mexico,' they told us, 'you can have this.' With that, they whipped out envelopes with $10,000 apiece in them for me and Stirnweiss. Then they told us to say nothing to McCarthy.

"We both said no, but agreed to talk with them again. A few weeks later, at this big dinner at the Waldorf-Astoria, we saw them again. We met with them upstairs in their suite. They were packing guns this time, which kinda scared me. They promised us Cadillacs, if we'd go with them. Again, though, they wanted us to go without telling McCarthy. Maybe I wouldn't have been so receptive to them if I was hitting better. But I had just gotten back from two years in the service and I was having a tough time adjusting to curveballs and getting base hits. I wasn't sure of my ability anymore. I was thinking this might be the most money I'll ever make in baseball, but after we left, Cora said to me: 'No way we're doing this!'

"Well, as it turned out, Larry MacPhail, who owned the Yankees then, had put a bug in the hotel suite and the next day when we came to the stadium, he called George and me into his office and told us he wanted us to testify against Pasquel and his brother in court. We protested, insisting that they hadn't done anything to us and we hadn't taken anything from them. So MacPhail suspended us—for two days. Considering what happened to all those other guys who took the money, we got off easy."

Baseball Commissioner A.B. "Happy" Chandler was able to put an effective end to the raids by announcing that any players defecting to the Mexican League would be barred from the majors for five years. In particular, Maglie (who would return to the Giants in 1950 and go 18-4, 22-6 and 18-8 over the next three seasons) lost five prime seasons that might have given him Hall of Fame status.

"Once again, Cora saved my life," Rizzuto said, "or at least my career."

He would go on to play 10½ more seasons with the Yankees, four of them—1950–53—as the starting American League shortstop in the All-Star Game. In 1950, he played in every game, batted .324, scored 125 runs and was a runaway winner of the AL Most Valuable Player Award. Ted Williams, when he served as a member of the Hall of Fame's Veterans Committee years later, said on numerous occasions the difference between those Yankee and Red Sox teams of the 1950s was Rizzuto. In the 1951 World Series against the Giants, Rizzuto batted .320, set a record with 40 chances at shortstop and took part in four double plays in one game. That was to be DiMaggio's last World Series and, with Joe's retirement, Rizzuto suddenly felt more and more isolated. These were Casey Stengel's Yankees now and the manager made that patently clear.

"It's no big secret Casey and I didn't get along," Rizzuto said. "The guys who came up with Casey were his guys. Joe and I both sensed that he wanted to put his own imprint on the team and make people forget about McCarthy. The first base thing with Joe [when Stengel asked DiMaggio to play first base in July of 1950—an abbreviated experiment that had disastrous results] was terrible. I'll never forget it. Then in '54 he started taking me out in the middle of the game. If he'd get behind in the first inning, he'd pinch-hit for me in my first at bat!"

So when Casey and George Weiss, the general manager, called Rizzuto into the manager's office before Old-Timers' Day, August 25, 1956, he probably shouldn't have been as shocked as he says he was at what they wanted to tell him. They had just reacquired Enos Slaughter, the veteran outfielder, from the Kansas City Athletics, on waivers, they told him, and they wanted his input as to who should go in order to make room on the roster. Rizzuto mentioned Charlie Silvera, the third-string catcher behind Yogi Berra and Elston Howard who had barely played a game. "No," they said, "we can't afford to go with only two catchers." He then mentioned a couple of second-line pitchers, only to get the same negative response. Finally, it dawned on him. They wanted him to reach the same conclusion they'd come to—that it was time for him to retire. For the good of the team, of course.

"Don't worry," Weiss said, "we'll give you a full share if we win the

World Series, and the day after you're released, you can still finish the season with us."

"I walked out of there in tears," Rizzuto said, "and as I'm heading out the door I see Stirnweiss, who was there for the Old-Timers' Game. He put his arm around me and said: 'Go back in there, get your money, grab your clothes and I'll take you home.' He took me up to Grossinger's in the Catskills, which was the smartest thing anybody could have done for me. No one could reach me and if they had, I'd have surely said something way out of line, ripping Weiss and Casey. Then, a week later, all the sympathy calls and letters started coming in, followed by the offer from WPIX to do a couple of innings on the air with Mel [Allen] and Red [Barber]."

A bitter end to one career suddenly became a sweet (if somewhat rocky, at first) beginning to a new career. He would come to idolize Allen as he had DiMaggio, and Allen would prove to be a far more willing and important mentor than Joe. Rizzuto would remain a fixture in the Yankee broadcast booth for 37 years—a genuine New York treasure, completely forgiven for his unabashed Yankee rooting mixed in around the umpteen birthday greetings and free commercial plugs for his favorite bakeries, delis, jewelry stores, golf clubs, etc., etc. In his rambling, barely coherent yet truly hysterical 1994 Hall of Fame acceptance speech—which closely resembled any of his broadcasts—he summed up by saying: "I've had the most wonderful lifetime that one man could possibly have."

"I really have," Rizzuto said, taking another sip of his coffee. "It's been unbelievable. I owe everything to the Yankees."

I suggested we go outside to take a picture. The bright, late-afternoon sunshine was streaming through the kitchen window and Rizzuto seemed to welcome the opportunity to get out of the house and take advantage of what was a beautiful afternoon. He led me through a side door into the garage where, from the back of his car, he pulled out two silver-foil birthday balloons.

"Don't tell Cora I'm doing this," he whispered. "She doesn't understand why I kept these things."

We walked around to the back of the house where, concealing much of a large window, a visitor couldn't help but notice this tall, sprawling orange-colored bush with berries on its branches.

"A huckleberry bush?" I said kiddingly, in reference to his favorite expression.

"Noooo, nooo," he said, chuckling. "I think Cora says that's a firethorn. It's funny, you'd come here at this time any other year and those berries would all be gone, eaten by the birds. But ever since the World Trade Center attack, the birds haven't come around . . ."

For a moment, he seemed lost in thought, gazing silently at the birthday balloons in his hand. Finally, he let them go, craning his neck to follow their ascent over the house, higher and higher into the brilliant, cloudless azure sky, until they disappeared from view.

"I guess that's it, they're gone," he said.

"The balloons," I replied.

"Yeah, the balloons."

He shook his head, as if to acknowledge the unintentional symbolism of the balloons and the towers. For more than a half-century Phil Rizzuto had lived the greatest life a man could ever hope to live and then, in a terrifying few minutes, he was left stupefied, first in front of his TV and then at the foot of his attic window, wondering what it's really all about.

"I'm an old man," he said, "and I've seen a lot. But this . . . this has really got to me. I thought I lost my innocence when I went into the navy. I never thought I'd lose it again."

ECHOES OF THE IRON HORSE, CRO, AND FAT FREDDIE FITZSIMMONS

MARIUS RUSSO

It seemed such an unlikely stopping off place, in this journey back though Yankee time, so far removed as it was from the clattering trains, urban bustle and the ghosts that still roamed the premises at 161st Street and River Avenue in the South Bronx. On the outskirts of Fort Myers, Florida, Marius Ugo Russo, lifelong New Yorker, winner of two World Series games two years apart and one of the last surviving teammates of Lou Gehrig, had at last been found residing in a retirement village with his wife, Stasia. It was February 2002, and some 150 miles to the north on Interstate 75, the Yankees had already begun spring training, although Russo was scarcely aware. His last Yankee spring had been 1946, and more than just the passage of time was responsible for his estrangement from the franchise that made him and ultimately forgot him.

It had been a frustrating search to find him. The Yankees

weren't even sure if he was still alive. The phone number and address they had for him in Elmont, Queens, proved to be no longer his—and none of the old Yankees in the New York metropolitan area who knew him had heard from him in years. Then I remembered Don Williams, the person who had first put Marius Russo's name in my state of consciousness.

A retired sportswriter from the *Newark Star-Ledger*, Williams often told tales in the press box about Russo, as if it were his special mission to keep the old left-hander's name alive. After all, there were those other, more celebrated Italian-American Yankees of that era, Joe DiMaggio, Frank Crosetti, Phil Rizzuto, as well as the core players of the prewar Yankee championship teams, Red Ruffing, Lefty Gomez, Bill Dickey, Red Rolfe, Joe Gordon and Charlie Keller, whose careers dwarfed Russo's barely six seasons in the Bronx. Williams had always hinted of a special relationship with Russo that transcended a sportswriter's affection for a favorite ballplayer of his youth, and I figured if anyone knew where the old pitcher could be found it would be he.

"Russ is like a second father to me," Williams related when I reached him by phone at his home in South Huntington, Queens, "and, yes, he's very much alive. You'll find him in Fort Myers. He moved there a couple of years ago. We talk by phone every couple of weeks. I always want to be sure he's doing okay. I lost him for over 40 years and I never want that to happen again."

The Williams-Russo story, it turned out, was just as poignant as Marius's remembrances of Gehrig's last days with the Yankees. They first met in 1941, just prior to spring training, when Williams was nine years old and bedridden awaiting an operation for Perthes disease, a rare childhood hip disorder in which the top portion of the thigh bone is degenerated. Russo was coming off a 14-8 season, having supplanted the aging Gomez as the left-handed complement to Ruffing at the top of the Yankees' pitching rotation, and was asked by a mutual friend if he would pay a visit to the stricken youngster.

"I was lying in bed one day and all of a sudden, the door to my room opened and there was Russ," Williams said. "I was a Dodger fan at the time, which he, of course, didn't know. He brought with him an autographed Yankee team picture. In it, he's sitting right next to Gehrig. I was overwhelmed. It was just an unbelievable gesture when you consider he didn't even know me. From that day on, we became close friends. When he went away to the army, he wrote letters to me, and through the years when he was with the Yankees, he'd get me team balls and pictures.

"The day I'll most cherish, though—and I've still got the picture— is the day Russ introduced me to Babe Ruth. It was in the winter of 1946 and Russ was working a second job at Gertz's department store in Jamaica [Queens]. Ruth was doing some sort of promotional appearance there one day and Russ had me come over to meet him. They knew each other, even though Russ didn't get to the Yankees until 1939, five years after Babe was let go to the Braves."

A couple of years later, Williams enrolled at Queens College, and as his interests expanded beyond baseball, he gradually lost contact with Russo, whose pitching career ended prematurely, at age 32, to a bum shoulder in 1946. Though he thought of Russo often, Williams, who got married, had a son and a daughter and fulfilled his childhood dream of becoming a sportswriter, just never seemed to get around to renewing the special bond they'd had. Then one summer day in 1996—July 19 to be exact—Williams was sitting in the den of his house in South Huntington, reading the newspaper when he turned to his wife, Pat.

"You know what today is?" he said to her. "It's Russ's birthday."

"Why don't you call him?" she replied.

"Nah," he said. "I don't even know if he's still living in the same place and if he is, he might not even remember me. Maybe I'll just drive by the house and if an old man is out in the front yard, I'll stop."

Williams did do that, but there was no sight of anyone at the house where Russo had lived on Norfolk Drive in Elmont for nearly 60 years. He shrugged and drove back home, wondering in silence if the old pitcher was still around. "Surely," Williams thought, "if he'd passed on,

I'd have heard or read about it." But it had been over 40 years and for all he knew, Russo had moved away and disappeared into time and the belly of civilization like so many forgotten old ballplayers. Pat Williams, however, suspected otherwise.

The next day, unbeknownst to her husband, she took it upon herself to pay a visit to the Russo home—only, unlike Don, she got out of her car and went right to the front door. Upon ringing the bell, the door opened and a woman, Stasia Russo, greeted her.

"Please come in," Stasia said, after Pat explained the circumstances of her impromptu visit. "Oh, Russ will be so excited to hear Donnie's fine and doing so well."

"Pat came home that afternoon and said to me: 'Guess who I just had a visit with?'" Williams said. "I was speechless. The last time I'd seen Russ was 1954 when he was working in a sporting goods store in Bethpage, Long Island. What really got to me, though, was when she told me Russ still kept my picture in his wallet—after all these years."

The sun was just beginning to break through the heavy morning fog, and the thick Florida sawgrass underfoot was still moist with dew as I got out of my car and approached the front door of the whitewashed ranch home that, I thought, must seem like another world away from 1940s Brooklyn. It had been approximately a 20-mile drive west, down Daniels Parkway from the Fort Myers airport, with just the one turn into the Myerling retirement community. To the right of the front porch, a bottlebrush tree with its distinctive furry red petals stood silent and unmoving, not unlike every one of the 61,808 fans at Yankee Stadium that long ago July 4 afternoon in 1939 when Lou Gehrig stepped to the microphone to deliver his immortal farewell address.

The front door opened and Marius Russo, looking fit and healthy, greeted me with a warm smile and a firm handshake. I had not seen him since the summer of 1991 at Yankee Stadium—when the Yankees held a commemorative day to honor Joe DiMaggio's historic 56-game hitting streak in 1941 and invited the Clipper's surviving teammates from that season—but aside from using a walker, he looked essentially the same.

"The Yankees didn't know if you were still alive," I said, prompting a soft chuckle from him.

"I'm not surprised," he said. "But here I am—not as mobile as I used to be—but other than this [nodding at his walker] I feel pretty good."

The walker, he explained, was the result of a bad hip for which surgery, at age 87, was no longer an option.

"I had the other one replaced 10 years ago," he said, "and there's no more pain in this one even though it's got bone meshing against bone. The doctors tell me I just gotta live with it, so I am."

He ushered me into the living room where Stasia was waiting.

"Where do you fellows want to talk?" she asked. "I see you have a notepad and tape recorder. Do you want to sit at the dining room table?"

"Let me show him around first," Russo said, leading me to a den just off the living room.

In lieu of wallpaper, above the desk in the room were pasted what looked to be nearly 100 black-and-white photos of silent movie stars.

"My hobby," Russo confessed. "You should see my silent movie collection. You probably know Donnie Williams has the biggest collection anywhere of Sinatra records. I like Frankie okay, but these people [pointing to the wall] have always been my passion. I grew up with them and they're still with me. I spend a lot of time in this room, adding pictures to this wall. Lot of good memories. I brought 'em all down from New York with me. We got so much room here, I've got a place for 'em now."

"What about your baseball memorabilia?" I asked. "Don't you have a place for that?"

"Oh, I didn't save much," he replied. "Stasia kept a lot of things, balls, magazines and stuff, that are all still in boxes. I got some pictures that are hanging in the lanai off the dining room. I'll show you them."

Stasia escorted us back across the living room to the dining room table. As Russo slowly made his way with his walker, his wife explained why, in the fall of 2000, they'd suddenly moved to the Florida tropics (without giving notice to the Yankees) after spending their entire lives in New York.

"Our daughter lives down here and she wanted us to be closer to her so she could look after us," Stasia said. "It's okay—I can't believe how much room we have here—but I miss my friends in New York. Russ is happy, though."

"Is that what you preferred to be called?" I asked him. "Marius does seem like a very formal name."

"Yeah, most everyone calls me Russ. That or Mario."

"What about your middle name—it's so unusual."

"You mean Ugo?" he said. "Nah, years ago it wasn't so unusual. There was a famous bicyclist, Ugo Fregari, who rode the six-day race at Madison Square Garden. Actually, I think my father gave me that name after an opera singer he liked in Italy."

Marius Ugo Russo was born in Bay Ridge, Brooklyn, in 1914 and grew up in Ozone Park, Queens, graduating from Richmond Hill High School. Although it was in the midst of the Depression, Russo's athletic ability—he excelled in baseball and basketball—helped him get scholarships, first to Brooklyn College and then to Long Island University. It was at LIU, in 1935, when he came to the attention of Paul Krichell, the sage Yankee scout whose reputation had been made a dozen years earlier with his signing of a "doughboy"-looking first baseman off the campus of Columbia University named Lou Gehrig for a bonus of $1,300.

Russo was pitching and playing first base at LIU when a local semipro coach, Ernie Wurthner, offered him his first paying job with a team that played across Long Island Sound in Mamaroneck, New York. It was Wurthner who alerted Krichell to Russo. In those days, scouts for major league clubs all had their own networks of semipro teams where they would arrange to have players of promise placed in order to retain control over them while further evaluating their abilities.

Krichell, in particular, used the Bushwicks club in Brooklyn, coached by one of his bird dog scouts, Joe Press, as a storage place for local talent. He placed Russo with the Bushwicks in 1935, where the catcher was a former Brooklyn Dodger, Charles Hargreaves, who also worked with Krichell.

"Hargreaves was smart and experienced in big league ways," Russo related. "He taught me a lot about pitching—things I never learned in college ball. He taught me when to let go of the fast one and when to hold it back. Krichell really knew what he was doing. He had all the angles covered. If he liked what he saw, he'd get you with his people and try to make you better. Then he'd sign you as a more finished product, at little or no expense to the Yankees."

In Russo's case, the signing cost to the Yankees was $750.

"My first spring training, in 1937, they had me report to the Newark team," he said. "That was their No. 1 farm team and I wasn't supposed to stay there. I was really ticketed for Binghamton in the New York–Penn League. But I guess Oscar Vitt, the manager at Newark, liked what he saw of me and convinced the Yankees to let me start there with him. I think it was mostly because they didn't have any other lefties there. I only know it was a great break for me."

Stasia emerged from the kitchen as Russo was talking and asked if we wanted some lunch.

"I'll order some pizza," she said. "There's a place just down the road from the community here and they make really great pizza."

Russo watched her as she disappeared back into the kitchen, then continued.

"The '37 Bears were one of the greatest minor league teams ever assembled," he said, "but you probably knew that. Almost everybody on that club went to the big leagues, including Charlie Keller, who led the league in hitting. He was only 20. We became lifelong friends. Stasia and I still see Charlie's widow, who moved to Florida—on the other coast—from Maryland after Charlie passed away."

He paused as if to reflect on some long ago memory of a cherished pal.

"There was also Joe Gordon, George McQuinn, Steve Sundra, Atley

Donald, Joe Beggs, Buddy Rosar . . . all gone now. We won the International League pennant by 25½ games, then rallied from an 0–3 deficit to beat the Cardinals' top farm team, Columbus, in the Junior World Series. I was only 8-8 that year. Beggs (21-4), Donald (19-2), Sundra (15-4) and Vito Tamulis (18-6) were the big starters."

Nevertheless, two years later, Russo joined Donald and Sundra on the Yankee pitching staff considered by baseball historians to be the best—and deepest—they ever had. Led by Red Ruffing's 21-7, no fewer than seven Yankee starters won in double figures in 1939—Bump Hadley (12-6), Monte Pearson (12-5), Lefty Gomez (12-8), Donald (13-3), Sundra (11-1), Oral Hildebrand (10-4) were the others—and conceivably Russo could have joined them had he not been inserted into the starting rotation so late in the season by manager Joe McCarthy. Down the stretch, Russo reeled off seven consecutive victories, including a 5–2 effort over the Chicago White Sox on September 21, which proved to be the pennant-clincher for the Yankees. Despite his starting pitching depth, McCarthy was concerned by the fact that Ruffing, Hadley, Hildebrand and Gomez were getting up there in baseball age. Gomez, in particular, within a couple of years was plagued by a stiff neck that prevented him from finishing games, and it was clear McCarthy was grooming Russo to be his primary left-handed starter.

"They started calling me Lefty when I was at Newark," Russo noted. "I think that was because Lefty Gomez was getting past his prime and they didn't have any other lefties."

The 1939 season—in which the Yankees won the American League pennant by 17 games over the Red Sox and swept the Cincinnati Reds in the World Series—was no doubt one of the most dominant in the team's history. In steamrolling to their fourth straight World Championship, the Yankees flexed their superiority in every facet of the game, leading the league in runs (967), homers (166), slugging (.451), complete games (87), shutouts (15), ERA (3.31), fewest runs allowed (556) and fielding (.978). They were an incredible 54-20 on the road and beat the last-place Browns (who finished 64½ games behind) all 11 games in St. Louis. Indeed, 1939 might well have been regarded as the greatest of all Yankee seasons had it not been so tempered by the tragedy of Gehrig being felled by the rare but fatal degenerative nerve disease, amyotrophic lateral sclerosis.

"Lou was carrying the lineup card to the plate when I got there," Russo said. "He'd taken himself out of the lineup and ended his [2,130] consecutive games streak a few weeks earlier. You could see, even with just that, he was really struggling. We didn't understand anything about the illness, just that it was really taking its toll on him."

Unfortunately, nobody knew anything about the illness, which is why an outrageous story by *New York Daily News* columnist Jimmy Powers, August 18, 1940, threatened to create a panic in New York. The Yankees were languishing in fifth place at the time and Powers speculated the cause of this uncharacteristic mediocrity from a team that had won an unprecedented four straight world championships was because they had been afflicted by a "mass polio epidemic." Though Powers admitted to having scant medical knowledge, he went on to suggest Gehrig's disease had infected all of his Yankee teammates. It was the height of irresponsibility on Powers's part and, as one might have expected, prompted Gehrig to file a $1 million lawsuit against the *News* in Bronx Supreme Court. The *News* issued an apology and the suit was settled out of court.

"We all had to go to the courthouse," Russo said. "The whole team was subpoenaed, although none of us was asked to testify. Needless to say, Powers didn't have much of a case. He was wrong all the way. I didn't like Powers anyway. He was a loudmouth. But Jack Smith, the *News*'s Yankee beat writer, was a nice fellow and we knew he had nothing to do with that awful article."

Although they were both native New Yorkers, signed and groomed for the Yankees by the same scout (Krichell), Russo didn't know Gehrig well. As a kid, he'd watched Gehrig play on the rare occasions when he and his friends ventured out of Ozone Park to Yankee Stadium, and, for sure, the Iron Horse's indomitable presence discouraged any thoughts on Russo's part of playing any more first base (his position in sandlot ball when he wasn't pitching) once he'd signed with the Yankees.

"Lou was always nice to me, and he always had a smile, acting as if nothing was wrong," Russo continued. "I have a picture of myself standing on the baseline while he was making his farewell speech in '39. There were a lot of tears that day, even more two years later when he died."

Stasia returned to the room, bringing with her a couple of cartons full of scrapbooks, photos, autographed baseballs and old magazines.

"That picture is in here somewhere," she said.

Russo stared indifferently at the memorabilia for a moment and then smiled.

"The little lady saved all this stuff through the years," he said. "I don't know what we're going to do with it."

"You have *grandkids*," Stasia reminded him.

Actually, the Gehrig farewell speech picture was framed and on the wall in the lanai, mixed in with all the other highlight photos of Russo's seven-year career. Russo lifted himself up from the dining room table and directed me to the other room.

"There it is," he said, pointing to the picture. "I still remember the lump I felt in my throat when Lou was talking. I suppose I won't forget that last spring training he had in 1939. Lou had been feeling really bad and didn't know what was wrong. We'd stay after the workout and Lou would be running in the outfield with us, and he couldn't understand why he was so tired. But he never complained. He just seemed to accept it all, whatever it was, with a smile."

After his auspicious breakthrough season, Russo earned a regular spot in the Yankee rotation in 1940 and won 14 games, second on the club behind Ruffing's 15. He won 14 again in 1941 and capped off what proved to be his best season with a victory over the Dodgers in the World Series. Of course, 1941 was most remembered for DiMaggio's 56-game hitting streak. It was impossible for DiMaggio's teammates not to get caught up in his remarkable feat, although Russo insisted the season always took precedence.

"We were all rooting for Joe to get his hit every day," he said as we stood in front of the 1941 team photo. "At the same time, though, we couldn't let ourselves get consumed by it. The game I most remember during the streak was, I think, No. 38. We were playing the Browns in New York and I had a no-hitter going until George McQuinn broke it up with a home run with one out in the seventh inning. I kiddingly blamed Tommy Henrich for not catching the ball even though it landed six or seven rows up in the seats."

Henrich had staked Russo to a 3–0 lead with a home run off Browns starter Elden Auker earlier in the game. By the eighth inning, however, DiMaggio had still not gotten a hit and, with the Yankees coming up for what was presumed to be their last at bats, Joe was scheduled to hit fourth. Johnny Sturm led off by popping out, but then Red Rolfe worked the side-arming Auker for a walk, bringing Henrich to the plate.

"For some reason," Russo remembered, shaking his head, "we bunted the runner over. Now here was Henrich, who'd already homered in the game, and he's *sacrificing!* No one could figure out why, other than the fact that maybe McCarthy, for the first time, was managing the game to help Joe keep the streak going. I later heard Henrich say he was afraid of hitting into a double play, depriving Joe of his last chance to get a hit. But with first base open, I'll never understand why the Browns didn't walk Joe instead. The whole thing was a little crazy. Sure enough, Joe got Auker for a base hit over third to keep the streak going."

(For the record, in his own autobiography, *Sleeper Cars and Flannel Uniforms*, with Tom Keegan, Auker insisted he never considered anything but pitching to DiMaggio. "I can honestly say, I didn't give a damn about the streak," he said. "If I had wanted to end the streak, I could have done that very easily. I could have hit him with a pitch. First base was open. I could have done that, but I was only thinking about getting him out and hoping we could come back and win the ball game.")

The year 1941 was a watershed season for Russo as well, although, like everything else, it got lost amid DiMaggio's streak, Ted Williams hitting .406, and the Yankees regaining their overall superiority in baseball after a one-year hiatus. Russo was 14-10, including that June 26 one-hitter against the St. Louis Browns and Auker. What was even more remarkable about those 14 wins in '41 was the fact that five of them came against the Red Sox, whose lineup consisted of some of the best right-handed hitters in the game—Jimmie Foxx, Bobby Doerr, Joe Cronin and Dom DiMaggio. It didn't figure a left-hander could be so dominant against them and yet Russo limited them to a mere 13 runs in those games. By 1941, he seemed on the brink of supplanting the aging Ruffing and Gomez as the ace of the Yankee rotation, and his 3.09 earned run average led the staff. He and Ruffing were named to the All-Star team.

"I'd have loved to have pitched in the All-Star Game," Russo said. "It was certainly an honor to be picked. But right before the game, I developed groin problems so I was there merely as a spectator. That was the game in Detroit when Ted [Williams] won it with his two-out, three-run homer in the ninth inning. Arky Vaughan, who was one of the best left-handed hitters of that time, hit two homers for the National League. I always said we could have used another left-handed pitcher."

In and around DiMaggio's hitting streak and league-leading 125 runs batted in, the Yankees once again waltzed to the American League pennant by 17 games, again over the Red Sox. The pennant race was almost secondary, but the World Series wouldn't be.

"The Dodgers," said Russo, his eyes now fixed on a picture of himself throwing the first pitch of Game 3 of the '41 Series to Pee Wee Reese. "The whole city was pretty fired up. I know I was. We hadn't had a Subway Series in six years and the Yankees had never played the Dodgers. We kinda knew it was gonna be special."

There had not been a special summer like this in Brooklyn since 1920, the last season the Dodgers had won the National League pennant. After two decades of mediocrity or worse, the Dodgers staged an aggressive September drive to the pennant in '41, establishing an Ebbets Field attendance record of 1,215,253, while also providing the first glimpse of brilliance in the managerial career of Leo Ernest Durocher. The 35-year-old Durocher was still giving himself occasional playing time at shortstop as the rookie Reese broke in, but it was his brassy leadership role from the bench that made him the new darling of Brooklyn.

Otherwise, these were the Dodgers of the bombastic impresario Larry MacPhail, who operated the team as he lived—for the moment. Their reign, as such, would be short-lived, just as MacPhail, in September of the following year, would resign as Dodger chief executive to join the war effort as a lieutenant colonel.

And also in that summer of '41, Brooklyn had its own San Francisco–born Italian hero in Dolph Camilli, who mirrored DiMaggio in winning the National League Most Valuable Player honors. Camilli batted a rather modest .285, but led the National League in homers (34) and runs batted in (120), scored 92 runs and had a .407 on-base percentage.

"I didn't know Dolph all that well, then or even later," Russo said. "He was a good paisan but he was in the other league and we really didn't ever see those guys. In a way, though, we were brought together again later in life when he and Buddy Hassett and some of the other old-timers petitioned baseball to include us all in the pension plan. Guys like Willis Hudlin, who helped keep the game going after Babe Ruth. In the end, we didn't get a lot, at least compared to the pensions the players who played after 1946 get. But it's $10,000 a year and I'm not complaining. Comes in handy. It's just too bad Camilli and Hassett didn't get to hardly benefit from it. They died shortly after baseball finally made the deal with us."

After splitting the first two '41 World Series games at Yankee Stadium—Ruffing hurled a six-hit, 3–2 Yankee win in Game 1 before Whitlow Wyatt returned fire for the Dodgers in pitching another 3–2 win in Game 2—Russo drew the starting assignment for the Yankees as the teams crossed boroughs to Ebbets Field. The Dodgers countered with the 40-year-old knuckleballer Freddie Fitzsimmons. The 5-11, 185-pound Fitzsimmons had been pitching in the major leagues since 1925, the first 12 years with the New York Giants, and though he was considered past his prime and had been used sparingly in 1941 (after leading the NL with an .889 winning percentage—16-2—the year before), Durocher decided to play a hunch that, between his savvy and unfamiliar knuckle curve, he could pose trouble for the Yankees.

Long before, Fitzsimmons had been tagged with the uncomplimentary nickname of "Fat Freddie" to which he said philosophically: "Maybe I just eat too much." In any case, it was an interesting match-up of contrasting pitchers and personalities—Fitzsimmons, the outgoing, fun-loving veteran right-hander with the trick pitch, versus Russo, the quiet, unassuming lefty with the more conventional fastball/curveball repertoire.

"My big day," Russo said, a reflective smile crossing his face. "I'd been in Ebbets Field as a kid, in the bleachers, but never on the field. Even though it was a bandbox, that didn't bother me. Once the game started, I put that all out of my mind."

So, too, did Fitzsimmons. The two of them matched shutouts through six innings when the Yankees literally caught a break, even if Russo didn't immediately. After Bill Dickey grounded out to second to start the Yankee seventh, Joe Gordon worked Fitzsimmons for a walk. Another grounder to second by Phil Rizzuto then moved Gordon into scoring position as Russo came to the plate.

It should be noted Russo hadn't allowed his hitting skills to diminish after becoming strictly a pitcher at LIU. He took pride in his hitting, even though he managed only 50 hits and no homers (but 25 RBI) in 235 career at bats.

"I was a singles hitter," he said, "but I enjoyed getting my whacks. There was no designated hitter in those days so we pitchers worked hard on our bunting and other things during batting practice."

Russo turned on a Fitzsimmons knuckleball and hit a smash back to the box that caught the portly veteran squarely on the knee. As Fitzsimmons writhed in pain—his kneecap had been broken—the ball came down safely into the glove of Reese at short, ending the Yankee threat.

"One of the hardest balls I ever hit," Russo said with no rancor 60 years later. "It would've scored a run if Fitzsimmons hadn't got in the way."

More importantly for the Yankees, it knocked Fitzsimmons out of the game, and the next inning they scored a pair of runs off his successor, Hugh Casey, on consecutive one-out singles by Rolfe, Henrich, DiMaggio and Keller. The Dodgers got one run back in their half of the eighth when Dixie Walker doubled and Reese singled—yet McCarthy made no move to replace Russo.

"Another complete game victory," I said to him. "It was a different game back then."

"Oh yeah, even though we had Johnny Murphy, one of the best relievers ever. McCarthy had so much confidence in me, even if I wasn't sure I could make it. I had a lot of help. Dickey was the best there was at calling a game. I learned everything from him. I never shook him off. He was the guy who really held us together. Everyone looked up to him on the team, not just the pitchers. I can't speak for the Ruth teams before me, or the ones that came after, but that '41 Yankee team was as good a team as I ever knew. There were no jealousies, which, I guess you could say, was the Yankee way."

"It still is today," I said, referring to Joe Torre's Yankees. "As Derek Jeter says, with this bunch you check your ego at the door."

"That's good," said Russo with a wry smile, "although I don't know about Steinbrenner."

If there was one, overriding characteristic I had noted about Russo it was his modesty. It didn't seem to matter to him if he'd become a forgotten Yankee World Series hero. Oh, he was proud enough of that four-hit, 2–1 win, he said, but in the big picture he was merely a support player to the real Yankee stars, DiMaggio, Dickey, Ruffing and Gomez.

"Who knows?" he said, "we might not have won that game if Casey hadn't failed to cover first on Henrich's infield hit [in the eighth]. That kept the inning going."

A far more egregious Dodger gaffe proved to be the turning point of the Series the next day. The Dodgers took a 4–3 Game 4 lead into the ninth inning with Casey once again on the mound, having come on in relief in the fifth. The Georgia-born right-hander, whose often devastating sinkers and curves were suspected of having more on them than just the right wrist action, retired the first two Yankee batters in the ninth on infield groundouts, and thought he'd succeeded in nailing down the victory by striking out a lunging Henrich on a 3-2 curve in the dirt. But the Ebbets Field crowd's exhilaration quickly turned to horror at the sight of the ball skirting past Dodger catcher Mickey Owen, as the alert Henrich dashed safely to first. Given new life, the Yankees pounced on the shaken Casey with a single by DiMaggio, a double by Keller, a walk to Dickey and another double by Joe Gordon, all of which accounted for four runs and a stunning 7–4 victory, en route to winning the whole Series.

"Mickey Owen's worst day." Russo sighed. "I thought it was a helluva spitball Casey threw to Henrich 'cause Owen always caught everything thrown to him."

When the Yankees lost to the St. Louis Cardinals in five games in the 1942 World Series, Russo was merely a spectator, having hurt his shoulder earlier in the season. The shoulder still bothered him for much of '43 as he won just five games, but McCarthy again showed his faith in him by giving him the ball for Game 4 of the revenge Series against the Cardinals. Russo justified it, tossing a nifty 2–1 seven-hitter over the Cardinals' 15-game winner, Max Lanier, and in the process contributed a pair of doubles.

Looking at the framed picture of himself and Lanier posing before the game, Russo seemed indifferent when I suggested all the elements of that '43 win—out-pitching Lanier, overcoming his shoulder problems and getting the two doubles—made it even more significant than the one against the Dodgers in '41.

"Not really," Russo said. "By '43, a lot of the fellas had gone to war. In particular, the Cardinals didn't have Terry Moore. We were without Joe and Gomez. I got the assignment because it was Lefty's turn. But it just wasn't the same. I went into the Army Signal Corps in February of '44 and didn't get out until December of '45. My shoulder was still bad, though. I wasn't that fancy to begin with. I had just two pitches. One was my 'Our Father' and the other was my 'Hail Mary.'"

He laughed quietly.

"I tried a change-up, but I never got it down. Control was my thing. After two years of inactivity, my ball didn't have the same sink to it and that was my best pitch. They sent me down to Kansas City in '46, but I couldn't pitch effectively. It was the same thing the next year and when they finally sold me to Seattle in the Pacific Coast League in 1948, I gave it up. Johnny Murphy was by then the Yankee farm director and he hired me to manage their Hornell, New York, team in Class D. Seven months away from my family was too much, though. I just didn't care for it."

So Russo walked away from the game for good. His lifetime record for six seasons in the big leagues was 45-34, with a 3.13 ERA, plus 2-0, 0.50 for those two World Series starts. He went to work, first for Gertz and later for 29 years with Grumman Aircraft on Long Island. Back then, baseball didn't set you up for life, not even after five decent years, including an All-Star selection and two World Series wins. And as Russo would also find out later, it didn't provide you with a pension either.

We had pretty much completed our walk-through of his wall of pictures when Stasia announced the pizza had arrived. Russo took his seat at the head of the dining room table and motioned me to help myself to a slice. As he mixed himself some salad, Stasia joined us, bringing with her another carton of yellowed, signed baseballs. Lying on top of the balls was a musty but otherwise remarkably preserved copy of *Look* magazine, dated May 5, 1942.

"You've got to see this," Stasia said, gently flipping through the pages. "Here it is! Would you believe it? An article by Russ!"

The headline across the top of the two-page spread read: "How to Pitch—By Marius Russo" and was accompanied by a sequence of photos of Russo in different pitching motions. While it may have been a war year with so many of the game's pitching stars, Bob Feller, Ruffing et al., overseas in the service of their country, there was still something to be said for being featured in this way by a national magazine with the prestige of *Look*.

"Yeah, it was pretty neat," Russo said grudgingly. "I think I even got $100 for it."

There was, I concluded, simply no escaping this man's understatement of himself and his accomplishments. He probably *did* get only $100 for writing the article, but 60 years later it was still no big deal to him. If not for Stasia, the magazine undoubtedly would have long since been discarded and forgotten. Fame was never what Russo was in it for. Winning was.

"I was very proud and lucky to be a Yankee," he said, "just being around and part of all those great guys, DiMaggio, Keller, Henrich, Ruffing, Gomez, Dickey, Rolfe and Gordon . . . I'd have to say Gehrig's class rubbed off on all of us. We were respected wherever we went. McCarthy always demanded that we wear a tie and jacket to dinner on the road. All our travel was first-class. We played cards on the trains, but never for a lot of money, just nickels and dimes. McCarthy didn't want anything to interfere with camaraderie."

We had finished our lunch, having each limited ourselves to one slice of the pizza, and the conversation returned to that '43 Yankee team, which despite the absence of DiMaggio, Gomez and Phil Rizzuto, managed to dispatch the Cardinals—who still had Stan Musial, Marty Marion, Harry Walker and the Cooper brothers, Mort and Walker—in five games. When I reminded Russo that Frank Crosetti (who had passed away at age 91 a few weeks prior to my visit) had gotten his shortstop job back in 1943 because of Rizzuto's call-up to the navy, a look of sadness crossed his face.

"I want to show you something," he said, getting up and heading off toward the bedroom in his walker.

I got up myself and waited in the lanai, again admiring all his vintage photos, when he reappeared a few minutes later, clutching a card in his hand.

"This is the last Christmas card I got from the Cro," he said. "Look at what he wrote."

It was a simple Christmas card, except for the personal inscription at the bottom, which read: "It was a pleasure playing behind you."

How touching, I thought, for a guy to think of writing something like this to an old teammate nearly 60 years later.

"That's why I got the ball over the plate," Russo said, with obvious pride, "so that everybody could get out of there as quickly as possible and not have to be late for dinner."

"Cro was past his prime when he played behind you," I said.

"Yeah," Russo said. "Rizzuto came up in '41 and played himself right into the job. Rizzuto and I lived near each other in New Jersey and I'd drive him to the Stadium. Years later, I told him if I knew he was gonna be such a big star I'd have bought a limo. But Cro stayed around and helped Phil break in and take his job. That's the way he was. I guess you could say that's the way the Yankees were."

Leaning on his walker, he scanned the wall of pictures, squinting his eyes as if in search of something. After a short period of silence, he finally said: "Now that Cro's gone, I guess I'm the oldest Yankee."

"You and Henrich," I answered, "and I believe you're the sole surviving member of the '37 Newark Bears."

"Too much sadness," Marius Russo whispered.

His eyes fixed on the wall again, in private thought, and as he turned away he said: "I've really got to get a picture of Cro up here."

THE WILD MAN OF WAKE FOREST

TOMMY BYRNE

I t had been more than 75 years ago and yet the memory of it was still clearly etched in Tommy Byrne's mind. Some things, he said, you never forget, no matter how young you might have been, and this was most definitely one of them.

He'd arisen early as usual that morning when, over breakfast, his mother informed him they were going to a baseball game and, not only that, they were going to meet someone really special. His parents were separated and Tommy lived with his mother and his brother, Ed, in a modest, four-room second-floor apartment on Greenmount Avenue in Baltimore, a couple of blocks from Oriole Park, where the International League team played its home games. He could not remember his mother ever being quite so excited about anything, but he quickly understood why.

"You have to realize," he said, "you lived in Baltimore, no matter how young you were, you knew about Babe Ruth. Those were probably the first two words we all learned as infants. So when my mom told me the Babe was coming to town with the New York Yankees, I was just as excited as she was."

The occasion was a spring training exhibition game between the Yankees and the Cleveland Indians, who were both barnstorming north from Florida. Byrne didn't know why they had chosen to stop in Baltimore, although he always figured the Babe had something to do with it, being that the owner of the Orioles, Jack Dunn, had been the one who'd signed Ruth to his first professional contract after watching him strike out 22 batters in a game for the local St. Mary's Orphanage team 10 years earlier. But the Indians also had a Baltimore native in second baseman Chick Fewster, who, as Byrne later found out, was his entrée to meeting Ruth.

"It seems my mom was friends with Fewster," he recalled. "I don't think she was dating him or anything, but she knew him, and over the years she'd tell me how it had been Fewster who arranged for our tickets—which were box seats right by the rail—and shortly before the game began, Fewster brought Babe over to meet us. I'll never forget that big hand of Babe's, which completely engulfed mine as he shook it. It was big, but soft, and the Babe had this big smile on his face. Then we watched him take batting practice, that quick, powerful left-handed swing of his, and it made a lasting impression on me.

"I'd had a baseball in my hand from the time I was two years old and everyone in my family said I was going to be a ballplayer. I could really throw—from my earliest years. I had a dog named Mike who would jump up into the fork of this big old poplar tree in our backyard and I'd throw a ball to him, over and over. My mother worried I'd hurt him because I could throw the ball so hard, but Mike was a tough old white shepherd and he waited there and caught all of 'em. When I saw the Babe hit, though, I wanted to be a hitter. Every kid in Baltimore wanted to be Babe Ruth. I just didn't realize it until later on that I was a lot more like him than other ballplayers in that I could pitch *and* hit."

I had arranged to meet him at his house, which was situated on the top of a hill alongside a golf course about two miles north of the Wake Forest, North Carolina, city limits on U.S. 1. Byrne, who had been the mayor of Wake Forest from 1975 to 1979 and 1983 to 1987, had built the house a couple of years earlier as part of the small community called Riverstone, which surrounds the Wake Forest Golf Club. Byrne and his friends had founded the club in 1965 and sold it in 1981. It was a large, handsome, brick-and-clapboard colonial house with a porch that stretched the length of the front of it, and a spacious garage on the side in which a white '98 Cadillac, a tan Lincoln and a golf cart were parked. As I got out of my car in his driveway, off in the distance I could see a foursome of golfers, approaching what was obviously a green.

Byrne greeted me warmly at the front door, inviting me in while immediately announcing we were going out to lunch. His wife, Mary Sue, he explained, had recently broken her hip and wouldn't be able to accompany us. (A year later, on Thanksgiving Day, 2002, she passed away in her sleep, shortly before their 63rd anniversary.) "But you'll like this place, I hope," he said. "It's not fancy or anything, just good ole southern barbecue."

He looked tanned and fit, belying his eighty-something years. He had always seemed a little taller than his listed 6-foot-1, and he didn't appear to have added many pounds to his playing weight of 182. A year-round, semidaily regimen of 18 holes of golf will do this for you, I figured. The day was sunny but cool and he was wearing a white golf sweater and a navy blue cap, which, across the brim, bore the inscription "U.S.S. *Ordronaux*"—the destroyer he'd served on for two years in World War II.

"Mostly, we did escort duty," he said, when asked about the cap. "Our job was to provide protection against subs. We were in the Atlantic and the Mediterranean and there *was* one trip in which we were one of the escort ships for President Roosevelt when he went to Yalta for his summit with Churchill and Stalin."

We walked around to the garage where Byrne instructed me to wait in the driveway while he backed his Caddy out for a 10-mile trip further north on U.S. 1 to a tiny wooden shanty on the side of the highway called Holden's Barbecue. The place was filled with the clatter of dishes and loud conversation when we entered, and Byrne immediately approached a large table behind the cash register where a group of eight elderly men in overalls and plaid flannel shirts were engaged in an animated debate over their plates of barbecue.

"This here's a reporter from New York," Byrne said, introducing me to the locals. "He's doing an interview with me for a book. You guys won't mind if we sit over there in the corner where it's a little more private."

He motioned for me to take a seat at the empty table on the other side of the room and after conversing with his pals for a few more minutes, he grabbed a couple of menus from the counter and joined me. Summoning the lone waitress working the room, he ordered the barbecue specials for both of us, assuring me that there was no better fare to be found anywhere in the state of North Carolina.

"So how," I asked, "did the kid from Babe Ruth's Baltimore wind up in North Carolina?"

"Well, as I told you, I knew I was going to be a ballplayer from the time I was five years old," he said. "I first started getting attention when I was pitching and playing first base and the outfield for Baltimore City College, which was actually a public high school. In the summer of 1937, the Tigers arranged for me to come to Detroit and travel with them. I got to know and really like all of them—Charlie Gehringer, Hank Greenberg and Mickey Cochrane, who was the manager then. They offered me a bonus of $4,000 to go to their minor league team in Beaumont, Texas, but I just had this deep desire to go to college.

"At the same time, I'd been offered a scholarship to go to Duke— which had a stipulation that I had to work in the cafeteria. I was ready to go there when a fellow I knew in Baltimore named George Bratt, who was close friends with the athletic director at Wake Forest, convinced me I should go to Wake. I'd never even heard of Wake Forest, but Bratt said: 'They'll give you a scholarship and you won't even have to work in the cafeteria.' I figured, if I go to Wake Forest and beat Duke, people will hear of me. So that's what I did. In three years, I beat Duke nine out of 10 times."

Meanwhile, the Yankees' chief scout for the southeastern region, Gene McCann, had been following him since his days in Baltimore. In Byrne's sophomore year at Wake Forest, McCann and his boss, Paul Krichell, came down to Raleigh and set up a meeting to talk to him about signing with them.

"They met with me and my college coach, John Caddell, in a hotel," Byrne said, "and while I expressed an interest in signing, I told them I still wanted to get a college degree. They didn't offer us any money, but what they did say was: 'Tommy, what we really want you to know is that we want you to sign with us and we look forward to you making your decision when you want to sign.' They were both complete gentlemen and great people and my coach really liked them. He was about 57, 58 years old then and he'd been around a lot of baseball people for a long time. As it was, I was living out there on his farm with him, and when I did sign, after my junior year, I called him from New York to get his approval. He died just a few days later. Fifteen years later, I bought that farm for his wife."

The Yankees gave him a $10,000 bonus plus $650 per month to go right to their flagship farm club in Newark, which, on its merit, was a terrific offer, except the Philadelphia Athletics were willing to go even higher. They would give him $12,000 and bring him right to the big leagues.

"I told the Athletics' scout, a big ole former catcher named Ira Thomas, I was going up to New York to see George Weiss and Ed Barrow and that if the Yankees didn't give me what I suggested, I'd sign with him for the $12,000. I told him right up front. The fact was, I wanted to be with the Yankees. When I got back to North Carolina after signing, Ira

Thomas was sitting right there on my coach's front porch in the hopes, I suppose, the Yankees didn't give me what I wanted."

While pitching for the Yankees might have been his driving ambition, Byrne also knew, privately, he wasn't ready to pitch in the major leagues. He would spend three seasons in Newark before the Yankees deemed him varsity-worthy, and even then, they had their reservations. For while he'd led the International League in winning percentage in 1942—17-4, .810—he'd also demonstrated an alarming lack of control, walking a league-leading 145 batters against 147 strikeouts in 209 innings. Of course, almost as intriguing to the Yankees was Byrne's bat. When he wasn't pitching for Newark, he was pinch-hitting a lot and finished the season with a .328 average in 64 games.

Said his manager at Newark, Billy Meyer: "Wild or not, he is the best prospect in the International League, as his record shows. There is no reason he can't get the ball over the plate in the majors."

It was nearly five years before the Yankees could start to make that determination. In the 11 games he pitched for them in 1943 before going into the service, he walked 35 batters and struck out just 22 in 32 innings, prompting Yankee manager Joe McCarthy's guarded use of him. ("I was strong as a bull but I just couldn't get any of that dinner chow," Byrne said.) McCarthy liked him, Byrne thought, but apparently didn't feel he could trust him, especially in the heat of a pennant race. The crusty manager did get a chuckle, however, out of the postcard Byrne sent him from Casablanca in 1945.

"We had pulled into Casablanca to take on supplies," Byrne said, "and while everyone was loading stuff on the docks, a friend of mine named Al Campalongo and I started throwing a softball back and forth. He was the catcher in all the recreation games I'd organized, and after a while I started really throwing hard, all strikes. Guys were up on the deck watching us. Then, just by coincidence, the ship's mailman came by and suggested I send a postcard to McCarthy, telling him how I was popping the ball on the dime over here. I never thought the card would get to him, but somehow it did and McCarthy was quoted as saying:

'Wouldn't you know, he's 5,000 miles away and finally throwing strikes. What good is that to me? That's my wild Irish Tommy.'"

He chuckled. All these years later, Byrne seemed to take special pride in the enduring legend of his wildness. He *did* drive managers to exasperation, but he had his moments, too, when he gave hint of being something truly special. In a span between the last three months of 1949 and the first two months of 1950, he was 17-2, and his 5.74 hits per nine innings in 1949 is the eighth lowest all-time. Five straight years, 1948–52, he led the American League in hit batters. He won 15 games for the Yankees in both 1949 and 1950 and in each of those seasons he also led the league in walks. He was on his way to doing it again in 1951, walking 36 batters in his first 21 innings, when Yankee co-owner Dan Topping had endured enough. After sitting through another of what had become a typical three-hours-plus Byrne outing, Topping, against the advice of GM Weiss and manager Casey Stengel, shipped the wild man to the last-place St. Louis Browns for a washed-up left-hander named Stubby Overmire and $25,000.

"Oh, Topping hated it when I pitched," Byrne said, laughing some more. "You know he was quite a man with the women and I think he always had a date waiting after the games. For all they made of my wildness, though, I always liked to remind people I was the only guy who ever led the league in walks three straight years and got a raise each time."

Stengel and Weiss always felt Topping had been too hasty in making the deal. In their minds, for all his wildness, Byrne had the kind of movement on his ball that, if ever harnessed, could make him a dominating pitcher. McCarthy thought the same thing and, in '46, assigned Byrne to Yankee catching great Bill Dickey in hopes of taming the wild man.

"I could throw harder than anyone on the team, and guys didn't want to hit against me in batting practice," Byrne said. "But Dickey, who was the first guy that ever caught me, told me: 'Your pitches are 10 inches out of the strike zone.' My fastball would go up and away and hit the glove and move it further out. The umpires didn't like me anyway, so it was always a ball. With Dickey's help, I learned a cut fastball that went the other way, in on the fists. That was the 10 inches! All the same, they kept me around all of '46 and never used me. I guess they just didn't want the 'wild man' to pitch."

The trade to the lowly Browns was a shock, but it was only the beginning of a three-year downward spiral for Byrne that seemingly had him headed for baseball oblivion. Suddenly, he no longer had either the power-laden Yankee offense or their customary trustworthy defense to help compensate for his wildness, and wins became hard to come by. After a 7-14 season in 1952, the Browns traded him to the Chicago White Sox for the flashy-fielding Cuban shortstop Willie Miranda. The White Sox were even less patient, selling him for $20,000 to another perpetual loser, the Washington Senators, in June of '53 after using him in only six games.

"Paul Richards, the manager over there with the White Sox, never really liked me much as a pitcher," Byrne said. "But for one game he sure did like me a whole lot as a hitter."

That was May 16, 1953. The White Sox were playing Byrne's old Yankee teammates at Yankee Stadium. As Byrne recounted it, he was sitting out in the bullpen when the White Sox, who had been shut out by Vic Raschi to that point, began mounting a rally in the ninth inning. All of a sudden, the bullpen phone rang and it was Richards, summoning Byrne to come in to the dugout.

"There were two out and the bases were loaded," Byrne said, "and Casey was bringing in Ewell Blackwell to replace Raschi. Vern Stephens was due up to hit for us, but I guess like a lot of other right-handed hitters, he didn't enjoy hitting against Blackwell, who had that buggy-whip side-arm delivery that scared the daylights out of a lot of guys. Still, Stephens had hit 10 grand slams in his career and I was surprised when Richards said to me: 'You ever hit this guy?'

"'Yeah,' I said, 'about 11 years ago.'

"'Well,' said Richards, 'how about going up and hitting one out of here?'

"So I go up there and, after getting the count to 2-2, I don't even remember swinging the bat, but I hit a line drive, twenty rows back in right field.

"Believe it or not, that was the second time I'd hit a grand slam homer with two outs in the ninth inning! The first time was in '51 when I was with the Browns. We were playing the Senators at old Griffith Stadium in September, and after fouling two straight breaking balls off Sid Hudson, I was waiting for a fastball and got it, hitting it over the left-center field fence, which was a pretty good poke in that park."

Byrne clearly regaled in the stories about his hitting prowess. For his career, he hit .238 with 14 homers and 98 RBI in 601 at bats, and was 3-for-10 in four World Series. His .378 career slugging percentage is the ninth highest of any pitcher in history. Oftentimes when he pitched, Stengel would bat him eighth or even seventh in the lineup, and his managers frequently used him as a pinch hitter.

I was about to ask him if he'd ever considered giving up pitching and becoming an outfielder—like Ruth did—when the waitress arrived with two heaping plates of barbecue, corn muffins and black-eyed peas. Byrne blessed himself, said a quick prayer of thanks and dug in.

Every table in the place was filled now and, peering through the front window, I could see a row of seven or eight pickup trucks had sandwiched Byrne's white Caddy in the dirt and gravel parking lot. The former mayor was in his element, taking in the buzzing small talk of Wake Forest football, local politics and the shrinking tobacco crops. All that was missing, I thought, was a jukebox playing a Hank Williams song. He may have once been a rich and famous pitcher for the New York Yankees, but, here, in this homespun place, among these rural folks of such modest means, he was just another good ole boy neighbor.

"Your stay in Washington," I finally said to him, "was about as short as your stay with the White Sox."

"Oh yeah," Byrne said. "I got sold over there and was reunited with Bucky Harris, my old manager with the Yankees. I'd made only six starts and hadn't won a game when Harris came to me and told me the old man,

Clark Griffith, who was owner, wanted to see me in his office. I went up there and Griffith tells me he's sending me to Charleston, their farm team. Seems they were bringing in a lot of Cubans and I was being chosen to make room for them. I had one day to go before becoming a 10-year man in the majors. Baseball was embarrassed, I think, but I went along with them because I hadn't done anything for the Senators."

"Did Griffith know you needed the one day?" I asked.

"Yeah, he'd been told by Will Harridge, the American League president," Byrne said. "But it didn't much matter to him. What he *did* say, though, that really surprised me was that he couldn't understand what happened to my *hitting!* That's why they'd acquired me! I think the old man remembered that grand slam I'd hit off Sid Hudson and thought I could be a first baseman."

The man, who only three years earlier had won 15 games for the Yankees and been selected for the All-Star team, was now back in the minor leagues, sent there, no less, by the Washington Senators—they of the motto "first in war, first in peace and last in the American League." He finished the season in Charleston, another last-place team, and then went home to North Carolina for some serious self-evaluation. Obviously, his career was going in the wrong direction and the wildness that had once been looked upon as a hindering but correctable flaw was now becoming his damnation.

"After the '53 season, I went down to Venezuela to play winter ball," Byrne said. "I had thought about a lot after going back to the minors, mostly that God had given me a lot of talent and I had to learn what to do with it to get the most out of it. I was determined to work on a slider down there, and it was amazing what I did in the short time there. I started changing speeds, changing up on my slow curve, throwing the slider when I was behind in the count. People weren't used to seeing me taking something off the ball."

While he was rediscovering himself in the islands, though, Byrne learned he'd be moving again for 1954. Griffith, it seems, had sold him to the Seattle Rainiers of the Pacific Coast League, an independent team that was not affiliated with any of the 16 major league clubs. The manager at Seattle was Gerry Priddy, who, like Byrne, had come up through the Yankee system in the '40s. In some ways, they were kindred spirits in that Priddy, a second baseman who'd attained All-Star honors at every level of the minor leagues, had never lived up to his potential either.

"It turned out to be the perfect spot for me," Byrne said. "Priddy was a first-year manager and he needed a veteran pitcher who could give him innings. I was ready and willing. I needed starts on a regular basis to work on my control."

It wasn't the big time anymore and his ego had definitely been bruised, but looking back, Byrne said, 1954 was the season of his life; the closest he ever came to emulating his Baltimore boyhood idol, Babe Ruth. He pitched 260 innings, the most in his professional career, was 20-10 with a 3.15 earned run average and, in 86 games as an outfielder–first baseman and pinch hitter, batted .295 with 7 homers and 39 RBI. Even more impressive to the scouts' eyes were his 199 strikeouts as a pitcher, which not only led the league but, for the first time in his career, exceeded his walks (118).

Charlie Dressen, who had been the third base coach for the Yankees under Bucky Harris in 1947 and '48, was managing the Oakland team in the Coast League in '54 and, toward the close of the season, got a call from his old friend, Casey Stengel, soliciting his opinions on players.

"The only guy out here who can help you," Dressen said, "is Byrne. I suggest you get him. He's a different pitcher than when I saw him with the Yankees. He's learned what it's all about."

Stengel immediately called his boss, Weiss, and urged him to get Byrne back. The Yankees were in the unaccustomed position of trailing the Cleveland Indians in September, and though it had become increasingly evident they wouldn't be able to overtake them this time, Stengel felt getting Byrne, if nothing else, would provide a needed boost to his aging starting rotation. Never before had the Yankees admitted they made a mistake on a front-line player, but on September 1, Weiss purchased Byrne from Seattle.

"I joined the Yankees in Washington," Byrne recalled, "and then we played a series in Baltimore before going back to New York. And don't you know, as I walked in the gate for my first game back there, who do you think was waiting there to greet me but Dan Topping! That's a true story! I never heard of an owner doing that, but there he was, and he actually apologized to me for trading me. I thought that was real class."

He paused in thought for a moment, a wide smile on his face. To this day, nearly 50 years later, there had not been a more satisfying moment in his life. If there was one thing about his career he didn't mind bragging on, it was that he was the only one the Yankees ever admitted they shouldn't have traded. All he ever wanted was to be a Yankee, the team of the Babe, and after having to refine his game in the bowels of baseball to prove his worth to them, they had deemed to give him a second chance.

"Excuse me," the waitress said, as he was about to continue. "Dessert? We have sweet potato pie special today . . ."

"Ohhh no, honey," Byrne replied. "We don't want any dessert. But we're gonna be here a while longer, if you don't mind, so you can just bring the check."

It was after one o'clock and all the locals had started filing out. Byrne looked around in search of his pal, B.P. Holden, the 80-year-old proprietor.

"Before we go, I want you to meet B.P.," he said. "He does one helluva business here. He's slowed down a little and his son pretty much runs the place now. Everybody comes here, even guys with ties and jackets. There's a Sprint office about 10 miles further up the highway and their executives come in here a lot. You see them sittin' there in their suits and you might wonder what in hell are those guys doin' here?"

"Is it true you used to talk to yourself on the mound?" I asked him after the waitress retreated to the kitchen. "Other players have said you deliberately did that to annoy and distract them."

"Is that what they said? Well, I guess I can't deny that. I was just a friendly guy. I'd do anything to get somebody's attention."

Ted Williams, in particular, told stories through the years about Byrne shouting things at him from the mound. And Mickey Vernon, the two-time batting champion with Washington, insisted that Byrne once hit him with a pitch in the on-deck circle.

"Williams was a helluva hitter," Byrne said, "and he enjoyed making his living against the Yankees. He'd be up there at the plate and I'd ask him about his family. I'd say, 'I understand you're not getting along so good with your wife,' stuff like that. Well, he wasn't! He'd yell at Yogi to 'tell that crazy left-hander to shut up and pitch.' Yogi would get up and walk around. He was enjoying it. I never did do it, but I often thought about going into my windup and just not throwing the ball.

"As for the Vernon thing, that did happen, and, once again, it involved Williams. We were playing in Boston and Casey brought me into the game in the ninth inning to pitch to Williams with two on. Vernon was with the Red Sox by this time and was in the on-deck circle as Williams was coming to the plate. While I'm out there on the mound warming up, Williams calls Vernon over from the on-deck circle and asks him to watch my pitches with him. They're both about three feet from the batter's box. I let them get a little bit closer, picked out my spot, and threw a pitch between their heads! Vernon dropped his bat and hit the dirt and Williams started screaming at me: 'You crazy SOB, I ought to come out there and squeeze your head in!' Yogi was laughing like hell. I yelled back to Williams: 'How was that pitch? Did you get a good look at it?'"

Williams did get his retribution. Two pitches into the at bat, he hit a line drive back to the box that caromed off Byrne's shins and rolled toward the third base bag. Byrne recovered, fielded the ball and threw Williams out by a step, but his leg was throbbing as he limped off the field. "The only thing that kept me from having a real serious injury was that the ball hit off the roll in my damn socks," Byrne said. "After the game, Ted sent Johnny Orlando, the Red Sox clubhouse guy, over to find out how bad I was hurt. I thought that was pretty damn nice of him, although I'm sure he said initially: 'The SOB deserved it!'"

Byrne doubled up in laughter telling it, and I imagined what the result would have been had the event occurred today—when batters seem to need only the slightest provocation to charge the mound. Today, Byrne would have been branded a headhunter of the worst kind. Back then, they just thought he was nuts.

He managed to get five starts for the Yankees that September of '54, winning three, including a shutout over Williams and the Red Sox. But the Indians couldn't be caught, winning an American League record 111 games, and for the first time since 1948, the world championship flag would not fly over Yankee Stadium. Still, Stengel had been impressed, noting Byrne's expanded repertoire of pitches. "They took one of my fellers away from me a few years ago," he told the writers, "but now I got him back with me and I'm glad of it."

In 1955, the Tommy Byrne Yankee comeback reached full flower. When Stengel assembled his troops in St. Petersburg that spring, the pitching staff had a very different look to it. The three mainstays of the five straight world championship teams of 1949–53, Allie Reynolds, Vic Raschi and Eddie Lopat, were either gone or almost gone. Raschi had been sold to the St. Louis Cardinals in February of 1954. Reynolds retired prior to the 1955 season because of a chronic back condition, incurred from a team bus crash in Philadelphia in 1954. Lopat was in camp in '55, but was bothered by a sore arm and in July of that year was waived to the Baltimore Orioles.

With the Yankees having failed to attain the World Series for the first time in six seasons, Weiss set about remaking the team and executed a mammoth 17-player deal with the Orioles in which he acquired Baltimore's highly regarded hard-throwing right-hander Bob Turley, along with another starting pitcher of promise, Don Larsen. In addition, the potential new ace of the Yankees was 25-year-old right-hander Bob Grim, who had been Rookie of the Year in 1954 after breaking in with a 20-6 season.

Crazy as it might have seemed, the guy Stengel felt most comfortable about that spring—other than Whitey Ford—was Byrne, whom he'd known since 1949 and in whom he'd witnessed the maturation as a pitcher the previous September. And then Grim came up with a sore arm and fell out of the rotation early. On any other club, that might have been a devastating loss, but Stengel had his lifeline in the 35-year-old Byrne, whose arm, nevertheless, had been slow to round into shape in '55 because of the heavy load of innings he'd logged the year before. It was just about the time when Grim had to drop out of the rotation, in May, and Larsen was sent to the minors, that Byrne stepped in—and began winning. He wound up with a 16-5 record, his .762 winning percentage the best in the league.

"He beat the other first-division clubs, Cleveland, the White Sox, the Red Sox, when it was them or us," said Stengel. "Without him, we don't win."

"My adrenaline was going pretty good that year," Byrne agreed, "and when we got to the World Series and Casey started me in Game 2, I was on cloud nine."

He beat the Dodgers 4–2 on a five-hitter to put the Yankees up 2–0 in the Series, and it looked like this was going to be the same script the Yankees and Dodgers had written over their five previous World Series encounters since '41: joy in the Bronx and the "wait til next year" lament in Brooklyn. But the Dodgers got all over Turley in Game 3 in Brooklyn, kayoing him in the second inning en route to an 8–3 win behind Johnny Podres, and the next day they did the same to Larsen, Turley's stablemate in the big trade with the Orioles. When they completed the sweep of the three middle games in Brooklyn, "next year" suddenly had the look of a real possibility.

But then Ford reminded the Dodgers of who both he and the Yankees were, with a brilliant four-hit, 5-1 win to tie the Series and send it to a decisive Game 7 with Byrne pitted against Podres.

"I wasn't really on top of my game in Game 7," Byrne confessed, "but I think maybe I might have had enough to beat them again if a lot of things hadn't happened. Sometimes, you have to think fate has something to do with it."

The Dodgers were winning 1–0 going into the sixth when Pee Wee Reese led off with a single. At that point, Dodger manager Walter Alston made the first of two pivotal decisions in the game by putting a sacrifice on with Duke Snider, his No. 3 hitter, who had led the Dodgers with 42 homers and the National League with 136 RBI. Snider laid down a bunt to the first base side of the infield which Byrne fielded and threw over to Moose Skowron, who was in a foot race with Snider to the bag.

"I wheeled and threw and for some reason Moose got his feet crossed up," Byrne said. "Snider hit his glove as they reached the base and knocked the ball loose. He made it look accidental."

Now it was first-and-second, nobody out, prompting Alston to sacrifice again, this time with his cleanup hitter, Roy Campanella. Carl Furillo was then walked intentionally to load the bases and with Gil Hodges coming up, Stengel elected to play the percentages, replacing Byrne with the right-handed Grim. The strategy failed when Hodges lofted a sacrifice fly to deep right-center.

"We certainly didn't think two runs was an insurmountable lead," Byrne said, "but then that Alston made the great move that, ultimately, won the World Series. He put that little left-handed Cuban [Sandy Amoros] into left field for defense in the sixth inning."

For the Yankees, Billy Martin led off the sixth with a walk and Gil McDougald beat out a bunt. Berra then hit a drive to deep left field that looked to be a certain game-tying extra-base hit. But Amoros, running hard toward the left field corner, reached out with his glove and snagged it. Then, as Amoros whirled and threw the ball back to Reese in shallow left-center, the Dodgers were able to complete a double play on McDougald, who was halfway between second and third when the catch was made. That proved to be the Yankees' last shot at breaking through against Podres, who went on to complete the 2–0 shutout that delivered to Brooklyn its one and only world championship.

"If Amoros had been right-handed he'd have never been able to make that catch," Byrne said. "They didn't have anybody else who could have gotten there and done that. We still felt we could get them, but it just wasn't to be. Afterward, Casey said he never should have taken me out, although I guess he felt it was the thing to do with Hodges coming up."

For reasons Byrne never quite understood, he was relegated to spot starting and middle relief duty in 1956. He started only eight games and was 7-3. His only World Series appearance that year was a third-of-an-inning relief call in which he surrendered a three-run homer to Duke Snider in Game 2.

"I didn't pitch that badly when I got to pitch in '56," he said, "but I hit even better (.269 with 3 HR and 10 RBI in 52 at bats). I think by then they were just looking to get younger in their rotation (Johnny Kucks had stepped up with 18 wins and Tom Sturdivant, another second-year starter, won 16), and Stengel thought I needed more rest."

By now, he was 37 and could see the sunset. In '57, Stengel used him almost entirely in relief, including twice in the World Series against the victorious Milwaukee Braves. He threw the final pitches of the season for the Yankees, as the last of four relievers Stengel used in the 5-0 seventh-game loss to the Braves' Lew Burdette. Only Byrne knew at the time that they were also most probably the final pitches of his career.

So it was probably an appropriate epilogue to Byrne's career that the Braves credited an errant pitch by the legendary wild man for turning the Series in their favor. The Yankees were ahead in the Series 2-1, and leading Game 4, 5-4, going into the bottom of the 10th inning. Byrne had come on in relief in the eighth and stood to be the winning pitcher as he walked to the mound for the 10th. Warren Spahn was due to lead off the 10th and Braves manager Fred Haney, who probably regretted allowing his tired ace to pitch the top of the inning (in which the Yankees took the lead on Tony Kubek's single and Hank Bauer's triple), summoned a pinch hitter. Vernal "Nippy" Jones was probably the least-known player on the Braves, a 32-year-old journeyman right-handed hitter whom they'd purchased from the minor leagues late in the season.

Byrne certainly didn't know anything about him when he peered in for Berra's sign. His first pitch to Jones was wild in the dirt, skirting back to the screen. As Jones made a halfhearted effort to skip out of the way of it, home plate umpire Augie Donatelli signaled ball one. Then, however, a look of puzzlement came over Donatelli's face as Jones quickly retrieved the ball after it bounced back from the screen. Presenting the ball to the umpire, Jones pointed to a black mark on it and maintained he'd been hit on the toe. The shoe polish mark, Jones insisted, proved his point.

"Awww, you had to bring that up," Byrne sighed, his face contorting in mock distress. "Here was Nippy coming up there with a cold jock strap. No way he was gettin' one down the middle. I threw him a curveball two inches off the plate. He raised his foot, the ball hovered and ticked his shoe, then rolled all the way back. Now, Yogi's looking for the ball and it's laying right there after ricocheting off the screen. I yelled to him: 'Get the ball!' But he never saw it. If Yogi had gotten the ball and thrown it back to me, I'd have put some more marks on it so nobody could tell the shoe polish. I told Donatelli that the ball had shoe polish on it before I threw it, but he didn't believe me."

Jones was thus awarded first base and Stengel replaced Byrne with Grim, who became the victim of a three-run winning rally by the Braves, climaxed by Eddie Mathews's two-run homer.

"If we'd have gotten out of that inning, we'd have won the Series," Byrne said.

"I hope you didn't get indigestion reliving it," I said.

"Nah," said Byrne. "It was just one of those things that happened. I don't blame myself for that loss. I made the one pitch and it was the right pitch to make."

He grabbed the check, put on his sunglasses and waved for me to follow him over to the table where B.P. Holden was now sitting by himself.

"This here's B.P.," Byrne said, introducing us. "We've been friends for 40 years. He's heard all these stories."

Holden got up and shook my hand and escorted us out the door to the parking lot. I waited by the car while the two of them exchanged small talk as Byrne caught up on the town news.

"I hope you liked it," he said, as we drove off. "Like I said, B.P.'s a good fellow and he runs a great place here. Maybe you can get him in the book. He'd love that."

"I'll try," I said.

As we headed down the highway toward his house, the conversation shifted from barbecue back to baseball. Byrne mentioned how he probably could have pitched for a couple of more years, but found it harder and harder to separate himself from this peaceful place among the pines and the friendly country folk. His family was growing, he said, and there were more opportunities here for him than prolonging his career as a big league ballplayer.

"When I sent my contract back after the '57 season, Weiss called me and asked me to come to St. Petersburg for spring training anyway," Byrne said. "So Mary Sue and I went down there and I talked to him. Weiss said, after '55, he'd be glad to pay me. I think he always felt he owed me something. He didn't believe I wanted to retire. But I'd gotten into the oil business, I had a couple of farms and I'd opened up a clothing store in Algiers, not far from Wake Forest. So he said to me: 'I could get you $5,000 more if you'd go to St. Louis and pitch for the Cardinals.'

"I told him: 'You don't understand, if I'm gonna pitch, the only place it's gonna ever be is for the New York Yankees.'"

He turned onto the winding road that led up the hill past the golf course to his house and parked in the driveway. We got out of the car and walked around to the front lawn where I said to him: "You're still in great shape, Tommy. I bet you could still bring it."

"Wanna see my windup?" he asked.

Without waiting for a reply, he gathered his arms by his chest, lifted his right leg, and in one swift and fluid motion, swung his left arm over the top of his head, went into his follow-through, and unleashed a fervid makeshift pitch. In that brief moment, we both stood there in silence, following the track of the imaginary baseball to one of Byrne's catchers of yesteryear. Whether it was Al Campalongo on the docks of Casablanca, or Berra in the smoke-filled haze of an October afternoon at Yankee Stadium, it really didn't matter. The grin of satisfaction on Tommy Byrne's face told you that, in his heart and mind, he knew he'd thrown a perfect strike.

LORD OF THE RINGS

YOGI BERRA

"You turn left on Highland Avenue and then it isn't too far, it just seems that way," Yogi Berra assured me. "When you get to the house, you'll see it."

The man to whom the "greatest living Yankee" torch had passed with the death of Joe DiMaggio in March of 1999 was giving me directions to his home in Montclair, New Jersey, as only he knew how—in "Yogi-speak." While I appreciated the directness of his directions, I nevertheless asked him to put Carmen, his wife of 53 years, on the phone, to provide the specifics that would assure me of finding the place.

"You mean Yogi's instructions are a little vague?" Carmen laughed.

"Oh, I'm sure they're right on," I said, "but I could use a little more detail, if you know what I mean."

Of course Yogi had known what he was saying. (He always did. It was just the rest of us who never could understand.) It *did* seem a lot further than it really was and I *did* see the house when I got to it. It is a stately, charcoal gray turn-of-the-century colonial, modest by the standards of a multimillionaire American icon. However, as Carmen noted, the house has four working fireplaces and is listed in the Historical Register. It was actually built around the steep, imposing spiral staircase, which is the first thing to catch a visitor's eye upon entering the front door. From 1959 until 1974 when they were raising their three sons, Larry, Tim and Dale, the Berras had lived in a large Tudor home in another section of Montclair, a house which Yogi—again accurately—described as being "nothing but rooms." But after the kids had grown up and moved out, Carmen wanted something smaller and more manageable and this was perfect—even more so when the Yogi Berra Museum & Learning Center was completed on the campus of the Montclair State University in December of 1998, providing a place for Yogi's baseball memorabilia, which was extensive.

It all seemed such a long, long way—in both time and culture—from the humble and spartan formative years of Yogi Berra's life in the predominantly Italian Hill section of St. Louis, Missouri, where his father, Pietro, and his mother, Paulina, eventually settled during the Depression, after migrating to America in 1913 from Malvaglia, a small village in northern Italy. Pietro Berra had worked as a farmhand and in construction in California and Colorado, saving all he could to send for Paulina. Upon coming to St. Louis, he got a job as a bricklayer and years later, on the occasions when he'd take young Larry (or "Lawdie" as Yogi was called in those days) to fights at the St. Louis Arena, he would remind his son of how he'd helped build the place.

Yogi was the youngest of Pietro and Paulina's four sons—a daughter, Josie, still lived in the original Berra house at 5447 Elizabeth Avenue on the Hill—and, as it turned out, he was the only one Papa Berra allowed to pursue a professional baseball career. Yogi often said, years later, his oldest brother, Tony, was probably the best ballplayer on the Hill. But because the family was so poor, the brothers were forced to forsake their baseball ambitions and drop out of school to take jobs that provided a guaranteed (if only slightly better than menial) wage at the local businesses such as the Johansen Shoe Co., Ward's Bakery and Ruggieri's restaurant.

Yogi was 14 when he quit school after graduating from the eighth grade, only, unlike his brothers, he couldn't seem to hold a job. He worked in a coal yard and on a Pepsi truck, earning $25 a week, all of it with the exception of $2 he would give to his mother to help support the household. The $2 went a long way, he explained, because he didn't have any time for girls. "If I'd see a girl I knew from school walking down the street, I'd cross over to the other side so I wouldn't have to talk to her. I was so bashful. All I was interested in was playing ball."

What were the odds of any kid, much less two, making it off the Hill to the major leagues? Yogi often asked that question when he was starting out with the Yankees, and Joe Garagiola, who had lived across the street at 5446 Elizabeth Avenue, was catching for the hometown Cardinals. The story of how the Cardinals took a pass on Berra after signing Garagiola to a $500 contract in 1942 is all part of the Yogi "business" lore.

"I was only 14, but I got a real break when Leo Browne, the commander of the Stockham Post American Legion team on the Hill, asked me to play in the Legion tournament," Yogi said, as we sat in the family room of the Berra home on Highland Avenue, which overlooked a steep wooded hill in the backyard. "Browne, I later found out, was friends with [Yankee general manager] George Weiss, and recommended me to him. That Stockham Post team went to the semifinals of the American Legion tournament two years in a row and we got a lot of publicity in the local papers. Joe played first base—he didn't catch much—and I played anywhere they put me. I didn't care. I just wanted to play. Joe was 16 when Branch Rickey, who was running the Cardinals, gave him $500 to sign.

"Our manager, Jack McGuire, spoke to Rickey about signing me as well, but Rickey would only offer $250. I wasn't jealous of Joe or anything. I just wasn't gonna sign for less than what he got. I later found out Rickey was leaving the Cardinals to go over to the Dodgers—when he sent me a telegram the next year and asked me to report to the Dodgers' spring training in Bear Mountain [New York]. But it was too late. Leo Browne had already talked to Weiss and the Yankees sent Johnny Schulte, one of their coaches who lived in St. Louis, over to the house to sign me—for $500."

Still, as Berra was to discover, much to his eternal dismay, there were strings attached even to that $500. He reported to Norfolk, the Yankees' Class B farm club in the Piedmont League, in 1943 and found out immediately that baseball, while it might be his passion, didn't pay all that much more than shoveling coal or hauling Pepsi. His take-home pay was $35 a week—and as for that $500 bonus, well, nobody would give him a straight answer as to where it was.

"They told me after I got there, I wouldn't get the bonus until I stuck the whole year out with the club," Berra related. "I wasn't too happy about that and I knew Pop wouldn't be either. I guess I shoulda read the fine print, but I trusted Schulte."

"I've heard from friends of yours that you never forgot that," I said, "and that's what made you the tough negotiator you've always been when it comes to your own value."

"Yeah," Berra said, "that's probably true. I know it made me mad. I lived in a boardinghouse for $7 a week and went on a hunger strike 'cause I didn't have enough money to eat on. I wrote home to my mom and she sent me some extra money for food—with a note saying not to tell Pop. Only on Sundays did I eat good when this lady used to come to the ballpark and bring us these big Italian hero sandwiches."

Otherwise, his first taste of professional baseball at Norfolk was pretty satisfying. He played 111 games, all at catcher, hit .253 with seven homers and, in one incredible day against Roanoke, knocked in 23 runs in a doubleheader.

"It seemed like every time I came up, there were people on base," he recounted. "We beat the hell out of 'em. The manager of Roanoke was Heinie Manush, the old Washington outfielder who's in the Hall of Fame. I think I got six hits in each of the two games, three homers, two doubles and a triple. It was on a Sunday, the day I ate good."

"When I heard about the 23-RBI day," said Carmen, "I figured he probably had a future."

Berra laughed at the memory. He'd never doubted his hitting, especially on a full stomach. His catching, however, was something else. He made 16 errors that season—tops among the Piedmont League catchers—and it was clear he had a lot to learn about the basics of the position.

"I was a lousy catcher," he said, "especially with my throws and blocking the plate. I did have a good arm. I just didn't know how to use it. Plus, I threw flat-footed. It wasn't until I got to the Yankees and they put me together with Bill Dickey did I learn how to really catch."

That was in 1949 when, in one of his original Yogi-isms, Berra was quoted as saying in praise of Dickey, the great Hall of Fame Yankee catcher: "He learned me all of his experiences." At Norfolk in '43, he was satisfied just to have caught a good game for his pitchers and not to have cost his team too many games with his errors.

"We had one pitcher on that team, Allen Gettel, who made it up to the Yankees in '45 and then bounced around in the majors for a few years with Cleveland, the White Sox and Washington," Berra said. "He had a kinda strange deal. He owned a farm near Norfolk and only pitched in home games. When the team went on the road, he had to stay home and work his farm. At that time, the farmers got out of going into the service. The first game I caught at Norfolk—it was a night game—the batter hit a pop foul that I lost in the lights. I yelled 'I got it! I got it!' Know how far that ball landed away from me? About 10 feet! Like I said, I was a lot more confident about my hitting. That was a dead ball league. I don't know what it was. Only one guy in the whole league, I think, hit .300. Jack Phillips, on our team, led the league in homers with eight and I hit seven. Then in the playoffs, they gave us live balls and I hit four home runs."

He was still answering to the name Larry then, even though sometime during those years he was playing with the Stockham Legion team on the Hill, he'd been unofficially ordained with the nickname that would be uniquely his the rest of his life. There have been numerous versions of how the "Yogi" thing originated, but as he affirmed on this day, the proper credit is due to Bobby Hofman, the 1950s New York Giants infielder, who grew up in the shadow of the Hill and played against Berra in those various American Legion sandlot games in St. Louis.

"One day I was sittin' along the basepath with my legs crossed—we didn't have no dugouts then—and Bobby walked by and yelled out: 'Look at Lawdie there! He looks like one of them yogis!'" Berra related. "That's the way it happened. The first baseballs I signed with the Yankees, in '46 and '47, I always signed 'Larry.' Then one day, the old umpire, Bill McGowan, asked me to sign a couple of balls for him and after I signed them, he came back into the room and hollered: 'Who the hell is Larry Berra?' I think that's when I started signing everything 'Yogi.' You didn't want to piss the umpires off."

At that moment, Carmen Berra, who'd been half-listening to our conversation from the adjoining kitchen, came into the room and said to her husband: "Tell him about the anniversary card."

"What about the anniversary card?" I asked.

"Aw, it's nothin'," Yogi muttered, a sheepish smile crossing his face.

"A few years ago, he sent me an anniversary card and signed it 'Yogi Berra,'" Carmen interjected.

"Why would you *do* that?" I asked him.

"I dunno," he replied. "I guess out of habit."

"I was actually kind of glad he thought to sign his last name," Carmen continued. "I wouldn't have wanted to confuse him with all the other Yogis I know."

They met in Stan Musial and Biggie Garagnani's restaurant in St. Louis in 1947. She was waiting tables there; he was having drinks with Musial and the other St. Louis Cardinals Hall of Fame outfielder (and idol of his youth), Joe Medwick, after a round of golf. She was beautiful—breathtakingly beautiful as far as he was concerned. He, on the other hand, was not exactly Tyrone Power—his short, squatty physique, large protruding ears and gap-tooth smile notwithstanding. It was a face only his mom could love—or so they all thought.

"I asked the bartender: 'Who's *that?*' Berra related. "He told me who she was and I asked him: 'Do you think she'd go out with me?'"

Carmen Short, who was of English ancestry, grew up in the central west end of St. Louis and knew hardly anybody from the Hill, which was in the southeast part of the city. She was teaching dancing at night and waitressing lunches at Stan and Biggie's as a second job.

"When he asked me, I told him no—that I didn't go out with married men," Carmen said.

"She thought I was Terry Moore," Berra said with a shrug, in reference to the Cardinals' graceful center fielder of that time, who, while he looked nothing like Berra (who did?), was, in fact, married.

Once Berra was able to convince her he was not Terry Moore, she agreed to go out with him. He took her to a hockey game for their first date—the beautiful swan and the ugly duckling—and from the get-go, she was just as smitten as he.

"I thought he was adorable," Carmen said. "He was good-looking and I knew he was going to be famous."

"Did you call him Yogi right from the beginning?" I asked her.

"No, not until our first son was born. From that point on, there was no confusion about two Larrys in the house. His most famous Yogi-ism was when somebody asked him why he didn't marry a girl from the Hill and he answered: 'They had their chance.'"

At the end of the 1943 season at Norfolk, Berra finally got to collect his $500 bonus, but there wouldn't be any opportunity to spend it. On the occasion of his 18th birthday, on May 12, he'd been served with a notice from his draft board in St. Louis. Because of the delay in getting the papers to Norfolk, he was able to finish out the season and then he enlisted in the navy because, as he said, "They told me I might have more opportunity to play baseball. That, and because it was easier." During boot camp in Bainbridge, Maryland, he volunteered for the amphibious division, even though he wasn't quite sure what it was.

"They had these boats that had rocket launchers on them," Berra explained. "The LSD, LCI launchers and all that [actually, he meant *LCSS* rocket launchers] . . . I was on a 36-footer, six men and an officer, when we invaded on D-Day. We stayed there, out in the water on patrol, for about 12 days while the army went in. From where we were, going back and forth from Omaha to Utah Beach, we couldn't see all the bloodshed that they showed in the movie *Private Ryan*, but I did see a lot of guys drown."

When the war in Europe ended, Berra was sent to submarine school in New London, Connecticut, where he finally got to play some baseball. It seems on his naval questionnaire he had listed "sports and recreation" as the type of duty he preferred after his tour overseas (who wouldn't?), and at New London they were starting up a baseball team, managed by former Cincinnati Reds outfielder Jimmy Gleeson. The team also included major league pitchers Walt Masterson of the Washington Senators and Cincinnati's Joe Beggs. (Beggs and Gleeson were also members of the fabled '37 Newark Bears Yankee farm team.)

"I reported to Jimmy Gleeson and told him I wanted to play ball," Berra said, "and he looked at me and said: 'You don't look like a ballplayer. What team did you play for?' He thought I was a wrestler. I told him: 'Norfolk, in the Yankee system.' He kept lookin' at me kinda funny and then said: 'Okay, let's see what happens.'"

As it so happened, Berra made quite an impression, not just on Gleeson but on the other teams New London played during that summer of 1945. One afternoon, they played the New York Giants, managed by Mel Ott, one of the greatest left-handed hitters in baseball history. Against Ace Adams, one of the Giants' top starting pitchers, Berra lashed out three hits, prompting Ott to ask Gleeson: "Who's that sawed-off little lefty hitter?" When Gleeson explained that Berra belonged to the Yankees, Ott reportedly replied: "Oh yeah? I'll give 'em $50,000 for him."

Apparently, word of that got back to Yankee president Larry MacPhail, who, the next year, sent Bill Dickey over to Newark (where Berra was now playing) to see this supposed $50,000 minor league catcher.

"I was told MacPhail said, 'who the hell is this guy they offered $50,000 for?'" Berra said, laughing. "Dickey was a coach then and I had a good night. He told MacPhail: 'Keep the kid.' I think he based that on what he saw of me as a hitter."

Indeed, it was hitting more than anything that earned him a promotion to the Yankees late in the '46 season after barely two years of minor league apprenticeship. He'd hit .314 with 15 homers and 50 RBI in just 77 games at Newark and clubbed two more homers in the seven games he appeared in for the Yankees in September. That convinced them they had to find a place for his bat in the lineup, and in 1947 he caught 51 games as the backup to Aaron Robinson and played 24 more in the outfield, hitting .280 with 11 homers and 54 RBI. Despite his still raw catching skills, Yankee manager Bucky Harris elected to start him over Robinson in Games 1, 2 and 4 of the '47 World Series against the Dodgers.

Game 4 turned out to be one of the most memorable in World Series history in that the Yankees' Bill Bevens had a no-hitter going with two outs in the ninth. It was hardly the neatest of no-hitters—Bevens had walked 10 and was leading 2–1—when pinch hitter Cookie Lavagetto finally broke it up with a two-out, game-winning two-run double off the right field wall.

In Game 3, Berra put the first line on his lengthy Hall of Fame résumé by becoming the first player in history to hit a pinch-hit homer in the World Series. It was struck off Ralph Branca, who, of course, yielded a far more historic postseason homer to the New York Giants Bobby Thomson in the 1951 National League playoff game. Nevertheless, Yogi could never resist needling Branca—who later became a lifelong pal—that *his* homer in '47 was bigger than Thomson's (even if it didn't affect the outcome of a game the Dodgers held on to win 9–8).

"They didn't have TV in those days," Berra said. "If they did, it might have been a bigger deal. We lost the game, but it was still nice. They still weren't sure about my catching, but they liked the way I could hit, and in '49 Dickey took care of the other part."

"You were quite a project for Dickey," I said.

"Well, he worked on just about every part of my game—throwing, blocking pitches, calling games. He taught me to throw off my front foot to get more on it—just like an infielder. The easiest ball to throw is the pitch inside 'cause the batter is gonna be jumpin' away. You can cheat like hell in there. He'd toss me balls to each side of the plate by the hour. Dickey actually used to tell guys in spring training to run on me so he could find out if I was learnin' what he was tellin' me."

He got up to demonstrate his footwork and as he waved his hands, I couldn't help but notice his fingers all looked normal. They weren't a catcher's typically gnarled fingers and there was no sign of any of them having ever been broken.

"I never broke a finger catching," he said, with a trace of pride. "I was lucky I guess. Other than the broken thumb I had in '49 when I got hit by a pitch, I didn't get hurt too much."

"All those games behind the plate, and never a broken finger," I said. "You *had* to have had some secret."

"Yeah," he said, grinning deviously now. "Falsies."

"*Falsies?*"

"I used to put 'em in my glove for extra padding. Nice 'n soft, that foam rubber. Today they make 'em out of plastic, so you can't use 'em in gloves anymore. Jim Hegan showed me that and he was one of the best catchers ever. Remember when they always used to say what soft hands he had? There was a reason for that. And Dickey taught me to catch with my throwing hand behind the glove to protect it."

It had been at the behest of Casey Stengel (who had taken over as

Yankee manager in 1949) that Dickey became Berra's personal mentor. Despite Berra's clumsiness and "wrestler-like" body, Stengel could see he had the instincts for catching, as well as a feel for the game and the right demeanor to work with pitchers. As the season progressed, Stengel frequently took pains to praise Berra's work behind the plate. Ironically, 1949 was the only season in the nearly 12 years he was the Yankees' No. 1 catcher that Berra sustained a major injury, missing nearly 30 games with a broken thumb. Otherwise, he was one of the most durable catchers ever, averaging over 140 games behind the plate from 1950 to 1956. And on June 24, 1962, at age 37, he set another endurance record—unlikely to be broken—when he caught all 22 innings of the Yankees' seven-hour marathon game against the Detroit Tigers. The game, which was ultimately won on a homer by reserve outfielder Jack Reed (who came to be dubbed "Mantle's legs"), achieved additional notoriety for holding New York TV viewers into *The Ed Sullivan Show*, which was the highest-rated program of the time.

"That was the only homer Reed ever hit in his career," Berra said. "I know *I* was happy, even though I knew we still had to hold 'em in the bottom of the 22nd. I'd arranged to take Mickey, Whitey and a couple of other guys over to my cousin's house in Detroit for homemade ravioli."

In fact, Berra perhaps had no one but himself to blame for the game lasting as long as it did. In the 11th, the Tigers were on the verge of winning it when he thwarted them with one of the great defensive plays of his career. The Tigers' Rocky Colavito had led off the inning with a triple, prompting Yankee manager Ralph Houk to order the next two batters walked intentionally to set up a play at any base. After Chico Fernandez lined out, Tiger catcher Dick Brown attempted to squeeze the winning run home, only to bunt the ball in the air behind home plate. Berra quickly spun around, caught the ball and tagged Colavito charging home to end the inning.

"I think I made only one other unassisted DP in my career," he said. "I'm not sure which was tougher—the 22 innings or the fact I was 37. Houk had used Ellie [Howard] as a pinch hitter in the 11th and [Johnny]

Blanchard was the left fielder the whole game, so we didn't have any other catchers. I just know I was pretty tired. Hungry, too."

Throughout Stengel's run of 10 pennants and seven world championships from 1949 to 1960, he referred to Berra as "my assistant manager"—and the sportswriters seemed to agree it was Yogi, above all, who was the pulse center of those great Yankee teams. They voted him the American League Most Valuable Player award three times—in 1951 when he hit .294 with 27 homers and 88 RBI; in 1954, when he hit .307 with 22 homers and 125 RBI, and in 1955, when he hit .272 with 27 homers and 108 RBI. Although those production numbers were impressive enough, they weren't overwhelming—a further testament to Berra's catching ability. In 1954, in particular, he won the MVP by a 230–210 point margin over Cleveland's Larry Doby, who had led the league in homers and RBI for a team that won a record 111 games and finished first. Long after they retired, Doby, a New Jersey native, would be an annual participant in Berra's charity golf tournament in Montclair.

"Did you and Larry ever have a discussion about that?" I asked him.

"Nah, no way," Berra said, waving his arm. "I don't know what goes into the voting. Look at Ted [Williams]—all the times he got beat out by Joe [DiMaggio]. Hell, he hit .406 in '41 and didn't win the MVP!"

"Yeah, but Joe hit in 56 straight games for a team that won the pennant," I countered.

"Okay," he shot back, "what about in 1950 when Phil [Rizzuto] beat me out? I hit .322 that year with 124 RBI and only struck out 12 times! If you ask me, that was my best year, but I didn't get mad."

He got up from his chair to stretch. A few years earlier, he'd had both knees replaced, the price paid for having caught 1,696 games in the major leagues. As he said, "I can't sit too long anymore." The knee replacements appeared to have made him an inch or so shorter than when he played, but his once "squatty body" was now trim, the result, no doubt, of his daily workout regimen, as well as his doctor limiting him to only three ounces of vodka a day.

"Four on the weekends," he was quick to remind me.

It was easy to see why Jimmy Gleeson couldn't believe he was a ballplayer, just as anyone who ever saw him hit couldn't believe the success he had. Ted Williams once said of him that he was "the best bad ball hitter I've ever seen"—a compliment Berra never could fathom.

"I don't think I was a wild swinger," he said adamantly. "I saw the ball good, maybe better than others. That was my style—if you see it, hit it. Don't matter where it is if you can see it. Joe Medwick was that way, too, and he was my idol when I was a kid. Maybe I got it from him."

I noted to him that, in spite of his reputation for going up there hacking and not being selective, he had only 415 strikeouts in 7,555 at bats, a rather remarkable 1/18.2 ratio for a power hitter.

"Dickey always said I coulda been a .300 hitter, but I didn't bear down all the time," Berra said. "He was right, I didn't. Nobody on base? Like Casey always used to say—'tra la-la, la-la' [he laughed]—I used to go up there just for the hell of it. I gave a lot of at bats away when there was no one on base. But when there were guys on, that was different. *I* was different."

A classic example of his ability to hit the ball no matter where it was pitched was an incident in a game he was playing while in the navy at New London, Connecticut. Gus Niarhos, a fellow catcher with the Yankees, was behind the plate with Berra at bat and a runner on first base. The pitch came in high and away and Berra reached out and smacked it into left field for a double. The astonished Niarhos turned to the umpire and said: "Cripes! That was supposed to be a pitchout!"

"You know it and I know it," the umpire replied, "but nobody told Berra."

As it was, he hit .285 lifetime, with 358 homers, 1,175 runs, 1,430 RBI and 2,150 hits over 2,120 games. More than anything else, though, his World Series record of 71 hits is what has come to define his career; why he is baseball's all-time Lord of the Rings, playing on 10 world championship teams from 1947 to 1962. Frank Crosetti will reign forever as baseball's ultimate "ring-master" with 17, but his last nine were won as a coach. As a player, Yogi stands alone with his 10 rings.

Berra played in more World Series games (75) than anyone, and almost every one of his 12 Series homers (3rd most all time) was a big one. In the Yankees' clinching 5–2 Game 4 victory against the Philadelphia Phillies in 1950, Berra singled home their first run in the first inning and hit a solo homer in the sixth. In Game 2 of 1956, against his favorite World Series mark, Don Newcombe, he hit a grand slam homer in the second inning that was not enough to avert a 13–8 Yankee loss to the Dodgers, but in the Yankees' triumphant, 9–0, Game 7, he victimized Newcombe again for a two-run homer in the third inning after Dodger catcher Roy Campanella had dropped his foul-tipped third strike. (He later added another homer in that game). He also hit a three-run homer in a losing cause in the seventh game of the 1960 Series against the Pittsburgh Pirates, a subject that, when broached, brought an instant frown to his face.

He was playing left field that day, having been displaced by then as the Yankees' No. 1 catcher by Elston Howard. In what will go down in the baseball annals as one of the most momentous World Series Game 7s, the Pirates jumped out to a 4–0 lead after two innings, only to have the Yankees come back with one run in the fifth and four more in the sixth (three of them on Berra's homer a few feet to the left of the right field foul line) to take the lead. They would add two more runs in the eighth to go up 7–4 before the Pirates retaliated with a five-run uprising in the bottom of the inning. Two things happened to shape that Pirate rally, which Berra, to this day, for different reasons, still cannot accept.

After pinch-hitter Gino Cimoli led off the inning with a single to right off Yankee reliever Bobby Shantz, Bill Virdon hit a hard grounder to short that, at first, looked like a certain double play. Suddenly, however, the ball took a bad hop, glancing off a pebble as it was later explained, striking Yankee shortstop Tony Kubek in the throat. Kubek was forced to leave the game, replaced by Joe DeMaestri, a past-his-prime refugee from the Kansas City Athletics, and now, instead of being two out and none on, there were Pirates at first and second and nobody out. When Dick Groat singled past third to bring Cimoli home, Stengel summoned right-hander Jim Coates from the bullpen to replace the left-handed Shantz, a curious move considering the next two Pirate batters, Bob Skinner and Rocky Nelson, both hit left-handed.

Nevertheless, Skinner was only up there to sacrifice—which he did, successfully—and when Nelson flied to Roger Maris in shallow right, the runners were forced to hold. For a moment, it looked as if Coates might pitch out of the jam, especially when he was able to get the dangerous future Hall of Famer Roberto Clemente to hit a slow chopper to first. Yankee first baseman Moose Skowron charged in to glove the ball, but Coates was slow in getting to the bag and Clemente was safe as Virdon scored. The next Pirate batter, catcher Hal Smith, hit a three-run homer to put Pittsburgh ahead 9–7.

"I probably felt as good about my home run [in the sixth] as any homer I ever hit," Berra revealed, "if only because it put us ahead. They said that was one of the only times they ever saw me show emotion. I was just wavin', tryin' to keep the ball fair like [Carlton] Fisk in the '75 Series."

The Yankees would tie the score in the ninth on singles by Bobby Richardson, Dale Long (pinch-hitting for DeMaestri) and Mickey Mantle, and Berra's RBI groundout. Whatever elation they might have felt in managing to get even again after the horrific turn of events in the eighth was short-lived, however. Two pitches into the bottom of the ninth, Pirate second baseman Bill Mazeroski stroked a high fastball from Ralph Terry over Forbes Field's left field wall.

"I still can't watch that replay," said Carmen Berra. "The saddest moment I ever had in baseball was sitting in the stands, seeing Yogi standing there in left field, helpless to do anything but watch that ball go over the fence."

"I really didn't think it was going out," Yogi said. "That's why my back was to the plate. My first thought was it was gonna hit the fence, which is why I turned to get ready for the relay. But what the hell? We had our chances. It probably never shoulda come to that. Coates didn't cover the bag—that was the third out in the eighth and Smith never hits the home run. And Tony getting hit in the neck—that was a double play. Outside of Clemente, Pittsburgh didn't have the heavy hitters we had. I think we outscored 'em 38–3 in the three games we beat 'em. Afterward, Mickey cried, and that was the only time I can remember not being able to bring myself to go over to the other clubhouse and congratulate 'em.

"You can't change it, though. It's done. Like [Mariano] Rivera makin' the wild throw to second in the ninth inning of the [2001] Yankees-Diamondbacks Series. When did you ever see that guy throw a ball bad? That's why it's never over till it's over."

A grin replaced the frown on his face at the uttering of his all-time-favorite Yogi-ism. He first used it in July of 1973 when he was managing the crosstown Mets, who were nine games out of first place. When they went on to win the National League pennant, the saying became the stuff of Yogi-lore. It would have been even more appropriate—and accurate—in 1964 when he was a rookie manager with the Yankees. That team, likewise, faltered during the summer as its uninspired play prompted critics to question Berra's ability to rally his troops, most of whom had been his teammates the year before. The Yankees also played an American League–record 26 extra-inning games in '64, adding further credence to his premise of things not being over till they're over.

He had privately harbored a desire to manage, probably going all the way back to the early '50s when Stengel began referring to him as "my assistant manager." While it never bothered him being the butt of jokes because of his funny way of speaking or the legendary stories of him reading comic books, he did have his pride. He knew that behind the clown image the media had created for him was a man of considerable baseball smarts. It was of no matter to him if the press mocked his ability to communicate. The players understood him. He wanted to be taken seriously.

And so when Yankee owner Dan Topping approached him in February of 1963 and broached the idea of him hanging up his cleats after the season and taking over as manager, Berra was very amenable—even though it would mean taking a $30,000 pay cut to $35,000. A secret plan was then put in place. Roy Hamey, the Yankee general manager, had informed Topping of his desire to retire at the end of the '63 season and everyone in the organization agreed the only man to replace him was the manager, Ralph Houk, who had won two straight world championships after taking over from the legend Stengel. Berra, soon to be 38, had already been relegated to backup catching and pinch-hitting duties, playing fewer than 100 games for the first time in 1962, and it would be a natural transition for him to sit next to Houk and be part of the in-game decision-making.

A week after the 1963 World Series, in which the Yankees were swept by the Los Angeles Dodgers and held to a total of four runs by the pitching of Sandy Koufax, Don Drysdale and Johnny Podres, a press conference was called at the Savoy Hilton hotel to officially announce Berra as the new manager. "We are losing a great player," said Topping, "and getting a great manager." (It would be only a few months later when, behind the scenes, Topping began seriously backing away from the latter part of that statement.)

For Berra, the press conference went smoothly as he answered to the satisfaction of the writers all the questions about his communication skills, close relationship with so many of the players and his lack of managerial experience.

"I've been up here 17 years, watching games and learning," he said. "If I can't manage, I'll quit. If I'm good, I'll stick around a little longer."

He went on to predict the '64 Yankees "are gonna be a terrific team—better than last year" and managed to drop one Yogi-ism on the assembled news hounds eager for some funny copy when he said: "I just hope I can stay in the same shoes as Houk did."

In retrospect, he was right about the Yankees being better than the '63 team. Under his guidance, they made it to the seventh game of the Series before losing to the St. Louis Cardinals. He was proven wrong, however, about everything else. If the bottom line is winning the pennant and going all the way to the seventh game of the World Series, then he did a good job as manager. But it wasn't good enough to allow him to stick around a little longer. And he didn't quit, he was fired—a decision that, evidence strongly suggests, Topping had made as early as August. As for Houk's shoes, well, they offered him a job in the front office as a "special advisor" to Houk, which he later politely declined.

The '64 Yankees, while still a "terrific" team on paper, were beginning to wear down from the ravages of age and injury at the core. The keystone combo, Bobby Richardson and Tony Kubek, had both expressed their desire to retire after the '64 season; Mickey Mantle was continually hobbled by bad knees, and, in late June, the perennial staff ace, Whitey Ford, was felled by a hip injury that later led to a sore arm. Ford was 10-1 with six shutouts on June 20, and only 7-5 the rest of the season. In addition, Ralph Terry, who'd been the No. 2 starter behind Ford with 23 and 17 wins in '62 and '63, slumped to 7-11 and was traded to the Cleveland Indians after the season.

Although the Yankees were either in first place or within a couple of games of it through the first three months of the season, there was this perception, at least, they were not playing up to their potential. Whether it was coming from Topping himself, or just a collective opinion of the beat writers, there was a growing feeling around the Yankees that Yogi was simply too nice a guy and that his ex-teammates were taking advantage of him. As the respected longtime Yankee beat man Harold Rosenthal wrote in the *New York Herald Tribune* after Berra's firing: "The oddest part is that Berra seemed to generate so little loyalty among the men he was called upon to lead even though his sometime superhuman bat had lined their pockets through timely homers over the years. He was singularly aware of this and baffled by it."

It was when the Yankees hit the skids in August, losing 14 out of 20 to fall into third place, five and a half games behind, that Berra's fate was sealed—whether he knew it or not. The nadir was the August 20 "harmonica incident" in Chicago. As the Yankee team bus was heading to O'Hare Airport after they'd suffered their fourth straight loss to the White Sox, backup shortstop Phil Linz began playing a harmonica. From his seat in the front of the bus, Berra ordered Linz to stifle it. Linz, however, didn't hear him and kept on playing after being impishly told by Mantle that Berra had said to play it louder. The enraged Berra bolted from his seat and charged to the back of the bus, screaming at Linz: "I said to put it away! You'd think we just *won* four games!"

According to Jack Clary in the *New York World-Telegram and Sun*, Frank Crosetti called the incident the worst he'd seen in 33 years with the team. "The 5–0 loss yesterday kept the Yankees 4½ games out of first place and all but finished their drive for a fifth straight American League pennant." How could he know? Remember, this was nine years before Yogi would reveal his No. 1 secret of life, "it ain't over till it's over."

"Phil and I never had any problems after that, really," Berra said, leaning back in his chair with his arms outstretched. "There were a lot of commercials and endorsements in the years after about that harmonica. Phil made all the money."

Instead of being the final nail, the harmonica incident served as a catalyst to one of the great Yankee surges to a pennant. All season, Berra had been forced to play a juggling act with his bullpen, depleted by injuries to Hal Reniff and Steve Hamilton, who'd combined for 82 appearances and 23 saves the year before. Rookie Pete Mikkelsen, a sinkerball specialist from Staten Island, stepped into the void and saved 12 games, but it wasn't until Houk swung the trade with Cleveland for veteran Pedro Ramos on September 1 that the bullpen really stabilized. Down the stretch, Ramos appeared in 13 games, recording seven saves. He yielded just three runs—and no walks—while striking out 21 in 21⅓ innings. Largely because of Ramos, the Yankees went 22-6 in September to win the pennant by one game over the White Sox.

Still, if Berra thought his season-long run of problems and misfortune was over, he was sadly mistaken. In the first game of the '64 World Series, Ford suddenly experienced a strange numbing sensation in his shoulder, later discovered to be a blocked artery, and did not pitch again. In addition, Kubek was sidelined for the entire Series with a sprained wrist and Mantle was still limping. The injury to Ford left Berra no choice but to start rookie Mel Stottlemyre (who had emerged as his best pitcher, winning nine games after being recalled from the minors in August) three times in the Series, the last time on just two days rest for Game 7. Despite all of this adversity, the Yankees evened the series by winning Game 6 in St. Louis, and rallied from a 6–0 deficit in Game 7 before succumbing 7–5.

Nobody could say the '64 Yankees didn't ultimately give their all for Berra, and there is nothing his critics could say he should have done differently in the World Series that would have changed the outcome. Considering his immense popularity and the way the team played over the final five weeks of the season, the notion of Topping and Houk going through with plans to fire him seemed unthinkable now. Even Berra thought he'd earned another year when the call came from Houk the day after the Series.

"Topping and Ralph called me in and said they were gonna make a change," Berra said. "I really thought they were gonna give me a contract for the next season. I thought I'd done all I could. We just came up one game short. We didn't get Ramos until September so he wasn't eligible for the Series, and Whitey gettin' hurt that first game was a blow. We had a lot of injuries, but the guys played good for me." (In particular, Joe Pepitone, who had his one and only 100-RBI season in 1964, later said Berra was the best manager he ever played for. Meanwhile, the final insult was their choice of his successor: Johnny Keane, the man who had just beaten him in the World Series, who then resigned as Cardinals manager.)

Yet, although he left shortly after his firing to take a job across town with the upstart Mets as a player-coach, Berra didn't seem to take personally the shabby treatment he'd gotten from the Yankees. At least not publicly anyway. (His revenge, however coincidental, was the fact that the Yankees did not go to the World Series again until he returned to the fold in 1976 as a coach under Billy Martin.) When he was fired the second time as Yankee manager—by George Steinbrenner—16 games into the 1985 season, he took it *very* personally, vowing he would never again set foot in Yankee Stadium until Steinbrenner sold the team. The year before, the Yankees had been eight games under .500 entering July, only to stage a dramatic second-half turnaround as Berra integrated three youngsters, third baseman Mike Pagliarulo, shortstop Bobby Meacham and outfielder Brian Dayett, into the lineup. In addition, Don Mattingly came into his own as a bona fide superstar that season and Dave Righetti made the successful conversion from starter to closer under Berra's guidance, registering 31 saves as Goose Gossage's replacement. The team fashioned the best record in baseball after the All-Star break (54-34), but because they were never in contention, it became increasingly apparent Berra had gotten caught up in Steinbrenner's cross hairs. At the start of the '85 season, Steinbrenner vowed Berra would be the manager "for the full season, win or lose."

Steinbrenner, of course, had made such hollow promises before. Nevertheless, when The Boss's axe fell in Chicago, following a three-game weekend sweep at the hands of the White Sox that dropped the team to 6-10, most everyone around the team was stunned. After all, it was barely two weeks into that "full season, win or lose" and Berra hadn't even had the use of Steinbrenner's newest marquee player, Rickey Henderson, who'd been sidelined by a hamstring problem. The Yankee players reacted in fury to Berra's firing and the accompanying announcement that Martin would be returning to the helm.

After GM Clyde King informed Berra of his dismissal in the visiting team manager's office at Comiskey Park that Sunday, Don Baylor, seeing Berra in tears, flipped over the spread table and Mattingly swung his bat in frustration at a garbage pail. (Martin, who knew Baylor detested him, quickly hired Willie Horton, the burly former Detroit Tigers outfielder, to be what he called "my discipline coach." In fact, everyone in the Yankee party knew he'd brought Horton in to serve as a bodyguard to protect him from Baylor.) But the height of the team's anguish over the firing was the bus ride to O'Hare Airport where Yogi was let off to catch his flight back to New York.

As the bus pulled away, and the players gazed somberly out the window at the sight of Yogi walking by himself into the terminal, Dale Berra could be heard sobbing in his back-row seat. Yogi, for his part, said only that he felt he deserved more than 16 games, especially since he hadn't even had the services of Henderson. Otherwise, he said, he was looking forward to playing golf and doing some traveling with Carmen. And, oh, yes, he told friends, don't expect to ever see him at Yankee Stadium again, as long as "that guy" is still around. Nobody needed to have him clarify who "that guy" was.

He maintained his stance for 14 years when, finally, the feud was ended in a peace accord brokered by the Yankee beat reporter for WFAN radio, Suzyn Waldman. On January 5, 1999, Steinbrenner made the trip from Tampa to the Berra museum in Montclair and personally apologized to Yogi for the manner in which he'd fired him. "I know I made a mistake by not letting you go in person," said Steinbrenner, in reference to having Clyde King do his dirty work for him in 1985. "It was the worst mistake I ever made in baseball. To get Yogi back, I'd come in a rickshaw across the George Washington Bridge."

Yogi, for his part, accepted the apology (as well as a sizable donation from The Boss to the museum) and said simply: "It's over."

As additional "restitution," Steinbrenner arranged for a special day in Berra's honor, July 18, 1999, which also happened to be Joe Torre's 59th birthday. A number of Berra's '50s teammates were invited back to Yankee Stadium to share in the festivities, including Don Larsen, whose perfect game he'd caught in the 1956 World Series. A crowd of 41,930 turned out in Berra's honor, only to be treated to something even more eventful and dramatic than the "welcome back" party for the beloved Hall of Fame catcher and heir to DiMaggio's "greatest living Yankee" title.

With Yogi and Larsen looking on, David Cone, ignoring the stifling 97 degree heat and then a 33-minute rain delay, equaled their feat by retiring all 27 Montreal Expos in order for the 16th perfect game in baseball history. As opposed to Larsen, who needed 97 pitches for his perfecto, Cone honored Yogi's retired number in twofold by using only 88.

Afterward, Berra said—as only he could say: "We re-created our game before the pregame, then he did his for real."

Certainly, no one could blame Berra for feeling the way he did about Steinbrenner. But what about the way Topping and Houk—who'd been his teammate and friend—treated him in 1964? Wasn't that even worse, given the fact he'd nearly won it all for them—with little support from them when the writers were all saying he'd lost control of the team in August?

"He *did* take it personally in '64," Carmen volunteered, "but that was a long time ago. I always found it kind of comical that they said the players were misbehaving. Did they misbehave any less before Yogi was the manager?"

"Obviously not," I said, "as Mickey confirmed on numerous occasions."

"The difference," Berra interrupted, "was that they at least told me to my face. Same thing with [club president M. Donald] Grant when I was fired by the Mets [in 1975]."

"Grant called me, too," Carmen said. "He called and said: 'Carmen, I hate to do this. You know we love you and Yogi, but we've got to make a change.'"

"Even though they told you to your face, was your relationship with Houk strained from that point on?" I asked.

"Yeah," Berra said. "I guess you'd have to say that. We smoothed things over through the years, but, yeah, it was tough. At least I was still young enough to get another job and that was probably a reason why I didn't let it get me down. The way I looked at it, the Yankees had given me a job they wouldn't even trust Babe Ruth with."

A valid point, I thought. He fell silent for a moment, glancing out the window where the sun had just about set and darkness had begun to envelop the picturesque, wooded landscape behind the house. In the patented words of Yogi, it had suddenly gotten late early, and, so, we decided to adjourn this session and reconvene later in the month, at the museum, where he could provide a personal tour down his memory lane. It is just that, too—a meandering 7,200-square-foot gallery of vintage photos, laminated newspaper clippings and assorted other memorabilia from his half-century in baseball—overlooking a 4,200-seat baseball stadium, which bears his name and is used by both Montclair State and the Jersey Jackals of the professional independent Northern League.

In the years after his retirement from baseball, Berra had dabbled in an assortment of side enterprises, including VP of the Yoo-Hoo soft drink company, a bowling alley with Phil Rizzuto and a racquetball club, but now his only business was the Yogi Berra business. Two of his sons, Tim and Dale, lease office space in the museum where they run the family mail order operation—LTD Enterprises (which essentially markets Yogi's signature logo on items such as golf shirts and caps, as well as his autographed memorabilia). Yogi is usually there 3, 4 days a week, signing balls and pictures, and during the 2001 American League playoffs, the switchboard at the museum was flooded with literally hundreds of calls from fans seeking a cap Yankee manager Joe Torre had been wearing after every game which bore the inscription "It Ain't Over Till It's Over."

"Yogi needs a place to hang out when he's not playing golf or on the road," said Carmen, "and the museum people are delighted because he's available to participate in their various educational functions."

Dale Berra was loading cartons of what appeared to be autographed balls onto a truck as I pulled up to the museum a few minutes before one o'clock on a cool, sunny April afternoon. We were originally supposed to meet later in the day, but Yogi had called to move it up because he'd forgotten about a dentist appointment.

"You're late," Dale said. "Dad's inside pacing. You know him. He's gonna get all over you."

Sure enough, Berra was looking at his watch as I entered the building through a back door that leads to his office. I secretly hoped he would ask me what time it was so I could come back with another of his more famous Yogi-isms: "You mean now?" Instead, he just smiled and made some kidding remark about how his time was limited for any more of my questions.

"I guess we should get right to it then," I said, pointing to the hallway entrance that led out to the museum.

The first thing a visitor notices is a giant, almost life-size, blowup of the famous photograph of Jackie Robinson stealing home on Berra in the first game of the 1955 Yankees-Dodgers World Series. Or rather, in deference to Berra, perhaps it should be described as Robinson's "attempt" to steal home. Because from that moment, and almost every waking moment of Berra's life to this day, he had adamantly maintained Robinson was out (home plate umpire Bill Summers's call to the contrary), and upon close scrutiny of the photo, Berra *does* appear to have the plate blocked as Robinson is sliding in.

"That's why we blew it up as big as we did," he said to me evenly. "So nobody's got any doubts."

Around the corner from the Robinson photo was a huge glass display case with all of Berra's product endorsements through the years. Most noticeable was the 1980s Miller Lite poster with a picture of Yogi holding a glass of beer, superimposed by the words: "Everybody I know drinks Miller Lite and if they don't, I probably don't know them." Not surprisingly, Berra's was the most popular of all the Miller Lite commercials of that time in which numerous retired athletes were the pitchmen. Of course, for nearly 20 years prior to that, Berra had made Yoo-Hoo chocolate one of the most popular beverages of choice in America.

Glancing at the huge "Yogi Berra's favorite drink" poster in the middle of the case, I asked him: "Did you really drink Yoo-Hoo?"

"Back then, I did," he said, "but no more. They changed ownership a number of times and it's different now. It was never the same after the Italian family sold it."

Then, abruptly changing the subject, he noted: "By the way, if you look in the back of that Miller Lite thing, I think Seinfeld is in there. He was just startin' out then."

We moved on to a case displaying the bronzed catcher's glove Berra used in Larsen's perfect game. In all, Berra caught three no-hitters in his career, the other two thrown by Allie Reynolds in the same season (1951).

"Just curious, did you stuff the falsie into that glove, too?" I asked.

"Oh yeah," Berra answered, smiling again. "What could you say? Larsen was really on it that day. When he got to the ninth inning, I told him: 'Let's get that first out, that's the most important thing.' We were only winnin' 2–0 and I was worried about the *game*, not the no-hitter. Remember, I was the catcher in '47 when Bevens had the no-hitter in that Series game with two outs in the ninth and Lavagetto pinch-hit the two-run double off the wall to beat us.

"When it came down to [Dale] Mitchell [the final batter, who struck out], Don shook me off a couple of times, but it was just as a decoy. We knew what we were gonna throw him. Right after the game ended, I gave Don the ball and a few days later I had Big Pete [clubhouse man Pete Sheehy] take the glove in to get bronzed. Hell, it's *still* the only one in World Series history and, to think, I almost had *two!*"

There were no visible mementos from the two Reynolds no-hitters, other than 3 or 4 pictures of the Oklahoma-born right-hander (who was the mainstay of the Yankee pitching staff from 1947 to 1954) in various display cases around the museum. Berra had always said his worst moment in baseball was dropping Ted Williams's pop foul behind the plate—which would have been the final out of Reynolds's no-hitter against the Red Sox in late September of 1951. Fortunately, for Berra, given a second life, Williams hit another foul pop, which, this time, Berra didn't drop. Throughout the '90s, when Berra served as a member of the Hall of Fame's Veterans Committee (the "court of appeals" for electing old-time players, managers, umpires and executives to the Cooperstown shrine), he openly championed Reynolds, which was not his style.

"I always thought Allie was as tough a money pitcher as there ever was," Berra said. "The argument against him was that he didn't win 200 games [he was 182-107 lifetime]. But Casey used him as both a starter and reliever. If he'd been just a starter, he coulda easily have won 200. He got penalized for doing what he was asked to help the team."

Like Berra, Reynolds was especially lethal in October—and against the Dodgers in particular. Reynolds was 7-2 with four saves and a 2.79 ERA in six World Series as a starter and reliever. Only Whitey Ford has more Series victories.

Berra waved me across the room to a glass case just inside the entrance foyer of the museum and, upon casting one's eyes on its contents, it was no secret why it was in such a place of prominence. *The rings.*

There they were, all 10 of them, from 1947 to 1962 accompanied by a magnificent silver humidor engraved with '50s Yankee signatures, a gold watch and assorted other trinkets. In those days of routinely winning world championships, Berra explained, the players were given a choice as to whether they wanted a ring or another selected gift of equal value.

"If I'd have known I was gonna win so many, I woulda taken the ring every year and had 'em cut down and put on a bracelet for Carm," he said. "But instead, I took the silver cigar box one year, a pocket watch another year and a Rolex another time. George replaced all these rings when he gave me that day at the Stadium, after we made up."

But through the years, the only ring he actually ever wore was the special one from 1953 with the No. 5 embossed over the diamond.

"Only the guys who played on all five of those championship teams [from 1949 to 1953] got these," he said, gently rubbing the ring. "The other guys got ones without the 5."

"I can see why that would be the one that means the most to you."

"Yeah," he said, "when the Yankees lost [in 2001 after having won three straight world championships from 1998 to 2000], I told Jeter: 'You gotta start all over again now.'"

He did not have to be told this display of rings behind him was what defined his professional baseball career; what set him apart from all the rest, Ruth, Gehrig, DiMaggio, Mantle and even Crosetti, who wore the Yankee pinstripes longer than any of them. Lawdie Berra, who came from so little, had been blessed with so much. Stengel had once said of him: "He could fall into a sewer and come up with a gold watch!" At 75, he had gracefully accepted the torch as the "greatest living Yankee," and beyond that, he remained one of the most recognizable and universally beloved people in America. He had been the ultimate "Yogi," even if he never fully understood that, and every weekend when he went to Mass, he thought of his mom and pop, who had sacrificed so much for him, and he thanked the Good Lord for having made this wonderful life necessary.

BREAKFAST AT LEFTY'S

CHARLIE SILVERA

To better understand the persona of all those championship Yankee teams from the '30s through the '50s, you need to go back to the sandlots of San Francisco, where, it could be argued, the dynasty was really spawned. Beginning with Tony Lazzeri in the '20s, a steady stream of extremely talented and polished ballplayers—Mark Koenig, Frank Crosetti, Joe DiMaggio, Charlie Wensloff, Jerry Coleman, Bobby Brown, Gil McDougald, Gus Triandos, Duane Pillette, Bill Wight, Lou Berberet, Woodie Held and, from across the Bay in Alameda, Billy Martin, Jackie Jensen and Andy Carey—spent their formative years honing their skills from dawn to dusk on those fields before ultimately going on to prosperous—even great—professional careers, mostly as Yankees.

As Charlie Silvera had assured me, many of the fields were still there—the 12-acre Funston Playground off Bay Street in the Marina

District (now called Mosconi Field after the slain former San Francisco mayor), where the grandstands have been preserved and the original light stanchions still outline the grounds; the "Big Rec," near the entrance of Golden Gate Park, where Joe Cronin, Crosetti, Dolf Camilli and other big league stars from the area would work out each winter before departing for spring training. It was a huge, all-grass meadow back then with five screens for batting practice. Now, it's divided in half with two well-groomed diamonds and separate grandstands, and still enough space to accommodate two games—as well as interloping Frisbee players in the far reaches of the outfields—all at the same time. And even just off Washington Square, the North Beach softball field— where the DiMaggio boys were regular participants in the pickup games when they weren't playing baseball over at Funston—remains, albeit in a considerably depressed state. It is almost entirely paved with blacktop now, with the exception of one corner that has been filled with sand and turned into a kiddie playground and indoor swimming pool. A 15-foot-high fence surrounds the site, giving it more the look of a prison yard than a historic old ball field.

"A lot of history on those fields," Silvera was saying. "We never quit playing. Looking back, I don't know if there was any city in the country that turned out as many big league ballplayers as San Francisco. We were proud of our city, proud of its baseball heritage. It was really a Yankee town, too; so many Yankees coming out of those sandlots."

And he was one of them.

Silvera, who was born in San Francisco in 1924, grew up in the Mission District and went to St. Ignatius High, near the University of San Francisco in the Richmond District, before signing with the Yankees for a $2,500 bonus in the spring of 1942. He would later spend eight full seasons with the Yankees as the backup catcher to Yogi Berra, picking up six World Series championship rings in the process. But as he said, he owed it all to his roots. His father was Portuguese and his mother (whose maiden name was Ryan) was Irish, and he remembers playing ball regularly at Funston from as early as when he was 10 years old, and also at Father Crowley Playground at 7th and Harrison where the Hall of Justice now stands. "My parents made sure I went first to seven o'clock Mass," he said, "and then I'd play ball, all day long."

And all the while, across those summers and throughout his high school years, the most constant presence in his life, other than his parents, was Joe Devine, the stocky, ruddy-faced Yankee scout who ruled the San Francisco sandlots as the man you had to impress to get your ticket to the one team that mattered; the team Joe D. played for. It was Devine who'd gotten the call in 1935 from Yankee general manager Ed Barrow, seeking his opinion as to whether the $25,000 and five minor league players the San Francisco Seals were asking for this acknowledged center field talent was worth the price. Barrow was concerned about reports DiMaggio had a knee problem and Devine had assured him: "Don't even think twice about it. This kid is ready for the major leagues—now." Before joining the Yankees in November of 1932, Devine had scouted for the Pittsburgh Pirates and delivered for them out of the San Francisco area three of the greatest shortstops of all time, Cronin, Dick Bartell and Arky Vaughan.

"Devine was like a father figure to all of us," Silvera related, "because he cared so deeply about who we were and what we were about, beyond just ballplayers. He made a point to get to know our parents before he'd ever consider signing us. Being that my mother was Irish, like him, he was especially close to her and took a personal interest in me. What really impressed us about him were his Yankee championship rings, and during the '42 season, when Ernie Bonham was on his way to winning 21 games for the Yankees, he'd show us the newspapers every time he pitched and say: 'There's one of my boys. Won another game.'"

Besides DiMaggio and Silvera, Devine was responsible for the signings of Coleman, Brown and McDougald off the San Francisco sandlots and was again the point man for the Yankees in their purchase of Gene Woodling from the San Francisco Seals after the lefty-swinging outfielder hit .385 to win the Pacific Coast League batting title in 1948. Woodling, nicknamed "Old Faithful" for his clutch-hitting ability by the legendary Yankee announcer Mel Allen, averaged .318 with three homers over 26 games in five World Series for the Yankees from 1949 to 1953; Coleman hit .275 with nine RBI in 26 World Series games from 1949 to 1957; Brown was a .439 hitter over 17 games in four World Series from '47 to '51, while McDougald was Rookie of the Year in 1951 and, that fall, became the first rookie to hit a grand slam homer in the World Series. In addition, Bonham, one of Devine's first Yankee signs, who grew up in the Sacramento suburb of Ione, won 21 and 15 games for the '42 and '43 World Series teams. Held, Devine's last sign, was traded by the Yankees to the Kansas City Athletics in June of 1957 (along with Billy Martin) for pitcher Ryne Duren and outfielder Harry "Suitcase" Simpson, and went on to hit 179 homers in 14 big league seasons.

It was no wonder that George Weiss, the Yankee farm director in the '40s before succeeding Barrow as GM, seemed so distressed that Devine's passing in the midst of the September 1951 pennant race (at age 56 from complications of a broken arm suffered in a fall) received so little notice in the press. "It won't be the same around here without him," Weiss said on the day the Yankees clinched the pennant. "The fans never read much about him, but he was as vital to our success as anyone in the organization. The material he got for us was only part of his contribution. To him, the Yankees were something more than just a baseball outfit; they were a deep part of his life."

They were all gone now, save for Silvera, who still resided in the suburb of Millbrae, nestled in the hills that overlook the San Francisco airport. DiMaggio, Crosetti, Bonham, Martin and Woodling had passed on, while the rest of Joe Devine's boys, Brown, Coleman and McDougald, had long since moved away from San Francisco. "If you really want to know about San Francisco and what it was to us," Coleman had told me, "you've gotta talk to Charlie. He remembers everything and, more importantly, he never left."

We had arranged to meet for breakfast at the one eatery in town unique to both San Francisco and baseball—Lefty O'Doul's restaurant at 333 Geary Street, just off Union Square in the heart of the city. O'Doul, a San Francisco legend, opened the place in 1958, the year the Giants moved to town from New York. A pitcher-turned-outfielder, O'Doul lived his whole life in San Francisco and played parts of 11 seasons in the big leagues from 1919 to 1934, averaging .349. In 1929, with the Philadelphia Phillies, he used the cramped confines of Baker Bowl (in which the right field wall was a mere 279½ feet from home plate) to his full advantage, winning the National League batting title with a .398 average and also leading the league in hits (254) and on-base percentage (.455). Three years later, he won another batting crown (.368) with the Brooklyn Dodgers. Periodically, there would be movements, usually generated out of San Francisco, to get O'Doul elected to the Hall of Fame, but despite his hitting prowess, he had only four full seasons in the majors as an outfielder. In '34, at the age of 37, he returned home to San Francisco when Charley Graham, the owner of the Pacific Coast League Seals, purchased his contract from the New York Giants for $25,000.

Graham offered O'Doul the job as player-manager for the Seals, which was perfect for Lefty in that it enabled him to spend most of his time in his hometown, doing what he loved most. It also enabled him to pursue his other passion—golf—on a more regular basis. O'Doul was regarded as one of the most accomplished left-handed golfers ever and once defeated US. Open champion Craig Wood in a $5 per hole stakes match. Over the years, O'Doul also organized numerous baseball barnstorming tours in Japan and was almost as big a celebrity in that country as he was in San Francisco. It is probably important to note Lefty's other favorite pastime, however, which was drinking. He could throw his bourbons down with the best of 'em, and it was, in fact, a thrown bottle of whiskey that effectively ended his playing career when it struck him in the face during a brawl in Hollywood's Roosevelt Hotel in 1941. Lefty underwent surgery to repair his extensive injuries, but was left with double vision.

As manager of the Seals from 1935 to 1951, O'Doul was quite the bon vivant in San Francisco. An impeccable dresser—he was said to own more than 200 ties and at least 20 to 30 tailor-made suits (most all of which were in varying shades of green, his favorite color)—he thoroughly enjoyed people and the fame he'd earned in his hometown. As such, his restaurant–piano bar was one of the most popular spots in the city until his death in 1969. On any given day, flocks of visiting team players could be found having lunch at O'Doul's. Everybody in San Francisco knew Lefty, even the bums to whom he'd nonchalantly toss a buck as he passed them on the street on the way to his restaurant. "They gotta eat, too," he'd say, "or drink." Joe DiMaggio, especially, revered him like a second father, and in the '40s O'Doul was regarded as baseball's greatest goodwill ambassador outside of Babe Ruth.

Though the restaurant changed hands a couple of times after Lefty's heirs sold the place upon his death, it remains the same as it was in 1958 (including many of the prices). The smell of the pastrami was already permeating the place when I arrived shortly before 9 A.M. for my breakfast meeting with Silvera. The walls were still proliferated with the black-and-white photos of Lefty and his hundreds of baseball friends and teammates. I chose a booth under pictures of Joe D. in a Seals uniform and Lefty with Tony Lazzeri. A few minutes later, Silvera arrived, wearing a bright multicolored sweater and a Yankee cap. Under his arm, he was carrying what looked to be a very vintage catcher's glove.

"I thought you'd get a kick out of this," he said as I greeted him. "You'd asked me if I had any memorabilia from my career. Well, this is about as good as it gets. This is the glove I used to warm up Don Larsen in the bullpen prior to his perfect game in the '56 World Series. It may not be quite as good as Yogi's, which was used in the regular game, but it means a lot to me. I feel I had a part in it."

The more we talked, the more it became evident to me that Silvera felt like the forgotten man among all those championship Yankees from the '50s. He may have been a seldom used backup catcher, but he was *there*, through all of it; the record five straight world championship seasons under Casey Stengel; October 4, 1955—the day "next year" finally came for Brooklyn, courtesy of Johnny Podres and Sandy Amoros; Joe D.'s last season and Mickey Mantle's Triple Crown season, and Larsen's perfecto.

"I was like all the other kids growing up in San Francisco in the '30s in that I wanted to be with the Yankees," Silvera related. "Devine started scouting me as a freshman at St. Ignatius. He lived six blocks from me and he knew my mother real well. None of the high schools in the city had a home field. We practiced at the Big Rec and, during the spring, we'd play our high school games at Funston on Tuesdays and Fridays and semipro games there on Sunday.

"I still remember when Bobby Brown moved to town. His parents bought a house right across the street from Funston and all he had to do was walk a couple hundred yards to the field. Naturally, we became good friends right away. Then, after a part-time Dodger scout named Charlie Wallgren had given me a job with their semipro team in San Mateo as a shortstop-outfielder for a dollar a game, Devine sent Bobby over there to tell me if I would come with him to the Keneally Yankees, I could catch. I was a senior by then and I made the move. I was on my way to being a Yankee."

Much like Yankee East Coast scouting guru Paul Krichell's Bushwicks club in Brooklyn, the Keneally Yankees were Devine's semipro team which he stocked with all his prospects and kept them playing over the summer and winter as he evaluated them until they were ready to be signed. An added enticement was the hand-me-down Yankee uniforms Devine had shipped from New York for his eager troops.

"One day, Coleman, Brown, Dino Restelli and myself all went over to San Mateo for a Dodger tryout camp and we wore our Keneally Yankee uniforms because they were all we had. They made us turn 'em inside out!" Silvera said. "During my sophomore and junior years, the neighborhood had a ball club that played in the summers at Mission Field. In order to get our baseballs, we'd sit behind the outfield fence at

Seals Stadium during batting practice and wait for the Seals or whoever they were playing that day to hit some out of the park. Then, they'd let us in and we'd take the batting cage down to left field and hit some before we dragged the infield. One day, Ferris Fain, who was only 19 years old, was playing first base for the Seals and he yelled at us: 'Get off the field you little bastards.' Years later, when he was playing for the Athletics and I was with the Yankees, I reminded him of what an SOB he was. Fain wasn't a bad guy, though. He wasn't a bad ballplayer either. Won a couple of batting titles in the '50s."

Seals owner Charley Graham was acutely aware of all the baseball talent Devine was culling, and did his best to try to keep the kids at home a while longer. He signed Crosetti to play shortstop for $35,000 in 1928, and, four years later, after the Cro helped the Seals win the pennant that season, Graham sold him to the Yankees for $72,000. The following year he signed another shortstop who'd grown up on Taylor Street in the North Beach area and was playing semipro ball with Sunset Produce. Only Joe DiMaggio, whom Graham corraled for the princely sum of $225 per month, was shortly relocated to center field after demonstrating one of the strongest throwing arms the Seals owner had ever seen.

"The Seals tried to sign me for $150 a month in 1942," Silvera said, "but Devine offered me $2,500 plus the opportunity to go away with Coleman and Brown."

Brown, however, had higher ambitions of someday becoming a doctor and elected to put off his professional baseball career to attend college. That left Coleman and Silvera and another Devine product, Bob Cherry, to take the long cross-country train ride from San Francisco to Wellsville, New York, the Yankees' Class D farm club in the PONY League. While it may have been a little tank town in the wilds of upstate New York, Silvera knew immediately he was a Yankee.

"In those days, they sent the hand-me-down major league uniforms to the minor leagues," Silvera said. "I couldn't believe it when I got mine. I had Gehrig's pants and Red Rolfe's shirt. Their names were stitched right in the flannel. That's when I first started wearing 29, which was my number the whole time I was with the Yankees. It ought to be retired—not for me, obviously, but for Catfish Hunter."

Silvera caught and played outfield and third base at Wellsville, hitting a so-so .254 in 75 games and then, like Coleman, joined the armed forces. Upon reflection, though, he figured he developed into a better ballplayer in his three years in the service than he probably would have had he played minor league ball all that time.

"We were stationed at McClellan Air Force Base in Sacramento," Silvera related, "where they'd assembled a baseball team of major leaguers that was pretty impressive. Fain played first, Gerry Priddy was at second, Dario Lodigiani at short, Bob Dillinger at third, Joe Gordon and Walt Judnich in the outfield and I got to catch. Here I was an 18-year-old kid with just a half-year of experience at D ball, and I'm playing with all these accomplished big leaguers and Coast League guys! That's when I knew I could compete."

The Yankees must have thought so, too, because when Silvera got out of the service, they sent him right to their flagship Triple A farm team in Kansas City in 1946 and told him he was now strictly a catcher. He spent two more seasons at Triple A, on loan from the Yankees to Portland in the Pacific Coast League where his manager was Jim Turner, who would later become the Yankees' pitching coach under Casey Stengel. After Devine, Silvera credited Turner with having the most to do with making him a big league catcher. In 1948, he caught 144 games for Turner at Portland and hit .301. He also led Pacific Coast League catchers in fielding, putouts and assists, convincing the Yankees he was ready for the Bronx. The call came in late September of 1948 when Berra's backup catcher, Gus Niarhos, broke his finger.

"I was not a power hitter," Silvera said, "and being that I hit right-handed, Turner knew I wasn't gonna be able to do much with that cavernous left-center field of Yankee Stadium. So he made me hit the ball to right field. He'd pitch batting practice to me by the hour at Portland, but he'd never throw me fastballs. All I got were curveballs and change-ups that I couldn't pull. My average improved from .247 to

.301 just by going the other way. Then he worked with me on my catching, teaching me how to position myself behind the plate and how to frame the ball. At one point in '48 at Portland I caught 80 straight games. Turner told me: 'You'll get tired, but you'll learn. You're gonna get two years experience in one.' He didn't have to do anything with my throwing. My arm was my best asset.

"So by the time I got to Yankee Stadium at the end of the '48 season, I was well schooled, although, years later, I got to see a scouting report on me written by Krichell. To say the least, it wasn't very flattering, but I believe that's because I was one of Devine's boys and, while it was never said, there was a rivalry there. I could catch and I could get a base hit, and when it came to power, well, I had three pretty good pinch hitters in Berra, [Johnny] Mize and Woodling!"

As it turned out, Silvera appeared in more games (58) his first season with the Yankees than any other, being pressed into regular duty late in the season when Berra suffered a broken thumb after being hit by a pitch by the St. Louis Browns' Dick Starr. He nonetheless felt confident he belonged, not just because of the valuable experience he'd gained in service ball and at Portland, but because DiMaggio and Crosetti made him *feel* comfortable. He was, after all, one of Joe Devine's San Francisco boys, like them.

"I first got to know Joe in the service when we were stationed together at Hickam Field in Honolulu. He was an icon in San Francisco, like Lefty, and I guess I was a little bit in awe of him when I first met him. But he liked me and we became good friends. He was always very good to my wife, Rose, and me. He'd take care of me for tickets or whatever through the years, and he'd invite me out to Toots Shor's with Billy [Martin] and Hank [Bauer]. And, of course, I got to meet Marilyn because of him. When they honored Joe for his 50 years as a Yankee, he invited Rose and I to be there. I always appreciated that. Joe didn't care if you were a backup. In a lot of ways, you could say we were all like family, the San Francisco guys I mean.

"I think Joe was instrumental in getting me to spring training with the Yankees in '46, too. He'd seen me play in Hawaii and he knew I had ability. Cro took me under his wing as soon as I joined the big club in '48. He'd take Coleman and me out to dinner and he'd talk to me about the press and how to deal with them. He told me how Yankees were expected to act. Cro was all Yankee. I learned right away the Yankee philosophy. We didn't believe in this 'get 'em tomorrow' crap. We got 'em today."

Silvera smiled at that. As he talked, ignoring the clattering of dishes in the kitchen behind us, I noted with amusement he had not bothered to remove his Yankee cap. I remembered how Billy Martin had always wanted the inscription "A Proud Yankee" placed beside his name on his gravestone, and there was little doubt of Silvera being one, too. The dozen or so people eating breakfast in O'Doul's on this morning looked like regulars from the neighborhood and, as such, were oblivious to this bespectacled, elderly gent in the Yankee cap with his old catcher's glove lying on the seat beside him. As a latter-day, card-carrying member of the New York baseball writers, my curiosity was piqued at Silvera's mention of Crosetti's warnings about the press.

"What did Cro tell you about the New York press?" I asked.

"Oh, just that they were tough. They were, but some were tougher than others. Joe Trimble of the *News*—your paper—he wrote a lot of tough things, unfair things, I thought. Then there was John Drebinger from the *Times*. Drebby. He was a sweetheart. One time in Boston I got hit right in the groin by a foul tip by Dom DiMaggio. I recoiled on the ground in pain. Only time I ever got a standing ovation! Drebby came to me after the game and asked me what had happened—as if he didn't know—and I came up with the perfect line for him. 'Just write there were two strikes on the batter,' I told him, 'and no balls on the catcher!' In all the years afterward, whenever I'd see Dom, he'd say to me: 'How's the equipment?'"

Silvera finished devouring his scrambled eggs and bacon and glanced at the picture of DiMaggio in the Seals uniform.

"It's common knowledge Joe didn't like Casey," he said. "Joe McCarthy was Joe's favorite manager, even though McCarthy made him play the last month of the '39 season with an eye infection and cost him his only chance at hitting .400. Joe was hitting .408 in late August and lost something like 30 points over his average and finished at .381. McCarthy told him: 'You don't want to be a cheese champion, do you?' We'll never know how much he would have hit if McCarthy had let him take a rest. I understood why Joe didn't like Casey—I think Casey had a certain favoritism for his own guys, and he *did* embarrass Joe when he had him play first base that time in 1950. But I always liked Casey, even though he hardly ever played me after that '49 season.

"You want to know why Casey was a great manager? We played 2, 3 men short every year, and still won. That's right. Three men short! In the early '50s, we carried two bonus babies, Frank Leja and Tommy Carroll, who had to be kept on the 25-man roster even though they were nowhere near ready for the major leagues. In '55 alone, I think Leja and Carroll got a combined total of five at bats! And, besides me, we had [Ralph] Houk as a *third* catcher behind Yogi. I'll never understand why they didn't just leave the third catcher at Newark or Kansas City. Houk might get in a half-dozen games the whole season and had one at bat in '54 when they finally took him off the roster in July. Like I said, Yogi was a horse. Meanwhile, we could have used those spots for an extra bat off the bench or another arm in the bullpen."

"Speaking of the bullpen," I said, "that was where you pretty much spent your entire Yankee career, no?"

"Yeah, I guess after a while Casey looked at me as more of an extra coach. They didn't have bullpen coaches in those days so I guess I was it. In nine seasons with the Yankees, I got in 201 games. What does that average out to?"

"About 22 per season," I quickly calculated. "But you did have your moments."

"Well, I guess my best moment was when I pinch-hit a single on June 17, 1950, against Stubby Overmire of the Browns. If you're wondering why I remember the exact date it's because that was my *first at bat of the season!* Imagine going two and a half months into the season before getting your first at bat? Anyway, the next day I couldn't wait to get the newspapers and turn to the averages in the sports page. There I was, at the top of the list, hitting 1.000!

"Casey called me 'Line Drive Charlie' and even though he didn't play me much, I know he liked me. I was a pallbearer at his funeral. One of the stories he always loved to tell was about how Ernie Lombardi stole second base off me in the Coast League. You know about Lombardi, of course?"

"Just that he was a Hall of Fame catcher, helluva hitter and the slowest man on earth," I answered.

"Right," said Silvera. "Well, that's why Casey relished telling the story. What happened was I was with Portland and Casey was managing Oakland. Lombardi was on first base for Oakland and Casey called a hit-and-run, with Dario Lodigiani batting. The pitch came in, high and inside, and I set up to throw only nobody was covering second as Lombardi just trudged into the bag. Casey just laughed and laughed and never stopped telling the story.

"After the Yankees traded me, I got a letter from Casey in which he said: 'I want to thank you for everything you did for the Yankees.' He signed it: 'Casey Stengel, manager.' I often wondered how many letters Casey wrote."

Silvera had made no bones about not being a power hitter. But for 482 career at bats, he batted a more than decent .282. I figured, too, there was a story to go along with the one home run he hit in his career, and I was right.

"Another date I'll never forget, for obvious reasons," he said, "July 4, 1951. The only time I ever caught both games of a doubleheader. I guess Yogi must have been hurt. We were playing Washington and I homered off Fred Sanford. I pulled the ball down the left field line and it landed about five rows into the lower seats. The funny thing is, I never hit a home run in batting practice—probably because I never tried. A couple of years earlier, Sanford had been with us. The Yankees bought him from the Browns for $100,000, which was a huge sum in those days. I saw him years later at a reunion of the '49 team and bragged on him how I hit the only homer of my career off him. For some reason, he didn't seem real thrilled.

"I have the picture at home of me shaking hands with Woodling at home plate after the homer and yelling: 'Somebody get the ball!' I gave another ball to the fan who caught it and I wrote on mine: 'No. 1 HR.' I guess, considering I never hit another one, I should've added: 'Onliest.' But I always said the Yankees had enough power hitters to absorb me."

The waitress had removed our plates and refreshed our coffee. Silvera was tapping his cup with his fingers as he talked and I couldn't help but notice the lone, gold, diamond-studded championship ring he was wearing.

"Which ring is that?" I asked.

"The '49," Silvera replied. "That was my first championship and, for that reason, it's the most special. As I said, I caught those six weeks when Yogi broke his thumb in August. I helped start the Yankee dynasty! I was buried, but I was there. There were eight of us who were on the team for the entire five straight years of championships from '49 to '53—Yogi, Woodling, Bauer, Reynolds, Raschi, Lopat, Rizzuto and me. I'm the one they always forget."

I looked at my watch. Breakfast at Lefty's was about to become lunch at Lefty's. We were the only ones left in the place and I suggested we take a sentimental journey around the room and look at all the pictures. Silvera agreed and as we walked to the end of the bar, he stopped in front of a picture of Lefty and Mantle that appeared to have been taken at a banquet.

"In 1952, they asked me to room with Mickey in spring training in a complex on St. Pete beach," Silvera said. "Yogi, Whitey, Joe Collins and Mickey were all staying there in separate rooms, and Mickey wanted to go out and party every night. So the club asked me to keep an eye on him. I asked them: 'Why me?' and they said, 'Because we can afford to lose you, not him.' By then, we were getting accustomed to winning every year. We'd already won three straight, and we were pretty confident about ourselves. I'd be sitting next to Woodling in the dugout in spring training and he'd say to me: 'What are you gonna do with your World Series money this year?' And, Billy, oh what a brash guy he was! He'd yell at opposing players—in the thick of the pennant race!—'Want some World Series tickets?'"

Climaxing those five straight world championships were the World Series victories over the Dodgers in '52 and '53, and after the Dodgers finally beat the Yankees in '55 for their only world championship in Brooklyn, the Yankees gained revenge by winning again in '56. Prior to all of this, the Yankees had beaten the Dodgers in the '41 and '47 World Series, and the core of those Dodger teams from '47 to '56—Jackie Robinson, Pee Wee Reese, Roy Campanella, Carl Furillo, Duke Snider and Gil Hodges—was essentially the same. I remembered, sometime in the late '80s, having lunch with Eddie Lopat, the junk-throwing but gifted Yankee left-hander of that era, and asking him what the difference was between the Yankees and the Dodgers.

"We just had that inner confidence we could beat them at anything," Lopat said, "tiddly-winks, bowling, whatever. It probably wasn't justified—those were great Dodger ball clubs—but we just felt that way."

"Was that true?" I asked Silvera.

"We were always confident, no matter who we played in the Series," he said, "but I believe there were a lot of factors that enabled us to beat the Dodgers all those times. A big part of it was we had power pitchers like Reynolds and Raschi who were effective in small ballparks like Ebbets Field. Plus, Yogi seemed to own their best guy, [Don] Newcombe. We played the game, and I guess I can say this with a little pride, the record shows the San Francisco guys did pretty good in the World Series."

Two months after the Yankees' 1956 World Series triumph over the Dodgers, Silvera, whose sole contribution had been to warm up the pitchers in the bullpen—most notably Larsen—was sold to the Chicago Cubs. He had played in only seven games that season, and, in Darrell Johnson, the Yankees had been developing a younger (and cheaper) backup to Berra at Denver, their new Triple A affiliate. Silvera saw it coming through all his idleness, and he understood.

"My skills were gone when I went to the Cubs," he said, "although the one thing about the Yankees in those days was that, no matter how far back you'd gone, they never traded you to a contender. After we won our fifth straight world championship in '53, Weiss traded Raschi to the Cardinals, who'd finished something like 22 games behind in the other league. Raschi had held out for more money and Weiss wanted to send a message to the rest of us. A lot of guys felt after we won 103 games in '54 and still finished second to the Indians, Raschi would have made the difference. He'd hurt his knee and lost something off his fastball, so who knows? I just know by the time they got rid of me, I'd lost my confidence from not playing. Then, on Memorial Day in 1957, I sprained my ankle in Milwaukee in a game against the Braves and that was it. I paid the price for all that sitting around."

Considering he was an accomplished defensive catcher, with an above-average throwing arm and acknowledged hitting skills (even without any long ball pop), Silvera, conceivably, could have had a much more fruitful career with a team that didn't have Yogi Berra as its No. 1 catcher. Indeed, had there been free agency in those days, it stands to reason Silvera would have landed a very lucrative contract elsewhere, before his skills deteriorated from inactivity.

"Have you ever thought about that?" I asked him, as we walked out onto Geary Street. "What you would have done if you could have been a free agent back then?"

"I'd have never left the Yankees," Silvera said. "Why would I want to be the first-string catcher for the St. Louis Browns when I could be a Yankee and be part of all those World Series? I was *there!* I had *success!* I was a spear carrier to the kings."

A HERO JUST THE SAME

JERRY COLEMAN

T here is no special section in the Elias *Book of Baseball Records* for achievements in the service of our country. If there were, you would find Jerry Coleman's name in a place of distinction alongside Ted Williams, Hank Gowdy (the Boston Braves and New York Giants catcher from 1910 to 1930) and an even lesser known Cincinnati Reds outfielder, Lloyd Merriman, as co-holders of the record for most wars fought during their careers—2. At the very least, Coleman stands alone among his military service/baseball peers as the all-time leader for most combat missions flown over enemy territory (57 in the Solomon Islands in World War II, and another 120 in the Korean War). For the latter, Coleman was awarded two Distinguished Flying Crosses, which, five decades later, he dismisses offhandedly as "merely the end product of being young and dumb."

To a later generation of veteran baseball people and fellow

broadcasters, however, Coleman is regarded as a hero of a different kind. At 61, he became a father for the third time, and 16 years later, he was still physically fit and distinguished looking, belying his approaching octogenarian status. "I have no explanation," he said, "other than hanging around young ballplayers all my life. Every February, as spring training approaches, my wife, Maggie, can't wait to throw me out of the house!"

We were having breakfast at the Grand Hyatt Hotel on 42nd Street on a cool spring morning in New York and, though it was 9 A.M., Coleman was dressed nattily in a herringbone sports coat and striped tie. Old habits die hard, I thought, as this is the way it was 50 years ago when jackets and ties were the required attire for ballplayers on the road. Coleman, who has been the San Diego Padres broadcaster since 1972 (with one year, 1980, removed when he ill-advisedly tried his hand at managing the club), would not be going to the ballpark for another six hours, but his day was already well underway.

"Jeez," he said, "I've been up since six o'clock, just lying around upstairs watching TV. I hope I didn't keep you waiting. So what is it we're going to talk about?"

"What it was to be young and a Yankee," I said.

Coleman put his napkin down and closed his eyes. For a good 15, 20 seconds, he seemed deep in thought, when suddenly he broke into a smile.

"Young and a Yankee. You bet I can relate to that. You want to know what the Yankees were to us? They weren't just a baseball team. They were a *religion!* It's really kind of appropriate we're talking about this, here in this place. Back in the '50s, this same hotel was the hotel where all the visiting teams stayed. It was the Commodore then. They'd come in by train to Grand Central Station, right underneath, and walk upstairs to check in. I always wondered what other players thought, coming into New York to play us. I can't imagine what it would have been to play for any other team than the Yankees."

In Coleman's nine seasons with the Yankees, 1949–57 (with most of

'52 and '53 removed by his return to combat duty in Korea as a marine bomber pilot), they won eight American League pennants and six world championships. It was the era that marked the passing of the torch from Joe DiMaggio, hero of Coleman's San Francisco youth, to Mickey Mantle.

"I was a product of Joe Devine's San Francisco Yankee incubator," Coleman said with a grin. "Bobby Brown, [Charlie] Silvera, Bill Wight and later on [Jackie] Jensen and [Gil] McDougald. Devine signed all of us after placing us with a Bay Area sandlot team called the Keneally Yankees. They were named after a friend of Devine's, a nondrinker who owned a bar in the Mission District."

But before all of them, there had been DiMaggio. Coleman was about to enter his senior year at Lowell High School in the summer of 1941 when an entire nation, straining desperately to divert its attention from the growing Axis menace in Europe and the Pacific, eagerly rushed to the newsstands for the evening papers to see if Joe got his hit.

"You have to understand. For us, Joe was everything. We felt San Francisco was the center of the universe because of Joe and the streak. Every day, the headline in the San Francisco papers was of Joe's streak. The war news was almost always played underneath it. This was the first great Italian-American to really make a name for himself. We were proud and I don't think there's any doubt—you could ask Silvera, Brown and the rest of them—we all wanted to be Yankees because of Joe."

Probably no one was more proud of Joe than Devine. It was Devine and Bill Essick, the Yankees' Los Angeles–area scout, who recommended the Yankees obtain DiMaggio from the San Francisco Seals, even though he'd hurt his knee in 1934. At the time, it was considered a risk considering the Yankees paid $25,000 and five players to the Seals for DiMaggio.

"But even with the bad knee, the Seals kept throwing him out there every day and Joe hit .341 for them that year," Coleman noted.

Of course everything changed December 7, 1941, when the Japanese bombs fell on Pearl Harbor.

"From that day forward," Coleman said, "my whole focus changed.

I couldn't wait to get out of high school and win the war. Two naval aviators came to our school to talk to our senior class. Those wings looked *that* big! [He stretched his arms to make his point.] I had a scholarship to play baseball and basketball at USC, but the war changed everything."

Nevertheless, Coleman did not tell Devine of his intentions to enlist. He had to wait until his 18th birthday anyway, so when the Dodgers asked him to attend a tryout in San Mateo a few days after the '41 World Series, he figured why not?

"They had all their top scouts there, Ted McGrew, Tom Greenwade, who later switched over to the Yankees and signed Mickey among others, and Jake Pitler, who later coached first base for them for a bunch of years. Afterward, they called me aside and said they'd give me $1,500 to sign, and another thousand if I made the team I was assigned to. There were some other incentives, too. The whole deal came to $2,800. I told them I had to get back to Devine first, which made my dad really upset. You have to remember. We weren't that well off and $2,800 was a lot of money to us. Imagine if I had signed with the Dodgers? A couple of years later they signed another second baseman by the name of Jackie Robinson. I'd have been just another infielder in a long line of infielders Branch Rickey sold off to Pittsburgh after he signed Jackie.

"Anyway, Devine told me he'd give me $2,800 in cash with no conditions. I was a Yankee and glad of it. Devine's idea of a Yankee was the whole package. He wouldn't sign anyone with any tarnish on his character or reputation. He always went into the homes to meet the parents."

He put his fork down and grinned again. "Yeah, we were all perfect."

Immediately after signing with the Yankees, Devine had Coleman assigned to the team's Wellsville, New York, farm club in the Class D PONY League. Coleman, Silvera and another product of the Keneally Yankees, Bob Cherry, boarded a train in San Francisco for the beginning of a great adventure as professional ballplayers.

"I think the trip took nearly three days," Coleman recalled. "We had to change trains in Chicago and when we were going through Ohio, some guy jumped on the tracks in front of the train and committed suicide! That delayed us another 3, 4 hours. When we pulled into Wellsville, all the lights were out in the station. We didn't know where we were."

Wellsville, in Coleman's eyes, was merely a summer hiatus anyway. He was 17 and impatient to be 18 so he could answer his new calling. Because his birthday was not until September 14, he needed to do something to pass the time. But for those three months that's all baseball was to him—a summer job, in waiting for a much bigger, and far more heroic job. After striking out his first six times at bat in professional ball and getting hit in the ribs with a pitch on his seventh, he settled in to hit .304 in 83 games, all of them at third base. It was an impressive enough beginning. Coleman just wasn't sure if it was an ending as well. Until Pearl Harbor, until the men with the big wings on their shoulders strode into his classroom that day, baseball had been practically his whole life. Silvera and Cherry would be going into the service after Wellsville, too. They just didn't look forward to it the way Coleman did.

"We were kicked in the ass on December 7," Coleman said. "That's the way I saw it and I was going into the V-5 Program, which was a 1½-year course in naval aviation. When I think about it now, I was only 17 and the Germans and Japanese would have never surrendered if they'd have known what they were up against. I had already passed the test. I just couldn't go until my 18th birthday. I got home to San Francisco and, on September 14, went down to the ferry building at the end of Market Street and offered up my body for my country."

For the better part of the next three years, home for Coleman would be a tiny coral and sand strip of land in the middle of the Pacific Ocean, about 100 miles north of Bougainville, called Green Island. It was nothing more than a landing strip from which two dive-bomber squadrons launched daily missions on Japanese strongholds in the Solomon Islands. Their planes, single engine SBD Dauntlesses with 1,300 horsepower engines, were scarcely heavier than the 1,000-pound bombs they carried.

"The 341 *Torrid Turtles!*" Coleman mused. "That was our squadron's name. Can you imagine that? No dragons, or tigers. *Turtles!* Don't you think they could have come up with something a little more fearsome than that? There was this picture on the side of our planes of a turtle carrying our bombs. It wasn't a bad existence as long as you didn't mind bathing and drinking out of your helmet with the rainwater. There was no other water there, even though we were in the middle of the Pacific."

"Wasn't there some trepidation getting into those little planes every day and then flying them over enemy territory?" I had to ask.

"Nah," Coleman replied. "Like I said, we were young and dumb. Besides, those planes were durable. They could take a beating."

After the Solomons there were more missions over Luzon and Mindanao, for which Coleman brought home the Distinguished Flying Cross as well as a small booty of other assorted air medals. He returned to San Francisco in January of 1946 unscathed in either body or mind. He had done what he was supposed to do. Maybe it was dumb luck that he came home with nothing more damaging than a few bullet holes in the wings of his SBD Dauntless. Every time he looked at his first lieutenant's bars he felt accomplished. Best of all, he was still young— and ready now to be a Yankee.

"I've always felt that was my biggest luck of all," he said, poking at his scrambled eggs.

He batted .275 in 134 games, mostly at third base, for Binghamton, the Yankees' Class A Eastern League farm club, in 1946 and got promoted to Triple A Kansas City the following season where he hit .278. Modest figures both, and the Yankees still weren't sure what they had.

"When they sent me to Newark in 1948, and my average slipped to .251, my manager there, Bill Skiff, told me: 'Learn to use your bat and quit cigarettes. You're too small.' I'd never had anyone tell me that," Coleman said. "In the service, I wanted to be Clark Gable and Errol Flynn. That's why I smoked. It was the social thing to do. With the Yankees, it was always power, power. So I got a leaded bat and used it in batting practice. I knew I wasn't going to be a power hitter, especially after I saw that left field fence at Yankee Stadium, but I'd learned how to handle a bat, hitting and running, at Wellsville, and then I watched Bobby Brown; how he'd choke up. I adopted a moderate choke style. That's how I made the big club."

In the spring of 1949, the postwar Yankees were a team in transition. The failure of Bucky Harris to repeat his 1947 world championship triumph resulted in his firing as manager, despite the Yankees having won 94 games in 1948 and finishing third, just two games behind the eventual world champion Cleveland Indians. Dan Topping and Del Webb had bought out their volcanic partner Larry MacPhail and, with their blessing (especially Webb's), GM George Weiss hired Casey Stengel, who had just managed Oakland to the Pacific Coast League pennant, to succeed Harris. Stengel was 58 years old, but his whitening hair and heavily lined face, undoubtedly the product of thousands of late-night imbibing sessions, made him look much older. And while he came with high grades from Devine and Essick—the Yankees' West Coast scouting gurus who had watched him regularly in the Coast League—in major league circles he was regarded mostly as a clown who had shown no hint of genius in his unsuccessful earlier managerial tenures with bad Brooklyn Dodger and Boston Brave teams in the late '30s and '40s. Upon the announcement of Stengel as Yankee manager, Dave Egan, the acerbic *Boston Daily Record* columnist, wrote: "Ladies and gentlemen, the Yankees have now been mathematically eliminated from the 1949 pennant race."

It was a veteran Yankee team Stengel inherited, and one on which he clearly wanted to put his stamp. Coleman began to sense this midway through the spring when, after he thumped a line drive into deep center field, the new manager started asking questions about him. Soon, he was playing every day, switching from third to short to second as Stengel evaluated the incumbents there, Billy Johnson, Phil Rizzuto and Snuffy Stirnweiss. Then, on opening day, the luck Coleman insisted had been his guardian through all those bombing missions (after first making him a Yankee, of course) cast favor his way again when Stirnweiss suffered a deep spike wound on his hand. Coleman had made the team as the backup utility infielder and now suddenly he was Stengel's second baseman.

"I said to myself, 'why me?'" Coleman recalled. "I had only played about 39 games at second in the minor leagues. I felt I was just lucky to have made the team. That's why I wore 42 my entire career. Back then, any number above 39 was the minor leagues. I was frankly scared to death and in my first game I proved it. We were playing Washington, second game of the season, and here I am at second base and wouldn't you know the first guy up, Gil Coan, hits this stinking little grounder that goes right through my legs. My first play in the big leagues and I booted it big time."

To say the least, it was an inauspicious start to what would ultimately be the most memorable season of Coleman's career. Indeed, if you asked any of the eight players—Allie Reynolds, Vic Raschi, Eddie Lopat, Yogi Berra, Phil Rizzuto, Charlie Silvera, Gene Woodling and Hank Bauer—who were with the Yankees throughout the entire record five straight world championship seasons under Stengel, 1949–53, they would, to a man, maintain that 1949 was the most special. There are a lot of reasons for that, not the least of which was the dramatic and defining manner in which the Yankees won the pennant, needing—and getting—a sweep of the Red Sox to erase a one-game deficit on the final weekend of the season.

It may not have been the best team Stengel managed in New York, but was almost certainly the most heartwarming one for the grizzled skipper. Without the presence of a .300-hitting regular—Tommy Henrich's .287 led the club—and with DiMaggio sidelined almost the entire first half with bone spurs in his right heel, it still had the look of a war team. (DiMaggio made his debut June 28 at Boston and smashed four homers in three games to lead the Yankees to a sweep of that series.) In addition, Yogi Berra broke a thumb and missed 50 games, and even Johnny Mize, the great slugging first baseman acquired

August 22 from the Giants for pennant insurance, tore his shoulder and missed the final month. Considering all those setbacks, it was almost a miracle the Yankees spent only four days out of first place the entire season. Those, however, came in the final week when the Red Sox, who had trailed by as much as 12 games in July, surged into the lead by taking two games from the Yankees at Fenway Park on the next-to-last weekend, and beating them a third straight day in a makeup game at Yankee Stadium on Monday.

The September 26 makeup game win, which thrust the surging Sox into the lead, was decided on a hotly contested play at the plate in the eighth inning. Leading 6–3 going into the eighth, the Yankees allowed the Red Sox to complete a four-run winning rally on a series of critical mistakes. Snuffy Stirnweiss (who had gone in to play second after Coleman was pinch-hit for in the fourth) bobbled what appeared to be a certain double play grounder by Johnny Pesky to allow one run to score. On the next play Yankee reliever Joe Page failed to cover first base on a hard-hit grounder by Ted Williams to the right side, creating a bases-loaded, no-out situation. After a sacrifice fly by Vern Stephens tied the score, Red Sox manager Joe McCarthy ordered Bobby Doerr, his hard-hitting second baseman, to squeeze. Doerr bunted down the first base line, but Henrich, an outfielder by trade, hesitated slightly in fielding the ball, and his subsequent throw home to Yankee catcher Ralph Houk was a tad late as Pesky slid under the sweep tag.

Houk, the decorated war veteran, went ballistic at home plate umpire Bill Grieve's safe call. Storming around the plate, Houk flung his cap and mask to the ground and raged at Grieve, as did Stengel and Page. The veteran umpire showed remarkable restraint—which would not likely be the case today—in allowing the Yankees to air their beef without ejecting anyone. He later said it was too important a game to have any of the key participants thrown out. However, as Grieve and the other umpires walked past the Yankee dugout on the way to their dressing room, Yankee right fielder Cliff Mapes cursed him and accused him of throwing the game to the Red Sox. For that, Mapes was fined

$200 by the American League office and ordered to publicly apologize to Grieve (which he did) or face an indefinite suspension. Houk and Stengel were fined $100 for their excessive arguing.

Two days later, the Yankees regained a tie for the lead, only to fall behind by a game with two to go when they lost to the Athletics September 30 as Boston won.

Saturday, October 1, a crowd of 69,551 at Yankee Stadium came to salute DiMaggio, still weakened by a bout of viral pneumonia that had sidelined him for nearly two weeks leading up to the pivotal final weekend series. When the Red Sox got off to a 4–0 lead after three innings, it looked as if the day, which had begun in celebration for the Yankees' greatest star since Babe Ruth, was going to end as a funeral procession for their season. Stengel must have sensed as much. In what initially seemed like a desperate gamble, he yanked Allie Reynolds after the Yankee ace and ultimate competitor walked three batters and gave up another single to right in the third. As Reynolds left with the bases loaded and the Yanks trailing 2–0, into this crisis Stengel summoned Joe Page, his principal reliever, who would have been considered a closer in those days before the term became fashionable. Obviously, this was not a closer situation, unless, of course, Stengel was somehow banking on Page closing out the Sox over the final six innings.

It turned out this was precisely what he had in mind. With the pennant and everything else for which the Yankees had seemingly overachieved in Stengel's maiden season on the line, the manager determined he was going to go down with his best. The free-spirited left-hander Page had, to that point, appeared in 59 games for Stengel in '49, winning 12 and saving 27, a Yankee record that would last until Luis Arroyo notched 29 (mostly for Whitey Ford) in 1961. No other reliever in baseball in '49 had more than 10 saves.

"Page was absolutely as cool and oblivious to pressure as they come," Coleman said. "Everything was fun to him. I'll never forget him walking past me at second base on his way to the mound that day and yelling over: 'Check out that blonde sitting behind third base!' I thought: 'This is over.' I never imagined how long Joe could go."

Initially, Coleman's fears about Page's concentration and focus seemed well founded and Stengel's big gamble seemed doomed. Page walked the first two batters he faced—the second, Billy Goodman, on four straight pitches—to force in two more runs. At that point Stengel came to the mound and asked his reliever if he was all right, to which Page replied: "Of course. I'll get us out of this."

Page proceeded to strike out the next two batters, Birdie Tebbetts (swinging on three high fastballs out of the zone) and Mel Parnell, a good-hitting pitcher, also on three pitches outside the zone, to leave the bases loaded. From there, he took complete charge, yielding just one more hit over the remaining six innings. The Yankees, meanwhile, came back against the lefty Parnell and his successor, right-hander Joe Dobson. It was a homer by the right-handed-hitting Johnny Lindell (whom Stengel had elected to keep in the game despite the switch of Dobson for Parnell) that finally put the Yankees ahead 5–4 in the eighth. Page then closed it out in the ninth to pull them even with the Red Sox with one game to play.

"The next day we had [Vic] Raschi and, I have to say, a kind of quiet confidence we would somehow find a way to win—just like we'd been doing all season long," Coleman said.

The Red Sox countered with Ellis Kinder, their ace who had already won 23 games, four of them against the Yankees. Kinder, a good ole boy right-hander from Jackson, Tennessee, was called "Old Folks" by his teammates, not necessarily because he was old (he was only 35), but because he *looked* old. Kinder's perpetually reddened face was heavily lined, the result no doubt of the hard-drinking lifestyle he maintained. (He died in 1968 at age 54 of cirrhosis of the liver.) The fact that this game was probably the most important he would ever pitch in no way deterred Kinder from his appointed rounds of the New York nightspots after Saturday's Red Sox loss. He partied hard Saturday night, as his teammates hoped he would. According to

Kinder's friend Arthur Richman, the longtime baseball executive who was then a baseball writer for the *New York Mirror*, Vern Stephens and Al Zarilla approached him in the Red Sox clubhouse after Saturday's game and instructed him to "take Old Folks out and get him good and drunk tonight because he always pitches better after a bender." Richman obliged, delivering a very intoxicated Kinder, along with a woman companion, to his hotel room at the Commodore at 4 A.M.

Phil Rizzuto was the first batter to greet the remarkably fresh Kinder the next day and lined a triple past Johnny Pesky at third into the left field corner. Henrich followed in typical fashion—for him. With the Red Sox infield playing back, conceding the run, the Yankee they called "Old Reliable" choked up to make sure he got a piece of the ball and hit a soft bouncer to second that scored Rizzuto easily.

If Kinder was experiencing any undue after-effects of his long night of imbibing, he certainly didn't show it. If anything, Rizzuto's leadoff triple served as his wake-up call as he settled in to shut the Yankees down on two hits into the eighth, matching zeroes with Raschi while masterfully mixing his fastball and bread-and-butter straight change with pinpoint control. With Kinder due to lead off, all the Yankee eyes were on the Red Sox bench at the start of the eighth, and when Boston manager Joe McCarthy signaled for rookie Tom Wright to pinch-hit, there was a sense of anticipation all around.

"More a sigh of relief," Coleman said. "Kinder was absolutely brilliant that day. We never could hit him and he showed no sign of tiring. Needless to say, we gave full approval to McCarthy's decision."

It would prove to be just another of the many fateful Red Sox decisions in the 80 years—following the sale of Ruth to the Yankees in 1920—that resulted in their being denied the pennant. Wright managed to draw a walk from Raschi, but Dom DiMaggio followed by grounding into a double play. The inning ended with the Yankees still ahead 1–0 and Kinder out of the game. With two left-handed hitters, Yogi Berra and Henrich, due to lead off the Yankee eighth, McCarthy once again summoned Parnell, his Saturday starter, to relieve Kinder. Parnell had been used extensively down the stretch by McCarthy and his fatigue was immediately evident.

Henrich had always had success against Parnell anyway and he walloped his first fastball deep into the right field seats to make it 2–0. Kinder sat on the Red Sox bench, silently fuming as Berra followed with a single and McCarthy lifted Parnell in favor of Tex Hughson, a right-hander in whom he'd shown almost no confidence all season. Hughson got DiMaggio to hit into a double play, but Lindell and Billy Johnson singled and Cliff Mapes was walked intentionally to load the bases for the rookie Coleman. On a letter-high fastball, Coleman turned and sliced the ball off the trademark into shallow right field toward the line—too far away for either second baseman Bobby Doerr or the right fielder Zarilla to catch. Zarilla made a valiant effort, racing in and diving at the last instant, the ball hitting the ground just in front of his outstretched glove. All three runners scored on the fluke hit and suddenly it was a 5–0 game.

"I was almost ashamed," Coleman said. "I mean, I came in afterward and everybody was patting me on the back and congratulating me for what I felt was just a lucky hit. Yeah, there it was, that Coleman luck again."

The Red Sox were down, but not quite dead. In the ninth, thanks in large part to a triple by Bobby Doerr over a clearly struggling DiMaggio's head in deep left-center, the Red Sox were able to stage a last-ditch three-run rally. Though the ball was hit hard, DiMaggio normally made those catches effortlessly. Two runs scored on the play and DiMaggio signaled to the bench to come out of the game.

"That was as memorable a moment in that game as anything," Coleman related. "Joe taking himself out. He was sick, but he played anyway. He was a very proud guy as everybody knows. He was a special person. His body just quit on him after the war and even though he had a great season in '48 (leading the league in homers and RBI), he wasn't nearly the same player. He had an imperial presence, like no one else in any sport. He always knew who he was. Mickey was always a kid and it ruined him, but Joe never lost his dignity. I'll always think of him in a blue suit with a shirt and tie."

After Zarilla flied out to Mapes, Goodman singled up the middle to score Doerr, closing the score to 5–3. Now it was Tebbetts again, representing the Sox's last chance; Tebbetts, who had always been the most vocal Red Sox bench jockey, who had taunted the Yankees prior to Saturday's game about Sunday's game being unnecessary. Raschi, now seething at what he perceived to be this freak Red Sox rally, waved Henrich off as the first baseman strolled over to offer some reassuring words. Moments later, Tebbetts hit a pop-up in foul territory behind first base. Coleman began making a run at it, only to be called off by Henrich, who squeezed it into his glove and raised his arms in celebration.

"As long as I live, my greatest thrill in baseball will always be Birdie Tebbetts popping up to Henrich," Coleman said. "We were picked everywhere from fourth to eighth that year. Nobody thought we had a team good enough to win."

The '49 World Series against the Dodgers was almost anticlimactic. Starting with Henrich's ninth-inning homer that beat Don Newcombe 1–0 in Game 1, the Yankees disposed of the Dodgers in five games. Reynolds shut the Dodgers down on two hits in that game and would later come back to throw three and a third more shutout innings in relief of Eddie Lopat to save the Yankees' 6–4 Game 4 victory.

"Winning the pennant had been such a desperate race," Coleman said, "and then, so quickly, we beat Newcombe and we just seemed in charge. I was in the clubhouse putting some drops in my eyes in the bottom of the ninth. I never saw Henrich hit it out. I just heard the roar and the next thing, everybody was rushing up the runway."

The Baseball Writers Association voted the 1949 American League Rookie of the Year award to Roy Sievers, the St. Louis Browns outfielder who hit .306 with 16 homers and 91 RBI. Coleman, who hit .275 and led American League second basemen in fielding, finished third. But the *Sporting News* named Coleman its top rookie.

"Didn't they always say the *Sporting News* was the 'bible of baseball'?" Coleman laughed. "I know I believed that."

The 1950 World Series was even easier for Stengel's troops, a four-game sweep of the Philadelphia Phillies in which Raschi out-dueled National League MVP Jim Konstanty 1–0 in Game 1 and Reynolds out-dueled Robin Roberts, 2–1, in the 10-inning thriller in Game 2. Only in Game 3 did the Phillies ever have a lead, rallying for single runs in the sixth and seventh to go up 2–1. In the Yankee eighth, however, Coleman started the Yankees' tying rally by drawing a two-out walk. Two more walks, to Berra and DiMaggio, loaded the bases and when Phils shortstop Granny Hamner fumbled Brown's grounder, Coleman scored. In the ninth, Coleman would climax a two-out rally off reliever Russ Meyer by singling home the winning run. His '50 Series totals, a .286 average, two runs scored and a Series-high three RBI, earned him another hero's honor—the Babe Ruth Award.

"I was involved in every run in the first three games," he said. "Just one of those things. The same story. In all my World Series games I made only one error. That's something I'm most proud of. Defense was my game."

How could he know that 1950 season would prove to be the peak of his career? He'd hit .287, been selected to the All-Star team and capped it by winning the World Series hero award. Baseball was his life now. He was one of Casey's boys and there was every reason to believe he would fulfill his destiny as the greatest Yankee second baseman since that other San Francisco product and idol of his youth, Tony Lazzeri. How could he know a year later he would be back flying warplanes?

"When they called me back to Korea, I was like all of us who thought we'd done our duty in World War II," Coleman said. "My attitude was 'let's just get it over with.' I never thought it would affect my career. Looking back, though, the highlight of my entire life was those five years in the service. They were far more important than anything else I ever did."

This time there would be close calls, summoning up all the

Coleman luck that hadn't been spent over the islands in the Pacific. Once, he was flying his Corsair attack bomber onto a landing strip when a crippled Sabre Jet was called in at the same time due to a mixup in the control tower. A crash was averted with only inches to spare when the pilot of the faster jet gunned out of Coleman's path. A second narrow escape occurred when his motor conked out on him after he was 100 feet above his takeoff strip. His plane was carrying 3,000-pound bombs, which he didn't dare to jettison. Instead, he dangled hopelessly in the air before a gliding crash landing in which the plane flipped on its back. The straps on his crash helmet entangled around his neck and only the quick action of a navy corpsman saved him from choking to death. Miraculously, the bombs didn't detonate in the crash.

"You really never know if you've had any close calls unless you're shot down," Coleman insisted matter-of-factly. "I guess the closest I ever came was on a training mission in which 10 to 12 planes were on a bombing run. My bunkmate and best friend, Max Harper, was flying right in front of me when his plane blew up. There was nothing I could do but follow it all the way down to mark the spot where it crashed. I had to stay with him, till I knew. He left a wife and five kids.

"When I got discharged in September of '53, the Yankees pulled a lot of strings to get me back in time to finish the season with them. But I was in no shape to play baseball. I was down to 150 pounds. So I just hung around and watched them win their fifth straight championship. They held a day for me on September 13. There were 50,000 people at Yankee Stadium and I guess it should have been the greatest day of my life as a Yankee. Instead it was the worst."

"How was that?" I asked.

"When I got to the Stadium, they told me Max Harper's wife was there. She wanted me to tell her he was dead. She wouldn't accept it from anyone else but me."

As he related the story, he paused and his eyes suddenly began to well up with tears. He took out a handkerchief and wiped them.

Embarrassed at this impromptu and unintentional overflow of

emotion, he said: "I can't believe I'm breaking up like this. You'll have to forgive me . . . I haven't talked about this in 40 years."

He had made it all sound so mundane—getting up in the morning every day, climbing into these rickety little planes loaded with bombs, and flying over enemy territory. Just another guy going to work, only that guy didn't have so many ways to die.

"Nothing is quite as desperate as your life," he agreed.

But when I opined that he and all the rest of them who risked their lives for their country were genuine heroes, he waved me off.

"We were scared just like anyone," he said. "We weren't heroes. The only heroes I know are dead."

After Korea, Coleman was never the same player and, by 1955, Stengel had a new favorite second baseman, a brassy, hard-nosed kid who, coincidentally, also hailed from the Bay Area: Billy Martin. Martin, Stengel said, "had intangibles," meaning he wasn't the greatest hitter but he would inevitably get a big hit when it was needed, and he wasn't the greatest fielder but he made all the plays that had to be made. Most of all, he had a knack for winning and the manager always said it was no coincidence the Yankees won world championships in all the years Martin was with them—and didn't in the two years, '54 and '55, he was in the service.

In '55, Coleman missed three and a half months of the season—after breaking his collarbone April 22 and then suffering a concussion after getting beaned by Chicago White Sox pitcher Harry Byrd on July 20. Between Korea and the injuries, there was just too much missed time. He never again attained regular status, despite Stengel's affection for him, and when the 1957 season ended, Weiss came to him with an offer he knew he was not going to be able to refuse. Although he was only 33, the Yankees wanted him to retire. After nine and a half years, they felt he could better serve the club with his brains, in the front office, working in the player development department.

"What happens if I don't take this job?" he asked.

"Well, in that case," Weiss replied, "we could trade you. Bobby

Richardson has showed us enough to handle second base. We've got to give him a full shot."

"I weighed all the issues in my mind," Coleman said. "It was decent money Weiss was offering me, and besides, who wanted to play for another team? I'm just glad I never got to be GM."

He laughed at that and stood up. We had encapsulated Coleman's life in a couple of hours over bacon and eggs and coffee. Now he had to go about his day, visiting with old friends in the city he still considered his second home before heading out to Shea Stadium.

"I've been with the Padres for 29 years now," he said, "but in my heart of hearts, I'll always be a Yankee."

With that, Jerry Coleman straightened his tie and strolled jauntily out the front door of the Hyatt onto 42nd Street, disappearing into the scurrying crowd of rush-hour commuters who, of course, had no idea there was suddenly in their midst a genuine American hero.

SLICK AS THEY COME

WHITEY FORD

I t had been almost 20 years since he last saw the old neighborhood, and, so, as we drove down Northern Boulevard, the principal artery that bisects Astoria and Jackson Heights, Queens, Whitey Ford admitted to being a little confused, and begged for patience as he tried to get his bearings. He thought he knew where he was, but the buildings along the busy thoroughfare all looked different now and his eyes squinted, desperately trying to find a familiar landmark.

"Right over there!" he said, finally, a note of triumph in his voice. "On the left! That was where the old Madison Square Garden Bowl was. At least I think that's where it was. No wait, it was up there a little further. We saw some of the great fighters there—Abe Simon and Joe Louis . . . Henry Armstrong, Barney Ross. They also had these midget auto races there and a lot of times the fumes from whatever it was they used to keep 'em going would spill through the whole neighborhood. On the couple nights a week they had the races, if the wind was blowin' the right way, we could get asphyxiated in our apartments if we didn't keep the windows closed."

It was approximately ten o'clock on a brisk and windy October morning. Joe Torre's Yankees were in the midst of another postseason—the second round against the Seattle Mariners—but this was an off day and Ford hadn't planned to attend any of these games anyway. ("I'll wait till the World Series," he said confidently.) He had picked me up in his white Cadillac at Shea Stadium, home of the Mets, having explained "it's a good meeting place despite being enemy territory" in that it was almost equidistant from his home now in Great Neck, Long Island, and his home then in Astoria. Despite the biting wind, he was wearing only a summer-weight blue sports jacket, a white knit golf shirt and light wool navy slacks. He seemed as oblivious to the cold as he was to the '50s rock 'n' roll tunes blaring out of the car radio.

"As I said, the Bowl was a little bit further up," he continued, slowing down and craning his neck to get a better view of the left side of the street. "Right here, this was all a great big open space on this side with about five ball fields on it. They weren't real pretty or anything. Some of them didn't even have backstops, but you could put a home plate there. We didn't care, and there was always plenty of room to play there."

The mid-'40s. America was just beginning to readjust to peacetime. Ford's father, Jim, worked for Consolidated Edison, the electric and gas power conglomerate, and while he never had the opportunity to play pro ball and didn't seem to share the same passion for baseball as Ford's uncles, Rudy and Bob, he'd gained a reputation for being one of the better players on the company's local sandlot team. Later on, Jim Ford and his friend Jack Rogers bought a bar called the Ivy Room, about five blocks from one of the first apartments the family lived in—on 34th Avenue. Ford's mother, Edith, worked in Manhattan as a bookkeeper at the A&P on 53rd Street and Second Avenue and later at Equitable Life Insurance in the city, where young Eddie already had a job himself.

As he turned off 34th Avenue onto 42nd Street, he pointed to a well-kept, pale yellow brick apartment building.

"Here's where I first lived for about 10 years," he said. "We played roller hockey in the street here. There was never any cars during the day. Joanie [his wife of 50 years] lived at 42-15, on the fourth floor. I was 16 and she was 12. She had great legs. That's what attracted me most about her. We moved three or four times when I was growing up there. I guess every time the rent was due."

It was a predominantly white neighborhood of second-generation Irish, Italians and Poles and it was therefore only natural that Precious Blood, the Catholic church on 38th Street between Broadway and 34th, was the center of activity. The church and the Thomas Quinn Funeral Home round the corner. On the top floor of the funeral parlor was the draft board. A few of the older Italian kids in the neighborhood, Sam Mele, and the Cuccinello brothers, Tony and Al, had already gone on to professional baseball careers. Mele, in particular, had been a baseball and basketball star at New York University and Ford remembered his dad taking him to see him play. Upon graduation, Mele signed as an outfielder with the Boston Red Sox, played 10 years in the big leagues, and later managed the Minnesota Twins to the World Series in 1965.

Another Italian kid, whose family owned the beauty salon on 34th Street, made it even bigger, but not in baseball. Anthony Benedetto had a different calling. He loved music and would sing at weddings and perform at some of the small clubs in the area.

"It wasn't until after he left the neighborhood that he changed his name to Tony Bennett," Ford said. "Kind of like me, going from Eddie to Whitey, only I think his new name did a lot more for him than mine did for me. He was older than I was and I didn't get to know him real well until years later. In the early '70s he'd perform at this big place out on Long Island, the Colony Hill, and I'd go out there and have lunch with him. He and Perry Como were my favorites."

Those spacious grass-less fields of his youth were gone—every one of them, he noted—replaced by the concrete and asphalt of factories, car dealerships, short order food joints and assorted Kmart, Wal-Mart and Walgreen discount chain stores. After the war, the Madison Square Garden Bowl was torn down, and U.S. Steel and Ronzoni factories replaced it on Northern Boulevard. "Now they're gone, too," Ford said.

In the fifty-year evolution since he left, progress had surely come to Astoria—which, itself, is now called Long Island City—and if Ford wondered where today's neighborhood youths played their baseball—if they played baseball, that is—he didn't say anything.

"Over there," he said, pointing now to the right side of the boulevard, "off to the right is Jackson Heights. They had a field there where we played the Jackson Heights Dukes in the Queens-Nassau League for 16- and 17-year-olds. A kid on Jackson Heights named Bruce Caldicott—who later became a good friend of mine—went 2-for-3 off me in one game. They wrote it up in the paper the next day and he kept that clipping in his wallet, showing it off all the time. Thirty years later, we were both members of the North Hills Country Club in Manhasset and he still had the damn clipping. We'd be having drinks at the bar and he'd whip it out and show everyone. Then he died a couple of years ago. At the funeral, I stood over the coffin with his wife, looking down at him in this brown suit, and I said to her: 'Does he still have that clipping in his jacket pocket?'"

We were heading west on 34th Avenue now and Ford noted how "10 or 12 blocks further down near the East River" was where the Greeks all lived, among them Billy Loes, a right-handed pitcher whom scouts rated about the best they'd ever seen in Astoria. The Dodgers gave him a record (for them) $22,500 bonus in 1949 (three times what Ford got from the Yankees), and while Loes would wind up pitching 11 years in the majors, the first five with the Dodgers as a frequent World Series opponent of Ford's Yankees, he never lived up to his ability. The most games he ever won in a season was 14 and in a famous quote that most reflected his quirky, blasé attitude toward baseball and life in general, he once explained: "You never want to win 20 because then they'll expect you to do it every year."

"They always said Billy should have been a left-hander," Ford said, "but we're not all crazy."

The local school in Astoria, Bryant High, didn't have a baseball team, so Ford, who had begun playing in earnest at age 13 in the summer sandlot leagues, decided to enroll at the time in Manhattan School of Aviation Trades. By his own account, he was neither a good student nor a good mechanic. His most notable accomplishment at Manhattan School of Aviation was his near perfect attendance record, which he maintained only because of his fear of losing his eligibility to play baseball. One of his high school teammates was a second baseman named Vito Valentinetti, who would go on to a major league career as a pitcher with the Chicago Cubs and Washington Senators. Ford was the first baseman and, as he said: "What were the odds of that? The second baseman and the first baseman both making the majors, but as pitchers?

"We played on a field underneath the 59th Street Bridge. At night the winos drank there and threw their bottles on the hard ground when they were done. I always told people we didn't play on grass, we played on *glass*."

But while the school enabled him to play baseball, it was a decision he said he regretted to this day.

"For one thing," he said, "it was a vocational school and didn't prepare us for college. Plus, there was all that traveling by bus back and forth from Astoria to the city, which was an hour's ride each way. And even though we got to play ball, the competition between vocational schools wasn't nearly as good as the academic schools. And it sure wasn't as good as the summer league teams we played as the 34th Avenue Boys."

The 34th Avenue Boys were Astoria's team in the Queens-Nassau League. The fathers of the section's more talented players had organized the team, given it its name and bought uniforms for the kids. They stayed together as a team for 3, 4 years—until Ford graduated high school. It was that last summer after his senior year in high school—1946—when Ford began to realize a career in professional baseball might actually be in the offing for him. The previous spring he had gone to his first major league tryout camp—at Yankee Stadium. He doesn't remember exactly how or why he got the invitation. He just remembers Paul Krichell, the Yankees' venerable New York area scouting guru, was there, as were a few former Yankee players. Among them was Johnny Sturm, the first baseman on the 1941 world champion Yankee team, who at that time was working for the organization in the scouting and player development department after breaking his wrist in spring training.

"I remember that day real well," Sturm told me in a telephone interview from his home in St. Louis. "I was sitting in the dugout with the mayor, Fiorello La Guardia, when the Yankee batboy came over and introduced this 16-year-old kid to me. 'John,' he said, 'I want you to meet Eddie Ford here. He's from Astoria and he wants to be a first baseman just like you.' I took one look at him and I said: 'This little guy? He'll never make it as a first baseman. They got guys like [Jimmie] Foxx and Hank [Greenberg] playing first base, big guys who hit home runs.' So the batboy says: 'Well, he pitches, too,' to which I said to Ford: 'Son, you better stick with pitching and forget about first base.'

"I never saw him again until the 25th anniversary of the '41 team at Yankee Stadium. By then, he'd already had a Hall of Fame career as a pitcher. I've always liked to think I might have had a little part in that."

Ford said he recalled meeting Johnny Sturm that April afternoon, but his decision to concentrate solely on pitching was reached later that summer when the 34th Avenue Boys found themselves in a bit of a bind because their best pitcher had surpassed the age limit in the Queens-Nassau League. Though he enjoyed first base and fancied himself as a more than decent hitter, Ford had privately been preparing himself for the eventuality of becoming a full-time pitcher. On the corner of 34th Avenue and 33rd Street, there was a candy store where the kids all hung out. On the side of a store was a brick wall, which Ford used as a backstop on which to practice his pitching.

"There it is," he said as we turned off 34th Avenue onto 33rd Street. "Look at that. It's still there."

Sixty years later, the candy store was all boarded up and appeared to be nothing more than a storage building. The brick wall on the side was covered with graffiti, although in the middle of all the mindless spray-paint scribbling there was a box imprint which, presumably, served as a latter-day strike zone target for the new generation of Astoria youths without a field.

"I used to throw tennis balls up against that wall by the hour," Ford related. "They were better than the old spaldeens 'cause you could get a better grip on them."

He stared silently at the wall for a few seconds, then turned and looked down 33rd Street, as if in search of something—or someone—from his distant past.

"So this is where it really all began?" I asked, interrupting his thoughts. "The pitching part, I mean."

"Yeah," he said, "pretty much."

With Ford as their primary pitcher, the 34th Avenue Boys went 36-0 that summer of '46. The Queens-Nassau League played all Sunday doubleheaders and the 34th Avenue Boys played all their games on the road because there wasn't an available field in Astoria.

"Years later," Ford said, "I'd always get a kick when guys from the area would come up to me and say they beat us. 'Not that summer, you didn't,' I'd tell them."

Turning onto 34th Street from 35th Avenue, he pulled the car over to the side of the road, alongside a long gray building.

"P.S. 166," he said. "I played my very first baseball here. They had a field in the back . . . let's go look at it now . . ."

We got out of the car and walked around the corner, the cold, shrill wind hitting us in the face. Ignoring the frigid gust, Ford walked briskly down the street, then stopped and shook his head. Where once there had been a field, now stood a building, attached to the grammar school.

"I'd heard they made an addition," he said softly. "I wondered where it could be. This was the only open space by the school. Now it's gone. What a field it was—100 feet to the left field wall and 120 feet to the right field wall! We'd play softball there and hit balls off those walls and feel like we were big-leaguers."

We got back into the car and drove around back onto 34th Avenue, which prompted the conversation to return to that championship summer of '46 when Ford became a pitcher forever and signed with the Yankees.

"Like I said, we won all our games and went to the championship game in the Polo Grounds, which was sponsored by the old *Journal-American*," he said. "It was quite a finish to the season. Our opponents were the Bay Ridge Tigers from Brooklyn. The game was 0–0 going into the 11th inning. I pitched for us and had a two-hitter, but the other pitcher, a kid named Lou D'Angelos, had a no-hitter into the 11th. In the bottom of the 11th, I led off with a double and the next guy up singled me home and we won 1–0."

There were at least a half-dozen scouts at the game, mostly from the East Coast major league teams, Dodgers, Giants, Phillies, Red Sox and Yankees, and in particular, Ray Garland, one of Krichell's area bird dogs who had been following Ford all that summer. Ford surmised Garland called Krichell immediately to inform him of the budding competition.

"Afterward, they all began calling the house," Ford related. "The Dodgers were the first and they offered $1,000. After that, the bidding started going up until it got to $5,000—the Yankees' offer. Krichell and one of his assistants, a guy named Harry Hess, came over to my house to close the deal, but first they wanted to take me over to Brooklyn to see a couple of their farmhands who were pitching for the Bushwicks, their semipro club, in Dexter Park. When we got back to the house to sign the contract, my mother comes out of the kitchen and says: 'The Giants scout, Jerry Monte, just called and offered $6,000.'

"I'm sure Krichell thought he was being set up, even though my mother would never have thought of anything like that. He was furious and he screamed: 'You already said you'd sign with us!'

"'I know,' I said, 'but $1,000 is a lot of money.'

"So they kicked it up to $7,000. They paid me the first half, $3,500, when I went to Yankee Stadium a couple of days later. That turned out to be the day Yogi and Bobby Brown were making their debuts with the Yankees. After the game, Krichell introduced Yogi and me, saying: 'Larry Berra, this is Eddie Ford.' That was probably the first and last time we were ever introduced like that!"

The gradual evolution from Eddie to Whitey, he said, came after he signed with the Yankees.

"I'm not sure exactly how it happened, except that Lefty Gomez, who was my manager at Binghamton in 1949, started calling me Whitey and it gradually stuck. I was still signing baseballs 'Ed' in 1950, my first year in the big leagues, but after that I guess I was always Whitey."

Then, in the mid-'50s, during the height of his carousing days with Mickey Mantle and Billy Martin, he got his "Slick" moniker. Casey Stengel, it seemed, had come to calling all three of his late-night desperadoes "my whiskey slicks" and eventually it became a term that was solely attributed to Ford.

"I guess because I was from the city—you know, the city slicker— that Billy and Mickey played off that and started calling me Slick," Ford said. "They both called me that right up to the end . . ."

The thought or mention of Mantle's and Martin's early deaths, both alcohol-related, was not something he'd ever cared to dwell on. They *were* like brothers, the three of them, and you always got the feeling Ford was uncomfortable talking about being the sole survivor. Tales of their drinking escapades have become the stuff of legend through the years, most notably the May 16, 1957, incident at the famous New York nightclub, the Copacabana. Ford, Mantle, Martin, and Yankee teammates Yogi Berra, Hank Bauer and Johnny Kucks were all partying it up at the Copa, celebrating Martin's 29th birthday, when suddenly a fight broke out and a patron at the next table, a delicatessen owner named Edwin Jones, claimed he was cold-cocked by Bauer. No witnesses ever came forward to corroborate the guy's charges and the case never went to court. However, the incident was the last straw for the Yankee management, which viewed Martin as a bad influence on

Mantle and Ford anyway, and a month later he was traded to the Kansas City A's.

"Billy always used to get upset over the fact that he always got in trouble in bars and nothing ever happened to me," Ford said, chuckling. "He and Mickey never seemed to realize I'm a professional drinker. I grew up in bars and I always knew when I'd had enough and when to get out of 'em. To this day, I don't know what really happened that night at the Copa. I just know we were there watching Sammy Davis and at this next table, these guys started making racial remarks at Sammy and Bauer told them to cool it. One of them challenged Bauer and the two of them went to a back room where, before the rest of us got there, the guy was knocked out. I know Hank didn't do it, but it got in all the papers how we were fined $1,000 each. Billy wound up being the scapegoat and he didn't even organize the party. I did.

"Mickey and I had adjoining suites on the road. I always slept late and he got up early. I always got my rest. Like I said, Billy and Mickey weren't professional drinkers."

Maybe subconsciously that, too, had something to do with the Slick thing, in that Ford *was* slick in the way he was able to avoid the inevitable trouble and after-effects of all the late-night imbibing that dogged Martin and Mantle their entire lives. All things considered—the 236 wins he managed to amass as much with cunning and control as with any overpowering stuff in 15 plus seasons in the majors; the outward cool he always exhibited—Slick was the perfect nickname. But he only answered to it among that inner circle of close-knit comrades, and when Martin and Mantle passed on, so, too, did the Slick seem to fade into memory.

"That was kind of our thing," Ford said. "We'd call each other that."

He had turned onto Broadway now, another of the main thoroughfares crisscrossing through Astoria. On the right-hand side was the Quinn Funeral Home, one of the few remaining landmarks from the old days, and he smiled at the sight of it.

"Yeah," he said, "we spent plenty of nights here—and one not-so-great morning, too. That was in 1951, when I stopped in to the draft board on top just to inquire about my status. They told me I was getting called up the next week."

Before that happened, however, he'd already more than made good to Krichell on that grudging $7,000 bonus. They sent him to Butler of the Class C Mid-Atlantic League in 1947 where he went 13-4. The following season he was 16-8 at Norfolk of the Class B Piedmont League. Then in 1949, under Gomez's tutelage at Binghamton, he got everyone's attention in the organization by going 16-5 and leading the Eastern League with a 1.61 ERA. On the back of his 1954 Topps baseball card, there is an "inside baseball" comic strip panel in which Ford is depicted on the telephone to the Yankees from Binghamton, advising them to call him up to the majors.

"Did you really do that?" I asked.

"Oh yeah," he said. "But it wasn't bein' cocky or anything on my part. It was in September and our season was over. I just wanted to keep pitching and that was the first year I really felt like I was good enough to pitch in the majors. So I called Krichell and asked him if I could come up."

"He must have thought you were pretty brazen, no?"

"Well, I know he'd had his scouts watching me pitch in the playoffs and I know they went back and told him they had a helluva prospect. So, in a way, I think he admired me for asking, although I'm sure he was probably giggling under his breath."

The following season, Ford didn't have to call the Yankees. In late June, he was 6-3 at Triple A Kansas City when they called him. In Allie Reynolds, Vic Raschi and Eddie Lopat, they had three of the premier starting pitchers in the American League, but Krichell's scouts were convinced he'd had enough minor league apprenticeship and recommended his call-up. Stengel agreed, although he was careful to spot the 21-year-old lefty against the softer teams on the schedule. Ford responded by reeling off nine straight wins.

"I started out pitching mostly against Washington, St. Louis and

Philly," he recalled. "Then after I won a few games, Casey let me pitch against some of the better teams, Chicago, Detroit. The win I remember most in that streak was a game against Detroit in mid-September. The Tigers were in first place, a half game ahead of us, so it was a pretty big game. Dizzy Trout was pitching for the Tigers and we were 1–1 going into the ninth. I was scheduled to lead off and Casey let me hit. I got a walk and we went on to score seven runs. We won that game 8-1 and it put us back in first place. We never trailed again."

"Imagine that ever happening today?" I said. "Being allowed to hit in the ninth, I mean."

"You got that right," he shot back. "I'm watchin' the Cardinals-Diamondbacks playoff game the other night and [Tony] LaRussa lets Morris hit in the eighth inning and McCarver starts screaming on the air: 'I can't believe LaRussa is letting his pitcher hit with only seven outs left in the game!' So what? The kid pitched two shutout innings after that! I said to myself: 'What are these guys getting to be?'"

His one loss that rookie season was in the final week, after his nine straight wins.

It was a September 27 relief appearance in Philadelphia against the Athletics, who were still managed by their 88-year-old patriarch and founder, the grand old man of baseball, Connie Mack.

"I relieved Eddie Lopat in the seventh inning," Ford recounted. "I don't know why Casey put me in. We were winning 2–1. I gave up a run in that inning that tied it. It was still tied in the ninth with a runner on and Sam Chapman, a notorious fastball hitter, at the plate for the A's. Ralph Houk was catching and we must have thrown eight curveballs in a row and the eighth one Chapman hit out to end the game."

He laughed at the memory of it. As it turned out, that was to be the second-to-last win in Mack's managing career, which began in 1894.

"You gotta be kiddin'," Ford exclaimed. "He didn't manage after that year?"

"The guy was 88 years old," I pointed out.

"I know," Ford said. "He was somethin' else. Standin' there in that dark blue suit with the top hat, the starched, collared shirt and the bow tie. It was *so hot in the dugout!* I don't know how he did it."

The Yankees clinched their second straight American League pennant under Stengel the next day and finished three games ahead of the Detroit Tigers. The 1950 World Series, though over quickly, was a closely contested affair in which the Yankees swept the Philadelphia Phillies, but won the first three games by margins of 1–0, 2–1 in 10 innings and 3–2. With a commanding 3–0 lead in games, Stengel elected to give his lefty rookie sensation a chance to win the clincher. After being staked to a 2–0 lead in the first inning, Ford shut the Phillies out through eight. But in the ninth, after the Yankees had increased their lead to 5–0, Willie "Puddin' Head" Jones led off with a single to left-center for the Phillies and Del Ennis was hit by a pitch.

Ford dug in, getting Dick Sisler to ground into an infield force-out and striking out Granny Hamner. He was now one out away from capping a sensational debut season by hurling a shutout to win the World Series. With runners at the corners, Phillies catcher Andy Seminick lofted a fly ball to left field that Gene Woodling lost in Yankee Stadium's tricky late-afternoon autumn shadows. The ball dropped in for a base hit, allowing both runners to score, and when Mike Goliat, the next batter, also singled, Stengel came out of the dugout and waved in Allie Reynolds from the bullpen.

"As I walked off the mound, with Reynolds coming in and Casey standin' there waitin' for him, I heard this booing," Ford said. "I thought they were booin' *me* and I said to myself: 'Shit, I shoulda had a shutout and they're booin' me!' Then I realized, when I got in the dugout and Casey walked off the mound the booing got heavier that they were booin' *him*. Hell, I'd left about 60 tickets for the game for my family and friends. I think it was all of them."

Baseball glory, however, was short-lived. A month after the Series, Ford found himself at the army induction center on Whitehall Street in the lower end of Manhattan. He would spend the next two years at Fort

Monmouth, New Jersey, including a 13-day furlough to marry his neighborhood sweetheart, Joan Foran, on April 14, 1951.

"Right over there," Ford said, pointing to a Popeyes Chicken restaurant on the left side of the road. We had swung around to Steinway Street, another main road in Astoria, heading back to Northern Boulevard. "That chicken joint. That used to be Donohue's Bar, where Joanie and me had our wedding reception in the catering hall upstairs. I was on furlough and it was fortunate I didn't get sent away any further than New Jersey. That was when I first met Mickey. Casey knew about the wedding and I guess he decided to have the team stop there on the way back to the Stadium from an exhibition game they'd played against the Dodgers at Ebbets Field. We're all in Donohue's when the Yankee bus pulls up. The whole team got out except the rookies like Mickey. They were too shy to go in, so after a while Joan and I went out to the bus to shake their hands and thank them for coming. Years later, Mickey told me the highlight of that day for him was meeting Joan, not me.

"What I remember most about the whole surprise appearance of the Yankees was Joe D. and Tommy Henrich scooping up a couple of drinks on the table as soon as they came in and staying about a half-hour. The neighbors couldn't believe it. *Joe D. on Steinway Street!* Krichell was there, too. He gave me a $500 gift. I guess he'd forgotten about that extra thousand he'd had to give me to sign."

If only Krichell's boss, GM George Weiss, had been as charitable when it came to parting with the Yankee dollar for the hired help. When Ford got discharged from the army in November of that year, he discovered to his dismay that Weiss had a very short memory when it came to the players' accomplishments.

"It really pissed me off that I made only $2,500 that first year," Ford said. "The minimum was $5,000 and I'd only been there half the year. The Yankee players were good to me and gave me a full Series share of $7,500 when they probably really shouldn't have. But I didn't get that until after I was already in the army. So now after bein' in the army for two years, I come out and I'm really in good shape and Weiss sends me a contract for $6,000, a $1,000 raise, just before spring training '53. I said: 'Shit, I'm 9-1 and I helped win the World Series and they give me a $1,000 raise? That's when I knew Weiss was a cheap sonovabitch.

"I finally said to them: 'I'm not going for any less than $9,000!' So they got it up to seven and I said: 'Nope, I won't go for any less than eight thousand.' That's when they called me back and said: 'If you're not on the next train to St. Petersburg we're gonna drop you back to $6,000.' So I wound up with a $2,000 raise. I have to laugh when I think I can make that in a half-hour now signing autographs at a card show."

That, of course, was the way it was in those days, before the advent of Marvin Miller and the players union a decade and a half later. Back then, players had no agents to do their negotiating for them, and the owners, without any constraints of free agency and salary arbitration, not only had the upper hand but an iron hand. Beginning in 1954, Ford would be selected to the All-Star team in seven of the next eight years. His .690 winning percentage (236-106) is the highest of any pitcher in the 20th century and he still holds the all-time record for most wins (10) in the World Series. Despite all those Hall of Fame accomplishments, the most he ever made in any one season was $78,000 after going 24-7 in 1963.

Under Stengel, Ford pretty much pitched on a five- or six-day regimen, early on the fifth man in what was ostensibly a four-man rotation behind such stalwarts as Reynolds, Raschi, Lopat and Tommy Byrne. From 1950 to 1960, he started over 35 games only once—in 1955 when he led the American League with 18 wins and 18 complete games in 39 starts. But when Ralph Houk replaced Stengel as manager in 1961, the first pronouncement he made was that Ford would be pitching every fourth day. Ford made 39 starts in '61 and led the league in wins and innings pitched. For the next four seasons, he started 38, 38, 39 and 37 games respectively and won a total of 74 games.

"With Casey, I'd often go six days between starts, with Monday always being an off day," Ford said. "My turn always seemed to fall on

Monday. I don't know why Casey did it that way. We had a lot of good pitchers in those early years—particularly our big three, Reynolds, Raschi and Lopat. I wish I could have pitched every fourth day. The Indians had a staff to equal ours—Bob Lemon, Early Wynn and Mike Garcia—and our pitching coach, Jim Turner, who really ran the pitching for Casey, felt their pitchers wore out at the end of the year. So Casey stretched it out. I hated sitting in the dugout watching so many games I thought I should have been pitching."

If nothing else, the extra day of rest allowed for Ford to further enjoy the New York nightlife and the status that came with being a Yankee—and a prominent one as well. For sure, he had status in the one joint that mattered most in those days, Toots Shor's, described in Lawrence Ritter's book on New York's sporting life, *East Side, West Side* as "America's unofficial headquarters for male sports celebrities during the '40s, '50s and '60s." Shor was a loud, rotund, often boorish host, a heavy drinker who took sublime pleasure in insulting his patrons. The insults were actually his form of affection and they flowed as freely as the booze every night, to almost every big-time celebrity you could name, Sinatra, Jackie Gleason, Bob Hope and his special favorites, the Yankees.

"Mickey and I went to Toots's a lot," Ford recalled. "But after a while Mickey didn't go with me that much. I think he got tired of Toots's bullshit. But I liked Toots and he liked me and during the off season, especially, I'd end up there."

The one thing about Shor was he knew baseball as much as he knew the restaurant business—maybe even more considering he managed to run his place out of business twice and died broke. Like the best of scouts, though, he could spot a budding Yankee star and, in 1950, it didn't take long for him to recognize this cocky young left-hander from Queens was going to be the real deal.

"Even though I was a rookie, I'd go in to Toots's place," Ford said. "Remember, I grew up in New York and that was the place to be. Toots kind of adopted me early on. During the World Series that fall, he rode on the train with us to Philadelphia. He had Dizzy Dean with him and on the trip back, after we won the first two games down there, I said to Dizzy: 'Now I know how you won all those games in the National League.' Dizzy got real pissed at me, but Toots got a big kick out of it.

"I was at Toots's the day he and Gleason had one of their famous drinking contests. I was having lunch and afterward Toots brought a bottle of bourbon to the table and gave Gleason a bottle of J&B. It was quiet in the place. I wasn't tryin' to keep up with them. I just watched in amusement as they went at it drink for drink. At about 4 P.M. Gleason got up to go to the bathroom and passed out in the middle of the floor. A waiter came over to help him up but Toots waved him away and told him to just leave him there. Later, the dinner crowd started coming in and Toots told 'em to drag Gleason into the pantry and let him sleep it off there."

They all felt immortal then and why not? They were all in the prime of their lives, famous and successful, admired and envied. How does the song go? *Those were the days my friend, we thought they'd never end?* Ford certainly never thought of his career ending. It had, after all, always come so easily to him. From the moment he arrived in the big leagues that late-June day in 1950, he started winning and never stopped. There was never a doubt he could pitch with the best of them and while he was at it, he partied with the best of them, too.

So when that feeling of numbness suddenly came over his shoulder in the sixth inning of the first game of the 1964 World Series against the Cardinals, he was first mystified and then, very quickly, terrified. *What's wrong with me?* What *is* this?

"It was the most frightening thing that ever happened to me," Ford said. "Elston [Howard] threw the ball back to me and I didn't even have the strength to grab it! I *knew* I couldn't throw it. When I got back to the dugout, I couldn't feel a pulse in my left arm. I thought I was having a heart attack! They did tests at the hospital and found out an artery was blocked. They decided to send me to Dr. Denton Cooley, the famous heart surgeon, in Houston. He didn't want to make a big deal of it. He said: 'We're gonna put a clip on your spine which keeps the capillaries open.' The next year they did a bypass where they cut a vein out of my leg. That worked fine in 1966, but then in '67 my elbow kicked up and I quit in the middle of the season.

"Eighteen years in baseball and I hadn't saved a dime and then Lee MacPhail, the new general manager, told me they'd pay me till the end of the month. Other than my pension, which I couldn't collect for another 25 years, that's what I got from the Yankees for my 18 years with them—two weeks severance pay."

The New York street hustler in him wasn't enough to sustain him in the world of business either. The five years from the end of his career to his induction into the Hall of Fame in 1974 were, by his own admission, the worst of his life. He came to realize if he was going to make the sort of living to which he'd been accustomed, he had to stick to what he knew best and that was baseball. And in that regard, the nostalgia craze, combined with his Hall of Fame celebrity, served him well. He discovered he could make big bucks on the card show circuit—$35 for his autograph on a photo or a baseball, $60 on a bat or jersey—and in the '80s he started a Yankee fantasy camp in Fort Lauderdale with Mantle, before branching out on his own.

"I got no complaints," he said, "except about not gettin' the education I shoulda had. I've had fun my whole life."

The nostalgic journey to his Astoria roots concluded, we had found our way back onto the Grand Central Parkway, heading east. Off in the distance you could see Shea Stadium with its blue and orange Mets trimmings. Ford glanced at his watch as he drove, oblivious to the song that had suddenly come across the radio—"The Boy from New York City" by the Ad Libs.

"How ironic," I thought, as I listened to the radio's blare: *"Ooh-wah, oo-wah, cool, cool Kitty, talkin' 'bout the boy from New York City . . ."*

As we pulled up to the press gate at Shea where I'd left my car, Ford announced: "I've got an appointment, so I hope you got everything. It'll probably be another 20 years before I go back to Astoria."

For him, the trip had been more out of curiosity than any

sentimentality. While he had always gladly regaled in the tales of his celebrant and intoxicating youth, there was no sense of regret nor any longing to relive them. Rather, having arrived at his seventh decade, Whitey Ford could be viewed as a man clearly comfortable and content with who he was and how he got here. His fellow rogues, Mickey, Billy and Toots, were all gone, but he had survived, still the same wise-cracking, self-assured son of the city. Between his conquest of all those batters without the benefit of a 95-mile-per-hour fastball, and his evasion of all those demons that lurked within the depths of a whiskey bottle, you got the feeling Ford always knew the secrets to his survival were his cool, his street smarts and his slickness.

ARLENE ALONE

ARLENE HOWARD

Some twenty-one years after his death, Elston Howard would undoubtedly have felt a great sense of pride and satisfaction knowing his widow, Arlene, was still holding forth in the home on Edgemont Place that the city fathers of Teaneck, New Jersey, once tried to keep them from occupying.

It remained a stately, if somewhat dated, two-story home in what was still regarded as one of the more upscale neighborhoods in one of Bergen County, New Jersey's, oldest, most affluent and most liberal communities. There was really no reason for Arlene Howard to even be here after all this time, especially considering she still burned with the memories of how they had betrayed and insulted her all those years ago. And yet, as she conceded, maybe that was precisely why she *was* still here, honoring her husband's memory while still subconsciously extending her middle finger to any of the remaining hypocrites who had tried to deny her this house and this piece of property in this supposed all-American city.

She'd forgotten our appointment when I arrived at the house shortly after noontime on a late-June afternoon in 2001.

"Oh," she said, upon opening the door and seeing me standing there, legal pad, tape recorder and camera in hand. "Today was the day, wasn't it? You'll have to forgive me. I'm a mess. This *place* is mess! If you don't mind . . . otherwise, if you want, we can reschedule."

I told her I didn't mind. After all, despite her protestations, she had scarcely aged a bit since the last time I'd seen her at a Yankees' Old-Timer's Day celebration a couple of years after Howard's death. As for the house, the only outward disarray about it was the trio of painters dangling from scaffoldings—"getting it back in shape," she explained, for a forthcoming Fourth of July gathering of family and friends.

"I'm not sure how much longer I want to stay here," she continued as we sat down at the dining room table. "It's just Cheryl and me left here now and she travels a lot with her work in show business. It's really a lot of work keeping the house up."

As if losing her husband, in the midst of what should have been the prime of their lives, wasn't tragedy enough, two of her three children had also gone, well before their time. Karen, her youngest daughter, had been born with cerebral palsy and managed to live to 31 before succumbing to complications of the affliction in 1991. Elston Jr., the eldest, died at 38 in 1994, angry and embittered, Arlene surmised, over his failure to follow in his father's footsteps as a professional ballplayer. The father and son became estranged in the late '70s after Elston Jr. busted out as a baseball player at the University of Alabama (his third college) and returned home to Teaneck without earning his degree.

According to Arlene, Elston Jr. "left his father with a broken heart" when he abruptly packed up and left the family home that summer, leaving only a note, never to return. There would be no deathbed reconciliation with his father either.

"Elston Jr. was in Florida and we called him and told him he had to get home when Elston was dying in Lenox Hill," Arlene recalled. "But by the time he got there, it was just a couple of days before Elston died, and by then, he wasn't really able to communicate much. So, no, they never reconciled."

And so, it had been left to Cheryl Howard (who inherited all of her mother's beauty) to maintain the family ties to baseball and the Yankees with her periodic appearances at Yankee Stadium performing the national anthem. Otherwise, her show biz career took her away from home for weeks and months at a time.

"I need to get a smaller place," Arlene acknowledged, "although a part of me keeps me here, maybe in defiance, you could say, out of what we went through to move in here."

It was 1963 and America had only just begun to undergo its social and racial awakening. In May, President Kennedy had had to send National Guard troops into Alabama to force Governor George Wallace to adhere to federal school desegregation orders, and a couple of weeks earlier Dr. Martin Luther King had led a march down the streets of Birmingham to protest the city's racial barriers. Later that summer, more than 200,000 peaceful demonstrators, led by Dr. King, descended on Washington, D.C., to demand passage of civil rights legislation. The South was the focal point of America's blind prejudice and inherent bigotry. A century after the Civil War, little had changed insofar as equality and tolerance for the descendants of the slaves, primarily in old Dixie. Or so it seemed anyway.

Howard, the first African-American to play for the Yankees, was the American League Most Valuable Player in 1963 and, as such, he was also quite the honored celebrity in his adopted hometown of Teaneck. The mayor, Matty Feldman, had proudly introduced him as his friend and confidant at all the various political banquets about town. Ellie Howard was a *Yankee* after all, and not only that, he was *Teaneck*'s Yankee. Of course, all of this was going on when the Howards were living on Howland Avenue in the north section of town in which a scattering of black families happened to reside. No one, Feldman especially, ever bothered to make a point of the fact it was also the *only* section of town in which they happened to reside.

"I'm not exactly sure what or who it was that drew us to Teaneck," Arlene said. "During the season, we were living at the Concourse Plaza in the Bronx and we had a home in St. Louis. I really had wanted to live in Manhattan, but Elston would have none of that. I know we had met Al Hibbler, the great jazz singer, and his wife, Jeanette, at a party and they lived in Teaneck and invited us out. Plus, my doctor in New York knew a lawyer who lived in Teaneck. So we wound up buying this beautiful split-level on Howland Avenue. But then we had two more kids and we needed a bigger place.

"People were still very prejudiced back then—in Teaneck and everyplace else—not just in the South. We knew that. Because of that, our lawyer suggested we have the builder buy this piece of land on Edgemont Place, which was restricted, and build the house for us. There was no way blacks were going to be permitted to buy in this area, although Elston had been honored by the town on a number of occasions. It didn't matter you were a Yankee. You were black. But we wound up being betrayed by the architect, who had to know everything about the house, and he told the mayor, Matty Feldman, who also betrayed us.

"I'll never, ever forget that day when Matty Feldman came to our house on Howland and said: 'You don't really want to live in that neighborhood' and proposed that we move to the west part of town. It was probably state property. The neighbors, when they found out, had gotten together and evidently asked Matty Feldman to intervene for them; to see what he could do to keep us out. I was incensed. *You pass judgment on me!* To this day . . . I shouldn't hold on to it, I suppose. We defied them."

"Nevertheless, you had to be wary about moving into this house," I countered.

"No I wasn't," she replied firmly. "I was furious. *How dare they!* We had to go by the place every day during the construction to check out what the opposition was doing. There'd be spray-painted 'nigger' . . .

all that. Even the bricks, they scratched it into . . . and we had to have them changed. Anyway, we built the house and the ones who couldn't deal with us moved out and we really did have 17 happy years here."

They were not exactly childhood sweethearts, although it was close. They grew up in the same predominantly black Compton Hill neighborhood on the south side of St. Louis. Howard, the son of a high school principal, and Arlene Henley, four years his junior, one of five children of a steelworker. Howard had been a four-sport star at the all-black Vashon High School ("Everybody knew Elston," she said). Colleges from all over the country offered him scholarships and though the year was 1947, and Jackie Robinson had just joined the Dodgers to break baseball's color barrier, big league scouts were already following him around, too.

His hometown team, the St. Louis Cardinals, had won the World Series the year before and they invited him to a tryout. But it didn't matter how much he'd impressed their scouts. They were told unequivocally: No blacks.

A few days after that tryout, George Sisler Jr., the Cardinals' assistant director of scouting, lamented over lunch to *St. Louis Globe-Democrat* columnist Robert L. Burnes: "I have been watching the best young prospect I've looked at in years—a big, good-looking kid just coming out of Vashon High. I worked him out for two days, and I'd stake my job on his ability to make it, but I can't sign him. I spent the whole morning pleading my case. I argued that now that the Dodgers have signed Robinson, everybody is going to fall into line . . . but I was turned down."

The Cardinals didn't "fall into line" until 1952 when they signed Tom Alston, a 6-5, 210-pound first baseman out of North Carolina A&T. Alston proved to be a bust, appearing in just 91 major league games from 1954 to 1957, and it was probably no coincidence the Cardinals, one of the last National League teams to integrate, didn't make it to another World Series until 1964. Ironically, that also happened to be the World Series that marked the end of the Yankees' dynasty, during which they had won nine pennants and four world championships after breaking their own color line with Howard in 1955.

Because Robinson had played for the fabled Negro League Kansas City Monarchs before signing with the Dodgers, Howard decided to sign with them and forget about plans to go to college and major in premed (his mother's dream). It was while he was playing for the Monarchs that he finally got around to dating Arlene. He played three years for the Monarchs as an outfielder–first baseman and occasional catcher, hitting .283, .270 and .319 with good power, and after his last year with them, the Yankees signed him in July of 1948 for a modest $7,500 bonus.

When he won the AL MVP award in 1963, Howard looked back on his Monarch years and his signing with the Yankees with a sense of amazement. "I really couldn't believe I was major league property," he said. "At the time, I was primarily an outfielder and first baseman. I caught some, too, but if anybody ever told me I was to become a Most Valuable Player as a catcher, I would have told the guy he was nuts."

After serving two years in the army in the Special Services Corps, Howard was assigned by the Yankees in 1953 to their flagship Kansas City Blues farm club in the American Association where, they told him, they wanted him to concentrate on catching. However, the Yankees were loaded with catching prospects at that time—among them Gus Triandos, Hal Smith, Lou Berberet and Cal Neeman, all of whom went on to major league careers with other teams. As a result they elected to farm him out to the independent Toronto Maple Leafs of the International League. As the Leafs' No. 1 catcher and part-time outfielder, Howard hit .330 with 22 homers, 16 triples and 109 RBI, earning him selection as the league MVP. It was the sort of performance that made it impossible for the Yankees to keep him in the minors any longer.

By 1955, eight years after Robinson's historic debut with the Dodgers, the Yankees were one of only four teams out of the majors' 16 (the Philadelphia Phillies, Detroit Tigers and Boston Red Sox were the others) that had not yet integrated. In response to the frequent charges that they were prejudiced and determined to remain the "lily-white" Yankees, team owner Dan Topping replied indignantly: "How can anybody accuse me of Jim Crow-ism when [as owner of the football New York Yankees] I signed Buddy Young, the first Negro in the All American Football Conference? We are eager to get a Negro player. But we are not going to bring one up just to meet the demands of pressure groups."

Despite Topping's impassioned defense of the Yankees' attitude toward black players, a 1949 letter from one of chief scout Paul Krichell's bird dog scouts (which surfaced into collectors' hands during the renovation of Yankee Stadium in 1974) suggests otherwise. In the letter, Joe Press, who operated the Bushwick semipro club in Brooklyn (which Krichell used as a way-station operation for potential prospects), complains to his boss that he was not allowed to sign black players.

"It is quite hard for me to understand your complete turn-around as far as the Negro baseball players are concerned," Press writes Krichell. "Within the past two years I have given you reports on practically every player, with the exception of a very few, who have since signed with other teams. You could have had practically all of them, just for the asking. A few of those I mentioned to you were Art Wilson and Orestes Minoso and there are still more of these whom, in my opinion, would fit in Organized Baseball without any trouble. They are Piper Davis, infielder, and Mays, outfielder, both of the Birmingham Black Barons."

If not the "smoking gun" of an unwritten, unstated "no-blacks" policy, the Press letter is certainly preserved evidence of the Yankees having passed on a chance to sign Willie Mays. Still, as GM George Weiss said coldly in 1953, echoing the words of his boss, Topping: "The Yankees are not averse to having a Negro player, but we are averse to settling for a Negro player merely to meet the wishes of people who insist we must have one. The first Negro player in Yankee uniform must be worth having waited for."

And, quite obviously, that player was not going to be Vic Power, a flashy-fielding Puerto Rican first baseman who was unquestionably the best prospect in the Yankee system in 1952 and '53 at Kansas City. For despite hitting .331 with 100 RBI in '52 and then .349 with 93 RBI in '53, Power didn't even get invited to spring training. As he said with both sadness and a trace of bitterness years later: "I never had a Yankee hat, never wore a Yankee uniform. At the end of the '52 season, they brought me to Yankee Stadium to take a physical and gave me a ticket to watch a game against the Red Sox. That turned out to be the game Allie Reynolds pitched a no-hitter. I had a front-row seat, but that was as close as I ever came to the Yankees. They never even invited me into the clubhouse."

Instead of bringing Power to the big leagues after his second straight sensational season at Triple A in 1953, the Yankees traded him to the Philadelphia Athletics in a 10-player deal that brought them pitcher Harry Byrd, a former American League Rookie of the Year, and first baseman Eddie Robinson, who had both driven in over 100 runs and been selected to the All-Star team in each of the previous three seasons. In response to the jettisoning of Power, Weiss insisted: "His race had no bearing on the trade. We're not going to keep anybody just because he's a Negro. That wouldn't be fair to the white players. I can't see why a Negro should be separated from a white man in a deal or anything else. And besides, we still have Elston Howard."

By now, the Yankees' vision of what they wanted in a black player had become readily apparent. No way could he be like Robinson, outspoken, angry and increasingly intolerant of baseball's foot-dragging on integration. Nor could he be any sort of a fiery-type holler guy. His off-the-field credentials had to be impeccable as well. Power, it was said by the Yankee operatives, was a showboat. Not only that, he dated white women.

"Vic *was* a showboat," Arlene said, smiling, "and his wife was very light-skinned. Then again, so, too, was I. It was just the stupidity and the prejudice of the times."

While he was at Toronto in '54 Howard became engaged to Arlene. Newspaper reports at the time claimed Maple Leafs owner, magazine mogul Jack Kent Cooke, had given him the money to buy the engagement ring.

"I don't think that happened," Arlene said. "What happened was Mr. Cooke sent Elston to a jeweler friend of his who probably gave him a good deal. It was a beautiful emerald-cut diamond."

"Do you still have it?" I asked.

"Oh, yes. But I put it in a heart. Do you want to see it?"

Without waiting for a response, she reached underneath the white cotton long-sleeved T-shirt she was wearing (which bore the monogram "Skin Deep," a black modeling agency in Paris) and produced a necklace with the diamond attached to the center of a heart.

"It's so beautiful," she repeated, rubbing it gently. "I don't know why I did it."

On October 15, 1954, the Yankees announced they had purchased the contract of Elston Howard from Toronto and as the *New York Times* reported: "He is expected to become the first Negro to wear a Bomber uniform after the start of the American League season. That will depend on whether the big fellow impresses manager Casey Stengel sufficiently to be retained on the club, but there is evidence Howard will succeed."

Although they were married December 4, 1954, Arlene Howard did not accompany her husband to that first Yankee spring training in St. Petersburg, Florida, perhaps because she sensed the indignities he was to incur.

"That first spring he stayed in a boardinghouse because the team hotel didn't accept blacks," she said. "St. Petersburg was really terrible. You couldn't even go to the beach. Blacks seen on the beach were likely to be arrested. St. Louis was segregated, but we never had signs—'Whites Only' everywhere."

"I can just imagine how rough it was on him," I offered. "How *was* he treated?"

"By his teammates?" she replied. "Great. They were absolutely great. Phil Rizzuto befriended him immediately. He later called Phil 'my great white father.' And Casey was fine. But the media was something else. One time, the Yankees had a party at the St. Petersburg Yacht Club but because they didn't accept blacks, Elston wasn't allowed to go. Instead of Elston making a big fuss about it, he just sort of ignored it. One writer from the *Amsterdam News*, Jimmy Hicks I think his name was, wrote a scathing article in which he said Elston wasn't acting like a man; he was being like an Uncle Tom and because they didn't invite him he just hung his head and walked away."

"They wanted him to be more like Jackie; to be more militant, didn't they?"

She nodded.

"Elston wasn't a flaming crusader," she continued. "He just really wanted to play baseball and he really wanted to play for the Yankees because, let's face it, no matter what you say about them, they were the best. He didn't care what people had said about them and their racial attitude. To him, they were the best team in baseball and he wanted to be part of that."

Because of that, he was criticized by people of his own race who accused him of "selling out" in embracing the Yankees as he did. Jackie Robinson, however, was not among them. According to Arlene, years after their respective breakthroughs, Robinson and Howard talked about what they had both had to endure.

"You had it much tougher than I did," Robinson said.

"Why would you say that?" Howard asked.

"Because," said Robinson, "when I signed with Brooklyn, Branch Rickey wanted me. He sought me out. But the Yankees, from top to bottom, *didn't* want you!"

Unintentional as it may have been, when Howard finally did make his Yankee debut, it was almost as if they tried to sneak him into a game in hopes that no one would notice.

The 1955 season opener against the Washington Senators was postponed by rain. The next day, the Yankees annihilated the Senators 19–1 but Howard did not play. Nor was he in the starting lineup for the second game of the season, April 14, against the Red Sox (which the Yankees lost 8–4). In the sixth inning, however, Yankee left fielder Irv Noren was thrown out at the plate trying to score from second on a single by Jerry Coleman. Infuriated at the call, Noren rushed home plate umpire Bill McKinley and bumped him, prompting his ejection. After the inning, Howard was sent out to left field by Stengel to replace Noren. He came to bat for the first time in the eighth and singled. Not surprisingly, in the next day's newspaper accounts, Howard was barely mentioned.

And yet, whether it was baseball's ultimate shame or merely blind indifference, Jackie Robinson's debut for all players of color, April 16, 1947, was equally ignored—incredible as that might seem today. Rather, most newspaper accounts of that day centered around Pete Reiser's game-winning double for the Dodgers, along with references to Dodger manager Leo Durocher's suspension for his association with gamblers. Dick Young's game story for the *Daily News* did not get around to Robinson until the last paragraph, when he referred to him as "The majors' most discussed rookie" without ever mentioning that he was black. Arthur Daley did not mention Robinson until the second part of his column in the *New York Times*, while Bob Cooke, in the *Herald Tribune*, noted almost off-handedly: "A number of observers had been attracted by the presence of Jackie Robinson, Brooklyn's Negro first baseman." And in the *New York Post*, Arch Murray dismissed Robinson's debut in the fourth paragraph of his story thusly: "Jackie Robinson, the first colored boy ever to don major league flannels, started at first base and batted second for the Dodgers."

"Being a Yankee in those days wasn't easy for *anyone*," Arlene said. "Casey was a tough manager and they were expected to win every year. He used to threaten them all the time, to send them down to the minors or whatever."

Stengel, as Howard would quickly come to realize, was a product of another time. Born in Kansas City in 1890, a part of his America had included a casual, unthinking disparagement of blacks. It wasn't bigotry, just a kind of blind indifference. Stengel was prone to occasionally use racial epithets, which, forty years later, would have earned him banishment from baseball—as it did Los Angeles Dodgers general manager Al Campanis. Campanis's life and reputation were ruined in just two minutes when, on ABC's *Nightline* show with Ted Koppel, April 6, 1987, he tried to explain that the reason there weren't more blacks in management positions in baseball was because they "lacked the necessities." Stengel was far more blunt when it came to assessing Howard that spring of 1955.

Noting that Howard's one apparent drawback was his lack of speed—which in the grizzled manager's opinion made him much more suitable for catching than playing the outfield—Stengel reportedly remarked: "They finally get me a nigger and he can't run!"

"I heard that," Arlene said, "and Elston told me about how Casey would yell things from the bench about Jackie stealing bases against them in the World Series—things like 'throw that nigger out.' But he would catch himself, realizing that Elston was there. I think Casey went out of his way to be nice to Elston. He gave him his chance and encouraged him to catch. I don't remember any overt prejudice from Casey. Back then, there were the victory parties—the Yankees were always having victory parties. And we'd go and Casey always called me 'the starlet.' I'd dance with him and Elston would dance with Edna, Casey's wife, and it was a whole big jolly thing.

"So what I do remember are only the kindnesses, like that first year when I was pregnant and the team went on a tour to Japan after the 1955 season. Both Merlyn Mantle and myself couldn't go because we were pregnant. All the other wives went and I was in the delivery room and Casey paid for the phone call, insisting that Elston call me. I remember, too, whenever a baby was born, we'd always get a gift from Edna."

No matter what the perception of the Yankees' upper management's attitude toward blacks, the players, coaches and even Stengel (in his own way) were color-blind. The Yankee way then, as it was nearly 50 years later under Joe Torre, was to work together toward the common cause of winning. Older players in their twilight willingly worked to groom their successors—as Frank Crosetti did with Phil Rizzuto in 1941, Eddie Lopat with Whitey Ford in 1950, Jerry Coleman with Bobby Richardson in 1957 and Joe Girardi with Jorge Posada in 1998 and '99—and coaches did the same. In Howard's case, it was Hall of Famer Bill Dickey, a born and bred son of the South—from Little Rock, Arkansas, via Bastrop, Louisiana—who taught him all the finer points of catching.

"He was the most patient man I ever met," Howard had said of Dickey in a magazine article. "He was more than a coach. He talked to me like an uncle. He had this patient way of explaining things. He made me feel like there was nothing impossible for me. All he ever wanted in return was that you pay attention and try as hard as you could. I didn't disappoint him there. I really was not much of a catcher at the start, but I never stopped trying. I'm more proud of trying hard than I am of anything else. Bill Dickey taught me that."

And while Stengel may have made disparaging remarks about Howard's lack of speed, he could not conceal his immense admiration for his arm. "He's got one of the greatest arms I ever saw," the manager said, "and he's gonna be a great catcher."

The problem was the Yankees already had a great catcher in the durable, future Hall of Famer Yogi Berra. In 1955, Berra was right in his prime, having just won his third American League Most Valuable Player award in five years. In 1958, Howard won the Babe Ruth Award as the Most Valuable Player in the World Series against the Milwaukee Braves—but as an outfielder.

Upon being shut out 3–0 by Warren Spahn in Game 4 (in which all three Milwaukee runs came as a result of Yankee left fielder Norm Siebern losing fly balls in the treacherous late-October afternoon sun and shadows of Yankee Stadium), the Yankees were down 3–1, a deficit no team had overcome in the Series since the 1925 Pittsburgh Pirates. Stengel sent Howard out to left field for Game 5, a move that Elston made inspired with a diving catch of Red Schoendienst's blooper in the sixth inning. Coming up throwing, he was then able to double off Billy Bruton at first to blunt a budding Milwaukee rally and preserve a 1–0

Yankee lead. Though he hit only .222 for the Series, that play was regarded as the turning point in the Yankees' comeback to the world championship.

"I know Elston was always very proud of getting that Babe Ruth Award, especially because it was really for his defense," Arlene said.

Still, it was defense as an *outfielder*, and the prospects of ever getting to catch on an everyday basis seemed dim. Berra, who averaged nearly 145 games behind the plate from 1950 to 1956, was still regarded the Yankees' No. 1 catcher in 1960—by which time Howard was 31 and into his sixth season with the club. He'd played over 100 games in each of them, but as Stengel's swingman, bouncing between the outfield, first base and catcher.

"It was frustrating for Elston, waiting for Yogi to move on," Arlene said. "I don't know if Elston ever felt that way, but I felt it was calculated by the Yankees; that they weren't sure if a black man could catch, and he was an outfielder and they switched him to catching and why? His best years were frittering away. He'd come home and he'd be very moody. Of course, he didn't show any of that emotion publicly because that was the way he was."

Much as Stengel had sung Howard's praises as a catcher, the old man could never bring himself to totally displace Berra as his No. 1 receiver. It wasn't until Ralph Houk took over as manager in 1961 that Howard was told he was the Yankees' No. 1 catcher. As opposed to Stengel, who seemed to take pleasure at chiding and even ridiculing his players in public, Houk was the consummate players manager and he wasted no time in putting his stamp on the Yankees. Shortly after being named Stengel's successor, Houk announced Whitey Ford would pitch on three days rest instead of four and informed Howard that he would handle the bulk of the catching with Berra backing him up and playing left field.

Howard responded with his finest season yet, leading the team in batting (.348) along with 21 homers and 77 RBI.

"That year he would have finished second in the [AL] batting race except he didn't have enough at bats," Arlene related. "I know that was frustrating for him, too. As great a season as that was for him, the MVP year, I'd say, was his real breakthrough year."

The Yankees won the American League pennant for the fourth straight season in '63, third straight under Houk. Their margin of victory was 10½ games over the Chicago White Sox and there was really no contest as to who the MVP was. Mickey Mantle broke his foot that year and was limited to just 65 games, while Roger Maris was also hampered by injuries throughout and hit .269 with 23 homers in just 90 games. It was therefore left to Howard to carry the Yankee offense—which he did with .287 average, 28 homers and 85 RBI—and he was unquestionably the best catcher in the league, winning Gold Glove honors. A breakdown of Howard's '63 season showed he either won or tied games the Yankees eventually won with clutch hits on 10 occasions.

"Do you have a place in the house with all of Elston's awards and memorabilia?" I asked her.

"Oh yes," she said. "Would you like to see it? That's where the MVP award is."

She got up from the dining room table and motioned for me to follow her upstairs. At the top of the stairs, she led me into a dimly lit room which appeared to be her office. Looking around at the baseball pictures on the wall and a stack of bats in one corner, I sensed it had once been her husband's office, too. Hanging prominently above the desk was the MVP award.

"Would it be okay if I took some pictures?" I asked.

"Of the room?" she said.

"Of you *and* the room," I replied.

"Oh my gosh!" she shrieked. "Without any makeup? Give me a few minutes to fix myself up."

She was still an exquisitely beautiful woman, defying her years much as she defied her neighbors forty years earlier. Her face, even without makeup, bore no telltale visible lines and the long-sleeved T-shirt she had chosen to wear on this day seemed most appropriate since she still maintained a model's figure. *What is it with these '50s*

Yankee wives? All of them—Carmen Berra, Cora Rizzuto, Joan Ford, Arlene Howard—having maintained their youthful beauty. Could it be that Gus Mauch, Stengel's venerable team trainer all of those years, had some sort of secret youth potion he dispensed to the team's stars to bring home to their wives?

"I honestly don't think that'll be necessary," I said to her.

She shrugged and reached up and took the MVP award down off the wall, cradling it in her arms.

"This, I know, was his greatest thrill," she said. "I always wondered how many others he might have won had he been the No. 1 catcher sooner. He was 34 when he won this and his best years were behind him."

In '64, Howard caught 146 games, and while he led AL catchers in fielding and putouts, his home run count fell to 15. Nevertheless, it was a performance that earned him a raise to $70,000, which, to that point, was the highest salary ever paid a catcher, including Berra, Roy Campanella of the Dodgers or any of the other Hall of Fame receivers.

"I know Elston took a lot of pride in that," Arlene said, "but at the same time you have to realize there were still a lot of players making more than that who weren't catchers."

Meanwhile, as with the Yankee dynasty itself, 1964 proved to be the beginning of the end for their first black player. The following season, he missed two months after undergoing surgery for the removal of bone chips in his elbow and was never the same player again. Two years later, he would find himself in another World Series, not with the Yankees, but, rather, with, of all teams, the hated rival Boston Red Sox. In August of 1967, Houk approached Howard and told him of the Red Sox's interest in him.

His skills had eroded to the point where he was back to being the No. 2 Yankee catcher, behind Jake Gibbs, the former University of Mississippi quarterback to whom the Yankees had paid a (then huge) $105,000 bonus in 1961 to convince him to forsake a pro football career for baseball. Howard was batting under .200, but as Houk explained, the Red Sox, who hadn't been to a World Series since 1946, valued his defense, experience and the leadership he could provide. "They feel they can win it with you handling their pitchers," Houk told him. "We're not going anywhere and this will be a great opportunity for you to get yourself another ring."

Still, Howard wasn't so sure.

"Everybody had gotten old and the Yankees were not anywhere close to what they had been," Arlene said. "But he had been promised he would finish his career with the Yankees and he really didn't want to go. That's why I think they offered him a coaching job with them when he retired. I wanted him to go because I had no love affair for the Yankees. I liked Boston anyway and under the circumstances, I said 'why not?' It turned out to be a good experience because the Red Sox did win and then he got to play the World Series against the Cardinals and we got to go home to St. Louis again."

And it was also at that World Series that Howard got the one and only offer he ever wanted in baseball—beyond the Yankees initially extending him the opportunity to play for them.

"He dearly wanted to manage, with every fiber in his body," Arlene said. "It was at that World Series in St. Louis Elston and I had breakfast together with Bill Veeck, who was out of baseball at the time, but was in the process of trying to buy the team in Washington. Veeck asked him: 'If I get this team, would you consider being my manager?' Unfortunately, it never came to pass because they wouldn't sell to Veeck. They didn't like him because he was too liberal, too progressive for them."

He played one more year with the Red Sox before coming back home to the Yankees and the promised coaching job. It was during his final season that he introduced a unique device called the batting doughnut which, nearly a half-century later, is as much a part of baseball as resin bags. The ringed weight, which hitters place around their bats for their warm-up swings in the on-deck circle, was developed by Howard in conjunction with a Bergenfield, New Jersey, firm called General Sportcraft Ltd. As more and more hitters gave it their endorsement, Howard and his partners got a patent for it and it looked like they were in for a windfall.

"They should have been," said Arlene, "but what happened was the bat companies infringed on the patent and made their own, flooding the market with them. Then they started using them in Japan. Even though they had the patent, Elston and his partners simply didn't have the resources to fight the big bat companies in the courts, and so they made a little money in the beginning but that was about it."

Howard left the legal wrangling over the doughnut patent to his partners. By this time, his playing career over, he had other ambitions, the seeds of managing having been planted in his head by Veeck. Unfortunately, as he was to find out in the ensuing years, the only man who apparently thought he could manage wasn't in the game. Howard remained entrenched as a brain trust lieutenant with the Yankees, coaching first base and the bullpen, until 1978. He never gave up on his dream of managing, although, with each succeeding year of no offers, or even interviews, he was left no choice but to accept the reality it was never going to happen.

"I guess the biggest disappointment for him came after Houk left [in 1973]," Arlene said, ignoring a painter suddenly ascending on the scaffolding outside the office room window. "Everybody thought that when Ralph retired or whatever that he would get the job. And then, when it happened, they hired somebody [Bill Virdon] out of the blue—from outside the organization. I remember flying back from St. Petersburg one year, sometime after that, and George Steinbrenner happened to be on the same flight. He invited me up to first class to sit with him, and in the conversation that took place I told him how much Elston wanted to manage. His excuse was: 'Well, Elston's too good for that. I have something else in mind for him.' Of course, that was when he was hiring two managers a year."

"In truth, George never had a high regard for managers," I ventured. "So he probably meant it, even if it sounded like he was giving you a line. He knew if he hired Ellie, he'd have to fire him and he probably didn't want to be the first guy to fire a black manager."

"Whatever," she said. "I just know Elston *did* want to manage and, in that respect, he died brokenhearted."

He was only 51. Prior to the 1979 season he was diagnosed with an extremely rare (and ultimately incurable) condition called Coxsackie virus, which attacks and inflames the tissues that line the heart. He was hospitalized for an extended stay that season, and, upon his release, was given a job in the front office by Steinbrenner. The doctors had told him, however, his illness was a progressive one. On December 14, 1980, after another prolonged hospitalization, he died of cardiac arrest.

His friend Bill White, a former first baseman for the Giants, Cardinals and Phillies and a pioneer in his own right as the first black broadcaster in the majors and later the first black league president, said of him: "We went through a lot of things together—things like being told we were not good enough to live with other people. Ellie didn't complain, but we complained for him."

Now, all these years later, in this same house, which cowardly and bigoted neighbors had deemed Elston Howard not good enough to live in, his widow still complains for him. She has chosen to remain alone, save for the periodic company of her only surviving daughter, the fierce protector of her husband's legacy. At his funeral, she was overheard telling a couple of close friends: "Death no longer has any fear for me, believing that I could be with my husband again afterward."

"I still feel the same way," said Arlene Howard, still radiant, still fervent in her convictions and still very much in love with the man who quietly and with a minimum of fanfare broke what many feel was baseball's toughest of all color lines. "Nothing has changed."

THE MAJOR IN WINTER

RALPH HOUK

He was 82 now, a lion in winter, living in peaceful retirement in a sprawling but secluded golf course community in central Florida. Nevertheless, there was a feeling of trepidation on my part as I approached the front door of the large adobe-style ranch home, privately wondering if, sometime during my visit with Ralph Houk, I was suddenly going to find myself gasping for air at the bottom of his swimming pool.

Houk, a decorated war hero who'd earned two battlefield promotions along with the Silver Star for his bravery under fire during the Battle of the Bulge, had similarly risen from seldom used third-string catcher on the Yankees in the late '40s and '50s, to make the unlikely rise to Casey Stengel's successor as manager in 1960. He would go on to direct the Yankees to world championships in 1961 and '62 and another American League pennant in '63 before again being elevated to general manager. When he first became Yankee manager, there was a headline in one of the national sports magazines that screamed: "Don't Mess with the Major!" and as umpires and, especially, sportswriters would later come to learn at their peril, it was an accurate warning. (The Yankee players had already gotten a hint of this from an incident on the train from Kansas City to Detroit after the club had clinched the American League pennant in 1957. During the celebratory revelry, Ryne Duren, the bespectacled, hard-throwing and equally hard-drinking relief pitcher, got a little too rambunctious and accidentally knocked a cigar out of Houk's hand. Houk, who was a coach by then, responded by hauling off and punching Duren, opening up a cut over the pitcher's eye in the process.

But for all his ferocity, he was still regarded as the consummate players' manager who would protect them at all costs, even if it meant lying about their human frailties, getting himself fined and suspended for verbally abusing umpires or, worse, getting physical with a writer. And almost to a man, his players loved him for his loyal and combative nature. In his later years as manager—with the Yankees again from 1966 to 1973 and then the Detroit Tigers and Boston Red Sox—his teams didn't win so much and his fits of temper became more volcanic, to the point where, in June of 1975 with the Tigers, he was actually arrested, jailed and charged with one count of assault by a *Baltimore Evening Sun* sportswriter.

My own experiences with Houk, as a neophyte baseball writer covering the Yankees for United Press International in the early '70s, were relatively tame. He didn't know me, and my questions to him were usually of the softball nature—not game-related—in regard to a feature story I might be writing about one of his players. And, so, the worst indignity I ever suffered from him was having tobacco juice spit on my shoes as I sat next to him in the dugout—a semi-intentional (if rather disgusting) gesture I later found out from my veteran colleagues at the *New York Daily News*, Dick Young and Phil Pepe, to be almost a badge of honor. "That's Ralph's way of saying he accepts you as part of the fraternity," Pepe told me reassuringly.

So even though it had been more than 15 years since he'd retired from managing, I wasn't sure how he might react to having any old wounds reopened. He had been inexplicably estranged from the Yankees after resigning as manager in 1973, the year George Steinbrenner bought the team from CBS, and, his strained and sometimes stormy relationship with the press being what it was, he hadn't been much for interviews. But considering he'd been such an important figure in Yankee history as Stengel's successor, manager of the latter-day Murderers' Row '61 team of Roger Maris and Mickey Mantle, and later as the GM who presided over the firings of Yankee icons Yogi Berra and Mel Allen, it was rather sad to think he'd been seemingly forgotten in the transition of Yankee fans from then until now. I couldn't help but wonder if he felt forgotten, too.

Then again, so much of Houk's tenure with the Yankees after the epic '61 season had been marred by unpleasantness. In his two autobiographies, Red Barber, the venerable Hall of Fame broadcaster who finished his career with the Yankees, hinted at Houk's fingerprints being on the Allen firing. (As it was, Allen, the acknowledged all-time "Voice of the Yankees," went to his death in 1996 without ever getting a satisfactory answer as to why he was unceremoniously let go after the 1964 season.) Barber also accused Houk of being disingenuous with him—*Oh Red, you know you're our man*—at the same time the Yankees were looking to ease him out and bring in Joe Garagiola as the No. 1 announcer in 1965.

"I see you found it all right," he said, upon opening the front door and ushering me into the foyer. His handshake was firm, and he looked fit in his white knit golf shirt and khaki slacks, and in reasonably good shape for a man of leisure. His once blond hair was now a shade lighter, closer to white, and there were more lines in his face and neck, but he definitely didn't look his age, and I sensed he could still pack a healthy wallop if provoked. It had been a long time since that had happened, though, and Houk seemed genuinely at ease as we sat down at a table in the glass-enclosed sunroom at the rear of his house. A par-three golf course wound around the community, and as I'd made my way in on the meandering road that led to Houk's street, I'd noticed a small lake where an elderly man was fishing.

"You really are tucked away back here in the middle of nowhere," I said to him.

"Yeah, Bette and I like it here," he said, in reference to his wife, who was watching TV in another room. He met her in 1947 at the University of Kansas in Lawrence where they both grew up. "It's quite a contrast from where we lived in New Jersey when I managed the Yankees, but my pastimes now are golf and fishing and I get to do both whenever I want right here."

It was early February, unseasonably cool, even for Florida's winter standards, and in a few days, the area would start to fill up with baseball people. The Cleveland Indians, Detroit Tigers, Atlanta Braves and Kansas City Royals all trained within a half-hour of Houk's community, while an hour to the west on Interstate 4 was the Yankee complex in Tampa. When I noted this to Houk, however, he shrugged.

"I haven't gotten around to any of the camps in a couple of years," he said, "and I really should. I like seeing all the guys who played for me."

"What about the Yankees?" I asked. "Have you been over to see them since they moved to Tampa from Fort Lauderdale in '96?"

"No," he said, with a trace of resignation. "Nobody's ever asked me."

Houk grew up on his father's 160-acre cattle farm on the Kansas River, about 40 miles from the Missouri-Kansas border. His father's four brothers all played semipro baseball for a local team called the Belvoirs, and when he was 11, his Uncle Charlie, who managed the team, took him to a tryout for a team in the Lawrence Twilight League, for kids ages 11 to 18. He made the team as an outfielder, but his second year, the team catcher came down with the measles and the coach, who'd noticed his exceptionally strong throwing arm, handed him a mask and chest protector and asked him to take over the receiving chores. He was pretty much a catcher from that day on.

There was no baseball at Lawrence High School until Houk's senior year, so as a freshman, sophomore and junior he concentrated all his athletic energies as a quarterback for the football team. In his senior year, he totaled 72 points and led the team to the state championship, which prompted college scholarship offers from Kansas and Oklahoma. But by then, Houk had grown more and more partial to baseball, having graduated from the Lawrence Twilight League to his Uncle Charlie's Belvoirs, and on the weekends he played for the Lawrence sandlot team in the prestigious Ban Johnson League. His throwing arm had particularly caught the attention of the roving major league scouts, and then, in the national Ban Johnson tournament in Kansas City that summer of 1938, he showed them he could do it all. In the first game of a tournament doubleheader, he had three hits, blocked two runners from scoring at the plate and threw out another on the basepaths. Among the more than interested observers in the primitive, roofless grandstand behind home plate were the Yankees' Midwestern scouting supervisor Bill Essick, and their other top area scout, Bill Skiff.

As the story has been told, after Houk's third hit, Essick instructed Skiff to run interference for him with the other bird dog scouts by regaling them with stories about his '30s Yankee teammate, Babe Ruth. In the meantime, Essick slipped away and waited for Houk under the grandstand with contract and fountain pen in hand. The bonus was $500, which, as Houk would recount in his 1962 book *Ballplayers Are Human Too*, "was big money then since the bushes were full of ambitious, hard-driving kids like me."

The next spring, he reported for spring training to the Yankees Class C Western Association club in Joplin, Missouri, only to have his ego deflated when the manager, former New York Giants catcher Bubber Jonnard, decided he did not have as much ability as the other catchers in camp (or as much as he thought he had) and sent him to Neosho, Missouri, of the Class D Arkansas-Missouri League to begin his professional career.

"I was pretty pissed off," Houk remembered. "I hadn't really had much of a chance to show them what I could do. It was cold that spring and we had most of our workouts at the local YMCA. I'll never forget telling the manager there, a guy named Dennie Burns, that I was a .400 hitter in Ban Johnson. He said: 'Oh yeah? You're the new Rogers Hornsby, huh?' He told me I'd find out quickly I wasn't a .400 hitter once they started throwing me curveballs. But I finished the season at .286, which wasn't too bad in a four-team league where you saw the same pitchers over and over. I made the All-Star team, was voted the most popular player and got an Arrow shirt and a tie and was asked to crown the Cherry Queen. That was the highlight of my career!"

It was good enough to earn a promotion to Joplin, where he thought he *should* have started out, for 1940. His pay increased from $75 to $90 a month, and so, too, did his batting average. He hit .313 in 110 games and led the Western Association catchers in fielding and assists. More importantly, the Yankees were starting to take notice. They advanced him to Binghamton of the Class A Eastern League to start the '41 season, but then shipped him back to Augusta in the Sally League where he became fast friends with Joe Page, the free-spirited left-handed pitcher who would go on to play a pivotal role as the Yankees' closer on their 1947 and '49 world championship clubs. Besides teaming up on a no-hitter with Page that summer at Augusta, Houk said he helped Page refine his spitball. According to Houk, Page had experimented with the spitter, but couldn't control it. As the season went on, Houk kept a stash of black dirt in his rear pocket and whenever Page would get in trouble, Houk would rub the dirt on the ball to help give it more dip. Because Houk chewed tobacco, the umpires assumed that was the reason for the balls becoming discolored.

By 1941, Houk was ready—at least in his mind—for advancement to the upper rungs of the Yankee farm system, but as he said: "The Japanese and the Nazis had other ideas." When he came in from hunting in the snowy Kansas woods that Sunday morning of December 7, his brother Harold met him at the farmhouse door, ashen-faced. "Pearl Harbor's been bombed," he said. "It looks like we're going to war."

Realizing he would surely be drafted before the next baseball season, Houk tried to enlist in the coast guard, only to be rejected for color blindness. Since the army didn't have color blindness tests yet, he and Harold decided to enlist there, knowing at least they had a baseball team. They had been stationed at Fort Leavenworth, Kansas, for only a few months when they'd had their fill of grunt duty and applied for Officers Candidate School. Both were accepted and Houk was assigned to an armored division in Fort Knox, Kentucky. Upon making the grade to second lieutenant, he was sent overseas at the end of 1943, to the Second Front in Wiltshire, England. A few days after D-Day, he landed on Omaha Beach with the 89th Cavalry Reconnaissance Squadron of the Ninth Armored Division.

Less than two years removed from the security of his Kansas farm and the carefree times in those rustic lower minor league ballparks, Houk was dodging aerial bombardments, fording streams, testing bridges and guiding Allied tanks inexorably across the Western Front of Europe. He received a Bronze Star when a piece of German shrapnel nicked him in the thigh sometime—he doesn't remember when or where—during the liberation of Paris. The war had taken a turn by then, and now the Allied forces were moving toward Berlin. In the Ardennes forest in December of '44, Houk's ranger battalion was patrolling for any lingering German resistance when suddenly they encountered a wave of panzer divisions, forcing them to fall back across the hills to Waldbillig, a small town in Luxembourg.

"That was the Battle of the Bulge," Houk related, "and the Germans were trying to make their way into Bastogne. We more or less got overrun in this little town of Waldbillig and were pretty much surrounded. I was kind of right in the mix of it, directing some tanks, and in order to direct their fire, I probably had to expose myself to some fire.

"It was real cold and I was wearing this heavy trench coat and, unbeknownst to me, some bullets went right through the coat. We were getting shelled pretty heavily and when two of our lieutenants of other platoons were killed, I was suddenly in command of the remaining forces. I was using this little house as a command post, and with the German tanks coming at us, firing 88s, I finally had to withdraw from the direction of the fire I had sent in from our tanks. My machine guns and mortars were then able to cut down the Nazi infantry, coming on foot in the snow, and, for that, I guess, they awarded me the Silver Star. I just know it was a real mess, a lot of people killed."

After the Germans withdrew, Houk and his troops continued their drive to the Rhine River. Houk was riding in a jeep with a driver and a gunner in the back. As they started up a small hill, Houk had gotten out his map case to try to determine where they were when he heard the crack of a rifle shot and a ping against his helmet. He instinctively ducked under the front seat, only to hear his driver say to the gunner: "They got Lieutenant Houk!"

"We were basically on a reconnaissance mission and I was riding in the lead jeep," Houk recalled. "I thought I'd been hit—I heard a tick—but I didn't know what had happened. So as I slumped over, my driver pulled the jeep around this big barn with haystacks. I sat up and looked at my helmet and saw this big hole in it and said, 'Jesus, was I lucky!' I still have the helmet. Would you like to see it?"

"Absolutely," I answered. "I've got to believe that's a little more meaningful trophy than anything you ever won in baseball."

"You're right about that," Houk answered.

He disappeared into another room and reemerged a couple of minutes later holding in his hands this battered green army helmet with a hole, two inches in circumference, through the front of it.

"The bullet nestled right in here in the webbing," Houk said, turning the helmet upside down. "A miracle, I guess. About the closest I could have come to buying it."

"Your number just wasn't up," I countered. "Whether you knew it or not, there were more men for you to lead—in a game, not a war. You were certainly prepared for it."

"Well, I think you definitely learn the feelings of men when you see people killed right in front of you; when you're riding in a jeep as I was a while after that incident, and you see a part of a guy's head shot off in a jeep right next to you. You learn a lot about people and how they react when the pressure's on 'em. You just have a feeling for people and I think that helped me as a manager, especially when things went bad.

"The worst thing for me as far as the war was the first time I saw dead people . . . when we landed at Omaha Beach and there were still people floating around there . . . and then later during the Battle of the Bulge, when you saw dead guys frozen in the snow. It wasn't very pretty. And I think all of that kind of stayed on my mind when I'd be on a losing streak and I'd go back to my room and say, 'Wait a minute this ain't that bad.'"

"It was always said of you that you were a players' manager, whatever that means," I said.

"Yeah, I never quite knew what that meant either," he said. "I know a lot of people said, 'Well he wouldn't knock his players to the press.' Well, that's true. I always felt you could get a lot more out of a player if you brought him into the office and discussed the thing with him in private and kept it out of the papers. The simple reason for that is that most players are young, and they have dads and moms. Or they have sweethearts. Or wives. This stuff about the player gets in the papers and they read that, it's gonna really bother the player and it's gonna affect his performance."

In his 20 years as a manager, in which he won 1,619 games (ranking him 13th all time), Houk probably had well over 1,000 players under his command. Only one of them, to his knowledge, ever took him on publicly—Jim Bouton, the iconoclastic Yankee pitcher in the '60s, with whom he'd had a celebrated contract dispute in 1964. It was bad enough Bouton took some swipes at Houk in his best-selling book *Ball Four*, but when he told tales out of school about other Yankee players, well, that, to the Major, was the unforgivable sin of baseball. Apparently, in his mind, it still was.

"Bouton and I don't get along," Houk said evenly. "He was only for himself. He was one guy who wasn't a team player. I realized that in '63, his second year with us when he won 21 games. There was a game in July in Kansas City and he had something like 17, 18 wins at the time. It was a real hot day and we had about a three-run lead with him pitching and he got into a jam. I took him out and brought in Steve Hamilton, who wound up losing the game. Afterward, Bouton made a remark to some writer that I didn't want him to win 20 games. He only worried about his pitching stats. I don't know if he ever changed. Everywhere he went after that, he got into trouble. Smart guy, but a funny-thinking person. He said bad things about Mantle in his book. I gave him his chance. I kept him on the team when the front office wanted to send him out."

For the first time in our conversation I could detect a bit of an edge to Houk's voice and, glancing warily at the swimming pool, I decided it might be a good idea to switch the conversation back to his playing career.

He spent all of 1947 with the Yankees as the backup catcher to Aaron Robinson and Yogi Berra, hitting .272 in 41 games. Though he would spend parts of the next seven seasons with the Yankees, that was by far the most games in which he would appear. The sum total of his major league career was 91 games, a .272 batting average, 20 RBI and no home runs.

"When I first joined the Yankees in '47, I had never seen a big league park," Houk said. "We came in from training in Cuba that year. I don't think anyone had expected me to make the Yankees, but somehow I did, and when the season opened, I was catching against left-hand pitching and Aaron Robinson was catching against right-handers. Yogi was in the outfield then, but they gradually started moving him behind the plate and he eventually took over the job from both of us. Then, later that season, they'd bring me in for defense, especially when Joe Page came into the game. But that's pretty much how it went for me and I just never did hit the long ball enough to make it as a regular."

"It had to be frustrating, sitting around in the bullpen, day after day, and never getting to play."

"I guess the thing that saved me was the bullpen," Houk said. "I had a lot of friends through the years out there. Plus, we were winning every year. You looked forward to that, and that check was usually bigger than my salary. Later, I heard there were a couple of clubs interested in me— you heard those things through the grapevine—and I wasn't sure what I wanted. But they never did trade me and late in 1954 Lee MacPhail, the farm director, came to me and asked me if I'd be interested in managing in the minors. I was surprised and I asked, 'Where?' Originally, it was gonna be Kansas City, but in '55 Kansas City went to the big leagues and the Yankees moved their Triple A farm club to Denver. So that's how I wound up in Denver. I still don't know how it all happened or what they saw in me. It wasn't as if I'd sat alongside Casey in the dugout picking up things all those years. I was in the bullpen. And I figured they were gonna send me to the low minors to start out."

Obviously, the Yankee high command, aware of his war record, had seen leadership and teaching qualities in Houk he might not have realized he had. For, in assigning him to Denver, they were entrusting him with the cream of their up-and-coming talent. The roster of the fledgling American Association Denver Bears franchise in 1955 included future major-leaguers Bobby Richardson, Woodie Held, Marv Throneberry, Whitey Herzog, Darrell Johnson and Lou Skizas. In addition, Don Larsen, whom the Yankees had acquired from the Baltimore Orioles in a huge 17-player deal the previous winter, was assigned to the Bears and went 9-1 before being called up to New York. Under Houk's direction, Denver finished third that year, and led the league in attendance.

An incident in late May 1955 only further convinced the Yankee brass they'd made the right decision in selecting Houk to manage their top prospects. The team had gotten off to a 7-25 start and was in last place when Bill DeWitt, the Yankees' assistant general manager, paid a visit to Denver and suggested they make some player purchases from the major league clubs when the rosters were to be pared from 28 to 25 in a couple of days. The meeting took place in a Denver hotel, and as DeWitt talked, Houk began to sweat. Finally, after listening to DeWitt discuss the various players he thought would be available, Houk said bluntly: "Bill, I don't want any new ballplayers. I just want time to work out our problems with the ones we have. I picked these players in the spring and I believe in them. I don't want any help."

The puzzled DeWitt had never heard of a manager refusing the front office's help to get him better players. He returned to New York and reported what Houk said to his boss, general manager George Weiss. "Okay, so be it," Weiss shrugged. "Let's see what he can do." Meanwhile, as the summer wore on, Houk's players began to justify the faith he'd shown in them, playing over .600 ball the rest of the year to finish at 83-71. The pugnacious side of Houk also got revealed that summer when, twice, he punched out one of his pitchers, a volatile left-hander named Ed Donnelly. But after the season was over, Donnelly was quoted as saying: "He was the greatest guy I ever played for. I felt like I'd go to the end of the world for him. He treated you like a man, not a kid."

Naturally, the Yankees were pleased at how Houk rallied the Denver team without their help, and they sent him back for 1956. Most of the same players were still there, only now they were joined by a couple more budding stars destined for successful careers in New York—shortstop Tony Kubek and right-handed pitcher Ralph Terry. The 1956 Denver Bears placed seven players on the American Association All-Star team—Throneberry (who led the league in homers and RBI), Richardson, Kubek, Held, Johnson, Terry and outfielder Bob Martyn—and finished second, 87–57.

During that time, the Yankees had two Triple A farm clubs, the other one in Richmond, Virginia, where Eddie Lopat, the old junk-balling left-hander who'd been Houk's teammate from '47 to '54, was managing. Although Houk swore he didn't know of any subtle competition being created by the Yankee front office, it was clear they were looking at both of them as potential successors to the aging Stengel. In retrospect, it seems just as clear Houk's performance in turning that 1955 team around had gained him a leg-up on Lopat in the Yankee brass's eyes since all their top prospects were assigned to

Denver, while Richmond was used primarily as a taxi squad outlet from where the Yankees would shuttle veteran backup players.

In any case, after the 1957 season, the Yankees brought Houk up as a coach under Stengel. Lopat, on the other hand, remained at Richmond in 1958 and was then made a scout the following year.

"To be honest," Houk said, "I looked at being brought to the big leagues as a demotion. I really enjoyed managing at Denver. I had also managed in winter ball at San Juan, Puerto Rico, in '57—I was the only American manager down there that season who didn't get fired—so it was pretty clear what I wanted to do. I coached those four years under Casey, and during the 1960 season, he got sick and they asked me to fill in for him for a couple of weeks. We all know what happened later. I'd heard rumors at the end of the season that Detroit and Kansas City were both interested in me to manage for them. I knew the general manager at Kansas City, Parke Carroll, personally. Then when we were in Pittsburgh for the Series, Roy Hamey [who was now the Yankee general manager], came to me and said: 'Don't be talking too much to that Kansas City club. There's a lot of things that may be happening here.' At the same time, Casey had said to me sometime earlier in the season that he sensed his time was coming to an end as manager and when it did, he'd be on my side for the job.

"Well, all this was happening so fast and then we blew that damn Series, and a few days after I got home, they called me and told me they wanted to talk to me downtown at [Yankee co-owner] Del Webb's suite at the Waldorf-Astoria, and not to say anything to the press."

On the morning of October 20, 1960, the Yankees called a press conference at the Savoy Hilton hotel to make official the naming of Houk as manager. Two days before, at the same hotel (but much larger room), they'd had a press conference purportedly to announce Stengel's retirement, except, when pressed by the media, the old man confessed to being fired, adding: "I wouldn't be a yes man for them!"

The headline in the *Daily News* that day said simply: "Houk, Former Catcher, 41, Will Be New Yank Pilot." So anonymously had

Houk toiled as the backup Yankee catcher those eight seasons and then as a minor league manager and first base coach, it was as if the *News* felt a need to identify him to its readers.

"I had no fear of managing the Yankees, even though I probably wasn't too familiar to a lot of the fans, and I was taking over for a legend," Houk said. "I'd had a lot of the players at Denver and I knew all the players on the club from having been on the coaching staff for three years. The biggest pressure I had, really, from the day I took over at the press conference was that everybody liked Casey. The fact that Casey had said two days before that he hadn't retired but was fired hurt me. A lot of the press started asking me: 'What are you gonna do? Are you gonna ask Casey for advice?' I loved Casey, but I was my own man. You have to be yourself."

From the get-go in 1961, Houk made that abundantly clear. (Ironically, his first move was to release Lopat as Yankee pitching coach and replace him with Johnny Sain, another former Yankee pitcher of the '50s.) One of the first determinations Houk made in spring training was to have Whitey Ford pitch every four days instead of five the way Stengel had mostly used him. Another thing was to appoint Mickey Mantle unofficial team captain.

"We'd never had a captain since Gehrig," Houk said, "but I called Mickey into my office that spring and said to him: 'We're not gonna have a captain, but you're going to be the leader of this club.' And the reason I did that was because I knew he was the one guy on the club everybody respected, whose only thought was to win. He was a guy who'd hit two home runs in a game and if you lost, you'd have thought the world had come to an end with him, and if he struck out three times and you won, he was the happiest guy on earth. That's the kind of guy I needed as a leader. I was fortunate, too, that DiMaggio came down to spring training that year as a special instructor for me. He didn't like Casey so it was the first time he'd been back in uniform since he retired. That's always been my good fortune in life. Even though I wasn't a star player, I always had star players backing me as a manager.

"As for the Whitey thing, I just felt we had the type of staff where I could go primarily with a four-man rotation and I had guys I could plug in there on that fifth day. Plus, in Luis Arroyo, we had a good reliever who could pick Whitey up in the eighth inning and save him some innings."

The Ford experiment couldn't have worked out more perfectly. Given the extra 10 starts, Ford fashioned his best season in '61—25-4 while leading the American League in innings (283). At the same time, Arroyo, the Puerto Rican left-hander whom the Yankees had purchased from the independent Jersey City team in the International League the year before—after he'd been cut loose by both the St. Louis Cardinals and Pittsburgh Pirates—emerged as the dominant reliever in the AL, winning 15 games and saving a league-leading 29. The winter Houk managed in Puerto Rico, he'd had Arroyo on his San Juan team and after watching the roly-poly lefty baffle the veteran hitters in that league with his screwball, he made a mental note to recommend him to the Yankees when he got home—which he did. But when it came to Houk's Midas touch in '61, nothing came close to Roger Maris breaking Babe Ruth's one-season home run record of 60 that had stood since 1927.

The Maris (and Mantle) pursuit of the Babe became the overriding story of 1961, to the point that the primary business at hand for Houk—winning the pennant—often got lost in all the media hoopla. Forty years later, Billy Crystal made a movie of the home run race in which Maris was portrayed as a reluctant challenger and Houk (played by character actor Bruce McGill, whose previous most notable part had been the lunatic biker in the classic *Animal House*) his constant protector and therapist.

"Was *61** a fairly accurate portrayal of that season?" I asked him.

"I thought the movie was fine," Houk said. "I thought they did a great job with Maris. But I didn't like the Mantle deal because they made him look in there like he drank too much and was a womanizer. And when he was playing, he wasn't nearly like that."

Mickey had been dead for nearly seven years, and his drinking and womanizing had become legendary—mostly through his own admissions. But it was of no matter to Houk, I thought. He still felt a need to protect his players.

"There was a scene in the movie where Topping comes to you and asks you to switch Mickey and Roger in the lineup. Did that happen?"

"No," Houk said firmly. "I have no idea how that got in there. I had a lot of *letters* to make lineup changes, but Topping or Webb never came to me and asked me to do that."

I mentioned to him a conversation I'd had with Gene Michael, the Yankees' chief player evaluator, earlier that winter about having players on your team chasing records. When asked if he thought the Yankees should go after Barry Bonds (who was a free agent at the time, having just raised the home run standard to 73), Michael said: 'Guys like Bonds and [Sammy] Sosa are great players, but ideally you don't want guys on your team who are breaking big records like that because it becomes a distraction and takes away from the team concept you're trying to keep.' He then pointed to the fact that the Yankees had won four world championships in the previous five years and none of their players had finished in the top two of the Most Valuable Player award voting.

"I agree with Gene," said Houk. "The home run thing was a real problem for me. It didn't become a real problem until the end when they got to the 50 mark. Writers would go to Roger and ask him stuff like: 'If you could win a game with a base hit instead of a homer, would you do it?' It was tough on all the other players. They'd do something to win a ball game and all the writers wanted to do was talk to Roger. People forget. We were in a tight pennant race that year. Even though we won 109 games, we didn't clinch it until the next-to-last week of the season [September 20]."

"So you had two things to manage that year," I said. "The team and the surrounding frenzy over the home run race."

"The biggest thing that happened was the time in Baltimore, after Roger had hit his 58th, and he came to me and said: 'I just don't think I can make it tonight.' That was the only time I had to really talk to him about the thing. I told him: 'All those people in the stands out there came to see if you're gonna hit a home run—more than the game.' Then I said: 'Will you do this? Go out in the field for the first inning and when you come in, if you still feel this way, I'll take you out and say you're sick?' He agreed and went out there and when he came in, I stayed way down on the other end of the bench and never went over to him to ask him if he wanted to come out. He stayed in and that night he hit another one.

"Roger was just a modest, small-town kid from the Midwest and he wasn't made for New York. There was a certain group of fans that was on him that year, too. You got the feeling they were rooting for Mantle to win. The biggest relief I had was when he finally broke it on the last day and we could get back to getting ready for the World Series."

As he was talking, a loud buzzing sound could be heard outside, which Houk ignored. A moment later, a man on a sit-down power mower went by the window, and continued on down the fairway that bordered all the homes on Houk's street. The subject of the '61 season had seemed to warm him, as well it should have. To this day, even after all the triumphs of the Joe Torre Yankees in the era of the three-tiered postseason, 1961 remains one of the greatest of all Yankee seasons. Beyond the Maris-Mantle home run race, the '61 Yankees hit a record 240 homers, 64 of them by their three catchers, Berra, Elston Howard and Johnny Blanchard. In winning 109 games, they had to overcome one of the great Detroit Tiger teams of all time, on which first baseman Norm Cash won the batting title (.361) and drove in 132 runs; Rocky Colavito had 45 homers and 140 RBI and future Hall of Famer Al Kaline hit .324.

Despite all the hitting, Houk had to do some major maneuvering with his starting pitching rotation after injuries and ineffectiveness plagued veterans Bob Turley and Art Ditmar. Houk broke in a pair of rookies, Bill Stafford and Rollie Sheldon (who combined for 25 wins) into the rotation, and veteran Bud Daley (acquired from the Athletics just before the June 15 trading deadline for Ditmar and minor league slugging prospect Deron Johnson) contributed eight wins over the last two months.

The season came down to a three-game showdown with the Tigers at the beginning of September and drew a record 171,503 fans to Yankee Stadium. Before 65,566 on a sultry Friday night, Ford, Daley and Arroyo combined to out-duel the Tigers' Don Mossi 1–0 in the wilting 90 degree heat. The next day, Frank Lary, the Tigers' renowned "Yankee Killer" who was seeking his 20th win, suffered one of his few losses to them when Maris hit homers 52 and 53 to power a 7–2 win. The Sunday finale, which drew 55,676, was the crusher for Detroit. The Tigers took a 5–4 lead into the bottom of the ninth, only to have Mantle tie the score with his 50th homer (and second of the day) and Howard win the game with a three-run bomb later in the inning.

"We only had one time when I got really concerned about our play that year," Houk said, "and that was when Turley was hurt and Ditmar wasn't pitching well and I had to change the pitching staff, working Stafford and Sheldon in. When they started pitching well, that really did it for us, and Daley, who's become sort of the forgotten man on that team, was a great pickup."

Houk's '61 Yankees continued their dominance in the World Series, dispatching the Cincinnati Reds in five games. Ford hurled a two-hit, 2–0 shutout in Game 1, and after the Reds' ace righty Joey Jay out-dueled Terry, 6–2, in Game 2, the Yankees swept the next three at Cincinnati. The 13–5 finale, in which Reds manager Fred Hutchinson frantically ran through eight pitchers, was a fitting culmination to the Yankees' record-breaking '61 season, and Houk became only the third manager in history to win a world championship in his first year.

The '62 season was another smashing success for the Major, even if it wasn't quite so dominant. Maris, who had won MVP honors in both '60 and '61, tailed off to 33 homers, but Mantle shook off numerous assorted injuries that limited him to 123 games and served as the inspirational leader Houk envisioned when he held that talk with him the previous spring. With 30 homers, 89 RBI, a league-leading 122 walks and a slugging percentage of .605, Mantle beat out Bobby Richardson 234–152 for the MVP award, the third and last of his career.

The Yankees went 96-66 (.593), the second lowest winning percentage of their 27 pennant winners to that season, and didn't climb into first place to stay until July 8 when they completed a three-game sweep of the Minnesota Twins. The Twins would dog them the rest of the year, but after losing eight of nine in August to have their lead reduced to two games, the Yankees got back on track and eventually won the pennant by five games.

The '62 World Series was likewise a much more challenging endeavor, and was decided, literally, by inches—after a decision by Houk that would have lived in baseball infamy had it backfired. In the first transcontinental World Series, the Yankees met the San Francisco Giants, who had won the National League pennant in a three-game playoff with the Los Angeles Dodgers. Once again, Ford got the Yankees off to a winning start by scattering 10 hits in the 6–2 Game 1 triumph. The Giants managed to snap Ford's World Series record scoreless inning streak at 33⅔, but a homer by Clete Boyer broke a 2–2 tie in the seventh and the Yankees added two in the eighth.

The Giants got even in Game 2 when Jack Sanford, their 24-game-winning ace, out-dueled Terry on a nifty three-hit, 2–0 shutout. The Yankees took two of the three middle games in New York, but whatever momentum they might have had was stalled by three days of rain in the Bay Area as the Series returned to San Francisco. When the weather finally broke, Billy Pierce, the little lefty who'd been a frequent tormentor of the Yankees through the '50s when he was with the Chicago White Sox, pitched a three-hitter, and the Giants knocked out Ford in the fifth inning en route to a 5–2 win that knotted the Series at three games apiece.

Game 7, which pitted Terry against Sanford, was a tension-filled World Series classic. After four scoreless innings, the Yankees broke through for a scratch run off Sanford when Kubek hit into a bases-loaded double play in the fifth. That was it, the only run of the game. The Yankees loaded the bases again with none out in the eighth, but came up empty when Maris hit into a force-out of Richardson at the plate and

Howard grounded into an inning-ending DP, setting the stage for the Giants' last stand—with their best hitters—against Terry.

The ninth began ominously for Terry when pinch hitter Matty Alou, leading off, beat out a bunt to second. But the righty, who led the American League in victories that season with 23, bore down and struck out Felipe Alou and Chuck Hiller. A reprieve, yes, but remember this was the same Terry who had yielded Bill Mazeroski's World Series–winning homer in 1960 and now was looking at the imposing middle of the Giant lineup—future Hall of Famers Willie Mays, Willie McCovey and Orlando Cepeda—to get the last out. It wasn't going to be Mays, who ripped a double to right which might well have scored the younger Alou with the winning run had Maris not executed the play with precision in his pickup of the ball and subsequent throw to the cutoff man, Richardson.

Now with runners at second and third, Houk had to make the decision of his baseball life. Did he play the percentages and walk the left-handed hitting McCovey to the empty base and take his chances with the equally lethal Cepeda? (In McCovey's previous at bat in the seventh, he'd scorched Terry for a two-out triple over Mantle's head off the center field fence.) Or did he give Terry some space to pitch around McCovey? By loading the bases, he knew he'd be setting up a situation in which Terry had to pitch to Cepeda, who was nevertheless 3-for-19 (.158) with no walks in the Series.

"I always respected Cepeda," Houk said now, "and I just felt he was about due. I thought McCovey would be real anxious, and I told Terry to just be careful with him. Ralph had a real good curve and I said: 'Let's make him fish.' The problem was he gave McCovey a pitch that was probably a little too good."

And McCovey hit a shot—right to Bobby Richardson at second. For an instant, the Candlestick Park crowd of 43,948 thought it was the World Series–winning hit, while a million Yankee fans watching on TV let out a collective gasp. But as Richardson said afterward, the ball, though hit hard, was right at him and wasn't nearly the tough play baseball lore made it out to be in the years afterward. He didn't have to leap for it. A couple of feet to the left or right, however, and the Giants win.

"A gutsy decision, pitching to McCovey," I said to Houk. "You have to know if it didn't work out the way it did you'd have probably been the most second-guessed manager in World Series history. 'How the hell could he pitch to McCovey with first base open?'"

Houk smiled knowingly. I figured this was something he'd thought about only a few thousand times since (while privately thanking the heavens above there wasn't any all-sports talk radio in those days).

"Yeah," he said, "I know that. But that's what managing's all about. You're always gonna be second-guessed, even when it works out."

Instead, to this day, he could take pride in being the only manager in baseball history to win world championships in his first two seasons. He might have made it three had the Yankees not run into the Dodgers' buzz saw pitching of Sandy Koufax, Don Drysdale and Johnny Podres in the World Series after winning a third straight AL pennant in 1963. In being swept 5–2, 4–1, 1–0 and 2–1, the Yankees were held to a collective .171 average in the Series with just five extra-base hits in the four games.

At LaGuardia Airport, after the Yankees returned home from Los Angeles, a defiant Houk got into it with a news-side reporter, Mel Juffe, from the *New York Journal-American*. Upon spotting Juffe attempting to question Yankee first baseman Joe Pepitone, Houk angrily interceded.

"Are you a sportswriter?" he demanded of Juffe.

When Juffe said he was a news reporter, Houk bellowed: "Then get the hell away from me if you don't know any baseball! You're nothing but a wise guy!"

Then, turning to the group of photographers excitedly popping pictures of the impromptu blowup, he shouted: "Do you see any blood while you're taking those pictures? We'll be back again."

Just not with him as manager.

A few days after the '62 season, Yankee owners Dan Topping and Del Webb had called Houk to a meeting at the Yankee offices. Roy

Hamey, who replaced Weiss as general manager shortly after the Stengel dismissal in 1960, was now himself retiring because of ill health. Topping and Webb had supposedly explored the major league landscape for a young exec who could lead the Yankees into the new era beyond Mantle, Ford, Berra, Howard et al., and concluded the best man for the job was the one they had right in front of them.

"They asked me if I'd do it," Houk said. "I had no intention of giving up managing for a desk job. I'd been with the Yankees since 1939 and Hamey came to me and said he was retiring and that he'd talked it over with Topping and Webb and was recommending me to replace him. I told him: 'I don't want it. I don't think I can do that.' But he persisted. He said: 'Look, Ralph: You've been in baseball all your life and we need someone who knows the organization and who can step in there and keep the continuity going here.' All that stuff. He told me all the good parts about the job and none of the bad parts. So I talked it over with Bette and told them if they really wanted me to do this, I'd do it. I agreed to manage the team again in '63 and groom Yogi to be manager."

Consider it the soldier in him. He had done the job for them on the field and now it was as if he was receiving another battlefield commission from his superiors. How did he know this was going to be the one mission handed him that couldn't be won? The Yankees' sickly performance against the Dodgers in the '63 World Series was an omen. The team was getting older as a unit and all the injuries were finally beginning to take their toll, especially on Mantle and Ford. Maris, too, began experiencing assorted physical problems—most notably a broken hand in '65—after his back-to-back MVP seasons in '60 and '61. And, as it turned out, the young pitchers Houk had cultivated, Stafford, Sheldon and even Terry, all had their careers curtailed by arm problems in subsequent seasons.

In past years, going all the way back to the '20s, the Yankees had always been able to sustain themselves in the face of age and injuries because of their vast scouting and player development resources. But the times, as Bob Dylan was singing, were a-changin' and with the introduction of the amateur draft in 1965, baseball evened the playing field for all the perennial also-ran clubs. In addition, behind the scenes Topping and Webb were negotiating to sell the team to CBS. It was the end of the dynasty, even if nobody around the Yankees, Houk especially, realized it.

"It was a job I never did like," Houk said. "What people never did understand was that, with the Yankees, the general manager was in charge of the stadium, broadcasting, all that stuff. Today, most of 'em just handle players. But it wasn't that way when I did it. I'd be sitting there in meetings, listening to stuff I knew nothing about. I worked hard at it, but I couldn't wait to get back on the field."

And to this day, he reiterated, the worst moment of all for him as GM was when he had to fire Berra—his friend, teammate and hand-groomed successor—as manager after the '64 season. Sometime during that summer of '64, as the Yankees floundered and bore scant resemblance to the powerhouse teams of '61 and '62, Topping concluded it had been a mistake to make the easygoing Berra the manager. The perception was that Berra had lost control of the team, and even after the Yankees rallied to win the pennant and take the St. Louis Cardinals to the seventh game of the World Series before losing, Topping felt a tougher, more experienced manager was necessary.

"Two of the hardest things I ever had to do in my life was tell Yogi he wasn't coming back and then, a year and half later, tell Johnny Keane he was being let go," Houk said. "That was tough. You know I'd been responsible for them getting Johnny Keane. When they said they were gonna have to let Yogi go—I loved Yogi, I'd have never let Yogi go—I called Johnny Keane right after the World Series. He'd just quit as Cardinals manager, after beating us, and I asked him if he'd agree to come over to us. My one connection with him was that he'd managed against me, with Omaha when I was at Denver, in the American Association. He was tough to manage against. He knew everything you were gonna do, and he'd been in baseball a long time. I felt he was the kind of guy they wanted."

Remembering my conversation with Berra about the firing, I asked him: "How do you think your relationship with Yogi was affected after this?"

Houk looked down at the table and paused in thought. In all the times I'd been around him, he'd always been the hard-bitten, uncompromising, unapologetic Major, but now a look of sadness came over his face and I detected a trembling in his voice as he relived that moment some 38 years later.

"Well, I don't know . . . for a long time . . . it was tough," he said. "As far as I know it's very good now. It was hard . . . because our wives liked each other and one summer we'd lived near each other and our kids all went to the same pool. You know, a lot of people don't understand baseball, and I think for a long time people thought I was responsible for firing Yogi. When you're the GM, they just tell you what to do. At the time they came to me, I don't know exactly when it was, things weren't going particularly well, and you say to yourself: 'What do you do now?'

"I was the GM when they let Mel Allen and Red Barber go, too. Christ, I had nothin' to do with that. What did I know about broadcasting? It was a real mess. I had to be the one to tell Yogi and I think he thought I was coming there to give him a raise. Worst thing I ever had to do. I didn't talk to him for a long time after that and every time I'd see him at some public function, I felt awful."

The next year, Berra went over to the Mets as a coach under Gil Hodges—and the Yankees began their long decline and didn't begin to get righted again until he returned to the organization in 1976. Houk, meanwhile, found himself presiding over an organization suddenly devoid of young, replenishing talent. In 1965, the Yankees plummeted to sixth place, 77-85, under Keane's direction—the team's first losing season since 1925. The next year was worse, as they dropped into last place, 70-89, for the first time since 1912. In late April of '66, with the club 4-16, Houk reluctantly fired Keane and reassumed the managing duties. But as uncomfortable as he'd been in the front office, this was not the scenario he'd envisioned upon going back down on the field.

"I knew we were having trouble when we couldn't replace Kubek and Richardson," Houk said. "We'd always been able to replace guys from within. The theory at the time was 'well, we didn't know they were both gonna retire this early'—which was true—but we didn't have anybody either. And the draft really hurt us. We were in real trouble and I knew it was gonna take a long time to get it back to where it was. I know I got a lot of criticism for playing Horace Clarke as much as I did, but he was a lot better ballplayer than anyone ever gave him credit for. He did a lot of things good but nothing great, and that was his problem. The only thing he didn't do good was make the double play. But he was better than they thought he was and, besides, I didn't have anyone else to play second."

Perhaps for that reason, Houk's fuse was decidedly shorter his second go-round as Yankee manager. During the championship years, '61–'63, writers instinctively approached him with caution, especially after tough losses, but his admonitions of them were usually limited to sarcastic responses or an occasional screaming outburst to questions he deemed imprudent. When the team failed to respond to his urgings, he became increasingly frustrated. There was a frequent need of someone on whom to take out his frustrations, and more often than not, that would be a sportswriter. Maury Allen, the Yankee beat writer for the *New York Post* all through the '60s, was the victim of one of Houk's most egregious confrontations.

"It was about three weeks after he'd taken over for Keane in 1966," Allen recalled. "The team was still playing horseshit and I wrote a column saying Ralph had lost some of his toughness. A lot of the players had been cutting up in the clubhouse and I think I wrote that Houk had become a marshmallow."

(I winced as he recounted this.)

"Anyway, the next day, Houk called me into his office and started screaming. Then he grabbed me around the neck, trying to hit my head against the wall. Between gasping for air, I managed to blurt out: 'Did you read it? Ninety-nine percent was how you were a great manager until now!' He shouted back: 'What the fuck does that have to do with anything?' Finally, Bruce Henry, the traveling secretary, heard all the commotion and burst into the office as Ralph had me pinned up against the wall. If I'd have been a couple of pounds lighter, I'd have been gone. Bruce probably saved my life."

"So what did you do?" I asked Allen. "Something like that happens today and there's a million-dollar lawsuit."

"Things were different back then," Allen said. "I had a wife and two kids to support and I needed the job covering the Yankees. I went to my sports editor, Ike Gellis, and he said: 'What do you want to do?' The crazy thing is, I liked Houk. He had this World War II macho image and he liked to show guys how tough he was when he'd lose it. I was also frightened of him. I never wrote about the incident. It was so common in those days . . . managers and players trying to intimidate writers. It remained an internal thing. The day after it happened, we were sitting on the bench in the dugout and Houk acted like nothing ever happened. I asked him a couple of questions, along with all the other writers, and at one point he winked at me. That was his way of saying he was sorry and that everything was okay between us."

Jay Dunn, an unobtrusive, soft-spoken reporter for the *Trentonian*, one of the suburban papers that covered the Yankees mostly just at home, had a similarly chilling encounter with Houk—over something far less offensive than calling him a marshmallow. According to Dunn, he was the inadvertent target of Houk's rage after the Yankees lost three out of four games to the Red Sox at Fenway Park in early August 1973 to fall out of first place.

"We didn't usually cover the team on the road," Dunn said, "but with the Yankees in first place that late in the season for the first time in so long, I talked my boss into letting me go to Boston for the four-game series. After losing two of the first three, Houk started Steve Kline, a long reliever who'd been on the disabled list earlier that year. Houk had brought him in to relieve a couple of times and he'd been decent, but Kline got bombed and the Yankees lost 10–0. It was getaway day and the team was going on to Detroit so most of the writers didn't get down to the clubhouse. There were only three writers, Jim Ogle of the *Star-Ledger*, Ray Fitzgerald of the *Boston Globe*, and myself in the manager's office talking to Houk.

"I let Ogle and Fitzgerald ask their questions and then I asked Houk: 'Do you have Kline penciled in for another start?' He glared at me, then picked up his spikes and slammed them against the wall. 'How the hell am I supposed to know now?' he screamed, loud enough for all the players in the clubhouse around the corner to hear. We all knew him to take it out on reporters and umpires, but I repeated my question because I thought it was a reasonable question. As I turned to go into that little walk area between the manager's office and the shower room, I felt something grab me on the biceps and spin me around. As he did that, he ripped a button right off my shirt, and then hollered: 'Don't you ever come back in here with your shit!'

"Fitzgerald was the only one who saw it. I was shaking. Then as I gathered myself in the clubhouse, picking up my notebook and pen which Houk had knocked out of my hands, Jim Hegan, one of his coaches, said: 'You better get your ass out of here!' I went upstairs to the press box and started writing my story—I wasn't going to write about what happened, but by now all the other reporters had heard there'd been an incident down there and wanted me to give them the details. After a while, Lee MacPhail, the Yankees GM, who was having a drink in the adjoining room, came over to me and said: 'Oh, don't pay any mind to Ralph. He's just upset over the loss. Tomorrow you and he will be buddies.' I didn't much care if that happened. For one thing, I was going back to New York while the team was going to Detroit. But then Elston Howard, who was also one of Houk's coaches, came all the way up to the press box and was much more assertive. He said: 'Ralph had no business doing what he did to you. You were only doing your job.' It was quite a contrast from Hegan, and the next home stand, I told Howard, right in front of Hegan, how much I appreciated it."

As for Houk, well, Dunn said, he got the same apology as Allen.

"He told Dick Young to tell me he was sorry, and that, when he saw me, we'd have a one-on-one," Dunn related. "A few days later, I was with the group of reporters in his office at Yankee Stadium and in the middle of the session he looked at me and winked. We never did have our one-on-one."

All these years later, I figured there wasn't a whole lot to be gained—and more likely a lot more to lose—in rehashing these incidents with the Major. Suffice to say, if he wasn't about to offer any public apologies then, he certainly wouldn't now. Still, there was this curiosity. Did he do these things for effect, as a show for his players that he was fighting for them? Or did he really have a burning disdain for the writers?

"I really don't know what that was," he said. "I do think television did a bad thing for writers. Before television was big, writers would ask more questions relative to the team. But then it got to the point where writers would want to talk about stuff that happened on television. Mostly bad stuff, and I suppose that kind of grew on me. Their editors wanted them to go and find something that was gonna make news. I think I *was* probably really mad, though, when I got after them."

New York has always had the reputation for being the toughest newspaper town in America. But it was two years after he left the Yankees that Houk was finally called to task—and charged with assault—for accosting a writer. He was managing the Tigers and, during a road trip to Baltimore in late June of 1975, Phil Hersh, a baseball beat writer covering the Orioles for the *Baltimore Evening Sun*, alleged that Houk had slapped him about the head. An arrest warrant was issued and Houk was brought to the Northern District police headquarters in Baltimore where he was charged with assault. After swearing out the complaint, Hersh said: "I want to see future baseball writers protected from this kind of treatment." The charges were dropped two months later when Houk appeared in court and issued a public apology to Hersh.

At the mention of the Hersh assault incident, Houk straightened up and reassumed the role of the Major.

"That was one time when he really deserved that," he said, his voice rising ever so slightly. "That was our first trip into Baltimore and after we lost the first game he wrote an article which said my team had no chance of winning the pennant and was playing that way. Well, I couldn't wait to get to the ballpark after reading that. As soon as I got there I called over to [Oriole manager] Earl Weaver and asked him: 'Who is this guy, Hersh?' and Weaver said: 'Oh, Ralph, he's bad. He's bad news. I read that article.' So I said: 'When he gets to the park, tell him I want to see him.'

"It was getting close to game time when Hersh comes into the manager's office where I'm sitting and he says: 'Earl says you want to talk to me?' And I say: 'Did you write this article?' He says: 'That's my name on it, isn't it?' Well, that did it. I didn't hit him, but I grabbed him. I had spikes on. I pulled him out of there into the clubhouse. The players were all hollering and clapping and I pushed him out the door. Well, you know what happened. The next morning they arrested me for assault and threw me in jail for a few hours. I finally got out of that mess.

"Believe it or not, though, there were a lot of writers I liked. Even Maury Allen, who I had a few laughs with years after he called me the Bronx monster or something like that."

He laughed, which put me more at ease. I sensed he kind of enjoyed reliving all his old tempests and so I decided to push the envelope with him and ask him about the night in May of 1967 when he allegedly punched out the actor-singer Gordon MacRae on the dance floor of the Empire Room in the Waldorf-Astoria. In the newspaper account the next day, varying witness accounts said Houk became offended when MacRae was dancing with Bette Houk and planted a kiss on her lips. It was reported that after MacRae attempted to placate the irate Houk, the Yankee manager socked him, flooring the entertainer and leaving him unconscious for nearly two minutes. MacRae, awakened in his sleep by a reporter, was quoted as saying: "I must have slipped. Ralph and I are old friends. I danced with his wife. Hell, as a matter of fact I danced with *him*, too."

"What can I say?" said Houk, laughing again. "It's all true."

Although the Yankees began to make a gradual improvement after the rock-bottom '66 season, they had clearly fallen to second-class status in New York, especially after the Mets' "miracle" 1969 season in which the once "lovable losers" '62 expansion team rose from seventh place to world champions under the direction of the popular ex–Brooklyn Dodger Gil Hodges. The great '61 Yankee team of Mantle and Maris was but a distant memory, and Houk, fair or not, was now the out-front symbol of the worst Yankee era in anyone's memory. Topping and Webb were gone and no longer accountable for having allowed the franchise to decay. In their place was the cold, corporate CBS and its designated Yankee president, Mike Burke, a flamboyant son of Ireland whose trademarks were his flowing white hair and his stylish hippie wardrobe. It was Burke who had engineered the disastrous trades of Maris to the Cardinals in 1966 for third baseman Charley Smith and, that same winter, third baseman Clete Boyer to the Atlanta Braves for outfielder Bill Robinson. But it was also Burke who'd saved the Yankees from being hijacked to New Jersey by negotiating the 1973 renovation of Yankee Stadium with New York Mayor John Lindsay for what eventually escalated into a $120 million boondoggle to the city.

By 1972, the Mets were routinely drawing over two million customers per year, while the Yankees were heading for their first season of less than one million since 1945. Burke, realizing the corporate consequences of this dire turn of events for the franchise his bosses, CBS chieftains William Paley and Frank Stanton, had purchased for $11.2 million, sought to remedy it. Unbeknownst to Houk and GM Lee MacPhail, Burke had a lunch meeting in early May of 1972 with Tom Villante, a former Yankee bat boy in the '40s who was now an innovative and well-connected executive with the powerful BBDO advertising agency. Villante's principal account at the time was Schaefer Beer, which had replaced Ballantine as the Yankees' primary TV and radio sponsor, and Burke wanted to tap his creative mind as to how best to restore fan interest in the Yankees.

"Burke called me to have lunch," Villante recalled, "and he was very concerned about the Mets and how they were taking the town away from the Yankees. We initially talked about bringing back Billy Martin—who was then with the Tigers—as manager. At that time, there still hadn't been a black manager and Burke brought up the idea of the Yankees making that groundbreaking move. I thought it was great idea and when he asked me for some suggestions, I immediately thought of Frank Robinson, who was then closing in on the end of his career with the Dodgers. Looking back, I wonder now why neither one of us thought of Elston Howard, who was right there on the Yankee coaching staff, except that Robinson was such a towering presence in the game and a no-nonsense guy, while Ellie was perceived as maybe being too nice to manage.

"Anyway, Burke loved the idea and said: 'That's great, let me run it past Willie'—which is what he called Paley. A couple of days later, he called me and said Paley was all for it and asked if I could serve as an intermediary for them with Robinson and feel him out about the job. It was a very delicate situation since Robinson was the property of the Dodgers and the Yankees couldn't put themselves in a place where they'd be guilty of tampering. So I said: 'Okay, I'll do it,' and then checked the schedule to see when the Dodgers would be coming east. It turned out the closest they were coming to New York was Atlanta.

"I knew Frank from my past connections with the Dodgers when Schaefer was their sponsor and I called him and asked him if he could meet with me when the Dodgers came into Atlanta. I think he thought I wanted to talk to him about a commercial. Anyway, I went to Atlanta to meet with him and as I'm walking through the hotel I run right into Junior Gilliam, who was now a Dodger coach but who I'd known for 15 years. He sees me and says: 'What are *you* doing here?' When I told him I was there to see Frank about something, Junior assumed, too, it was for a commercial and said: 'He's my *roommate!* Whatever commercial you're putting him in, you've got to put me in, too!'

"So, I had the meeting with Frank, and he said he'd be very much interested in the job. I told him this had to be kept in utmost secrecy—that no one could know—and that if he told anyone, the Yankees would emphatically deny it. He never told a soul—to my knowledge to this day. But what happened was, the Yankees went on a hot streak in July and August of that year and climbed back into the pennant race. Once that happened, Burke realized he couldn't make the move. He asked me to call Frank and explain the situation, which I did. Frank was great about it. He said to me: 'I've been watching the newspapers every day. There's no way they can justify firing Ralph.'"

The Yankees eventually slumped back to fourth place, 79–76, that strike-shortened season, and the following year, as Berra heaped further insult on them by managing the Mets to the World Series (having been entrusted with the job by them upon the sudden death of Hodges in 1972), Houk's troops slipped under .500 (80–82). CBS, acknowledging its failed stewardship, sold the team in January of '73 to a syndicate headed by Cleveland shipbuilder George Steinbrenner for $8.8 million—$3.4 million less than what it had paid for it nine years earlier. As for Houk, the change of ownership didn't change the way he thought about things. His patriarch, MacPhail, had left to become president of the American League, and he had grown weary of the losing and the seemingly impossible task of getting it back to what it was. Worst of all was the daily booing he was taking from the Yankee fans. *How soon they forget!*

The assumption was that when he resigned as manager after the '73 season, it was because he saw the coming storm in Steinbrenner; that the virtual autonomy to which he'd been accustomed in the previous two ownership regimes was over.

"I know that's what people always thought," Houk said, "but it wasn't the case. George and I never had a problem. It was the booing that really hurt me. I just decided it had gotten too far. George said:

'You're making a mistake, Ralph. I'm gonna go out and get some ballplayers and make this team great again.' And he did, bringing in Catfish and Reggie. That'll make you good in a hurry! But I didn't know him. I was never fired in baseball. I suppose if I'd stayed, though, he'd have gotten me eventually."

"Probably," I said, "but you might have won at least one more championship, too."

"That's maybe my one regret," Houk said, an uncharacteristic trace of melancholy in his voice. "The Yankees were a great thing for me. I owe an awful lot to the Yankees. They're what made me. I was there for the best and worst of times . . . and after I left, they started going out and buying all those good players. Sometimes I wonder what would have happened if I would have stayed. You know I've never made it to the Hall of Fame and I see Lasorda in there and I see Weaver in there and it makes me wonder . . . I won more games than a lot of guys in the Hall of Fame. It is kinda funny that I've never been thought of . . ."

He was never one to seek or feel due any personal glory. *He'd won the Silver Star, for godsakes,* in his mind for only doing what he was supposed to do. But now, in the mellowed winter of his years, the Major felt a need to state his case (to a sportswriter, no less). He accomplished something none of the rest of them—Weaver, Lasorda, even Casey—ever did, winning two world championships and three pennants in his first three years as a manager. He is also one of four managers—Joe McCarthy, Bucky Harris and Frank Chance are the others—to have managed both the Yankees and the Red Sox—but the only one of them not in the Hall of Fame. And in his second term at the Yankee helm, he stood guardian to the franchise under siege, as if he were back at Waldbillig, deploying his troops and dodging enemy fire as best he could. He'd been the ultimate Yankee company man whose final reward had been a farewell of boos. All he asked for now was to be remembered for the times his teams had given them cause to cheer.

JASON'S SONG

MEL STOTTLEMYRE

Yankee Stadium was in the midst of being drenched by a gray, piercing rain, and although no official announcement had come down from the offices above, it was becoming pretty much a given there would be no game on this night. It was 4 P.M. and ordinarily Mel Stottlemyre, the Yankees' pitching coach, would be out in the bullpen observing one of his pitchers throwing, or working on mechanics with his other pupils. In the late-afternoon hours leading up to game time, the bullpen was his office, but with the inclement weather making for a likely postponement, Stottlemyre had agreed to alter his routine and spend the idle time talking about his life as a Yankee—then and now.

Going all the way back to his days as a player, circa 1964–75, he was never very comfortable talking about himself or, especially, his teammates. A private man by nature, with a rural, small-town upbringing, he never seemed to truly trust the media. As pitching coach, it was always as if he viewed their periodic requests for analyses of his flock a requirement of the job yet, by the same token, an intrusion into his world.

But after being diagnosed in the spring of 1999 with multiple myeloma, a rare form of blood cancer for which scientists have not been able to find a cure, his desire to remain in the background of the Yankees' latest dynasty, as Joe Torre's loyal and quietly efficient aide-de-camp, was forever compromised. In April of 2001, having completed four months of chemotherapy on top of a complex stem-cell transplant procedure and being informed by his doctors that he was, for the time being, "cancer-free," Stottlemyre found himself on the front page of the *New York Post*. "Mel's Miracle—Yankee Coach Triumphs Over Rare Cancer" the tabloid proclaimed in detailing Stottlemyre's courageous but still uncertain battle with the dreaded disease.

When presented with the initial diagnosis, Stottlemyre was understandably stunned. For one thing, it was not the first time cancer had invaded his immediate household. Twenty years earlier, his youngest son, Jason, had lost a five-year struggle with leukemia, and now this cancer was said to be just as insidious, only more problematic in that doctors knew so little about it. At first, Stottlemyre and his wife, Jean, were merely numb. They asked themselves the usual question, with an addendum: Why us . . . again? Then, in the ensuing days, as the doctors laid out all the options for fighting it, the couple determined to learn everything they could about this thing called multiple myeloma.

"One of the reasons I was able to keep such a positive outlook was because of what I'd learned about the disease and how far I realized they'd come in the methods of treating it," Stottlemyre said. "Between that and the strength I got from Jean and my boys, I was able to stay upbeat throughout the whole ordeal. Of course, lying in the background of my mind, there was always Jason and what he'd had to go through."

He had suggested we talk in the dugout, rather than the clubhouse where privacy is normally hard to come by, especially on rainy days when there was no pregame batting practice. Aside from a couple of Yankee security men, and a grounds crew worker occasionally wandering by with a rake or a shovel, the dugout was deserted. Stottlemyre placed his clipboard down on the padded bench and removed his Yankee cap, revealing a full complement of thick, healthy-looking brown hair.

"You've got more hair now than before the chemotherapy," I noted.

"Yeah, I guess I do," he laughed. "Everybody's mentioned that to me, although I don't recommend what I had to go though to get it."

He grew up in the tiny town of Mabton, Washington, population 900, approximately 150 miles southeast of Seattle across the Cascade mountain range. In the continental United States, it is about as far as you could be from New York City, which made Stottlemyre's childhood rooting interest in the Yankees all that more curious.

"Believe it or not, growing up I was a huge Yankee fan," he related. "They may have been on the other side of the continent, but we followed them through all their championships. My brother, who was 17 months younger, was a Dodger fan and we had quite a rivalry, especially since the Yankees and Dodgers met in all those World Series. I'd have to say, Mickey was my favorite player, too. Who'd have ever believed I'd actually be playing with him a few years later?"

His signing by the Yankees out of Yakima Valley Community College in the summer of 1961, for the princely sum of $400 per month (no bonus), was almost an afterthought on their part. Eddie Taylor, the scout who signed him, had actually been following another pitcher for Yakima Valley, a left-hander named Andy Erickson. As Stottlemyre explained it, he and Erickson would often pitch doubleheaders and that enabled Taylor to see just as much of him. Taylor would later say it was Stottlemyre's determination and character that most impressed him about the tall, skinny right-hander. On the night Taylor consummated the deal, he drove to the Stottlemyre house in Mabton in a car he'd borrowed from the coach at Yakima Valley, Bobo Brayton.

(It was Brayton who taught Stottlemyre the sinker that would be his meal ticket pitch to 164 victories in his 11 seasons with the Yankees, and years later, Mike Hampton would say it was that same sinker—which Stottlemyre taught *him* while pitching coach with the Houston Astros in 1994—that transformed him into the pitcher able to command a $121 million free agent contract from the Colorado Rockies.)

"I had talked to Eddie earlier in the day—he'd visited me at a farm where I was working—and I told him I had to talk it over with my dad before I signed," Stottlemyre said. "If you're writing about the deal I got, don't forget to include the bus ticket from Toppenish, Washington, to Modesto, California, where the Yankees had an instructional camp. I threw batting practice for them for about a week there and then they shipped me off to Harlan, Kentucky, their Class D team in the Appalachian League.

"The only other player on that club besides me who got any big league time was Arturo Lopez, who played a little bit in the Yankee outfield. Half that club was White Sox and the other half Yankees. It was weird. We had two managers and something like 21 pitchers, half-and-half. It was one of those joint-agreement operations. The managers would play their own players, but with Harlan being a depressed coal-mining town, and some real rough people living there, they were afraid to lose there. So they'd play their best players at home, no matter what team they were on. The other guys, who needed to get some playing time in, they'd play on the road. It was really strange."

He was 5-1 in eight games at Harlan and, from there, moved rapidly though the Yankee system, belying the small price they'd paid to sign him. In 1962 at Greensboro, he was 17-9 and led the Carolina League with 241 innings pitched. All of a sudden, the Yankee player development people began to realize they might have something here in the guy Eddie Taylor had told them "might not be overpowering but has a great will to learn."

From Greensboro, it was right to Triple A Richmond in 1963 even though the Yankees still weren't quite sure if he had all the right stuff to make it to the majors. "I could never remember being able to throw real hard," he said, "and up until about 1962 there was considerable doubt in my own mind that I'd ever amount to much as a professional pitcher."

As a sometimes starter and long relief man, Stottlemyre was a so-so 7-7 in his first season at Triple A, but upon returning to Richmond in 1964, he began to find his niche—or, more precisely, refine his sinker. At the advice of his old American Legion coach in Mabton, Del Bethel, he changed the grip on his sinkerball. Instead of holding it across the seams, he started holding it *on* the seams and was surprised to discover the extra dip that gave it. Similarly surprised were the Triple A hitters. By early August of '64, Stottlemyre was 13-3 and had reeled off 10 straight wins.

Meanwhile, there were problems in the Bronx. The Yankees, who had changed managers from Ralph Houk to Yogi Berra for '64, were experiencing a lot of inner turmoil and were trailing the Baltimore Orioles and the Chicago White Sox in the standings. They were also beset with injuries, most notably the sore hip incurred by Whitey Ford. Desperate for a starting pitcher, Houk, who was now the GM, consulted with all his scouts and player development execs. The consensus was to bring up Stottlemyre, despite the fact he wasn't even on the 40-man roster and had not been in the major league camp in spring training.

"I was really kinda shocked when they told me I was going up, although for two weeks the people at Richmond had been talking about the possibility because they knew the problems they were having in New York. I was just hoping to get called up in September for a look-see. I'd have to say Jean was even more nervous because it was the first time she'd had to pack up and move in the middle of a season. We had Mel Jr. by then and she had to get a U-Haul and drive from Richmond up to New York. We spent our first night in New York at the Concourse Plaza Hotel in the Bronx and then we got an apartment in Ridgewood, New Jersey."

The irony of Stottlemyre being recalled to replace Ford was that, in 1950. it had been Ford who was called up to the Yankees late in the season and who made an equally significant contribution to their winning of the American League pennant. Just like Ford, who was 9-1 in the Yankees' stretch drive of 1950, Stottlemyre made pitching in the big leagues look so easy, going 9-3 with a 2.06 ERA, as the pitcher most instrumental in the team overtaking the Orioles and White Sox en route to their fifth straight World Series. Berra would later say: "Without Mel, we probably wouldn't have won it. He had that great sinker and he had great control and he didn't scare. He was my best pitcher at the end of that year."

"I had already been pretty much on a roll at Richmond and even though I hadn't pitched an inning in the big leagues, my confidence level was pretty high," Stottlemyre said. "I don't know why—what the reasons were—but I felt very comfortable right away. The players I was most petrified of, Mickey, who'd been my hero, and Elston Howard, came up to me the first day I was there and really made me feel at ease. I'd never seen Yankee Stadium except on TV and all of a sudden, there it is, and the first time I'm in uniform, I'm in the lineup. I beat the White Sox 7–3 and it was a big win for us because we were trailing them in the standings. I never saved a lot of balls during my career but I do have the one from that game."

Thanks to the major infusion they got from Stottlemyre, and a no-less-important one from veteran reliever Pedro Ramos (who came over from Cleveland in September and filled the void in the injury-depleted Yankee bullpen by saving eight games down the stretch), the Yankees were assured of a few more—much bigger—games in October. On September 17, Stottlemyre beat the Los Angeles Angels 6–2, to pitch the Yankees into first place by two percentage points over idle Baltimore and Chicago. They never relinquished the lead after that and went on an 11-game winning streak to take command of the race.

Though his team was still ravaged by injuries, Berra at least had his starting pitching in order for the World Series against the St. Louis Cardinals. But then, even that went awry on him when Ford developed an arterial blockage in his arm while losing Game 1 and was done for the Series. Again, it was left to the rookie Stottlemyre to rescue the

LEFT:
YOUNG JOE D. AND THE IRON HORSE: Joe DiMaggio was just beginning his Yankee career when he received some words of wisdom from Lou Gehrig. (PHOTO FILE, INC.)

BELOW: *40's STYLIN':* That's Phil Rizzuto behind the wheel of a British Austin on display at Yankee Stadium as part of a promotion with Alexander's Department Store in 1949. With him are Charlie Silvera and Joe Collins (leaning on the hood). (NY YANKEES)

TWO LEFTIES COMPARING TRICKS: *Marius Russo (left) and Tommy Byrne, both members of the Yankees' starting rotations in the '40s, discuss pitching secrets.* (NATIONAL BASEBALL HALL OF FAME)

SAN FRAN DANDY:
Backup catcher Charlie Silvera, one of the many San Francisco sandlot products who had a role in the Yankees' unprecedented streak of championship successes 1949 – 53.
(DIAMOND IMAGES)

A YOUNG CHAIRMAN MEETS AN EQUALLY YOUNG SCOOTER:
This photo of Frank Sinatra with Phil Rizzuto was believed to have been taken when the Chairman of the Board took some time off from shooting Take Me Out to the Ballgame *with Gene Kelly in 1949.*
(DIAMOND IMAGES)

THE KEYSTONE KIDS: *Phil Rizzuto (left) and Joe Gordon formed the keystone infield combo for the Yankees in the '40s.* (NY DAILY NEWS)

CASEY'S SECOND: *Yankee manager Casey Stengel holds two fingers aloft in celebration of his second straight world championship for the Yankees in 1950. Surrounding Stengel (left to right) are Phil Rizzuto, Cliff Mapes, Tommy Byrne, Joe Page and Yogi Berra.* (UPI)

JERRY COLEMAN'S BITTERSWEET DAY: *War hero Jerry Coleman was saluted by the Yankees with a day in his honor upon his discharge from Korea in September of 1953. As Coleman later related, it was both the best and worst day of his life in that, after the ceremonies, he had to console the widow of his best friend, Max Harper, whose plane was shot down right in front of him.* (NY YANKEES)

TOP: *SPRINGTIME FROLICS:* *Whitey Ford, Ralph Houk and Yogi Berra (left to right) run laps after a spring-training workout in the early '50s at Miller Huggins Field in St. Petersburg.* (DIAMOND IMAGES)

BOTTOM: *THE PREACHER AND HIS 'VETTE:* *Devout Christian Bobby Richardson, hardly one who believed in living in the fast lane, accepted this Corvette from* Sport Magazine *as MVP of the 1960 World Series. Richardson is the only player from a losing team ever to win the Series MVP.* (NY YANKEES)

RIGHT: *YOUNG ELLIE:*
Elston Howard strikes a batting pose at Huggins Field in his first spring training with the Yankees in 1955. Howard made the team that spring as the first black Yankee. (NY YANKEES)

BELOW: *ONE MAN'S FAMILY:*
Elston Howard and his wife, Arlene, and their three children at their Teaneck home in 1960. That's Karen in Elston's arms, Elston Jr. is sitting on the sofa, and Cheryl is standing next to her mother; only Arlene and Cheryl survive today. (NY YANKEES)

MICK AND SLICK: *Hall of Fame Yankee teammates Mickey Mantle (left) and Whitey Ford share a few private thoughts shortly after Ford announced his retirement in 1967. The two pals were inducted into Cooperstown together in 1974.* (NY YANKEES)

PASSING OF THE BATON: *Yogi Berra takes over as Yankee manager from Ralph Houk (who has his arm around him) at a press conference at the Savoy-Hilton Hotel, October 24, 1963.* (NY YANKEES)

TOP: *THE CLIPPER COUNSELS JOE PEP: If only Joe Pepitone had listened to the wise words of fellow paisan Joe DiMaggio. Unfortunately, Pepitone's Yankee career fell far short of the promise it held when this photo was taken before Game 1 of the 1963 World Series.*
(NATIONAL BASEBALL HALL OF FAME)

RIGHT: *HAIR GUY: Joe Pepitone introduced the hair dryer to the baseball clubhouse and that, sadly, is the thing for which he has been most remembered through the years.*
(NY DAILY NEWS)

BIG BRAWL IN TOWN: *Joe Pepitone is right in the middle of this 1963 fracas, precipitated when Indian pitcher Gary Bell hit him with a pitch.* (UPI)

BEFORE BRAVE-RY: *Even Bobby Cox, shown here in a 1968 photo, was once "young and a Yankee." The longtime manager for the Atlanta Braves, winner of an unprecedented 11 consecutive division titles from 1991 to 2002, grew up as a player in the Yankee system.* (NY YANKEES)

TOP: *MEL'S BOYS:*
Yankee pitching great Mel Stottlemyre is shown here with his two sons, Todd (left) and Mel Jr., both of whom went on to have pitching careers of their own in the majors. A third son, Jason, died tragically of leukemia in 1981.
(NY YANKEES)

RIGHT: *CONGRATS FROM AN IDOL:*
Growing up in tiny Mabton, Washington, Mel Stottlemyre rooted for the Yankees and especially Mickey Mantle, who is shown here congratulating him after his Game 2 victory over Bob Gibson and the Cardinals in the 1964 World Series.
(LOU REQUENA)

PRIDE OF THE NEW YANKEES

Bobby Murcer and Ron Blomberg

NEW ERA COVER BOYS: Sports Illustrated, *in its July 2, 1973, issue, billed Bobby Murcer (left) and Ron Blomberg as the cornerstone players of the Yankees' perceived return to championship prominence.* (NEIL LEIFER/ SPORTS ILLUSTRATED)

BOBBY AND BILL BEFORE THE FALL (-ING OUT): *Bobby Murcer solicits advice from new Yankee manager Bill Virdon in the spring of 1974. A few weeks later, Murcer was moved by Virdon from his accustomed center field to right, in what was the beginning of the worst season of his life.* (NY YANKEES)

BONUS BOY: *Ron Blomberg, whom the Yankees billed as the "great Jewish hope," signs his contract as the No. 1 player selected in the 1967 draft. Blomberg's parents are standing behind him, while the Georgia-bred outfielder/first baseman is flanked (left to right) by Yankee executives Mike Burke, Lee MacPhail and Johnny Johnson.* (NY YANKEES)

DESIGNATED HEBREW: *Both Ron Blomberg and the Yankees hoped and believed he'd have a Hall of Fame career, but a series of injuries doomed that.* (NY YANKEES)

REGGIE'S FINEST MOMENT: *Reggie Jackson connects for his third homer in Game 6 of the 1977 World Series against the Dodgers. This one, a monster shot into the black-painted area in dead center field of Yankee Stadium off knuckleballer Charlie Hough, tied Reggie with Babe Ruth as the only players to hit three homers in one Series game.* (NY YANKEES)

MR. OCTOBER AND "THE VOICE OF GOD": *Reggie Jackson shares a story in the clubhouse with venerable Yankees' public address announcer Bob Sheppard. It was Reggie who (appropriately) gave Sheppard the nickname "the voice of God."* (LOU REQUENA)

SPIRIT OF '78: *Three of the mainstays of the Yankees' remarkable comeback team of 1978, which rallied from 14 games back to win the AL East and eventually a second straight World Series: (from left) Ron Guidry, Lou Piniella and Willie Randolph.* (NY YANKEES)

GEORGE AND HIS GUYS: *Owner George Steinbrenner always has high expectations for the Yankees in spring training. This photo of the Boss, flanked by manager Lou Piniella (right) and coach Gene Michael—two of his longtime "favorite sons"—was taken in the spring of 1986 at Fort Lauderdale.* (NY YANKEES)

TWO FOR THE TITLE: *Don Mattingly (left) and Dave Winfield waged a spirited battle for the American League batting title in 1984. Mattingly won, .343 to .340, with a 4-for-5 performance on the final day.* (LOU REQUENA)

LEAVIN' TIME: *Paul O'Neill cleans out his locker at Yankee Stadium for the last time, after returning home from the 2001 World Series. The man George Steinbrenner called "my warrior" had an outstanding nine-year Yankee career, finishing 11th on the team's all-time list in RBIs (858), and 12th in average (.303), doubles (304) and homers (185).* (NY DAILY NEWS)

besieged and broken old champions. He would make three starts in the Series, all of them against Cardinal ace and future Hall of Famer Bob Gibson, and he would distinguish himself throughout, even if he ultimately was unable to deliver the crown for them. To this day, he said, he still considers his Game 2 8–3 win over Gibson in St. Louis the defining performance of his career.

"It was a blow to us that Whitey wasn't going to be able to pitch anymore in the Series. He was our definite leader and everybody sort of had a depressed feeling," Stottlemyre recalled. "All the events happened so fast that season and I didn't really think too much about it. I just reacted to the moments as they came. That particular moment was a great opportunity for me. I just looked at it as a very important game in a World Series everybody wants to be in. I tried to treat it as just another game, even though it wasn't. I definitely had trouble sleeping the night before. It was my boyhood dream on my boyhood team and so many of the guys I'd dreamt about and worshipped as a kid were still there.

"What I remember most about that first start against Gibson, other than winning it, was the fact that Gibson had this reputation of being such a fierce competitor and how difficult it was for him to even take a picture with me. The day before, when they always had the next-day starters pose for publicity pictures together, he didn't want any part of it. I still have that picture at home and I've joked with him about it, as we became good friends. But that day, I was scared to death of him."

If he was, he fooled the Cardinals. The game was 1–1 after five innings, the kid Stottlemyre's enticing sinkers measuring up to Gibson's intimidating heat, and then in the sixth the Yankees broke the tie on an RBI single by Tom Tresh. The Yankee lead was 4–2 when Gibson was removed for a pinch hitter in the eighth and, with Stottlemyre still in full command, with 13 ground ball outs to that point, they put the game away with a four-run rally off the Cardinal bullpen in the ninth.

In their next match-up, Game 5, Gibson got even, dominating the Yankees with a 13-strikeout performance that put the Cardinals ahead in the Series 3–2. Nevertheless, Stottlemyre earned even more respect by limiting the Cards to one earned run over *his* seven innings. Three days later, the two of them were back again for the deciding Game 7, only this time, it finally all caught up to Stottlemyre, who was knocked out after four innings when the Cardinals went up 3–0 on three singles, a walk and a botched double play by the Yankees. Gibson showed the ill effects of the short rest as well, getting roughed up for nine hits by the Yankees, but managed to hang on for the complete-game 7–5 win.

"Game 7, I have to admit, I finally got real nervous because I suddenly realized there was no tomorrow, and that the whole Series . . . the whole season hinged on that one game," Stottlemyre said. "I remember thinking going into the game I might have a slight advantage over Gibson because he was such a power pitcher and I relied on my sinker. To be honest, I don't have much recollection of that game, maybe because I don't want to, although the one play I do remember was in the fourth inning when I gave up the three runs. I could have been out of that inning with a 3-6-1 double play when Tim McCarver hit a grounder to Joe Pepitone at first. Pepi made a good throw to second, but the runner took Phil Linz out and he made a wide throw back to first. I came over and dove for the ball and landed on my right shoulder. Fortunately I wasn't injured."

How could he know this would be his one and only World Series as a player? After all, all he'd known about the Yankees, going all the way back to his days as a young sandlotter back in Mabton, was that they won every year. It was a given. And so many of those same heroes of his youth were still there. He had shown uncommon poise and cool for a rookie thrust onto a veteran championship contingent in need of a lifeline, but he was naive to the reality of the game, which was that even heroes grow old and dynasties are the product of constant replenishing. The Yankees had managed to do that for more than 15 years in this latest dynasty, as Mantle followed DiMaggio, Ford followed Allie Reynolds, Tony Kubek followed Phil Rizzuto, Bobby Richardson followed Billy Martin, Clete Boyer followed Gil McDougald,

Ellie Howard replaced Berra, and Pepitone replaced Bill Skowron. Now, however, time—and the rest of baseball—had caught up to them, for reasons both within and out of their control.

In August of 1964, it was revealed the Yankee owners, Dan Topping and Del Webb, were preparing to sell the team to CBS for $11.2 million. As the news sent shock waves through baseball, the question immediately arose: Did Topping and Webb know something? Did they sense the coming change in baseball—the advent of the amateur draft—was about to dramatically close the gap between the haves and the have-nots, at the same time they realized privately they themselves had sown the seeds of Yankee neglect?

When the Dodgers and Giants left New York for the West Coast after the 1957 season, it stood to reason the Yankees would now own the town, and yet their attendance actually *declined* in 1958, from 1,491,784 to 1,428,428! And with the birth of the Mets in 1962, it would decline even further—to 1,308,920 in 1963, even though the National League expansion team in Queens quickly established itself as about the worst aggregate of baseball players in the history of the game.

And while the Yankees were still winning, they were clearly in a state of decline as injuries and age had caught up to their mainstays, Mantle, Ford, Howard and Kubek, and suddenly there were no adequate replacements in sight. While nobody in the front office cared to admit it, the testimony to the eroded state of the Yankee farm system was that the '64 season had to be saved by a rookie held in such little regard he was not even invited to the major league camp in spring training and had been left off the 40-man roster, available to be drafted by any other organization in baseball the previous winter.

Compounding this alarming development was the fact that, in 1965, baseball elected to implement the amateur draft, meaning the Yankees could no longer sign the high school and college players of their choice. Rather, they would now have to wait their turn in hopes those players might still be available when they got to pick. It no longer mattered to have superior scouts like Paul Krichell, who'd signed Lou Gehrig, Phil

Rizzuto, Marius Russo and Ford off the New York sandlots; or Eddie Taylor, who'd found Stottlemyre in the Washington hinterlands. The playing field was about to be made level for the lower-revenue clubs, most of which had been accustomed to spending a third of what the Yankees allotted annually for scouting and player development.

But Stottlemyre certainly had no awareness of the front office already making cutbacks in these areas. He was 22 years old, in the major leagues barely six weeks, and already he'd pitched three World Series games. This was the life he'd imagined . . . the Yankee life. Looking around the Busch Stadium visitors' clubhouse after that final Game 7, he watched Mantle, Maris, Ford, Howard and the rest of those heroes he'd grown up idolizing, dressing silently. They had just been vanquished, but he had no doubt they would rise again.

"When I got home to Washington and heard the news that Yogi had been fired, I was completely dumbfounded," he said. "I didn't know what to tell people when they asked me if there'd been a problem. There certainly wasn't a problem to the best of *my* knowledge. I later heard it had been in the works before I came up. I guess they didn't expect the Yankees to get to the World Series. I just know I loved Yogi and he was tremendous with me.

"The next year, there was a lot of negative reaction to some of the things Johnny Keane did. The first couple of times he removed Mickey for a defensive replacement late in the game and he'd let him run all the way to center field and then send a guy out there. Boy, guys were not very receptive to that. So he lost favor with a lot of guys early on. Plus, Maris was hurt most of the year and Kubek retired. Then in '66 everything went really bad and after the season, Maris and Clete were traded and Bobby retired. I guess I knew better than anyone else we didn't have very much at the Triple A level to replace these guys, but I couldn't foresee it all falling apart as fast as it did. Nobody could. In my first three years, we went from first to fifth to tenth. These weren't the Yankees I knew."

Or anyone else knew for that matter. The Yankees of the mid-'60s were impostors, none more so than Mantle, who stayed at least four years too long at the urging of the front office and, by doing so, cost himself a lifetime .300 batting average. The other holdovers from that last '64 Series club, Pepitone, Tom Tresh and Jim Bouton, never fulfilled their promise. Only Stottlemyre, it seemed, bore any resemblance to the glory that was past. His replacing of Ford as the ace of the staff in the '64 Series, it turned out, was permanent. Whitey came back to win 16 games in '65, but Stottlemyre won 20 and led the American League in complete games (18) and innings. Three years later, Ford had retired and Stottlemyre was 21-12 for a fifth-place Yankee team on which Mantle played first base in his final season.

On July 20, 1965, Stottlemyre achieved a feat unmatched by any other pitcher in the history of baseball: He won his own 6–2 decision over the Boston Red Sox with an inside-the-park grand slam homer in the fourth inning. Although he hit only .160 (120-for-749) lifetime, Stottlemyre's pride in his hitting was obvious by his accurate recall of having 26 extra-base hits, seven of them homers. This one was so special to him he listed it in the Yankee yearbook a few years later as his greatest thrill in baseball.

"I hit it off Bill Monbouquette," he said, "and two years later he got traded over to us. Monbo was a great guy, with a great sense of humor, and I listed that in the yearbook as a kind of a joke. Believe me, it didn't compare to winning my World Series game in '64. But Bill never let me forget that. What happened was, the bases were loaded and they had a kind of strange defensive alignment. Well, maybe it wasn't so strange, considering it was me batting. Yaz (Carl Yastrzemski) was playing real shallow in left and the center fielder (Jim Gosger) was shaded way over to right. I hit a line drive into left-center that bounced off the wall back to the monuments that were on the field at that time in the old Stadium. Everybody scored easily on the play and as I was rounding third, I looked and saw Frank Crosetti waving me home. I was out of gas, but I kept on going. I didn't slide in at the plate as much as I collapsed!"

"Most pitchers, especially today, are not regarded as especially good base runners," I said.

"You're right," Stottlemyre said, "but back then, before the designated hitter, we were required to work on all parts of our game. One thing I could always do was run and I'm really proud of having twice been sent in to pinch-run for Mickey. I've saved both of those box scores at home all these years."

Ever so gradually, the Yankees began returning to respectability as the '60s gave way to the '70s, and while there may have been no Mantles, Kubeks, Richardsons or Howards coming through the system, there were pitchers, particularly Stan Bahnsen, a 6-2 right-hander out of the University of Nebraska who won Rookie of the Year honors with a 17-win season in '68, and Fritz Peterson, an affable and happy-go-lucky left-hander, who won 20 in 1970 and settled in as the No. 2 starter in the rotation behind Stottlemyre. From 1968 to 1971 the Yankees' "Big Three" starters, Stottlemyre, Peterson and Bahnsen, combined to average about 45 wins per season. In the absence of a super slugger that had been the staple of nearly all the Yankee teams going back to Babe Ruth, the pitchers were the driving force in this apparent renaissance in the Bronx.

They might well have been the guiding force in returning the Yankees to supremacy, except for two dramatic and totally unrelated events, which prevented that from happening.

After the 1971 season, in which the Yankees finished a disappointing fourth in the American League East, 21 games behind, it was determined by the front office something had to be done about the offense, which had ranked 11th out of 14 teams in homers. In particular, they needed to plug a long-standing glaring deficiency at third base where the incumbent, Jerry Kenney, had hit just .262 with no homers and 20 RBI in 1971. Since the ill-conceived trade of Boyer in 1966, the Yankees had gotten a total of 22 homers out of his third base successors, Charley Smith, Bobby Cox and Kenney, over the next five years. (Of those three, Cox, at least, went on to a highly successful major league career as manager of the Toronto Blue Jays and Atlanta Braves.)

Lee MacPhail, the farm director under Yankee GM George Weiss in the 1950s who had been lured back to the organization by CBS after a successful term in Baltimore as head man of the Orioles, decided the only way to rectify this nagging third base problem was to sacrifice pitching. After failing in his efforts to obtain Don Money, a 14-homer man for the Philadelphia Phillies in 1970 who had slumped in '71, MacPhail agreed to send Bahnsen to the Chicago White Sox for their second-year second baseman, Rich McKinney. McKinney had hit only eight homers in '71, but was thought to be an up-and-coming player. MacPhail's scouts had also told him that McKinney was a born hitter who shouldn't have any trouble making the switch from second base to third.

It turned out all the Yankee reports on McKinney couldn't have been more wrong. He was a dismal failure in New York, appearing in only 37 games in 1972 after being replaced at third base by the personable, flashy rookie Celerino Sanchez six weeks into the season. Bahnsen, in the meantime, went on to win 21 games for the White Sox. In his autobiography, *My 9 Innings,* MacPhail confessed: "The Bahnsen-McKinney trade was the worst of my career. The mistake was made because I did not know McKinney well enough."

But if the disaster of the McKinney trade was the product of MacPhail not knowing enough about the player, it was nothing compared to what they didn't know about Fritz Peterson, and the shocking event that led to his demise as a Yankee fan favorite and successful pitcher. On March 5, 1973, the customary tranquility of spring training was abruptly interrupted when Peterson and Mike Kekich, another left-handed starter on the club, announced to their disbelieving Yankee teammates and the rest of the world they had decided to trade wives . . . and kids . . . and dogs. While both pitchers were regarded as your typical "flaky left-handers," this was something so bizarre that no one, not even their closest friends on the team like Stottlemyre, could fathom it.

After the initial jokes—Dick Young in the *New York Daily News* noted that the two pitchers had actually agreed to the swap on December 14 and therefore "did it before the inter-family trading deadline"—reaction from within, especially from the other Yankee players' wives, ranged from sadness to anger to disgust.

"They were, I thought, two of my closest friends," Stottlemyre said, "and that's why I thought it was so strange that two guys who were that close to me could possibly pull this off without me knowing it. Because of the type of personalities they were, always fooling around and pulling pranks on each other, even if they had thrown hints at me, I thought nothing of it. It was just a real shock to me. Jean was even more shocked and it bothered her a lot. She was tremendously upset. We were close friends with the wives, too."

Stottlemyre had actually been given advance notice of the "trade" a few weeks prior to spring training when Kekich, who lived in Portland, Oregon, called him and told him he'd be driving through Seattle and wanted to stop over for a visit. Stottlemyre told him he was welcome to stay as long as he wanted, but Kekich replied: "That's okay, we won't be staying long. Haven't you heard about the trade?"

"I said: 'What trade?'" Stottlemyre related, and Mike said: 'The inter-team trade! Fritz and I have traded wives and families! He went on to say he had Chip—who was Marilyn Peterson—with him, and I said: 'Sure you do, but go ahead and stop.' When I got off the phone, I said to Jean: 'You're not gonna believe what Mike just said to me.'

"I'm about two and a half hours from Portland, but sure enough, in about that time the two of them pull up to the house. I looked out the window and I said to Jean: 'You're not gonna believe this, but it's Mike (Kekich) and Marilyn Peterson.' I thought: 'Well, if we wait a few minutes, Fritz and Susanne Kekich will show up and we'll all have a good laugh at the joke because that's the sort of thing they were always doing to everybody. But they were there for a couple of hours and nobody else ever showed up. When they left, Jean and I looked at each other and said: 'Can this really be true?' Later that spring, it really started having an effect on Jean. She'd been out in the backyard of the house we were staying in and she heard one of the neighbors say: 'I wonder if *they're* like that!' I suppose it was a natural reaction."

In commending the New York media for its handling of the Peterson-Kekich affair, MacPhail conceded the incident adversely affected the two pitchers and the Yankees as a team. Peterson went from 17-15 in 1972 to 8-15 in '73, while Kekich was sent to the Cleveland Indians in June of that season. A year later, they were reunited when the Yankees traded Peterson over to Cleveland in the beneficial multiplayer deal that netted them first baseman Chris Chambliss and right-hander Dick Tidrow, who became key players on their '76-'78 championship teams.

[A footnote to the Peterson-Kekich affair: As of 2002, Peterson and the former Susanne Kekich were still together, living in a suburb of Chicago. Mike Kekich and Marilyn Peterson never married and split up shortly after spring training in 1973. Marilyn eventually remarried and, some 20 years after the scandal, was reportedly living in the same Bergen County, New Jersey, town she and Kekich had inhabited. For Kekich, the wife-swapping episode was the beginning of the end of his pitching career, after which he remarried, graduated from a Mexican medical school and became vice president of a health services company that administers in-home medical tests and counseling.]

By then, of course, Stottlemyre should have grown accustomed to constant change around the Yankees. In January of 1973, CBS announced it was selling the team to a syndicate headed by Cleveland shipbuilder George Steinbrenner, marking the third Yankee ownership in the nearly 10 years Stottlemyre had been there. At the end of the season, Houk resigned as manager—MacPhail had been elected president of the American League in 1973 and left as GM shortly after the sale of the team to Steinbrenner—and, so, another new management team was in place as well. And as Stottlemyre was soon to discover, the new bosses did not care if he'd been the best pitcher on the team since the day he arrived in August of 1964. As far as they were concerned, the CBS years had represented a failed regime—the worst decade in Yankee history—and they were determined to eradicate it.

Stottlemyre was already the highest paid Yankee when, in the spring of 1974, he found himself engaged in the first holdout of his career. The new Yankee GM, Gabe Paul, had offered him the same $80,000 salary as the year before, when he led the 80-82, fourth-place Yankees in wins with 16. Stottlemyre's original asking price was $90,000, but as he later explained, "I felt I should have had at least a cost of living raise." Paul, on the other hand, had been slow to move. Finally, after a two-hour meeting in the Yankees' executive trailer in the spring training complex, they agreed on a token raise to $87,500. "Now, I hope to have a real good season so I can become the Yankees' first $100,000 pitcher," Stottlemyre told reporters at the announcement of the new contract.

There was nothing but smiles on that day, Paul draping his arm around Stottlemyre's shoulder as the two emerged from the trailer. Stottlemyre had gotten only a hint of what was to come in the couple of weeks he'd been holding out for his token raise. Despite having been in baseball in every front office capacity from traveling secretary to GM since 1928, Gabe Paul was, first and foremost, a businessman. His job, the way he saw it, was to limit the players' compensation in every way he could in order to maximize the ball club's profit margin. Loyalty and sentiment were not Gabe Paul attributes, as Stottlemyre soon came to discover after hurting his arm, June 11, 1974.

"We were playing at Shea Stadium in '74 as Yankee Stadium was being renovated," Stottlemyre recalled. "I was pitching against the Angels and Frank Robinson was the hitter. I had just thrown him a curveball for a strike and I tried to throw another one and get a little further on top of it. But when I did that, I actually felt something pop in my shoulder. I had tremendous pain."

He had torn his rotator cuff, the kiss of death for any pitcher, especially then, before doctors had devised reconstructive surgery procedures which, in recent years, have been able to salvage careers to the point where pitchers are as good or better than what they were. In Stottlemyre's case, they told him surgery wouldn't help and to just shut it down and rest it until next spring. Over the winter, he was given further reassurance from Paul, who told him that, despite the bleak outlook, he could take all the time he needed to try to bring the arm back in spring training and that, regardless, the Yankees wouldn't make any decision on him until May 1. With that in mind, as well as the faint hope from the doctors that he "might be able to pitch with some pain," Stottlemyre reported to Fort Lauderdale in the spring of '75 and put himself on a limited workout regimen, in which he would throw 10 to 20 minutes of warm-up pitches daily under the supervision of Ford, who was now the pitching coach.

Then on March 31, the next to last day of spring training, Stottlemyre was out fishing in the Everglades, in nearby Loxahatchee, when he got an unexpected visitor in the person of Yankee traveling secretary Bill "Killer" Kane.

"We had just come in and Killer was waiting there as we got out of the boat. He said Gabe wanted to see me as quick as possible back at the stadium," Stottlemyre related, his eyes suddenly shifting out onto the field where the rain was showing no sign of subsiding. "My first thoughts were that somehow they'd probably traded me. One of the reasons I didn't think anything else was because I hadn't thrown much and Gabe had promised me I had until May 1 to make the roster. My arm was still hurting and I was still having a tough time throwing. But when I got back there and went to see Gabe in the trailer, it turned out he wasn't trading me, he was releasing me. I remember him telling me: 'You can call some other clubs, if you want,' to which I said to him: 'You mean you haven't even called any other clubs?' The reason he hadn't, I think, is because this had been a spur-of-the-moment decision. He'd suddenly realized if they kept me on the roster one more day they'd have had to pay me my $30,000 in severance."

It was about as cold and unceremonious a parting as there could be for a player who'd been a Yankee icon, the one remaining symbol of the glory years. Through all the CBS lean years—the "Yankee depression" as it was—along with the ownership upheavals and roster overhauls,

Stottlemyre had been the one bastion of Yankee stability and consistency. In the meantime, his family had grown. Mel Jr. was now 11, Todd 10 and the baby, Jason, was four. There could not have been a worse time for a man to get fired from the only job he'd ever known, but that, in effect, was what the Yankees were doing to him. His final won-lost record of 164-139 was far superior to the teams he'd pitched on. His 2.97 ERA ranks eighth all-time in the Yankee annals.

"The word 'release' was really very damaging to my thoughts," Stottlemyre said. "The fact that I hadn't been able to throw in a game, I felt they at least owed it to me to come to me and say: 'Look, we're thinking about giving you your release. You've got nothing to lose. Go out and see if you can throw.' I hadn't thrown an inning all spring and was just taking it as slow as I could because I thought I had until May 1. I suppose I should have seen it coming. During those times, I'd be throwing off the practice mounds, Whitey, who was the pitching coach, said to me two or three times: 'Be careful, Gabe's out to get you.' I think that was a message, not that I could have probably done anything about it.

"I left with real, real bitter feelings. I was just as upset at George as I was with Gabe. Even though George was banned from the everyday dealings of the ball club at the time, I held him responsible. I felt he could have stepped in and done something . . . or at least seen to it that it was handled a little better. I felt I deserved that and I made a lot of statements about him that I had to eat 20 years later. When they decided they wanted me to come back to be Joe's pitching coach, George called me himself and apologized. That really meant something."

He paused in his thoughts, as if the remembrance of it had conjured up some of that old bitterness. His fortune had been to have ridden the last wave of prodigies from the ever fertile Yankee farm system before the '60s decline and fall of the empire. He'd come back to the Yankees in 1996, the same year they started winning championships again, after another 15-year lull, and it was as if he'd truly come full-cycle. Thirty-two years between Yankee World Series for him, but once he did get back, they came in a flurry. Now, with four world championship rings in six years, he'd decided this would probably be his last season. This time, however, he'd be leaving the Yankees on *his* terms.

"I feel good, really good," he said, "but after 9/11, like everybody else I looked at myself and my life in a whole different way. I want to spend more time with my family. Jean's been traveling around practically her whole life with me and, as much as baseball has been a part of our lives and as much as I love what I do, she deserves to have me home with her in Seattle full-time."

A few of the grounds crew workers had run out onto the field and were sweeping the standing water off the tarpaulin now. Then, all of a sudden, the stadium was filled with organ music coming over the public address system. The gates weren't scheduled to open for another hour, but Eddie Layton, Steinbrenner's longtime in-house Yankee organist, was tuning up in the unlikely event he would have to provide rain delay entertainment for the fans.

As Layton launched into a soft rippling of "New York, New York," I said jokingly to Stottlemyre: "Eddie's playing your song."

"In a lot of ways it *is* my song," Stottlemyre replied. "I did have ten very happy years on the other side of town as the Mets' pitching coach."

"Yeah," I said, "but even then you were always a Yankee, at least in the eyes of New Yorkers."

"You re right," he sighed. "After I was released and went home to Seattle, I went to work for the Mariners as a minor league pitching coach and in the five years I spent with them, it was strange. Everywhere I went and everybody I met still identified me as a Yankee. Then I spent those 10 years working over there with the Mets and I can't tell you how many times people came up to me and said, 'We love having you here but you belong back on the other side of town."

"I tried to lose that feeling for a while, but surprisingly my family members kept me from losing it. My little guy that I lost, Jason, was born into it. The Yankees were his only team. When I was working for Seattle and I'd take him to a game, to see the Yankees when they'd come in, he'd tell me: 'I know you have to root for the Mariners, dad, but I'm rooting for the Yankees.' Thurman Munson was his favorite player and Jason would always tell me how much he wished I'd go back to the Yankees."

It was in December of 1976, Stottlemyre remembered, when Jason started having some flu symptoms and was run-down. When the aching and overall weak feeling persisted for a couple of weeks, Mel and Jean, at the doctor's suggestion, took him to the hospital in Yakima for tests.

"A couple of days later, they called us in to tell us the news," Stottlemyre said, clearing his throat. "They had done a bone marrow test and they had concluded he had leukemia. They spelled it out to us that it wasn't gonna be real good. They tried to paint a somewhat positive picture for us; that it was the type they were having some success dealing with, and we tried to remain as positive as we could about it. He was in remission two times and battled it for five years, back and forth from Yakima to Seattle. We still deal with it. I can't make anyone fully understand that, until you lose a child. Every time I hear the name Jason I get a flood of memories."

At that moment, we were interrupted by Rick Cerrone, the Yankees' publicity director, who had come down from the clubhouse to inform us the game had been postponed. Stottlemyre nodded, grabbed his clipboard and got up to go. Walking down the dugout toward the ramp, his white Yankee pinstripes a contrasting silhouette against the gray heavy mist still falling on the field, I was prompted to ask him one last question.

"Do you think," I said, "there would have been anyone more happy than Jason about your reconciliation with the Yankees?"

"I kinda doubt it," he said. "I have to believe he's looking down at all this . . . all these championships . . . and there's a real big smile on his face."

GOD'S HALL OF FAMER

BOBBY RICHARDSON

Your name may not appear down here
In this world's Hall of Fame
In fact you may be so unknown
That no one knows your name;
The headlines here may pass you by
The neon lights of blue
May never come your way,
But if you love and serve the Lord
Then I have news for you.
This Hall of Fame is only good
As long as time shall be;
But keep in mind, God's Hall of Fame
Is for eternity.
This crowd on earth they soon forget

The heroes of the past
They cheer like mad until you fall
And that's how long you last.
I tell you friend, I wouldn't trade
My name however small,
That's written there beyond the stars
In that celestial Hall,
For all the famous names on earth;
Or glory that they share;
I'd rather be an unknown here,
And have my name up there.

"A fellow by the name of Walt Huntley wrote that poem and sent it to me sometime back in the early '60s," Bobby Richardson was saying. "He was an active layman in the People's Church of Toronto and he enclosed it in a fan letter. I was so impressed with it that I started using it in various speaking engagements. It seemed like every time I used it, somebody was deeply touched by it and when I read it at Roger's funeral, Mickey said to me afterward: 'You've got to promise me to read that at my funeral, too.' Mickey especially loved the line about how 'they cheer like mad until you fall and that's how long you last.' He really related to that."

We were sitting on the second-level deck of an elevated, framed house in Myrtle Beach, South Carolina, overlooking the tidal marshes. Off in the distance, a small fishing boat was trolling the inlet while across the dune-lined road in front of the house, you could faintly hear the soft crashing of the ocean's waves. Richardson and his wife, Betsy, had been given use of the house for the weekend by one of the benefactors of the Fellowship of Christian Athletes' golf tournament at which the former Yankee second baseman was to serve as the celebrity host. It was early November, and although the day was overcast and seasonably cool, Richardson, ever the native, was clad in shorts and a lightweight parka.

On the table next to him was a Bible along with a stack of papers, on top of which was a mimeographed copy of the aforementioned Huntley poem. I had remembered it from that scorching August day in 1995, at the Lover's Lane Baptist Church in Dallas. Richardson, fulfilling the promise he made to Mickey Mantle at Roger Maris's funeral in Fargo, North Dakota, nearly 10 years earlier, had recited it once again in his role as the Yankees' "designated preacher" and principal euologist at the services for The Mick.

"You really have gotten a lot of mileage out of that poem," I said.

"Well, I just really think there's so much there," Richardson replied. "The first time I used it was in the '70s at an Oklahoma Hall of Fame banquet for the late, great athlete Jim Thorpe. Johnny Bench was there and he memorized every line from it. Every time I see him, he'll recite it to me."

From the very beginning—in 1957 when he arrived for good as the second base heir apparent to Billy Martin—it had become evident to the old-guard Yankees of Casey Stengel that Bobby Richardson was different from the rest of them. He wasn't the typical jock athlete indifferent to the gifts God bestowed on him; he didn't drink, he didn't smoke and he didn't cuss. He was 21 and married happily to his Sumter, South Carolina, hometown sweetheart, the former Betsy Dobson, who was only 17. Not only that, he kept a New Testament Bible in his locker, and during idle moments might even be observed reading it while the conversation across the room among the other Yankees featured tales of late-night escapades and boozy triumphs. And his best friend on the team, Tony Kubek, the all-purpose man who now seemed to be gradually settling in at shortstop, was much like him insofar as their mutual sharing of Christian values. They'd come up together through the system, each achieving All-Star status at Triple A Denver in 1956, when Richardson hit .328 and Kubek .331. Kubek, a gangly, shy farm boy from the dairy land of Wisconsin, was single but eschewed the bar and party scene that in most cases captivated a young, unattached, famous Yankee.

Someone—no one could ever remember who it was—dubbed them the "Milk Shake Boys" but if it was meant to be a mocking of their clean-living image, they weren't offended, and it stuck.

In the ribald Yankee clubhouse, theirs was one corner where temperance had its place. Pete Sheehy, the venerable custodian of the Yankee clubhouse since the days of Babe Ruth, saw to that. Right away, he knew Richardson and Kubek were a different breed and, so, he strategically set them up, side by side, out of earshot of the profanity, next to the old-school coach, Frank Crosetti, who concerned himself only with the game day preparation and the accounting of the baseballs.

"Pete was amazing like that," Richardson said. "He put Tony and I right there on the left side of the clubhouse as you walked in and we couldn't hear anything that was going on at the other end of the room. The other guys all knew how we were about things; that we loved the Lord, and they respected that. I used to bring my kids into the clubhouse a lot and they'd invariably go right over to Mickey's locker. One time, though, Hank Bauer motioned to my son Robbie, who was only two at the time, to come over to his locker and take a sip of beer. 'C'mon' he said, 'this'll help you grow up to be a man.' I said something to Hank about not to do that, but he persisted and kept offering Robbie a sip of the beer. He was just fooling around, but then he realized I was serious. We later apologized to each other, but I guess that was the first real time the other players came to know what I was about."

They would kiddingly call him "Preacher" and the "Right Reverend" but those were really terms of endearment. And after a while, especially on the chartered flights, he would often find himself in the company of teammates seeking his counsel and even prayer.

"I had permission from the club to fly home on off-days before and after road trips," Richardson recalled, "and once, while I was home, the team's charter developed some sort of engine or turbulence problems. The guys all looked around and said: 'Where's Bobby?' From then on, they always wanted to make sure I was on the flight. Those were the times they'd come over and talk."

He laughed at the recollection of it. Maybe if he hadn't been as good a player as he was, as valuable a contributor to the seven World Series teams he played on in his 10 full seasons as a Yankee, he wouldn't have been held in quite the same high esteem as he was. Ralph Houk, his hard-bitten manager at Denver in '56 and then mostly with the Yankees from 1961 to 1966, once said of him: "It's difficult to talk about Bobby. You start to get embarrassed because he forces you to talk in superlatives. He was the finest type of all-around player I ever managed. From the first time I had him in the minors until I had him in the big leagues, he never caused me a minute's loss of sleep. Not only was he marvelous on the field, but his influence on his teammates was beyond measure."

As far back as his freshman year in high school in Sumter, Richardson knew he wanted to be a Yankee. That summer, his American Legion baseball team won the regional championship in Charlotte, North Carolina, and after the game the coaches took them to the movies where they saw *Pride of the Yankees,* the classic heart-wrencher in which Gary Cooper portrayed doomed Yankee first base great Lou Gehrig. "That was the first time I came to recognize what a great organization the Yankees were," Richardson said. "I just really admired Lou Gehrig."

Three years later, in 1951, as Richardson had developed into a full-fledged prospect, he began receiving correspondence from the Yankees, in particular their *Play Ball* instructional book with Phil Rizzuto on the cover which they used to send out to all the young players they were interested in signing. When it came time to sign, 12 of the then 16 major league clubs offered him identical contracts for $4,000, which made his decision easy.

"In those days, if you received more than $4,000, you had to go directly to the big leagues and spend two years on the roster," Richardson said, "so nobody wanted to go over that. Leon Hamilton was the one scout who was really courting me for the Dodgers. He put a lot of pressure on me. He was in town all the time. He even gave my girlfriend—who wasn't Betsy at the time—a glove. But I had made up my mind a long time before I was going to sign with the Yankees. I never thought about it maybe being a lot harder to make their team. Shortly after that, Hamilton signed Junior Gilliam for the Dodgers and he always told me that was because he couldn't sign me.

"After I signed, the Yankees wanted me to come to New York and work out with them for three days. There was a fellow who lived in Sumter, a Coca-Cola Bottling Co. executive named Fred Heath who had close ties to the Yankees, and he arranged to take me up there. We took a Pullman—it was the first time I'd ever been on a train—and when we got there, we checked into the hotel New Yorker and I took a cab out to Yankee Stadium. When I got there, Frank Crosetti was sitting in front of the locker next to the one they'd assigned to me. He looked at me and said: 'Those the only shoes you got, kid?' I said: 'Yes sir.' And he said, 'Well here's a new pair you can have.' That was my first pair of baseball spikes. Later, I went out onto the field where the Yankees were taking batting practice. I couldn't get over the size of the Stadium. I'm standing there, this scared-stiff 17-year-old boy, not daring to pick up a bat, when Mickey comes over to me and puts his arm around me and says: 'C'mon, kid. Take a few swings in the cage.'"

(There was, of course, no way for him to know that unexpected gesture of kindness from the budding Yankee star was, in fact, the beginning of a lifelong friendship; an odd-couple bonding if there ever was one, that would nevertheless endure unabated in spite of Mickey's wayward indulgences and infidelities. And that it would end some 42 years later with the two of them praying together at the dying Mantle's bedside at Baylor University Medical Hospital in Dallas.)

After returning home to a hero's welcome in Sumter, Richardson was dispatched by the Yankees to their Norfolk farm in the Class B Piedmont League where he hit an undistinguished .211 in 29 games—all at shortstop.

"I was just outclassed," he sighed. "What had happened was the regular shortstop at Norfolk, guy named Dick Sanders, had been called into the reserves and the manager there, the old Dodger Mickey Owen, told me: 'You're my shortstop.' I couldn't wait for Sanders to get back and that was about the closest I ever came to quitting. It was also the only time I ever remember my father taking a trip out of Sumter. The Yankees wanted to send me to Class D Olean, New York, and I wanted to come back home. My father talked me into staying, and right after that, my high school coach wrote me a letter with the verse from Matthew 6:33 which says: 'Seek ye first the kingdom of God and His righteousness and all these things shall be added unto you.' In the letter he said some things to explain that the Lord will be with you and it'll work out, and that kind of encouraged me, too. So I said, 'I'll go to Olean,' and as soon as I got there, I fit right in and wound up hitting .412 in the 32 games I was there."

Because of that turnaround, the Yankees invited him to their instructional league the following spring, where he first caught the eye of Stengel. He made enough of an impression then to convince the Yankees to send him to Binghamton, a class above Norfolk, in 1954 and as a full-time second baseman he hit .310 and led the Eastern League in hits and made the All-Star team. A year later, he was in the big leagues—albeit briefly—as a mid-August infield replacement for Gil McDougald, who had gone down with an injury.

Another All-Star season at Denver in '56 earned him permanent residence in the Bronx in 1957. But it was not until Martin was exiled to the Kansas City Athletics on June 15 in the aftermath of Billy's infamous birthday bash at the Copacabana nightclub a month earlier, that Richardson began to feel he might have a long future with the Yankees.

"You have to remember they had a bunch of infielders—good infielders—back then," he said. "Besides Billy, there was McDougald, Jerry Coleman and Andy Carey, who had all been around on their championship clubs, and Jerry Lumpe and Woodie Held, who'd come up through the system like me."

The day of the Martin trade, the Yankees were in Kansas City, in the midst of a weekend series against the A's. As Richardson remembered it, Martin spent nearly an hour in Stengel's office after the game. "Then, as I was sitting on the bus that was to take us back to the Muehlebach Hotel where we were staying, Billy got on and sat down next to me and said: 'Okay kid, it's all yours.'"

At the time, Richardson thought Martin meant just the second base job, but as it turned out he meant his coveted No. 1 as well.

"When we got back to New York," he said, "Big Pete [Sheehy] came up to me with the No. 1 jersey and said: 'This is the number you'll wear.' I'd been wearing 29. It was a very humbling experience because I felt for Billy. I looked at him as a true Yankee. He was Stengel's buddy and he spurred all the other guys along. He was very calm when he talked to me on the bus and I could tell he was sad but he'd evidently worked through all his emotions when he was inside with Casey."

While the trading of Martin was a prelude to Richardson becoming the Yankees' regular second baseman, the position didn't officially pass to him until two years later. Coleman, who had been sharing second base duties with Martin since 1950, retired after the '57 season at the Yankees behest to go to work in the team's player development department. But McDougald (who, along with Pete Rose, shares the distinction as the only players selected to the All-Star Game at three different positions) was still playing the bulk of his games at second. Finally, in '59, Stengel decided to use McDougald more as a utility man and installed Richardson as his everyday second baseman. Richardson responded by hitting .301 in 134 games and getting selected by Stengel as a backup infielder on the American League All-Star team.

He had clearly come a long way from being one of Stengel's favorite targets for derision and ridicule. As he had done with the aging Phil Rizzuto, Stengel would often overtly disparage Richardson's hitting, by batting him ninth in the lineup behind good-hitting pitchers like Tommy Byrne or Don Larsen, or by pinch-hitting for him in the early innings. "Look at him," the old man once said of Richardson, "he don't smoke, he don't drink, nothing. But he still can't hit .220!"

So it was therefore sort of ironic Richardson's most celebrated output of hitting—the record 12 RBI he amassed as the surprising

MVP of the 1960 World Series against the Pittsburgh Pirates—wasn't enough to save Stengel's job. Half of those 12 RBI had come in Game 3 when Stengel had him hitting seventh in the lineup, one game-breaking opportunity away, Richardson feared, from being removed for a pinch hitter.

The Series was tied at one game apiece, but for reasons Stengel never fully explained to anyone's satisfaction, he'd held Whitey Ford back until Game 3, thus precluding any chance of the Yankee ace getting three starts. The Yankees got right at it for Ford against Pirate starter Wilmer "Vinegar Bend" Mizell, knocking him out of the box in the first inning with three hard-hit singles and a walk. Elston Howard then beat out a slow infield roller against reliever Clem Labine to score Mantle with the second run of the inning and set up a bases-loaded situation for Richardson.

"As I was kneeling in the on-deck circle, I kind of anticipated, 'he's gonna pinch-hit for me,'" Richardson said. "I saw Johnny Blanchard sitting there in the dugout as I started up to the plate and I waited for Casey to yell 'hold that gun,' which was his way of saying 'c'mon back and let Blanchard hit.' Well, as I got to the plate I didn't hear it and when I looked down at Crosetti in the third base coaching box, I knew why. Crosetti gave me the bunt sign. Now you and I both know that's not a good play, squeezing with the bases loaded and one out."

Nevertheless, Richardson obliged—or at least *attempted* to oblige. Squaring around the first time, he popped the ball up into the stands behind home plate. His second attempt was equally futile, this one landing on the screen. After that, he was at least able to work the count to 3-2, at which point Crosetti yelled to him: "Hit the ball to right field and stay out of the double play." Even that, though, he wasn't able to do.

"Labine threw me a fastball up and in," he related, "and I was able to get around on it and hit it good. As I'm rounding first base, Gino Cimoli, who was playing left field for the Pirates, had gone all the way back to the wall, leaped, and was looking in his glove. I thought he'd caught it. I thought he was looking at the ball in his glove. When I saw the umpire signal home run, I was surprised although I imagine Stengel was even more surprised, given the fact I'd hit only one home run all year and had just 26 RBIs. A grand slam. Then, when I came up the next time, the bases were loaded again and by this time we were leading by 7–0 and I honestly tried to hit a home run. I said, 'Let's see if I can do that again. Instead, I hit a line drive to left field that scored two more runs and I guess that's a record that still stands—six RBIs in a single World Series game. I know that because my son Robbie called me after Game 6 of the Yankees-Diamondbacks Series—which I hadn't seen—and reported how [Arizona's Danny] Bautista had five and they took him out of the game!"

The 1960 World Series will forever be regarded as one of the bitter chapters in Yankee history. To a man, they believed they were the far superior team—their three victories, 16–3, 10–0 and 12–0, were three of the most lopsided games in Series history—and, overall, they outscored the Pirates 55–27, out-hit them 91–60 and out-homered them 10–4. But in the end, it was Bill Mazeroski, Richardson's equally unheralded second base counterpart, who settled it for the Pirates with his lead-off game-winning homer in the ninth inning of the wild Game 7. Years later, Mantle would maintain that loss was the low point of his Yankee career and nothing remotely came close to it. To this day as well, Richardson felt no consolation at being named winner of the Corvette by *Sport Magazine* as the MVP of the Series—the only Series MVP ever to come from the losing team. Nothing made sense, least of all the preacher driving off in a sports car.

"You know, I'll tell you a funny story," Richardson said, getting up to stretch. "Ed Fitzgerald, who was the editor of *Sport Magazine*, wrote a fictional book about the Yankees in 1950 called *The Rookie,* and in this book, the second baseman for the Yankees is named Bobby Richardson!"

"You've gotta be kidding. How eerie is *that?*" I said.

"*Very* eerie," Richardson said."I didn't even know about it until years later when my son Robbie found the book. Anyway, all these years I always thought it was Fitzgerald who decided on the MVP. My part of it is, we're sitting in the clubhouse and we're sad, because we lost. It was my biggest disappointment and when they came up to me and said you've just been named MVP, there was no joy. I didn't care about any individual honor. If I'd been like Paul O'Neill, I'd have probably turned it down. As it was, I just felt empty."

The cool ocean breeze had begun to pick up a little and we adjourned to the living room where Betsy was sorting a load of laundry. Richardson offered me a glass of iced tea and poured one for himself. He had made arrangements to take us to the Grand Ole Opry Christmas show in downtown Myrtle Beach that night and excused himself to make a phone call to check on the tickets. As I waited for him to finish the call, I tried to envision him tooling around Manhattan in that Corvette—as noted playboys and previous Series MVPs, Johnny Podres and Don Larsen, had done.

"I know you probably wonder what I did with the Corvette," he said, reading my mind, as he put away his cell phone.

"Well, you've got to admit, it wasn't exactly *you*."

"I had a friend drive it home to Sumter for me," he said. "But when I got it, I realized I had two boys already and Betsy was expecting our third child and I couldn't get them all in the car. So I took it down to the local Oldsmobile dealership in town and traded it in for a Jeep. But later on I realized, *'Man, I shouldn't have done that.'* That was a wonderful award. Well, a young girl from a neighboring community bought it and put 9,000 miles on it and traded it back in to the Oldsmobile dealer. So now I thought: 'Betsy would really like to have that Corvette, and I went back and bought it back and gave it to Betsy."

Overhearing the story, Betsy came in from the other room.

"My reaction," she laughed, "was that, in our financial situation at the time, the last thing we needed was a sports car that only two people could fit in."

"The rest of the story," Richardson continued, "was that I used to sit next to Johnny Sain, our pitching coach, on all the plane trips and he had an auto dealership back in Arkansas. He said to me: 'I'll tell you what I'll do. I'll trade you a brand-new Chevy II station wagon for that Corvette.' So I traded the Corvette again and that's the last I ever heard about it. I don't know whatever happened to it after that, although I do know a good friend of mine in Sumter has a 1960 Corvette in mint condition and recently turned down $65,000 for it."

The combination of losing the '60 Series to a clearly inferior team, a year after failing to reach the Series for the first time since 1954, was sufficient ammunition for the Yankee owners, Dan Topping and Del Webb, to relieve the 70-year-old Stengel of his duties as manager. They had been grooming Houk for the job for six years and they feared losing him to another club, but as long as the immensely popular Stengel kept winning, it was impossible to move him out. In May of 1960, Stengel had been hospitalized for a couple of weeks after suffering chest pains and Houk ran the club in his absence. In one of his classic self-effacing quips, Stengel told reporters upon his release from the hospital: "They examined all my organs. Some of them are quite remarkable and others are not so good. A lot of museums are bidding for them."

So five days after the 1960 World Series, as Richardson was home in Sumter figuring out what to do with his new Corvette, his life as a Yankee was about to dramatically change when the club called a press conference at the Savoy Hilton hotel in New York, purportedly to announce Stengel's "retirement" and Houk's long-anticipated ascension to the manager's job. A nervous Topping beat around the bush in attempting to convey the idea that Stengel was voluntarily stepping down, but the reporters knew otherwise. And when asked directly if he had resigned or was fired, Stengel replied characteristically: "I don't know if I was discharged or what except that there was no question I had to leave." He later added with an equal trace of bitterness to another reporter's probing question about his "resignation": "I just know I'll never make the mistake of turning 70 again."

"When I heard about the manager change, I wasn't surprised," Richardson said. "Ralph was a coach and I'd played for him and I think because of Casey's age we didn't think too much about it. The next spring, though, there was quite a contrast. Whereas before you were always a little bit on edge and you had to figure out how you could please Casey, Ralph just patted you on the back and told you all he wanted from you was your best effort. That followed over to the regular season when, unlike before when I was in and out of the lineup, Ralph just came up and sat down next to me and said: 'It doesn't matter if you hit .150, .250 or .350, you're my second baseman. Remember, Ralph had had me at Denver when I'd hit .328 and he believed in my hitting ability."

"As opposed to Casey, who didn't," I interjected.

"Casey gave me my first chance and I'll always be grateful to him," Richardson said. "But after I stuck with the club, the way he'd do things . . . he'd just get you so mad you wanted to prove him wrong. He'd knock you in the papers. I remember how he pinch-hit for me once in the first inning of a game in 1957. I walked right by him in the dugout and started heading to the clubhouse when he yelled: 'Where are you going?' I told him I was going home. 'Nah,' he said, 'you go out to the bullpen and warm up Ryne Duren.' He was a hard guy to figure out. To this day, I'll never understand why he didn't start Whitey in the first game of that '60 Series."

Still, there were other times when Stengel showed a softer, more compassionate side. As Richardson noted: "He did pick me for the All-Star Game in '57 and I'll never forget the last game of the '59 season when I was hitting .299 and needed one hit for .300. We had long since been eliminated so the game didn't mean anything, but Casey said before the game: 'We don't have a single .300 hitter on this team, so if you get a hit your first time up, I'm taking you out.'

"Well, we were playing the Orioles and Billy O'Dell, who lived in Newberry, South Carolina, was pitching for them. Billy and I used to go quail hunting together and we were friends. Apparently, the word had gotten all around, even to the Orioles, about me needing that hit for .300. So Billy came over to me and said: 'Don't worry, I'll be throwing one right in there for you.' Then, a couple of minutes later, Brooks Robinson came up to me and said: 'I'll be playing real deep at third if you want to bunt.' Right after that, their catcher, Joe Ginsberg, says to me: 'I'll tell you what pitch is coming.' Finally, if all that wasn't enough, the first base umpire, Ed Hurley, said to me: 'If you hit it on the ground, just make it close at first.' There couldn't have been a more complete fix on."

"So what happened?" I asked, my curiosity piqued that, even in a meaningless game, the 'Right Reverend' Richardson would have allowed himself to become involved in such a patently crooked scheme.

"I got my pitch and hit a line drive to right field that Albie Pearson made a diving catch on," he replied, laughing. Pearson was one of my closest friends in the game—we'd spoken together at church! He must have been the only person in the ballpark who didn't know I was supposed to get my hit!"

In retrospect, there can be no question now that the changeover from Stengel to Houk was both necessary and right for the Yankees, as it had an immediate positive effect on the entire ball club, which had seemingly been worn down by the old man's incessant gibes and increasingly questionable strategy. Houk's first season at the helm, 1961, turned out to be one of those magical and mythical seasons in which everything he did worked to perfection and his players achieved heights they could not have imagined.

In particular, Ford, responding to Houk pitching him every four days, won a career-high 25 games, while Roger Maris, who had never hit more than 39 homers in a season, broke Babe Ruth's 34-year-old record with 61. Even Mantle, who waged a compelling race with Maris for the homer record until being felled by a hip infection in September, hit 54 (the most of his career) and led the AL in runs with 132. The Yankees as a team steamrolled to the pennant, pulling away from the Detroit Tigers in early September en route to 109 wins, and set a major league record with 240 homers. In the World Series that fall, they dispatched the Cincinnati Reds in five games to further carve their niche as one of the greatest teams in baseball history.

Lost in all the homer heroics, Richardson hit a respectable .261 in '61 while playing all 162 games. It was the following season, however, in which he established himself as one of the truly essential Yankees as well as one of the premier second basemen in the game. Though Mantle won the last of his three Most Valuable Player Awards in 1962, he always maintained it really should have gone to Richardson, who finished second in the balloting after batting a career-high .302 and leading the AL in hits with 209. Batting first or second in the order all season long, Richardson led the Yankees in runs (99), doubles (38) and stolen bases (11), won his second of six straight Gold Gloves for defensive excellence and was elected the starting second baseman in the All-Star Game.

"Ralph was like a father to me," Richardson said, "and it's not surprising I had my best seasons under him. When I was at Denver, he let me take a week off to marry Betsy after the team president, Bob Howsam, had adamantly said no. And I remember, it was sometime around 1961 or '62, I was thinking of quitting baseball early and going to school to become a pastor, and I talked it over with Ralph. He said: 'You don't realize it, but you have far more impact as a baseball player. There will be many more doors opening for you because of baseball and you'll have many more opportunities to reach people.' I thought about it and he really made sense."

With Mantle sidelined for nearly 40 games with a knee injury, the Yankees' run for the pennant in '62 wasn't nearly as easy as the year before. They managed to hold off an up-and-coming Minnesota Twins team by five games and then got taken to seven games in the World Series by the San Francisco Giants. Or more precisely to seven games and two feet. In one of the most memorable and heart-stopping climaxes to any World Series, the Yankees' Ralph Terry (who had been the victim of Mazeroski's crushing Series-ending homer two years earlier) was clinging to a 1–0 shutout with two out, runners at second and third and Willie McCovey at the plate in the ninth inning of Game 7.

"Matty Alou had led off the inning with a bunt to the right side that I got to too late to make a play on him," Richardson recalled. "Then

Terry struck out both Felipe Alou and Chuck Hiller and it looked like he was going to wrap it up when Willie Mays doubled to right."

It took both a perfect cutoff of the ball and the ensuing throw by Maris in right to prevent Alou from scoring, and now Houk was forced to make one of those rock-and-a-hard-place decisions in which you might just as well flip a coin. With first base open, did he have the right-handed Terry intentionally walk the left-handed McCovey? That was the percentage move, although, by doing so, it meant bringing the equally lethal Orlando Cepeda to the plate with nowhere to put him.

"About the time Ralph and Terry were discussing at the mound what they were going to do," Richardson said, "Kubek comes over to me at second base and says: 'I hope McCovey doesn't hit the ball to you. You have already made two errors in this game and I'd hate to see you blow another one now.' Mays burst out laughing and I've got to say, it eased the tension for me, too."

The decision made to pitch to McCovey, the imposing Giant slugger proceeded to hit a scorching liner right at Richardson, who had played him perfectly. A foot or so to the right or left and it's a Series-winning gapper. A foot or so higher and the diminutive 5-9 Richardson most likely couldn't have gotten it, but as he said: "One of the great misconceptions that's been perpetuated through the years is that I had to leap up to catch the ball. What happened was, the ball had a lot of backspin on it and it looked like a base hit. But it came down in a hurry and I actually caught it chest high."

McCovey later insisted Richardson was actually playing him out of position. In a June 2002 interview with Murray Chass of the *New York Times*, he said: "No second baseman ever played me that close to second base because I was a dead pull hitter. When I hit the ball in that direction, I figure it's a base hit."

With two straight world championships under Houk, Richardson assumed this was just the beginning of another long run and that he'd never play for another manager. With his family growing, he wasn't sure how many more years he wanted to play anyway and he definitely couldn't foresee Houk leaving any time soon. But after winning a third straight AL pennant in 1963, the Yankees were swept by the Dodgers in the World Series, scoring a total of only four runs against the vaunted pitching of Sandy Koufax, Don Drysdale and Johnny Podres. Afterward, Houk shocked his troops by announcing he was leaving the field to go upstairs to the front office as general manager and that Yogi Berra would be taking over as manager.

The '64 season, though ultimately successful from the standpoint of another pennant, was one of the most tumultuous in Yankee history, culminating with Berra's firing after another seven-game World Series loss. From the outset, as Richardson remembered, Yogi had trouble making the transition from teammate to boss and for most of the summer, the team's perceived uninspired and lackadaisical play perhaps reflected a lack of discipline and dedication that Houk had instilled in them with his commanding style.

"I remember one of those first days in Fort Lauderdale that spring of '64 that Yogi came by the place Betsy and I were staying and said: 'Tomorrow, in the clubhouse, will be the first time I'll address the ball club,'" Richardson related. "He said: 'I'm going to set some rules—no swimming, no card playing, etc., etc.' And then he said, 'No, I'm only kidding. We're just gonna work hard together and have fun. How does that sound?' Well, it sounded good, but the next day in the clubhouse, he got through about three of those rules and there was this noise in the back of the room. It was Mickey, who got up and said, 'I quit' and started walking out of the room. Everybody laughed, but then we started out that season and things did not go well."

With three of their key operatives, Mantle, Ford and Kubek, sidelined for substantial periods of time with injuries, along with three principal relievers, Steve Hamilton, Hal Reniff and Bill Stafford, Yogi's Yankees found themselves in a three-way dogfight with the Chicago White Sox and the Baltimore Orioles. Things came to a particularly stormy juncture in mid-August when the Yankees lost four straight in Chicago to the White Sox (whom they had beaten 10 in a row earlier in the season) to fall four and a half games behind. On the bus ride from Comiskey Park to O'Hare Airport, the low-key Berra's fuse was finally ignited when backup shortstop Phil Linz began playing a harmonica.

"Prior to that series, we had been in Minnesota," Richardson said, "and Kubek and I had been invited out to the Billy Graham headquarters there. While we were being shown through, Tony picked up one of those little chorus books they used in the crusades. Well, Tony can't sing and I can't sing, but when we got back to our hotel room, Tony said: 'Man, I really like these. Let's try to sing them.' Before we did, though, we called Spud Murray, the batting practice pitcher, up to the room and he brought with him a harmonica. We sang for about three hours and the next morning in the coffee shop of the Radisson Hotel some of our teammates were sitting there and you could tell they hadn't slept much. We asked them what was wrong and they said there were some drunks in the room over their head singing all night. We laughed and when we got to Chicago, Tony went into Marshall Field's and bought four harmonicas. He gave one to me, one to Tom Tresh and the last one he gave to Linz.

"So now we lost the four games in Chicago, and Phil—who didn't play an inning of any of those games—was in the back of the bus and decided to choose this time to learn how to play the harmonica. When Yogi heard him, he jumped up and yelled: 'Put that thing in your pocket.' Unfortunately, Linz didn't hear him and when he asked what Yogi had said, Mantle, who was sitting across the aisle, yelled: 'He said to play it louder!' So Phil kept playing and this time, Yogi jumped up and now he was really mad. He grabbed the harmonica and threw it and it hit Pepitone, who started screaming for the trainer. There were a bunch of the reporters on the bus and, of course, it eventually got in the papers and became a whole big controversy."

"So what you're telling me," I queried, 'is that the Milk Shake Boys were indirectly responsible for the infamous Phil Linz harmonica incident?"

"I guess so," Richardson replied, chuckling. "But in the end, Yogi had the last laugh. The team got together after that and rallied to win the pennant. I think we went 22-6 in September to finish a game ahead of the White Sox."

If only that had been enough for Berra to keep his job. Unfortunately for him, the harmonica incident merely served to validate Topping's conclusion that Yogi had lost control of the team and that it had been a mistake to make him the manager. Even a hard-fought, seven-game World Series—in which Ford got hurt in the first game, Mantle played with a bad leg and Kubek was sidelined throughout—wasn't enough to convince the front office Yogi deserved to stay on as manager. For Richardson, the '64 World Series was all too reminiscent of 1960. Once again, he was the batting star in a losing cause, knocking a record 13 hits (that still stands). But his error on Dick Groat's one-out grounder to second in the sixth inning set the stage for Ken Boyer's grand slam home run that won the pivotal Game 4 for the Cardinals, and he popped up to second against a spent Bob Gibson, who won two of the three games he started, for the final out of the Series.

"Seven of those hits were off Gibson," Richardson said, with an obvious trace of pride, "but I did make the last out, with Maris on deck after Clete [Boyer] had homered to make it 7–5. The thing I felt most badly about was the error on the Groat grounder. Tony was not playing shortstop, Linz was. I did not field the ball cleanly and hesitated in my throw to Phil. If Tony had been playing short—we'd been playing together so long—he'd have just stepped on the bag and we'd have gotten one out. But Phil came flying across the bag, in anticipation of a double play, and because of my hesitation, by the time I got the ball to him he was already across the bag and the runner hit him and dislodged the ball. That loaded the bases for Boyer, and what it proved to me was the importance of playing together."

Just like in 1960, Richardson was back home in Sumter the day after the World Series, without an inkling of another managerial change. He had assumed that with the Yankees' strong finish and their game performance against the Cardinals in the Series, Berra had quelled the critics. So he was therefore as shocked as everyone else when Houk announced Berra was being relieved of his duties as manager and being replaced by Johnny Keane, the man who had just beaten him in the World Series. The shock, however, turned to anger when Richardson learned of the newspaper report that had fingered him as the player who undermined Yogi. Nearly 40 years later, the story still rankled him.

The day of the Berra-Keane bombshell announcement, Joe Trimble in the *New York Daily News* reported: "It's been no secret that Richardson, like his roommate, shortstop Tony Kubek, refused to associate with certain players off the field. The pair apparently were assured that a firmer hand would be guiding the Yankees next season. Thus, 'Richy' changed his mind about retiring to Sumter, S.C."

"I was home in Sumter when the calls started coming from New York with people saying, 'The headlines up here say you're responsible for Yogi leaving,'" Richardson said. "I called Joe on the phone and said, 'Not a word of that is true. I don't know where you got it from.' He said: 'I thought I overheard you and the sportswriter from Tennessee, Fred Russell, saying that you weren't going to come back if Yogi was manager.' I said: 'No sir, Fred asked me if I went out to eat after games with Yogi and Mickey and all the guys and I said that usually Kubek and I go out together but that's simply because we want to go to bed a little earlier.'

"Well, the thing really mushroomed and I got mail you just couldn't believe, from the Italians in New York and everything. And the problem was, once that story was out, it perpetuated itself. It still upsets me to this day because there isn't a person in baseball any dearer to me than Yogi. He did a great job in 1964, especially with all the injuries we had, and we were all shocked and upset when he got fired."

Those who believe in legends and mystique have maintained it was no coincidence the firing of Yogi Berra as manager in 1964 also marked the end of the Yankee dynasty—and that they did not return to the World Series until 1976, the year Yogi returned to the team as a coach for Billy Martin after a 10-year tour of duty across town with the Mets. Richardson smiled and nodded when I mentioned that to him. Certainly, life as a Yankee for him was never the same after Yogi's departure, and being a firsthand witness to the rapid deterioration of this once great team under the miscast and beleaguered Keane was painful.

"Johnny Keane was just a man of character," Richardson said. "He just didn't understand Yankee baseball. For instance, he would take Whitey out in the eighth inning of a tie ball game . . . pinch-hit for him. You just don't do that. You leave Whitey in there. But I think it broke his heart when he was let go in 1966. Betsy and I went to see him in Houston just before he died in 1967. We had a great visit together, but I could tell then he had a broken heart from that year and a half in New York. Nothing went right for him. He was more upset with himself because it just didn't work out."

It didn't help either that, in addition to Mantle and Maris experiencing dramatic declines under Keane, Kubek retired because of a neck injury after the '65 season and Richardson, in a pre-arranged agreement, was to leave after the '66 season. Kubek was only 29, Richardson 31. In agreeing to delay his retirement a year after Kubek's, Richardson signed a five-year contract for which he was paid $45,000 to play in 1966, and then $15,000 per year as a special assignment scout for the last four.

"Ralph had come back to replace Keane as manager in '66 and as we got to the end of the season—we were in last place—he told me he was going to play Horace Clarke at second base, to break him in," Richardson said. "They had a day for me in New York in which they drew 40,000 people a day after there'd been only about 400 at Yankee Stadium. We ended the season in Chicago and Ralph suggested that it might be a nice idea to have a team devotion on my last day. So that's what we did. We held it in the Bismarck Hotel there and the whole team came out. It was goodbye time."

He looked at his watch and motioned me to turn off the tape

recorder. It was just past noon and Betsy had prepared a spread of cold cuts and salads for lunch, to which we helped ourselves, and afterward I suggested we all walk it off on the beach. Not surprisingly, the beach was deserted, although a glint of sun had broken through the overcast skies to warm the air, and the sand felt good underfoot as we kicked off our shoes and began our trek along the wide, white expanse between the dunes and the ocean. For the first few minutes, we walked in silence, taking in the placid late-autumn afternoon on the South Carolina shore.

"Your friendship with Mickey," I finally said. "How was it you stayed so close despite such vastly contrasting lifestyles? His drinking and infidelities had to make it hard for you to maintain your relationship with him."

"I was never around Mickey on the road," he replied firmly. "But after we were both retired, we'd get together at the various functions each of us might be involved in. I was always there for him and he was always there for me. We grew up in similar circumstances, both of us being from the somewhat rural South. We both attended church . . . he just got away from it. He was my friend and I always enjoyed being with him."

"In that regard, there was probably never a more important time for Mickey than at the end for him."

"I guess," he said. "For me, it was a very emotional time. In July of 1995, I was in Dallas for a meeting of BAT, the Baseball Assistance Team. Mickey and I were both on the board of directors, but he was really sick by then, undergoing chemotherapy after having gotten his liver transplant. About 5:30 in the morning, the phone in my hotel room rang. Betsy answered it and it was Mickey. His cancer had come back and he said to Betsy: 'I m really hurting, Betsy. I want Bobby to pray for me.'

"When I got on the phone, we did have prayer together. The verse that I shared with him was Philippians 4: 'Delight yourself in the Lord. Find your joy in Him at all times. Have a reputation for being reasonable and never forget the nearness of your Lord. Don't worry over anything whatsoever, but whenever you pray, tell God every detail of your needs and then the peace of God, which transcends all human understanding, will keep constant guard over your hearts and minds as they rest in Christ Jesus.'"

Immediately after that phone conversation, Betsy Richardson called Mantle's wife, Merlyn, from whom he'd been estranged for years while he had carried on an open live-in relationship with his agent, Greer Johnson. It was after doctors had diagnosed him with cirrhosis of the liver and informed him he would need a transplant to save his life that he reconciled with Merlyn and now, clearly, he was seeking to reconcile with his Maker as well. Betsy and Merlyn spent some time together at Merlyn's home and then, a couple of weeks later, Richardson got a phone call from Mantle's longtime attorney, Roy True, informing him that Mickey had taken a turn for the worse and that the end was near.

"As soon as Roy called, within two hours Betsy and I were flying to Dallas," Richardson related. "When we got there, I went right to the hospital where Hank, Whitey and Moose Skowron were just leaving. Mickey was always upbeat after being with Whitey but when he saw me, he had this smile on his face and he said simply: 'Come over here, Bobby, I can't wait to tell you this. I've trusted Jesus Christ as my savior!'"

His voice cracking slightly, Richardson continued. "I looked at him, lying there, his body wasted away with all those tubes in him and I said: 'Mickey, I love you and I want you to spend eternity in heaven with me.'"

"I'm ready to go, Bobby," Mantle replied. "I've got a real peace."

He lasted a couple more days, but that was the last time Mantle was conscious enough to fully communicate. At the funeral, as promised, Richardson read the Huntley poem and then talked about his personal joy in knowing Mantle had won his greatest victory in his final inning. Before an overflow audience of more than 2,000 mourners, he revealed how Mantle had been asked by Betsy Richardson, "If the Holy God were here today and he would ask why should I let you in my heaven, what would you say?" According to

Richardson, Mantle had responded by reciting John 3:16: "Whoever believes in the Son has eternal life, but whoever rejects the Son will not see life, for God's wrath remains on him."

"The whole thing," said Richardson, "was very humbling. I was staying in a home that morning after he died and we got calls from *Good Morning America*, the *Today* show . . . everybody was trying to get to me. But I didn't want to do any television shows or anything like that so I didn't answer."

"You had been the ultimate teammate to him," I said.

"It was the biggest honor I ever received just to be asked. Nothing I've ever done . . . no award I've ever gotten could ever compare to that."

Listening silently, Betsy clasped his hand and the two of them walked a few steps ahead of me as we headed back to retrieve our shoes. I thought to myself: "How ironic it was that the smallest of those Yankees had seemingly been the one with the most inner strength." Long before it dawned on Mickey, Richardson always understood how "this crowd on earth they soon forget the heroes of the past."

THERE'S TROUBLE ON JOE PEPITONE'S LINE

JOE PEPITONE

"No problem," Joe Pepitone said to me, "when do you want to do it? I'm available just about any time."

"How about tomorrow," I said. "I'll come out to the house and we'll take it from there."

"Great," Pepitone replied. "Call me in the morning for directions. You can call as early as you want. I don't sleep late."

Despite his assurances, I decided to wait until nine o'clock to call him, only to get a busy signal. When I tried back a half-hour later, the phone was still busy. "I can't believe Joe Pepitone, of all people, doesn't have call waiting," I thought to myself. "After all, hadn't he been the one who sought to revolutionize clubhouse life in baseball by having a phone installed in his locker at Yankee Stadium?"

This was, of course, back in the revolutionary '60s, and long before the advent of cell phones. You have to understand. Pepitone *needed* the private phone. He got more phone calls to the clubhouse than all the other Yankees combined. It was also around the same time he'd introduced the hair dryer to baseball. Who'd've ever thought that would be his biggest contribution to baseball? Joe Pep, the hippest Yankee of them all, with his Nehru suits, jewelry and hairpieces was a true renaissance man.

But now his phone was busy . . . and busy . . . and still busy. Finally, after three hours of repeated tries, I gave up, only to be struck with a sudden sinking thought. What if something had happened to Pepitone? It's not like this was some preposterous notion. Ever since he was shot in the belly with a .38-caliber pistol by a schoolmate at Manual Training High in Brooklyn in 1958, we'll never know how many times Joe Pepitone nearly bought it. Heaven knows, he'd hung out with a goodly share of disreputable characters in his lifetime, many of whom, presumably, were quite capable—and equally willing—to curtail that lifetime.

I dialed the operator and asked if she could verify Pepitone's number for busy. After nearly a minute of waiting, the operator came back to me.

"I'm sorry," she said, "there's no conversation there. It appears as if there's some trouble on that line. I'll report it."

"Trouble on Joe Pepitone's line?" I thought. "If she only knew."

The title of his brutally honest 1975 "half-autobiography" (written with Berry Stainback), *Joe You Coulda Made Us Proud*, pretty much told it all about the man who might have been one of the great Yankees, if only he hadn't gotten so quickly caught up in the late-night neon of New York and allowed the wise guys' fast life to blind him to real life. Along with a constant bevy of beautiful women, he had this beautiful left-handed batting stroke, so perfect for Yankee Stadium and its inviting right field porch. And he could pick it at first base with the best of them, past or present, a reflexive attribute that was the by-product of all those 1950s summer afternoons of stickball on St. Mark's Avenue in Brooklyn.

"Those spaldeens came at you so fast," he said, "you had to learn how to react. They can't teach that today, but that's how I learned how to field."

Pepitone, with a capital "P" and that rhymes with "T" and that stands for trouble.

He never met a manager in 12 years in the big leagues he couldn't drive to exasperation. But when it was over, and Pepitone was merely a onetime celebrity ballplayer, it was the family and friends who loved him who were driven most to exasperation. It all kind of hit the breaking point on March 18, 1986, when Pepitone and two companions were arrested for running a red light in the wee hours of the morning on the mean streets of Brooklyn's Brownsville section. A search of their car uncovered about nine ounces of cocaine and 344 Quaalude pills, street value about $6,300, plus a loaded five-shot derringer.

Then there was the time he was found wandering semicoherent through the midtown tunnel that connects Queens and Manhattan at 4:30 in the morning on October 24, 1995. His brand-new Ford had been totaled, a mangled wreck lying in the right lane of the dimly lit tunnel, and both his eye socket and his jaw had been fractured. There was a bloody gash above his left brow and as he searched frantically for a cop or merely a Good Samaritan with a cell phone, all Pepitone wanted was an ambulance. To this day, no one knows exactly what happened; just like no one will ever know for sure what it was that drove Pepitone to take a two-day sabbatical from the Yankees in August of 1969—to go out fishing by himself on a friend's boat in Sheepshead Bay—during which time his friends and teammates feared the worst. We only know that, in all of those instances, he was under extreme duress.

So, yes, I had reason to be concerned the trouble on Joe Pepitone's line might be something darker than the operator's casual dismissal of it—which is why there was a great sense of relief when, upon trying again later that night, the phone was no longer busy and Pepitone picked up on the first ring.

"Oh, man," he said apologetically. "I don't know what happened. I musta knocked the phone off the hook while I was sleeping. I only know my wife came home from work at noontime and woke me up. She was frantic with me. Anyway, I'm sorry, man. Come on out tomorrow morning. I'll be here. I got nothin' planned all week."

For the past 12 years Pepitone and his wife, Stephanie ("Stevie" as he calls her affectionately, or "St. Stephanie" as he refers to her with knowing friends), had lived in this modest split-level home in Farmingdale, Long Island, about 45 minutes equidistant from the Park Slope neighborhood where he grew up in Brooklyn and Yankee Stadium in the Bronx (which he could still call his workplace after being kept on retainer in the Yankees' speakers bureau by owner George Steinbrenner). The Pepitones settled here in suburbia a couple of years after he was released from Rikers Island prison where he'd served a four-month sentence on two misdemeanor drug charges stemming from that 1986 arrest in Brownsville. Before that, flat broke, Pepitone had moved back into the Brooklyn home of his mother—the other "saint" in his life, eighty-something Ann Pepitone, who, he said, "still goes to Atlantic City every week to do her little gambling thing."

As I pulled into the driveway shortly before 11 A.M., he bounded out the front door—as if to instantly assure me that he really *was* here.

"How you doin' buddy," he said. "You'll have to forgive me. I'm nursing a three-day hangover."

Knowing Pepitone as I did, I figured he was just saying this for effect. He really *had* cleaned up his act, sort of, if nothing else for *her,* the saint he lived with, who had gone through her own form of hell these past 30 years they'd been married. Or, at least, I hoped so anyway. Because to know Joe Pepitone was always to like Joe Pepitone, which is really all he ever wanted out of life. He just never felt secure enough to believe people could really like him for who he was, a genuinely giving person—albeit an irrepressible rascal—whose only real weakness was the addiction to celebrity. It's what ultimately eroded his baseball career, and in a related way, what led to his meeting her, the former Stephanie Deeker, a resident of the Playboy mansion in Chicago, in 1970. He was barely a half-year removed from his mostly unfulfilled Yankee career, now a member of the Chicago Cubs, and she was a Playboy Bunny. He was living in an apartment in the Astor House, across the street from the mansion, and she, initially, rejected his advances. He'd already been married twice, and his reputation as a notorious New York playboy and associate with people notorious in a much more sinister way had preceded his grand entrance to Chicago.

And it *was* the grandest of entrances that somehow led to her eventually succumbing to his charms.

"I got sold from Houston over to the Cubs in July of 1970," Pepitone related, "and somehow this guy, who was a limo driver in Chicago and called himself the 'Fabulous Howard,' had heard about me. One day, at the Executive House where I was first staying there, this guy shows up and says to me: 'I'm the Fabulous Howard and your limo is waiting out front. I think we can do a lot for each other.' He's got this big stretch limo and, from that day on, he took me everywhere. Leo Durocher, the Cubs manager, went nuts when I offered him and his coach, Peanuts Lowrey, a ride home after a game one time and they came out and saw this guy waiting in the stretch limo. The Fabulous Howard was just looking for publicity, but that was okay with me. So was I. Anyway, I told the Fabulous Howard: 'As long as I go good, I'll keep you.' One day, he took me over to the Playboy Club and that's when I met Stevie."

He grew up in the Park Slope section of Brooklyn, which, in the '40s and '50s, was largely a blue-collar Irish-Italian neighborhood. His father, Willie—"Willie Pep" as he was called, after the featherweight boxing champion of the late '40s—worked construction after his own paper box company went bankrupt. Pepitone idolized the old man, who, in many ways, was the neighborhood enforcer—at least as far as the Pepitone family was concerned. Willie Pep was a loving father, whose human frailty was that he loved too much—to the point where his temper consumed him.

"My father would knock a guy out if he said anything about me,"

Pepitone related. "He was so high-strung, he just couldn't contain it. My mother worked most of her life in a clothing factory and my father was so jealous that if anyone even looked at her, he'd challenge him to a fight. She loved him like I loved him, but it was tough on both of us."

They lived in a four-story apartment building at 270 St. Marks Avenue, and in the summers Pepitone would play stickball and punch ball in the street with his younger brother, Jimmy. His other brother, Billy, was six years younger, and Willie Pep told him he was supposed to look out for both of them. Whenever either of them got in a fight and came home bruised and cut, Willie Pep took it out on Joe.

"He had this flare temper," Pepitone said, "and I knew that if he said to do something, I'd better do it. He beat the hell out of me a lot of times, but I also know that if he'd lived longer, I'd have never gotten in all the trouble I got in years later. He never drank. He never caroused, never stayed out. He was just very high strung and he'd drop you on a dime if you ever did anything to his family."

From the beginning, Pepitone was a pull hitter—and therefore never had his power judged by the number of sewers he could hit a ball. Four sewers, on St. Mark's Avenue, was a given home run, if only because it was out onto Vanderbilt Avenue where, as Pepitone explained, "you'd get run over by a bus trying to get the ball."

"I pulled everything," he said, "and most of the balls I hit went up into the fire escapes. If you were a pull hitter, you broke a lot of windows so you had to learn how to hit the ball in the street, but I could never do that. I had to go up on the roofs and get all the balls I hit up there. It was hot and heavy and balls would come at you at 100 miles per hour on one bounce. Guys from the neighborhood would be up there on the fire escapes throwin' down money, betting on the games. Teams from the Bronx would come in, in about 10 cars, to play us—real tough guys—and Puerto Rican and black teams. There were crowds on the steps all cheerin' and throwin' down money. It was like going to Ebbets Field—guys throwin' bottles out the window. Unreal. Sunday was the money games.

"One time, during a punch ball game, a guy was laying down some concrete on the curb and, after he got done, I went over and wrote in the cement: 'Joe Pep, 1955.' Years later, when I was in the major leagues, I'd take guys back to the old neighborhood and show them that piece of cement where the inscription was still there. When I did an interview with *Sports Illustrated,* I showed it to them, too. Then I went back about 10 years ago and it was gone. Just last week, I ran into a guy at a golf tournament who said he has that piece of concrete. Turned out his father was doin' some construction in the neighborhood and he saw it and just tore it up and took it home with him. I'm tryin' to get it back from him."

Baseball in Brooklyn was everything in 1950, the borough being consumed with the Dodgers, although, according to Pepitone, his was a family of Yankee fans. About the only time he ever went to Ebbets Field to see the Dodgers was in the early spring when they'd be playing the Yankees in a preseason exhibition game.

"Another time," he said, "I'm there with my father, sittin' in the center field bleachers. It had to be 1951 because Joe D. and Mickey were both playin' for the Yankees. I remember that because Mickey hit two homers that day. Anyway, I had this spaldeen on which I'd written 'I love you Joe D.' and I threw it out onto the field at him as he was standin' there in center field with his back to me. Well, damned if I didn't hit him right in the back! I wanted to die. He looked around to see who threw it, then reached down and just put it in his pocket."

"Your father must have been furious at you," I said.

"Nah," Pepitone said. "He didn't say anything. But it's a good thing Joe D. didn't come up into the stands. My father woulda hit him."

He laughed and then added: "Years later, I asked Joe if he remembered being hit in the back with a spaldeen in Ebbets Field. I told him I was the kid who threw it. He got a kick out of that, or at least I think he did."

From the origin of those stickball games, Pepitone had no doubt as to his true vocation. He was blessed with that swing and through the street games he developed his instincts. In his junior year at Manual Training High, he hit what was said to be the longest ball ever hit by a Brooklyn high school youth, in a game at Fort Hamilton High. It was a shot that cleared the fence 320 feet down the right field line, continued on over two tennis courts before landing on the street beyond and bouncing into a front yard.

"The field was right off the Belt Parkway," Pepitone related, "and nobody could believe how far this ball went, over the tennis courts and into some guy's front lawn. Anyway, they put a bronze plaque there that said: 'Schoolboy Joe Pepitone hit a ball in 1957 that landed here— the longest home run in high school history.' I never saw it, but my friends all insisted it was there for years."

When they weren't playing baseball on the streets and sandlots during those '50s summers, Pepitone and his pals (especially his best friend, the famed "Lemon"—Clement Sebastopoli, who was like an older brother) would head down to the Fox Theater and the Brooklyn Paramount for Alan Freed's Rock 'n' Roll shows in which many of the performers—Johnny Maestro and the Crests, Jay Black and the Americans—were locals like themselves.

"We had this song we'd sing to impress the girls," Pepitone said, launching into a few nostalgic bars of it.

We are the boys from St. Mark's you hear so much about
The ladies hide their pocketbooks whenever we come out
We carry knives and pistols and cigarettes too . . .

"We'd break through doors, and go down the aisles singing this song until the security guys threw us out."

By now the scouts were starting to come around as word of Pepitone's hitting prowess had spread throughout the five boroughs. In particular, a Yankee bird dog scout named Johnny King became a regular observer at the summer stickball games on the Madison High School field. King, who realized Pepitone's talent, ingratiated himself to Joe and his parents. After the games, he'd work with Pepitone on his running and throws from the outfield, teaching him finer points like his release. Pepitone played center field in high school and hit .600 his junior year. That summer he tried out for one of the best semipro teams in Brooklyn—Nathan's Famous Hot Dogs—and made it as a first baseman. The Nathan's team played about 100 games and Pepitone hit .390. King assured him he was going to get a nice bonus, perhaps as much as $75,000.

At the same time, however, Pepitone's father was creating a problem that eventually would affect that bonus. Sitting in the stands at all the games, the high-strung Willie Pep was continually unable to control his emotions whenever Joe would make a mistake in the field or strike out. He wanted so badly for his son to succeed, but his actions—he'd berate Joe and even smack him around after games and engage in fistfights with fans who would boo his son—merely impeded the boy. Finally, it came to a point where King and the other scouts concluded it would be in Pepitone's best interests if his father didn't come around to the games anymore. But when King called the house and relayed those sentiments to Willie Pep, the old man flew into a rage.

"I'm not making him nervous goddammit!" he screamed. "Who do you think you're talking to? If I can't go to the games, my son's not going either!"

Pepitone, listening to this conversation from the other room, was crushed. But before he could say anything, Willie Pep picked up a large ashtray and flung it at him. As Pepitone ducked, the ashtray hit a china closet and smashed into a hundred pieces, a dozen or so shards hitting him in the face. The pain in Pepitone's eyes was piercing from the tiny shards that had landed in them. For a terrifying moment, he thought he'd been blinded. Willie Pep, realizing what he'd done, collapsed in tears. Then, rushing to hug his son, he wiped the blood off Pepitone's face, eased him into the car and rushed him to the hospital, frantically tooting the horn as he weaved though the Brooklyn streets. The doctors successfully removed all the shards of glass from Pepitone's eyes and there was no permanent damage. According to him, from that day on, Willie Pep never again picked up his hands to him.

A few days before Joe's senior year baseball season was to begin, Willie Pep, who was only 39 and in great physical shape, suffered a severe heart attack. While he was recovering in the hospital, an incident occurred at Manual Training High that would put young Joe in the hospital, too—in equally critical condition. The school day was over and Pepitone was at his locker when another student named George O'Dell Jr. pulled out a .38-caliber revolver and began showing it off. Suddenly, he pointed it at Pepitone's belly and shouted: "Stick 'em up!" Just as Pepitone protested to O'Dell that the gun was loaded, it went off. Looking down, the stunned Pepitone saw the hole in his shirt and the pool of blood forming on his belly. As O'Dell ran off, crying, the other students called for help. A teacher quickly arrived on the scene and escorted Pepitone to the nurse's office where it was quickly discovered he'd been severely wounded. A priest was summoned to begin administering the last rites while they all waited for the paramedics to arrive to take him across the street to Methodist Hospital.

"It was bad," Pepitone said, "but I was lucky in that the bullet struck a rib and continued out my back without hitting any of the vital organs. But after that, a lot of the scouts dropped off. Cleveland, I was told, was gonna offer $75,000 and they dropped out. Same thing with the Reds, who wanted to sign me as a pitcher because they liked the way I could throw so much. Anyway, they kept the news of my shooting from my father, who was in Jewish Hospital a couple of miles away. But when he kept asking questions as to where I was and didn't get any satisfactory answers, he instinctively knew something was wrong. Finally, when they saw how agitated he was getting, they told him. Now he *really* was upset and when he refused to take sedatives, they reluctantly agreed to put him in a wheelchair and take him over to Methodist Hospital so he could see me. They wheeled him into my room that morning and we hugged and kissed, both of us crying like hell.

"I was in the hospital 12 days and was back playing ball at Manual Training a few days later. We played in Red Hook Stadium, which had no fences. It was 1,400 feet in right field to the street, and 1,000 feet to left field. You hit the ball over the outfielders' heads and just ran. My first game back, I hit one over the right fielder's head, which should have been an easy home run, but I was so weak I had to walk in from third base."

Upon his own release from the hospital, Willie Pep was no longer allowed to work. As a result, he'd sit home and brood. It was, as Pepitone said, as if his father had lost his manhood. He was miserable—and just as miserable to be around. Then one day, Pepitone and his father got into an argument and Willie Pep began screaming at his wife, who had attempted to intercede in the father-son tempest.

"That's when I had absolutely had it with him," Pepitone said. "I was furious and I just blurted out to my mother 'I wish he'd just die!' It was a Thursday night—I still remember it like it was yesterday—and the next morning we heard him snoring and he couldn't catch his breath. I ran inside and it was like he was just staring at me. But he was dead. I was devastated. To be honest with you, I'm devastated about it to this day. I remember my aunt saying to me—she was an old Italian—'God took your father to give you your life back.' So I always thought it was my fault. I really did. It was heavy. I loved him so much. He was a tough man, but he was good also. After he died, I didn't want to feel good, but it was a lot of pressure off me. I was sad, but I was almost glad. I was on my own now. My mother couldn't tell me what to do. She just gave me whatever I wanted."

Later on that spring of 1958, after proving he was 100 percent recovered from the bullet wound, the scouts renewed their advances and it came down to the Dodgers, Yankees and Phillies. The Phillies brought Pepitone to Shibe Park in Philadelphia where they worked him out and had him take batting practice against future Hall of Famer Robin Roberts.

"I hit three balls into the seats on him," Pepitone recalled. "He was just throwin' junk. The Dodgers offered me $10,000 more than anyone else, but my dad had been a lifelong Yankee fan and so was my Uncle

Louie, who woulda killed me if I didn't sign with them. So I got $23,000 to sign with the Yankees and spent almost all of it in about two months."

He wasn't supposed to report for the beginning of his professional career until the following spring, but a couple of weeks after he signed the contract, the Yankees called and told him they needed an outfielder for their short-season Class D Auburn, New York, farm club in the New York–Penn League.

"I was thrilled to go," Pepitone said. "I went up there and hit .321 in 16 games, which was only about 300 points less than what I'd just hit in high school. But I got a taste. Phil Linz was on that team and we both moved up through the system together. The next year, they sent me up to Fargo-Moorhead, North Dakota, in the Northern League and I led the league with 25 doubles. That earned me an invitation to spring training the following year where they sent me to Binghamton, which was one rung below Triple A. That was the Eastern League and it was a tough league. It was a disaster for me. It was the first time I was seeing sliders and after the great spring training I'd had—I think I hit 11 homers in 13 spring training games to make the Binghamton club—I got real depressed and was ready to quit after hitting just .260 with 13 homers there. Bill Skiff, the Yankees' assistant general manager, came down and got real pissed off at me when I told him I wanted to quit. He said: 'You want to go home? So go home then.'"

Pepitone stuck it out, then, in '61, got assigned to Amarillo in the Texas League, which, like Binghamton, was Double A. The results, however, were decidedly better. He hit .316 with 21 homers and also began playing first base. The Yankees took notice. So, too, did the "fellas" back in Brooklyn. It was sometime early in the '62 season after Pepitone had made the Yankees out of spring training despite the presence of longtime (and still very productive) incumbent Bill Skowron at first base—that a couple of "acquaintances" approached him with an offer he absolutely had to refuse.

"I used to know some people, you know, I'd see at the Copa, the old Italians," Pepitone said, "and one night I'm there and these guys say to me: 'Joe, next year you got that first base job—one way or the other. He can't play first base with broken kneecaps.' I said: 'C'mon, guys! Stop it! I'm gonna make it on my own! Don't worry about nothin'.' So they said, 'Okay, but either way let us know.' That's the way it was back then. Moose was my roommate, for godsakes! I told him about it later and we laughed. I don't think he believed it."

He laughed at what, 40 years later, was a tale so unbelievable as to be a script right out of *The Sopranos*.

It turned out, Pepitone was right about winning the Yankees' first base job on his own—without the need of any outside influencing enforcers. Nevertheless, his lust for the high life and recognition made for a quick but temporary detour.

"Mickey [Mantle] and Moose were the best of friends," Pepitone said, "and when I first got up there, I was out every night. Moose wanted to get his sleep and finally he got sick of me coming in at all hours of the night and put a lock on the door. He later told Mickey one night that I hadn't come home yet and Mickey came down and filled my bed up with shaving cream. That's what they used to do, these guys."

There was no question the personality of the Yankees was changing in the '60s, just as the nation's was. It was an anti-establishment time and the new Yankees, Pepitone, Linz and Jim Bouton, were all free-spirited rebels in their own way. They didn't bow to tradition or pay deference to the Yankee deities. They did their own irreverent thing and hoped the old guard, Mantle, Whitey Ford, Yogi Berra, Elston Howard, Skowron et al., would accept them for what they were.

"We all came up together," Pepitone said. "Jim was different. Phil was a little crazy and me, I just liked to laugh and have a good time. I'd have paid them to be able to play in the majors—and I did."

The irony of it was that Ralph Houk, the Yankee manager at the time, was about as old-school as you could get. A decorated war hero, Houk had come up through the Yankee system and spent seven years in the majors with them as a seldom-used third-string catcher before going back to the minor leagues to hone his managing skills. Pepitone, on the other hand, was something else. Houk could not abide Pepitone's recurring defiances of authority, but at the same time he recognized his vast talent and, like everybody else, could be seduced by his charm.

One classic example of that was the time Pepitone and Mantle were partying all night in Mickey's suite at the St. Moritz Hotel and forgot to leave a wake-up call to go to the team's exhibition game at West Point against the Army cadet team the next day. Bleary-eyed and still in a state of inebriation when they finally awoke around 10 A.M., they rented a limo to take them to West Point—not before dropping off their female companions at another Manhattan hotel.

"We brought a bottle of vodka with us and drank it all the way up," Pepitone recalled, "and when we got there, the limo driver pulled along the third base line. All the guys are standin' around wondering 'who the hell is this pullin' up in a limo?' Houk's got his hands on his hips and you knew he was really pissed. Then, Mickey opens the door and trips and falls out of the car onto the baseline. I'm just watchin' everybody's reaction and I can't believe this. They picked Mickey up and put him on the bench and just left him there. The game went 14 innings and Houk made me play all 14 of 'em in center field. I was lucky that was the worst of it for me.

"But the one confrontation I had with Houk I've never forgotten was the time I hit a pop fly to shallow left field and didn't run it out. The ball fell in and I was on first base when I shoulda been on second. When I came into the dugout afterward, Houk just gave me a look and spit some tobacco on my shoes. Then [Frank] Crosetti came over and told me Houk was hot that I didn't run that ball out. Next time up, same thing . . . ball hit in the same spot, drops in and I'm only at first base. I look in the dugout and Houk's spitting like crazy and I can almost hear him cursing me out. Then, two at bats later, I'm up in the ninth inning. Crosetti gives me the bunt sign from the third base coaching box. I step out because I don't want to bunt. Then I step back in and the next fuckin' pitch I hit out of the ballpark for a game-winning home run. Now I walk past Houk—everyone's congratulating me—and he spits tobacco juice all over my leg.

"When we got into the clubhouse, Houk calls me into his office. I figure he's gonna congratulate me. I go in there and he's on the other side of the room, taking off his shirt. He turns around and says: 'You crossed me three times out there today, now you gotta fight me.' I said: 'C'mon Ralph, are you crazy? I won the fuckin' game!' He said: 'You didn't run out two pop ups and you missed the bunt sign.' I said: 'Ralph, I'm sorry! I'm sorry! I don't wanna fight you! I promise it'll never happen again!' He just looked at me and said: 'Get the hell outa here!'"

"You'd have to agree," I said, "Houk was an old-line Yankee who had never seen the like of free-spirit guys like you and Bouton."

"Yeah," he said with a shrug. "I guess we *were* a little different than what he was used to. But times were changing then. Guys were startin' to grow their hair longer and I guess mine was even longer than most. I was always tryin' to straighten it. That's when I brought the hair dryer into the clubhouse and stirred up all that commotion. I plugged it in and turned around and all the other players are starin' at me. I could just imagine what they were thinkin'. 'Look at this fuckin' fruit cup.' Then they put the talcum powder in it that one time. Before long, though, everybody was usin' the hair dyer."

In his animated retelling of it, he kept running his fingers through his signature, vintage '60s thick, black hairpiece that covers his ears and neck. Some things about Joe Pepitone will never change.

"When did you get your first hairpiece?" I asked him.

"What happened was . . . it was '63 . . . I had my hair . . . and we're in Minnesota at the end of the year, closing in on the pennant. Houk says to me: 'If we win this thing, I'm gonna cut your hair.' So next thing you know, I hit a home run—me and Johnny Blanchard—in Minnesota and we win the ball game. Afterward, they all threw me on the trainer's table and Hector Lopez and Ellie Howard held me down and he cut my hair. Cut a big chunk out of it right down to the scalp and it never grew back. In my locker at Yankee Stadium—Y.A. Tittle used to use it with the Giants during the football season—I found this little partial hairpiece in the bottom of it. Tittle was almost completely bald, but I guess he used it. Anyway, I tried it on, I combed my hair over it and said: 'Sonovabitch! Look at this!' I shoulda kept it and had him sign it. It woulda been worth about $15,000 now. That was the first one. Then I started losin' my hair and I kept into wearing them."

"Just curious," I said, "when you were palling around with Sinatra, did you guys ever get around to comparing hairpieces?"

"Nooooo," Pepitone said, "shit, no! But Frank was good with me. I got introduced to him by Pat Henry, the comedian who opened for him all those years. I knew Henry from my days of hangin' around the Copa. One day, we ran into each other in the city. I was separated and dating this girl and he was living down the street. He said: 'I'm goin' out to see Frank tonight in Palm Springs. Why don't you come with me?' So I met him at the airport and we flew out to Palm Springs and I stayed at Frank's house for two weeks. Broads comin' and goin' all day and night. Fugettaboutit! I was like a kid in the candy store. I was livin' the life I loved!"

It was around the same time Pepitone introduced the hair dryer and hairpieces to the Yankee clubhouse that he attempted to have a telephone installed in his locker—which, of course, would have been another historic first. As he explained it to me all these years later, it was perfectly understandable given the fact that the one pay phone in the clubhouse—on which nearly 90 per cent of the incoming calls were for him—had been removed from the trainer's room.

"What happened was, they pulled the phone outa the trainer's room 'cause I was getting all these calls from the guys—I used to know all these wise guys—but I didn't know what the hell they were doin'. They'd call and say stuff like 'how's Whitey feelin' today'—he'd be pitching. And I'd say, 'I dunno, he's okay, I think.' And they'd ask me all these questions . . . about Mickey's knees and whoever was the starting pitcher that day . . . and the Yankees pulled the phone out because of that.

"So I said: 'Screw it. I want my own fuckin' phone.' So I called the phone company—what the hell, the Yankees were payin' for it—and I said: 'I'm Joe Pepitone and I want to have a phone installed in my locker at Yankee Stadium.' The next day, Houk's holding a clubhouse meeting, and there's a knock on the door. Pete Previte, the clubhouse guy, opens the door and in walks this phone guy, carrying all his equipment. He's got this belt with all these tools and stuff hangin' off it. Houk looks at the guy and says: 'Who the hell are *you?*' and he says: 'I'm from the telephone company. I got a work order here to install a phone in Joe Pepitone's locker.' Well, everybody starts laughing and Houk goes nuts. He yells at the guy: 'Get the fuck out of here! *Do you believe this shit!*' I had to take the guy outside and tell him to get lost before Houk killed him. Later that day, Roy Hamey, the general manager, calls me and says: 'What the hell is *wrong* with you?'"

"It was a reasonable question," I offered.

Pepitone laughed. It was a good thing for him he had talent. The Yankee high command recognized that and, as such, indulged his idiosyncrasies and wayward ways. At the same time, though, they became increasingly frustrated by his failure to reach his potential. There would be hints of greatness—a game-winning homer here or there; the two home runs he hit in one inning in his rookie season; the grand slam in the '64 World Series—but in the end, they were all too few and far between.

"My first full year, 1963," Pepitone said, "Houk called me aside and predicted to me that I'd hit about .270 with 25 homers and 85 RBIs. He was amazing like that. I hit .271 with 27 homers and 89 RBIs. He just knew. He also knew how to treat people. He knew the guys he had to pat on the ass and the other guys he had to kick in the ass. I fell into that latter group.

"One of my worst encounters with Ralph was that first season, in '62. We were in Baltimore and it was around one o'clock in the morning and I had a date with a stripper, who got off at two. Linz was my roomie at the time. So I'm getting dressed. I got a suit and tie on and sprayed myself with cologne and I go to the elevator and the door opens up and who's standing there but Hamey and Houk. Houk says: 'Where the hell do you think *you're* going?' I got to think fast here so

I said: 'Phil didn't get back to the room yet and I'm goin' out lookin' for him. Houk says: 'Get your ass back into that goddamn room' and he follows me down the hall to the room. So I open the door and Houk pushes his way in with me and there's Phil, still sleeping. I yell: 'Phil! How the hell did you get back into the room? What did you do climb through the window?' Houk said: 'That's it. You get your things together. Tomorrow you're gonna find your ass in Richmond.' The next day, sure enough, they sent me to Richmond.''

He got the message—that time anyway. His exile lasted 46 games at Richmond where he batted .315 with eight homers and 27 RBI to earn his recall to the Bronx. Although Yankee teammate Tom Tresh won 1962 American League Rookie of the Year honors, driving in 93 runs in 157 games, Pepitone also had his moments in the 63 games in which he got into the lineup. One of the highlights of his career, he maintained, was the May 23 game against the Kansas City Athletics when he hit two home runs in the eighth inning. And however abbreviated his rookie season may have been, he made a significant enough impression to prompt the front office to trade Skowron to the Dodgers in November of '62 for pitcher Stan Williams. The first base job was Pepitone's—and without any "outside" help.

"When I hit those two homers against Kansas City, they told me the only other Yankee to ever do it was DiMaggio," Pepitone said. "So I felt 'whoa! I'm in for a great career!' Then I hit the grand slam homer in the ['64] World Series and they told me I was like the 10th guy to ever do that. Yeah, I had my moments. You could put my whole '63 season in there, too. I hit .271 with 27 homers and was the only Yankee to make the All-Star team as a starter that year. That was a big thing for me. I was hitting .300 until the last month of the season and then it went down."

And in late August of '63, Pepitone was a central figure in one of the most celebrated baseball brawls of that time. The Yankees were playing a doubleheader against the Cleveland Indians and in the first game, Pepitone went 3-for-4. In the third inning of the second game, Indian pitcher Barry Latman hit him on the wrist with a pitch.

Pepitone assumed that was retribution for the damage he'd done to the Indians in the first game, but when Latman's roommate, Gary Bell, hit him with another pitch in the eighth, he decided to take matters into his own hands.

"I heard Birdie Tebbetts [the Indian manager] had told his pitchers: 'Every time you miss him'—meaning me—'it's gonna cost you $50,'" Pepitone related. "So now, I've already been hit by Latman and Bell's first pitch just misses me and I go down on my ass. I told the home plate umpire, Lou DiMuro, Bell's throwin' at me. DiMuro says: 'Just get up there and hit.' Next pitch is inside, then his fourth pitch he hits me right in the ass. As I'm goin' to first base, I'm cursing Bell and his whole family out. When I got to first, he yells: 'If you want me come and get me!' So I start charging for the mound and Fred Whitfield, the Indians' first baseman, grabs ahold of me. I threw him to the ground and started slugging him. Then, as I'm running to the mound, I see the whole Cleveland ball club comin' at me, but as I turned around, there was no one behind me! I don't know if it was a delayed reaction or what, but they finally all came out and it turned into a helluva fight.

"I always hated Gary Bell after that and then a couple of years ago, I wound up being in the same fantasy camp with him in Florida. He was one of the coaches there, like me. We ran into each other in the bar one night and he turned out to be one of the funniest and nicest guys I ever met. We were drinking together for three days."

In the 1963 World Series, the Yankees were swept by the Dodgers and held to three runs in the four games. Other than their own stellar (if luckless) pitching, the Yankees simply couldn't seem to do anything. The Series' final insult for them was a fielding lapse by Pepitone—already considered their best defensive player—in the fourth game. The score was tied 1–1 when the Dodgers' Junior Gilliam led off the seventh inning with a grounder to Clete Boyer at third. It should have been a routine out, except Pepitone lost sight of Boyer's throw in the sun's glare and sea of white shirts in the stands, and Gilliam wound up at third. An ensuing sacrifice fly to deep center by

Willie Davis brought him home with what proved to be the game-winning and Series-winning run.

"I saw the ball when it left Clete's hands, but then I lost it in those shirts," Pepitone said. "I had to live with that for a long time afterward, even though we had pretty much lost the Series by then, being down 0-3. And then came '64, the only year I had 100 RBIs. Yogi was the manager and he made me play every game. I loved playing for Yogi and I was probably more crushed than anyone when they fired him after the season—especially once I got to know Johnny Keane."

Keane, Berra's successor, was hired from the St. Louis Cardinals after beating the Yankees in that '64 Series. He had come strongly recommended by Houk, who had moved upstairs to the general manager's job. Houk had managed against Keane in the minor leagues years earlier, but it soon became evident that turning the club over to an outsider who didn't know or understand the personalities of this veteran team that had won five straight American League pennants was a huge mistake. As the team went into an immediate and dramatic decline, Keane clashed with just about everyone, none more so than Pepitone.

By 1965, Pepitone's high living had left him with a mound of debt and marital trouble, and his play began to reflect that. He was fined twice by Keane that year for showing up late to the ballpark. The following spring he was reprimanded—but not fined—for missing the team bus for a trip to Orlando after claiming he had a bad leg that prevented him from getting out of bed.

"He's got to prove to me he's a careful ballplayer instead of a careless one," the unsympathetic Keane said. "He knows the other players don't like it any more than I do. But there's no malice in this boy, no real badness. It's just time he grew up."

"Keane was just different," Pepitone said now. "He was tough on everybody, even Mickey. He accused me of fooling around with his daughter that spring [of '66]."

"Were you?"

"[Laughter] It wasn't my fault! I'd be layin' on the beach in Fort

Lauderdale and she'd come down, wearing her bikini, and she'd jump on me. And she'd be there talkin' to me. She said, 'Why don't we meet later and go out to dinner.' I said: 'Okay, we can do that, but we gotta keep it on the quiet.' We did, but she was always on the beach with me. But then Vern Benson, one of Keane's coaches, reported back to him that I was carrying on with his daughter.

"Nobody liked playing for Keane. He came in with all these situation plays and curfews and rules and he'd hold these meetings and scream at us. Who the fuck ever screamed at the Yankees? We never heard that. Mickey said: 'What the hell is this?' Then they fired Keane, what was it? Twenty games into the '66 season? He came into the clubhouse and he was cryin' in a team meeting and nobody fuckin' cared. Keane just got off on the wrong foot with that club and that was it. That was still a good ball club and it was terrible the way they let Yogi go after the season he'd had. Yogi knew the team, knew the pitching and knew the guys. Keane didn't know any of that. He was a National League manager. I remember one time, in '65, he took me out of a game after I'd hit two home runs in my first two times at bat! There was a left-hander pitchin' and he sent Phil Linz up for me. I was walkin' out of the dugout to the on-deck circle and Phil says he's pinch-hitting for me and he's laughin'. I went back and cursed out Keane and threw my bat down."

For all his misery playing for Keane, Pepitone won his only two Gold Gloves for defensive excellence in '65 and '66, and while the return of Houk to the manager's chair represented a return to the Yankee way, the team had deteriorated to the point where it didn't much matter who the manager was. Mantle's chronically creaky legs had rendered him a shell of the five-tool superstar player he'd been from '53 to '63 and the team seemed to be a reflection of him. As for Pepitone, much as he may have welcomed Keane's ouster, it didn't stop him from causing just as much grief for Houk.

In '68, missing 54 games due to a variety of injuries, Pepitone hit just .245. It was Houk's opinion—shared by the front office—that Pepitone's injuries were largely the result of his failure to be in top condition. By the end of the '68 season, Houk was platooning Pepitone at first base. Then, in August the following season, Pepitone drove Houk to the breaking point by twice going AWOL. On August 12 and 13, he was a no-show for the Yankees' games against the Twins, explaining later he had "personal matters that made it impossible for me to be at the stadium." Then, on August 29, after arguing with Houk before the game, Pepitone left the ballpark and disappeared for two days, thus becoming the first Yankee since Buddy Rosar in 1942 to be suspended by the club. When nobody heard from him, an all-points bulletin was issued and the Yankee players began fearing he'd met an untimely demise.

"I was just pissed off about a lot of things," Pepitone recounted, momentarily gazing out the dining room window at the swimming pool beyond. "Hell, I led the club in home runs in '69. But there were a lot of things going on at the time and I just decided I needed to get away from it all. I was out at Coney Island with some friends. We were at this beach club. I had given my car to one of my friends and I was gonna take a cab to the ballpark and then I just said, 'screw it.' I borrowed this 60-foot boat from my friend—we called him Freddie Bayside 'cause he owned this big company Bayside Fuel Oil—and I took it out into Sheepshead Bay for about a day. I came back to the dock—I was starvin'—and pulled up and all these cops are waitin' there for me. I know Ellie and the guys all thought I was dead somewhere inside a trunk."

Whether he realized it or not, that was the last straw for the Yankees. Even Houk no longer believed he was ever going to live up to his ability and, that being the case, the club decided to cut their losses and trade him. It did not matter if he'd just led the team in homers. They'd finally wearied of his antics and, on December 4, 1969, sent him to the Houston Astros for outfielder Curt Blefary. According to Pepitone, he had grown just as weary of the Yankees.

"It was time for me to go," he said. "We had a bad ball club and I'd been used to winning. I got a call from Bruce Henry, the traveling secretary, at my hair-styling salon on Flatbush Avenue in Brooklyn. He said: 'You've been traded to Houston. My first reaction was that I wasn't going, but my partner in the salon talked me into going. Can you imagine *me*—in *Houston?* I absolutely hated it. The Astrodome was hot, a big park where the ball didn't carry. My manager there, Harry Walker, was another Keane, preaching all that old-time shit. He had me leading off and told me to hit the ball to left. I don't know, maybe it was me all those years."

He lasted barely five months in Houston and, after another of his characteristic walkouts, was sold to the Chicago Cubs July 27, 1970. At first, it was a perfect marriage—Pepi and Cubs manager Leo Durocher, a colorful baseball character in his own right. With the Playboy Mansion, Fabulous Howard, the Rush Street nightlife and the "Friendly Confines" of cozy Wrigley Field, Chicago was definitely Pepitone's kind of town. He finished that first season with 26 homers and 79 RBI shifting between center field and first base. In '71, he hit over .300 (.307 in 115 games) for the only time in his career. But like New York, Chicago and its nightlife soon engulfed him. He was now making alimony payments to a second ex-wife and, with a $40,000 loan, opened up his own bar called Joe Pepitone's Thing on Division Street, just off Rush. The lounge made money the first nine months until it, too, began to consume him, and when a drug probe of all the bars in the area was announced, business fell off dramatically and Pepitone finally sold out.

It all began to unravel in 1972. Between his contentious alimony hearings, the problems at the lounge and an early-season batting slump, Pepitone began to experience stomach problems. On May 2, he asked the Cubs to put him on the voluntary retired list. Once again, he had dropped out. This one lasted a month, but when he came back, his teammates didn't exactly welcome him with open arms. And when Durocher was fired in late July of '72 and replaced by Whitey Lockman, Pepitone discovered he no longer had a kindred spirit in the manager's office. In a meeting with Lockman prior to the '73 season, Pepitone vowed to have a good year, assuring his manager he'd gotten his act together.

"I'm only 32," he told Lockman. "I'm in good shape and I can hit the ball better than half the assholes in this league."

"You don't have to sell me that you can play baseball, Joe," Lockman replied. "I know that. I've seen you. The thing is do you *want* to play? Do you *really* want to play. You got a lot of things to prove to a lot of guys on this club. Do you know what I mean?"

Apparently, Whitey Lockman was not a believer in Pepitone. The problem was he'd seen too much of Pepitone and, shortly after the season began, he started platooning him at first base with Jim Hickman. Finally, on May 19, the Cubs traded Pepitone to the Atlanta Braves for minor league outfielder–first baseman Andre Thornton, who went on to have a fine career, hitting 253 homers, mostly with the Cleveland Indians.

"This is best for all concerned," Lockman assured Pepitone.

Easy for him to say. He was getting rid of a headache. For Pepitone, who was forced to leave his new wife, Stephanie, in Chicago, it was the final message of a career unfulfilled. He appeared in only three games for the Braves and walked away from baseball again after the '73 season—this time for good—save the brief and traumatic flirtation in Japan the following spring which ended with a broken ankle and a plaintive, long-distance bylined plea in the *New York Times:* "Please don't let me die here."

His final numbers for 12 big league seasons—.258, 219 homers, 721 RBI—pretty much summed up the wise guys' lament: Joe, you coulda made us proud.

"Looking back," I asked, "do you ever think it's a wonder you're still alive?"

"If it wasn't for my wife and it wasn't for me—ultimately—and a couple of other friends like George [Steinbrenner], I know I wouldn't be here now," he replied. "I just went to extremes—with everything. I never put a needle in my arm, but I did my drugs and other stuff. I just made up my mind one day to stay away from it. My wife's been a recovering alcoholic for 18 years and if it wasn't for her getting straight, I'd still be fuckin' crazy or, probably, dead. Now I have some wine or a few vodkas with my friends, but as far as goin' out and stayin' out, that's gone. Can't do it. I feel good. I'm healthy and I want to do more things with family. That's what's happening."

Of course, those four months in the Rikers Island slammer had been a rude awakening for him and should have been sufficient incentive to give anyone a new perspective on life.

"When I went away for those four months it seemed like it was 10 years," Pepitone said. "I never want to be caught with anything or doin' anything or bein' with anyone that's gonna get myself locked up again. What you go through mentally and then comin' out and havin' people look at you. What about George? What he did for me when I got out? And when I was in there? He got me on work release. And then when I got out, he had a job for me with the Yankees. If I didn't have that—if it weren't for George and my wife, I'd be dead in the streets. You'd find me in an alley somewhere."

"Did you ask yourself: 'How did it all come to this?'" I queried.

"No," he said, "because I *knew* how it had. I'll say this: I didn't know what was goin' on in that car that night. I was just gettin' a ride home with these guys. When they searched the car they found the gun, which I knew wasn't mine. Then they found some 'ludes in the back seat. I'm sayin' to myself: 'I'm okay. The gun ain't mine' and I didn't know about the other stuff. Then I hear this applauding and the next thing I know they found, tied to the trunk inside the back seat, all this cocaine. They charged me with five A-1 felonies and if I was convicted on one of 'em, I had to do a mandatory 16 years. Thank God, I had good lawyers and a good jury. Their whole case was against me. The prosecutors had champagne ready. But that's what happens when you get involved with a little drugs and you meet certain people."

Despite being acquitted of the serious drug charges, the jury found Pepitone guilty of possessing the Quaaludes as well as the glassine envelopes used to package narcotics. At his sentencing, New York Supreme Court Judge Alan Marrus rejected a Probation Department recommendation that Pepitone be given probation and perform community service and instead issued a stern condemnation of him.

"At one time, you were a special person, Bronx Bomber; now you're an ordinary Brooklyn criminal," Marrus said. "Once a first-rate baseball player, you now stand before this court as a second-rate drug operator. I'm afraid you're going to be remembered more for the bag inside the car than the bag at first base. I have no reason to believe you've straightened yourself out."

It could have been a lot worse, and thanks to his influential friends like Steinbrenner, he was spared the hard time—even for misdemeanor charges—the authorities had striven to lay on him. Much of his prison time was spent in a work release program, on a ferryboat docked off Hart Island. Even so, as he went though the boring, daily ritual of unloading cargo, Pepitone looked back on his life . . . those carefree, intoxicating days with Mantle . . . the $500 tip nights at the Copa . . . even the effervescent twilight years in Chicago . . . and regretted only the people he'd hurt along the way in arriving at this place.

If nothing else, he thought, he'd done it his way, just not with nearly the degree of success and acclaim of his idol, Sinatra. Regrets? Oh yeah, Joe Pepitone had a few—really too many—to mention. But at least he still had his health, his home and a loving woman. And considering all he'd done to potentially blow all of that, life was good for the eternal incorrigible as he approached the early-retirement age of 62.

He offered me a tour of the house, and after checking out the pool, I followed him to the lower level where, sporadically displayed, were the few remaining pieces of memorabilia from his career. The first item that caught my eye was a huge picture of Pepitone and Joe DiMaggio, circa 1962. On one wall was the framed cover of the *Sporting News*, September 26, 1970, with Pepitone posing in his Cubs uniform underneath the headline: 'Funny Pepi Bum Joke to Cub Foes.' On another wall was a framed picture of the 1964 Yankee infield of Pepitone, Bobby Richardson, Tony Kubek and Boyer.

"It's kind of nice being safe at home, isn't it?" I said to him. "It's sure a long way from Rikers Island."

He nodded and put his hand on my shoulder.

"If it weren't for the Yankees, where would I be?" he said. "Everybody still knows me. I wish I could change the things that happened that hurt me, and my family. I always liked to smile, and I don't like people being pissed off at me. I just loved being noticed, hangin' out with the big guys. All my life, I still get flashbacks. I'll be drivin' and I'll see somethin' that knocks the shit out of me. You got to fight 'em off and I do. I learned that from my wife.

"But you know what? I had great times. I've had a great fuckin' life. I had my ups and my downs. I think if I'd had good times all the time, I'd probably be bored. I like fightin' back. I know what I coulda been. I know I made mess of a lot of things. It wouldn't have been that way if my father was alive. If he was alive, I'd have money today and I wouldn't have been married three times. You never think it's gonna catch up, but it does. You can't play ball without sleep."

Fitting words for his epitaph, I thought. Yet somehow Joe Pepitone was still here, still famous in his own right, still a Yankee, and, for the moment anyway, trouble-free.

DESIGNATED HEBREW

RON BLOMBERG

Maybe if he'd had a better understanding in the first place of what it meant to be the first significant Jewish Yankee, Ron Blomberg wouldn't have been quite so accepting of the fact that he never became the first [and only] *great* Jewish Yankee. That was who he was supposed to be after all—the long-awaited replacement for the great one who got away all those years ago, Hank Greenberg. And it didn't matter that he was, of all things, a *Georgia* Jew, even if that seemed so incongruous. From that June day in 1967 when the Yankees announced they had selected this hulking, 6-1, 200-pound left-handed hitting first baseman from DeKalb Junior College in Georgia with the No. 1 overall pick in the draft, the Jewish community of New York embraced him as its own.

"I remember the day I signed I had so many people in New York I didn't know calling me up," Blomberg said. "Large corporations calling me; clothing stores in the garment district, calling to say: 'We want you to come down and pick out some suits and shirts. We want you to be our savior. We've never had a Jewish Yankee.' "

Well, actually, there *was* one before him. Jimmie Reese, whose real name was James Herman Soloman, was a backup second baseman for the Yankees in the '30s after being sold to them along with shortstop Lyn Lary from the Pacific Coast League Los Angeles Angels for what was then a record price of $125,000. During his two years with the Yankees, Reese roomed with Babe Ruth on the road, or, more precisely, as he put it: "I roomed with his suitcase." It wasn't until decades later, however, that Reese attained his greatest notoriety as an aged coach and fungo master with the California Angels. Greenberg, on the other hand, was something else. One of the most prodigious right-handed power hitters in baseball history who won four home run titles (including 58 in 1938), Greenberg was born and raised in the Bronx, graduated from James Monroe High School and enrolled at NYU after failing to attract any decent offers to play professional baseball. It was while playing semipro baseball during the summer of 1929 after graduating from high school that Greenberg finally began attracting the attention of the major league scouts, in particular Paul Krichell, the Yankees' New York area and East Coast scouting chieftain. Greenberg initially wanted to sign with the Yankees, too. But then Krichell made the mistake of taking him to watch a Yankee game where Lou Gehrig (whom Krichell had signed a few years earlier off the Columbia campus) was in his prime as their first baseman.

As Greenberg explained it in his 1989 autobiography, written with Ira Berkow of the *New York Times:* "I was so awed at the sight of Gehrig kneeling in the on-deck circle only a few feet away. His shoulders were a yard wide and his legs looked like mighty oak trees. I'd never seen such brute strength and I said to myself: 'No way am I going to sign with this team—not with *him* playing first base."

Though Krichell offered him a bonus of $10,000, Greenberg opted for the $3,000 up-front cash deal to sign with the Detroit Tigers and another $6,000 when he reported upon finishing his freshman year at college. That was how the Yankees missed out on the greatest Jewish hitter ever to come out of New York. Blomberg, however, knew little about Greenberg and matter-of-factly admitted as much when the inevitable questions were posed to him at the celebratory press conference, June 20, 1967, at Yankee Stadium announcing his official signing with the Yankees for a bonus of $97,000. No doubt, the old-timers in the New York Jewish community wished this new hope from Georgia (who would soon be anointed by the New York press corps with the appropriate nickname "Li'l Abner" for his folksy innocence) had a deeper appreciation for his faith's baseball heritage. But because they had waited so long—nearly 40 years—for the second coming of Greenberg, they didn't really care *from where* he was coming.

It had taken him a couple of months to get over his fear of flying and airports in the aftermath of the September 11 terrorist attacks, but he was clearly at ease and in his element at the Yankees' 2002 annual Old-Timers' Day gathering. We had arranged to meet at the Millennium Hotel on 44th and Broadway where the Yankees had put up all the old-timers and their families for the two-day festivities. When I arrived for our appointment, shortly before 4 P.M., a small crowd of collectors was gathered on the sidewalk in front of the main entrance. One of them, I couldn't help but notice, was holding an 8-by-10 color photo of Blomberg with the inscription "First Designated Hitter" along the bottom border.

"The one thing they can never take away from him," I thought.

After waiting in the lobby for about 15 minutes, I looked around for a house phone to call upstairs to let him know I was here when he suddenly emerged out of the elevator.

"Sorry I'm late," he said. "Have you been waiting long? You know what happened? I was down the hallway visiting with a friend and we got to talking and I forgot all about what time it was. You know how that is?"

With Ron Blomberg, I knew how that was.

He never met a reporter he wouldn't talk to . . . and talk to . . . and talk to. Former Yankee manager Bob Lemon once said of the equally loquacious Tommy John: "If you ask him what time it is, he'll tell you how to make a watch." With Blomberg, if you asked him if he had a minute, he'd reply, with a forlorn look: "That's all?"

"Did you see all your fans out there in the street?" I said to him as we gravitated to a secluded table in the back corner of the hotel lounge.

"Oh yeah," he said, smiling. "I can't get over how they still remember me. It's such a thrill to come here and to see all these people and be treated the same way as the big stars. It's a thrill just *being around* the big stars."

"You *do* have your own place in baseball history," I countered.

It came—entirely by accident—at a time his career appeared on the rise after a somewhat sluggish start. After the 1972 season (during which the players staged a 13-day strike that caused the cancellation of 86 games) the baseball owners, concerned with the decrease of scoring, initiated the most dramatic rules change in the game's history with the introduction of the designated hitter. The DH was to take the place of the (traditionally weak-hitting) pitcher in the batting order and would not play in the field. It was decided by the owners the DH would be used on an experimental basis, and only in the American League.

As a result, late in the '72 season and over the winter, American League clubs began scurrying about for veteran accomplished hitters from the National League whose diminished defensive skills would no longer be a detriment. Most notably, the Boston Red Sox brought in Orlando Cepeda; the California Angels traded for Frank Robinson; the Texas Rangers for Rico Carty; the Oakland A's for Deron Johnson; and the Milwaukee Brewers for Ollie Brown. The Yankees, on the other hand, didn't feel they immediately needed to go fossil hunting in the National League for their designated hitter. The way they saw it, they had a natural DH in Blomberg, whose big-boned, heavily muscled body never seemed adaptable to the outfield—where he'd played almost exclusively in four years in their minor league system—and they were less than enthused with his defensive work at first base, his primary position for them his first two years in the majors. In addition, there was a growing concern among the Yankee brass about Blomberg's propensity for pulling muscles. They still liked his bat, though, especially against right-handed pitching.

With barely a week left in spring training 1973, Blomberg was sidelined by a pulled hamstring and limited to taking only batting practice. Yankee manager Ralph Houk approached him one morning and said: "Do you think you'll be able to hit four times on Opening Day?" Not quite comprehending what Houk was getting at, Blomberg replied: "Sure, I'll be ready, Skip."

"When Houk explained he wanted to use me as his DH, I didn't know what to think," Blomberg related. "I thought it was a gimmick, like a big pinch hitter. But I couldn't play in the field and, so, when Ralph made this proposal to me about just hitting, I jumped at it. Then, I wondered what I'd accepted. I said to [coach] Ellie Howard: 'What do I *do*?' He said: 'Just go up there four times, swing the bat and sit down.' I told Houk and the coaches I still wanted to take ground balls at first base and they said: 'No! Just hit!'"

There are those people whose every walk of their lives seems as if by accident. Blomberg was the epitome of this. He never understood why his being Jewish was a big deal to so many New York baseball fans. He was mostly unfazed at being the overall No. 1 pick in the 1967 June draft. And when fate bestowed the ultimate accident of baseball fame upon him with the start of the Yankees–Red Sox 1973 Opening Day at Fenway Park being scheduled earlier than any other American League game, Blomberg was oblivious to the significance of that.

"What I remember most about that game," he said, "was that it was freezing in Boston and while I was waiting in the clubhouse to hit, Vince Orlando, the visiting clubhouse man, gave me hot chocolate to stay warm. Luis Tiant was pitching for the Red Sox and he was hard enough to hit in normal conditions. But the cold was tougher on him than it was on the hitters and he had control problems that day. I was the No. 6 hitter and Tiant's wildness probably allowed me to come to bat in the first inning. The bases were loaded when I came to bat for the first time, and after running the count to 3-2, I drew a walk."

The scoreboard clock showed 1:53 when Blomberg had come to bat that first time and it was not until a cursory check was made of all the other American League games that it was officially determined Blomberg had been the first designated hitter. But it was not until after the game (which the Yankees wound up losing 15–5) that it finally began to dawn on Blomberg he'd done something truly historic (if, again, purely by accident).

"Here we were, having just gotten beaten 15–5, and there must have been 25 reporters around me in the clubhouse afterward," Blomberg recalled. "Then, in the middle of it all, Marty Appel, the Yankees' publicity director, came up to me and said: 'Let me have your bat. It's going to the Hall of Fame.' I said: 'Hall of Fame? Why?' And he said: 'Because this is history. You were the first-ever designated hitter.' I said: 'You gotta be kidding!'"

Despite Blomberg's initial success (he went 1-for-3 in addition to that bases-loaded walk), the Yankees had become convinced he couldn't hit left-handed pitching and, a couple of weeks into the '73 season, they followed suit of so many of the other AL clubs by purchasing veteran right-handed hitter Jim Ray Hart from the San Francisco Giants. For the rest of the year, the Yankees' DH slot was a platoon situation with Blomberg hitting a career high .329 with 12 homers and 57 RBI in 301 at bats (including 41 games at first base) and Hart batting .254 with 13 homers and 52 RBI in 339 at bats.

In periodic interviews over the ensuing years, Blomberg was fond of telling people he was in the Hall of Fame, an innocent enough exaggeration, even if he had seemed to grow entirely too accustomed to omitting the fact that it was his *bat* that had a place in Cooperstown. Certainly, he did become a historic figure in baseball history, and, just as certainly, the Yankees envisioned him becoming a player of Hall of Fame proportions. If only the designated hitter rule had served its other purpose—prolonging one's career by providing a safe haven from injury—maybe he'd exist in the Hall today in body as well as mind.

The irony was he'd been a multi-sport star in high school and junior college. His senior year in high school he was selected for *Parade Magazine*'s America basketball team and signed a letter of intent to go to UCLA to play for the legendary Johnny Wooden's perennial national champions.

"I had close to 150 basketball scholarships," Blomberg said, "but at the same time I knew I was gonna be a high pick in the baseball draft and if the Yankees took me, I was gonna sign with them. I had always been a Yankee fan. Mickey Mantle was my idol growing up in Atlanta and, being Jewish and living down South, I just figured it would be a perfect fit coming up to New York. Even though the Yankees were awful then, I saw it as the fulfillment of a dream when I signed with them in '67. Mickey was still there, playing first base. Joe Pepitone was there with his hairdo, and I got interviewed by Phil Rizzuto, Frank Messer and Bill White. It was an exciting time for me. The Yankees put me and my family up at the Hilton Hotel, and on the billboard outside was a sign that said: 'Welcome Ron Blomberg. Drafted No. 1 by the New York Yankees.' You have to understand, that was a big deal back then. The Yankees also got us tickets to see *Fiddler on the Roof* [what else?] and Michael Burke, the team president, was a real marketing guy, who also did a lot for me."

It took Blomberg four years to work his way through the Yankee minor league system to a permanent place in the Bronx where Burke could begin to work his marketing and promotional skill with his Jewish slugging prodigy. In particular, reports of Blomberg's voracious appetite had preceded him. While playing for Kinston, North Carolina, in the Class A Carolina League in 1968, he was hungry after a game and stopped at a restaurant in Kernersville, North Carolina, that was offering a free 72-ounce steak to anyone who could devour it, in its entirety, within one hour. Otherwise, the dinner cost $25. Blomberg took half the allotted time to earn himself a free dinner.

Another time, when he was in high school, a local McDonald's was offering a deal of a free hamburger for any patron who could produce a 1956 penny. Blomberg happened to have 28 of them—and used them all in one sitting of 28 burgers. There was also the story—confirmed later by his then wife, Mara—of Blomberg stopping off at a restaurant on his way home from Yankee Stadium in his rookie year for a "snack" before going out to dinner. His dinner plans weren't until 7:30 and, being that it was only 6:00, he was hungry. At the restaurant near his hotel in Paramus, New Jersey, he consumed two hamburgers, two steak sandwiches, a hot dog, two orders of potato salad and a pitcher of iced tea. Less than two hours later, he and Mara arrived at the restaurant where they'd made reservations and Blomberg had himself a full-course steak dinner.

"There were a lot of restaurants that banned me from eating there," Blomberg said, laughing softly. "I admit I could really eat. I guess it was something about my metabolism, but I never got fat."

Not long after he joined the Yankees in 1971, a flamboyant, millionaire record company executive named Nat Tarnopol—presumably with Burke's full approval—instinctively seized on the Blomberg appetite legend and began arranging appearances for the Yankees' celebrated No. 1 draft pick at delicatessens and restaurant openings all over the city. For his part, Blomberg established as his restaurant of choice the famous Stage Deli on Seventh Avenue, which, not coincidentally, was right next door to Tarnopol's Brunswick Records offices.

The president of Brunswick Records, Tarnopol was what you would consider a glorified baseball groupie. He had his own season box at Yankee Stadium—right next to the Yankee dugout and directly behind Houk's box—and, between his wealth and connections, was able to befriend many of the Yankee stars such as Thurman Munson, as well as opposing players and managers, whom he would often entertain at his mansion in Purchase, New York. But in Blomberg he saw a kindred Jewish spirit and, as such, took it upon himself to serve as his unofficial agent. According to Appel, Tarnopol enjoyed a free run around Yankee Stadium in those days and would frequently pop in, unannounced, to GM Gabe Paul's office with promotional propositions for Blomberg.

"Nat would say: 'Gabe, ya gotta have a day for Blomberg,'" Appel recalled, "and Gabe would brush him off by saying something like: 'He's only been here two years' to which Nat would retort: 'You don't understand, Gabe, it's the *future* you need to be concerned with!'"

Tarnopol, who was indicted in July of 1975 for income tax invasion as part of a federal probe into payola in the record business, died in 1987. His conviction on conspiracy charges was later overturned on appeal and, despite the scandal, Blomberg remained close friends with him.

"Nat Tarnopol was like a second father to me when I came to New York," Blomberg said. "He took me all over the city, to restaurants and clothing stores and he gave me a brand-new 450 SL Mercedes—just for being his friend! I got to meet a lot of famous people in the entertainment business through him—Jay Black . . . Frankie Valli . . . Soupy Sales. I think because of that, some of the other players on the team were jealous of me, especially in those early years with the team."

In fact, Blomberg's closest friends during his all too brief seven years with the Yankees were probably the writers who covered the team. On any given night on the road, he'd just as likely be seen dining with a group of the beat writers than any of his teammates. And because he was always such a refreshingly uninhibited quote, the writers would flock to his locker after games, even when he hadn't done anything to merit being interviewed. That, too, didn't sit well with his teammates.

After an ill-fated final tour of duty with the Chicago White Sox in 1978 led to his release with nearly $400,000 still due him on a three-year $600,000 deal, Blomberg made a public plea to the Yankees to bring him back—if nothing else for attendance reasons—in a column by Phil Pepe of the *Daily News*.

"Just give me a chance," he said. "Let me come down to spring training and look at me in the batting cage. The Chicago thing was unfortunate, but I'm not a troublemaker. I'm too nice a guy and maybe I'm naive. They don't have anything to draw fans. I'll draw fans. I'll say stuff nobody else says. What do they have now to draw fans? Lee Mazzilli [the Mets star at that time] has to get in a fight with Elliott Maddox. Elliott is a black Jew. What the Yankees need is a white Jew."

The reality of the situation—which Blomberg knew all too well—was that the Yankees had given him more than enough chances to reach his potential. Nobody wanted him to succeed more than Burke and, later, George Steinbrenner, if for no other reason than his box office appeal to one of the largest ethnic contingents in the metropolitan area. Unfortunately, every time success appeared to be within his grasp, his body betrayed him. Or, as was the case in his early years, he was done in by left-handers.

He was hitting .403 as late as June 28 in the '73 season, facing predominantly right-handed pitching, and he was featured on the cover of both *Sports Illustrated* and the *Sporting News* that summer. But as Houk pointed out a couple of weeks later, Blomberg had managed only three hits in 53 at bats against lefties from spring training until July 1. Still, the letters came pouring in imploring him to let Blomberg play every day.

"You would be amazed how many there are and how many stories are written about what a fool I am not to play Ronnie against left-handers," Houk said. "But I'd be foolish to take a chance of losing a ball game by doing it."

All these years later, Blomberg seemed to have a selective memory about his inability to hit lefties. As he remembered it, he never was given enough of a chance to hit against them to prove his critics' point.

"My first stop in the minor leagues—Johnson City, Tennessee, in 1967—two of my teammates who later went on to the big leagues, too, Cesar Geronimo and Rusty Torres, came to me and said they'd never seen a sweeter swing than mine," Blomberg said. "But when I got to Triple A with Syracuse a couple of years later, my manager there, Frank Verdi, told me he was only gonna play me against right-handed pitchers because he had a lot of veteran players there who had to play because they'd been with him the previous year. After that, I got this reputation for not being able to hit lefties. To this day, Ralph will tell you he didn't let me hit against lefties because he had too many other players."

He went on to expound about the day he hit a ninth-inning, walk-off home run off Sudden Sam McDowell, the most feared left-handed pitcher in the American League in the late '60s and early '70s. It was at Yankee Stadium, he said, and it won the game for the Yankees.

"The only reason Ralph let me hit against McDowell that day," he said, "was because he didn't have any right-handed pinch hitters left on the bench. After the game everyone was congratulating me and *still* Ralph wouldn't let me hit against lefties after that."

It was a compelling story. The only problem with it was it never happened. According to the record books, the only year it could have happened was 1971, McDowell's last year in the American League before he was traded from the Cleveland Indians to the Giants. Blomberg hit seven home runs in 64 games that year, but none of them came against McDowell. In fact, research of all 52 of his career home runs shows only two of them hit against left-handers—the first off former Yankee teammate Mike Kekich, July 1, 1973, and the other off Bill Butler of the Minnesota Twins, June 2, 1974.

Still, I didn't have the heart to challenge Blomberg on his Sudden Sam story. He'd made it sound so genuine with his impassioned detail, and I figured what was the harm if, in his own mind anyway, it really did happen. Just the way he said it did. With his teammates mobbing him afterward and the writers all eagerly chronicling the feat as the lead story in their newspapers that day while further editorializing the injustice of Houk not allowing him to use that sweet swing against all pitching. In this respect, I thought, Blomberg was still an innocent.

He had his pride, of course, but he could also poke fun at himself and his shortcomings and idiosyncrasies. Like the night he got up on the stage at the New York baseball writers dinner in 1975 and took part in a song parody (to the Broadway show tune "Bye Bye Birdie") about his inability to hit lefties. While he may have always believed in his heart he could hit them, he accepted the contrary opinion affably.

Bye bye Blomberg, John Hiller's in to pitch
Bye bye Blomberg, lefties are such a bitch
No more righties, lefties are all you'll see
Bye bye Blomberg, now here comes tough Bill Lee
You can't hit Paul Splittorff . . . or Cleveland's Hilgendorf
And we've seen Vida Blue make such a shmuck of you!

Ultimately, though, it was the injuries that doomed him to a footnote in Yankee history instead of a place in Monument Park. He hit .311 with 10 homers and 46 RBI in 90 games in 1974—almost exclusively against right-handers—and that proved to be his last "complete" season. His next three years with the Yankees he played a total of 35 games. The first major injury occurred in Milwaukee in early May 1975 when, swinging hard on a ground ball to Brewers first baseman George Scott, Blomberg felt something pop in his shoulder. At first, it seemed like just a strained muscle. Until then all of his assorted injuries had been minor in nature, nagging muscle pulls and strains. But a couple of days later, in Anaheim, Blomberg was taking batting practice before the Yankees' game against the California Angels and the pain in his shoulder intensified.

"At one point," he said, "Ellie Howard, who was watching me from behind the cage, yelled: 'Get out of there! You can't swing the bat!'"

The Yankees sent him for an arthrogram but the muscle was so thick and deep the dye could not penetrate fully to the injured area. Finally, it was determined the muscle was torn in the shoulder and doctors prescribed reconstructive surgery while also noting Blomberg had "unusually thick muscle development."

"It must be an injury only Jews get," he joked to reporters who visited him at his New Jersey home where he was consigned to recover for the rest of the season. "At least, with football players they can wrap them up and they can play. With me, there's nothing they can do that will allow me to swing a bat."

Nevertheless, some of his teammates, those who had never been particularly enamored with him and, especially, all the undue attention he got from the writers, outwardly disparaged him. There was predictable resentment, too, over his getting full World Series shares in 1976 and '77 despite not playing those entire seasons (save two at bats in '76). Graig Nettles, in particular, suggested in August of 1976 Blomberg hadn't done enough to rehabilitate himself from the shoulder injury, and bluntly recommended he go to winter ball if he was serious about learning to hit left-handers. And one time after knee surgery had wiped out Blomberg's 1977 season, Yankee longtime publicity director Bob Fishel walked into the clubhouse showing no ill effects of the cast on his leg from his own recent knee surgery and a couple of players remarked with cruel disdain: "At least Fishel's ready to play, even if Blomberg isn't!"

"Were you aware of some of your teammates resenting you?" I asked him.

"Oh yeah," Blomberg said, ignoring a waitress setting up all the tables around us. "But, like I said, it was just a few guys who were probably jealous of the attention I got. Thurman, Catfish [Hunter], Sparky [Lyle], Dick Tidrow . . . they were all great to me. I remember one time, there was this watermelon in the clubhouse and everybody knew I could eat two or three watermelons in one sitting. Unbeknownst to me, Tidrow had put some grain alcohol in the watermelon and, as I'm eating away on it, I'm starting to get a major buzz.

"As for the other ones, in '77 they just didn't know how badly messed up my knee was. It never came around after the operation. And I understand how some of them might have felt. They're the ones who got the team to the World Series both those years and I got a full share without doing anything. But, believe me, it killed me to have to watch those World Series on television and not being able to contribute."

In the opinion of Yankee insiders at the time, the knee injury—which Blomberg suffered running into an outfield wall at Chain O' Lakes Park in Winter Haven attempting to chase down a fly ball hit by the Red Sox's Doug Griffin during a spring training game, March 30, 1977—may not have been entirely unrelated to the second shoulder injury he incurred in spring training the previous year. Blomberg had injured the shoulder late in the spring of '76, but fearing the Yankees would put him on the disabled list again, he failed to tell manager Billy Martin about it. In the meantime, the Yankees had brought in 37-year-old Tommy Davis that spring to compete for the designated hitter job as well as possibly providing an extra right-handed bat on the bench. But on the last day of spring training, they reluctantly released Davis to get down to the 25-man roster limit. Then, later that night, on the plane ride from Fort Lauderdale to Milwaukee for the start of the season, Blomberg informed Martin his shoulder was aching again and he didn't think he could play.

Martin was furious. He had been the one to recommend signing Davis and he'd hated having to cut him. Now, in Davis's place, he suddenly had no one. From that day on, according to those close to Martin, the manager had no use for Blomberg. He'd always suspected Blomberg of divulging too much in-house information to the writers, but now he *really* didn't trust him. So when, the following spring, Blomberg was back trying to regain the DH job, Martin was determined not to have him on the ball club. At least that was how the theory went regarding Martin's decision to play Blomberg in the outfield that day in Winter Haven. Martin claimed he was merely trying to get Reggie Jackson (who was nursing a minor hamstring injury) some at bats at DH, but everyone knew Blomberg playing the outfield for the first time in more than four years was a disaster-in-waiting.

"What happened was, I didn't get my [first] shoulder operation until August of '75," Blomberg explained now, "and even though Dr. [Sidney] Gaynor said it was okay, I knew if I swung hard it was gonna kill me that following spring. So I took it easy all spring and whenever Billy would come to me and ask 'how's the shoulder?' I'd say: 'It's 110 percent.' I was afraid to tell him it was still bad.

"Then it popped on me again and the next day they released

Tommy Davis. Billy screamed at me: 'I thought you told me your shoulder was good? You really screwed me up good!' After that, Billy wouldn't talk to me anymore. The problem for him, I think, was that I had so much fan support in New York. So he put me in left field that day against the Red Sox and I hit the wall and, bam! My knee was a mess."

And that, in effect, was the end of Blomberg's Yankee career.

After being sidelined the whole '77 season, Blomberg, who was now a free agent, waited for the Yankees to make him an offer. In early November, they offered him a conditional contract. Even though he hadn't played in two and a half years, he'd hoped for something more substantial from them. Then, Bill Veeck, the promotions-driven impresario who owned the Chicago White Sox, called with an offer Blomberg could hardly refuse—three years, $600,000. Blomberg had also been talking to the Mets, but this was an offer no one, even Blomberg, in all his naïveté, could believe. He accepted immediately, not waiting for Veeck to have second thoughts, and that made for a particularly bitter parting. Said Paul ruefully after being informed of Blomberg's White Sox windfall: "We paid him two years for doing nothing and he got two World Series shares. The least he could have done was let us know his plans."

"It certainly didn't end the way anyone thought it would," I said to Blomberg.

"No, it didn't," he replied. "You know I was still limping when I signed that contract. I never wanted to be anything but a Yankee and yet, after getting that '77 ring by being on the disabled list all year, I knew I needed to make a change. To this day, I fantasize about playing in that World Series."

I believed that. In the final analysis, though, he didn't come close to fulfilling the dreams his adoring constituency held for him. Oddly, because of his designated hitter fame, they probably felt more deprived than he did. They never got their Greenberg, or anything even close, but he would always have his place alone in the history books.

"To this day," Blomberg said, glancing out the window at the collectors still gathered on the sidewalk, "I'll come up here from Atlanta and run into someone on the street and they'll say: 'You were the Messiah to the Jews in New York City.' They never say I didn't reach my potential, even though, deep down, I wish I could've played more. I remember how so many guys wore my uniform No. 12, and how Phil Rizzuto gave me the nickname 'Boomer' and the time Joe D. told me on an elevator at an Old-Timers' Day years ago: 'Boomer, I just want you to know I thought you were a super player!' It was great being idolized. And every year, on April 6, they remember what I did. I was a $125,000 question on *Who Wants to Be a Millionaire* and I've been a *Jeopardy* question for years.

"I guess I screwed this game up pretty good, didn't I?"

NOT MICKEY, BUT A PRETTY FAIR COUNTRY BALLPLAYER

BOBBY MURCER

S hortly after six o'clock on a Monday afternoon in late March 2002, Bobby Ray Murcer strode purposefully through the doors of the New York Yankee clubhouse at Legends Field in Tampa, Florida, executed a right turn into the locker room area and waited to introduce himself to the players who had just come in off the field from their pregame workout. Most of them already knew him as the homespun, dry-witted former Yankee outfielder-turned-broadcaster, but on this day, Murcer was carrying a briefcase and wore a solemn, well-ordered look on his face.

It had been nearly 20 years since Murcer played his last game, and in that time he'd forged himself a comfortable and prosperous baseball afterlife, working a limited TV schedule of Yankee games, amid various business and charity enterprises and commercial endorsements. For a couple of years in the mid-'80s, Murcer was also the president of his hometown Triple A Oklahoma City 89ers. He was, he said, a very fortunate and lucky man—unlike so many other former major league ballplayers who had since fallen upon hard times.

This was Murcer's mission today, as the chairman of BAT, the Baseball Assistance Team, a nonprofit, Major League Baseball–sanctioned organization, which raises and dispenses nearly a million dollars a year for the benefit of all segments of the baseball community. For nearly two weeks, Murcer had been touring the spring training camps, handing out information pamphlets about BAT and delivering his pitch for contributions from the current generation of millionaire ballplayers.

"It was almost 40 years ago when I first put that uniform on," Murcer began, pointing to a set of home Yankee pinstripes hanging in an empty locker next to him. "And when I had that uniform on I never felt more secure in my life. But when I took that uniform off, my security blanket left. I felt pretty alone, but fortunately for me, I was able to land a job almost immediately after I retired. I was one of the lucky ones, but I'm in the minority of the lucky ones. There are players out there, from the '40s, '50s, '60s, '70s, even the '80s, who missed getting a pension by just *days*. There's hundreds of them out there and that pension means a lot to 'em because a pension they'd be getting today would keep them from asking for assistance. We're doing what we can for all of these people in what we like to call the 'baseball family,' which includes former major-leaguers, front office personnel, Negro League players, umpires, even the women's professional baseball league from the '40s. We've got hundreds of grants, but more grants than money, which is why we need your help to keep this going. I want to tell you about the history of this foundation; how it was built and how these players can be reaping the benefits of it today . . . "

He went on for about 15 minutes as the Yankee players listened intently. At the conclusion of his presentation, Murcer distributed his pamphlets and donation cards and thanked the players for their time. He was still pumped up when he found me waiting in the corridor outside the clubhouse a few minutes later.

"This is probably the most important thing I've ever done in my working life," Murcer said, as we headed down the corridor to the media dining room. "I consider this their responsibility. I know that's a pretty tough word, but that's how I feel . . . that it's their responsibility . . . and I believe, in my heart, they'll embrace this organization once they really begin to feel like it's doing something important for the well-being of people who were just like them but who found life a struggle after baseball. That's the reason we're doing what we're doing—to educate them on who we are and to solicit their help."

All these years later, Bobby Murcer, silver-haired, baseball elder statesman, seemed genuinely comfortable with who he was, even if that never was quite who he was supposed to be. He had taken the same Oklahoma-to-Yankees path blazed by Mickey Mantle, only Mantle hailed from the rural, dirt-poor mining country while Murcer, the son of a jeweler, grew up more affluent and better educated on Whippoorwill Drive in the state capital of Oklahoma City. They were both signed as shortstops, by the same legendary scout, Tom Greenwade, with the same high expectations. Mantle's road to Cooperstown was a straight shot, through 18 seasons in the Bronx, during which he hit 536 home runs and a record 18 more in 12 World Series. Murcer gave hint of following a similar road with breakout seasons in 1971–'72–'73 before his career took an unhappy (some people might say cruel) detour, first to inhospitable Shea Stadium, the Yankees' tenant quarters during the renovation of Yankee Stadium, and then in exile to the windy and foreign environs of Candlestick Park in San Francisco and Wrigley Field in Chicago, where it all but dissipated. By the time he got his one World Series as a Yankee, he was 35 years old and just holding on as a platoon designated hitter.

Yet through it all Murcer insisted he never resented or felt pressured by the larger-than-life shadow Mantle cast over him—perhaps, for no other reason than it was by his own choosing.

"I came before the draft and because of that I could sign with any team," Murcer said. "The day of my graduation from Southeast High, there was a scout from just about every team in baseball at my house, so I never even got to go out and celebrate. They all had a time slot. I had already signed a letter of intent to go to the University of Oklahoma on a football scholarship as a halfback-quarterback in case it didn't work out for me in baseball.

"Besides Tom being just a wonderful man, the Yankees were the team I'd always had my eye on. Mickey had a lot to do with that, of course, but it was their history, their tradition . . . all that winning, all those great names . . . The Dodgers actually offered me more money than anyone else—$20,000—while the Yankees would only go to 10. For $10,000 less, back in 1964, that was big money in those days. In my mind, which was a kid's mind, I would make that up in World Series money anyway. Tom said they would also pay for my college education, which, they knew, in those days, I'd never follow up on."

As the final inducement, Greenwade arranged for Murcer to go to Kansas City and work out with the Yankees, who were going to be there for a series against the Kansas City Athletics. It was the first time he ever met his boyhood idol, Mantle, and Greenwade knew the $10,000 difference would become a pittance in Murcer's eyes once he got to ride the team bus, put on the pinstripes and take batting practice with the likes of The Mick, Roger Maris, Tony Kubek, Bobby Richardson and Elston Howard.

"What I remember most about that trip," said Murcer, "was that Mickey and Roger didn't stay at the same hotel as the rest of the team. Mickey got off a block before we got to our hotel, wearing a disguise. I mean Kansas City was absolutely crazy over the Yankees. There were thousands of people around our hotel. You couldn't move in the lobby. Here's this town in the middle of the United States and everybody who couldn't see the Yankees, living out in those prairies and farmlands, descended on Kansas City and, from my standpoint as an 18-year-old kid, that was pretty impressive. It was everything I thought it would be. I signed with them a couple of days later, right after I got home."

"Nevertheless," I countered, "Greenwade must have been a pretty slick salesman."

"He was a very soft-spoken man," Murcer said. "When we drove up to Kansas City, he told me about how he'd gone down to Commerce to see Mickey and how he'd talked to Mickey's dad. He'd also signed Elston Howard, out of St. Louis, and that impressed me. I'll tell you who Tom reminded me of—the guy who played Lou Gehrig in *Pride of the Yankees*—Gary Cooper. He always wore a suit and a top hat. He was a gentleman. He was legitimate in wanting to do what was right for a young kid, while, at the same time, he was doing his job for the Yankees. You trusted him."

Upon gladly taking the $10,000, Murcer's first stop in the Yankee player development system was Johnson City, Tennessee, in the short-season Class D Appalachian League. He finished up the 1964 season there, hitting .365 with 29 RBI in 32 games. The next year, he was moved up to A ball, with Greensboro, where he continued to demonstrate his major league hitting potential, batting .322. And even his 55 errors, tops among Carolina League shortstops, failed to sway the Yankee hierarchy's thinking about him as the eventual successor to Kubek.

"A funny thing was, the only injury I ever had in professional baseball I had that first year with Johnson City," Murcer related. "We were in Bluefield, West Virginia, playing a doubleheader. In the latter innings of the first game, there was a close play at the plate. I slid in and scored the run. But between games, my knee started swelling up and I couldn't play the second game. As the night wore on, the knee got so bad . . . I was having so much pain . . . I finally called the manager, Lamar North, who took me to the only hospital in town—the Bluefield Sanitarium. That was the name of it! Can you believe that?"

Murcer began laughing as he recounted the story. "Their first diagnosis . . . preliminary diagnosis . . . of my knee was that I had meningitis! I said '*Meningitis?* What does *that* have to do with my *knee?*' Anyway, I got my mom on the phone and told her this and she darned near had a coronary. Then they told me: 'No, what we think it is now is mononucleosis.' I couldn't understand what that had to do with my knee either, but they put me in a body cast from my knee all the way to my hip and kept me there in the hospital while the team left town and went home to Johnson City. After about a week or so, they took the cast off and shipped me up to New York to see the Yankee team physician, Dr. Sidney Gaynor, at Lenox Hill. That was my first time in New York City. They put me in a hotel that's probably not even there anymore, in Midtown, and there I was, this 18-year-old kid, fresh out of high school and the Bluefield Sanitarium, in the middle of New York City! Gaynor looked at my leg and diagnosed me with a bursa sac that had apparently busted. In those days, they didn't do anything for you in terms of rehab or anything. Gaynor just said: 'Oh, nature will take care of it. You'll be ready next year. Just go home and take it easy.'

"Well, darned if Gaynor wasn't right. I was fine the next year and never had another problem with it. Nature took care of it! Then at the end of the next season, I was in the big leagues! Toward the end of the season at Greensboro, Ralph Houk, who was the Yankees' general manager then, came down to watch me play, and in September they called me up and put me right in at short. I probably should have gotten a sense that things had really changed with the Yankees, the fact that they'd call a 19-year-old kid all the way up from A ball. I guess for the previous 40, 50 years, something like that would have been unheard of. Guys played in their system five, six, seven, even eight years before ever getting called up to New York."

Things *had* changed with the Yankees. Dan Topping and Del Webb, who had owned the team since 1947 and presided over its grandest era—15 American League pennants and 10 world championships—sold out to CBS in November of '64. Whether it was a blind arrogance or benign neglect, they had allowed the Yankees' infrastructure to deteriorate. The legendary scouting gurus, Paul Krichell on the East Coast and Joe Devine on the West Coast, had died and the Yankees hadn't seen to maintaining their networks. As a result, the pipeline of talent out of New York and San Francisco had all but dried up. Whether Bobby Murcer knew it or not, he *was*, essentially, the Yankee farm system in 1965.

"Kubek had retired," he said, "and Houk told Johnny Keane, the manager, 'If this kid Murcer can cut the mustard in spring training next year, he can make it.' That's about what happened. I made it in '66. They told me they wanted to start me off platooning with Ruben Amaro [a light-hitting utility infielder the Yankees had acquired from the Philadelphia Phillies for Phil Linz the previous November] and they'd asked Bobby Richardson to stay around one more year at second base to work with me at shortstop."

The Murcer "force feeding" project lasted only a couple of weeks when, despite their obvious depletion of talent, the Yankees determined he needed more minor league seasoning and sent him to Toledo of the International League. He found Triple A pitching a tad more challenging than what he'd seen in the lower minors and his 36 errors at shortstop again led the league. Nevertheless, the Yankees' projections for arrival in 1967 remained firm.

"And then I got drafted," Murcer said.

He missed two potential prime seasons of his career, but it could have been worse. Instead of being sent to Vietnam—where just about all of the draftees were destined during that turbulent period—Murcer lucked out and was assigned to a radio unit in Fort Huachuca, Arizona, where he taught other men to operate radios, in and around playing golf and softball on the base with a colonel who happened to be a Yankee fan. Murcer never asked for the favored treatment, but it only reinforced the near mythical view he'd always had of the Yankees.

When he got out of the service he reported to spring training in Fort Lauderdale in 1969 with nowhere near the fanfare and anticipation that had greeted him three years earlier. Rather, all the attention leading up to that spring was on Mantle, who, at 37 with increasingly brittle legs, was coming off his worst season, in which his anemic .237 batting average had dropped his lifetime mark under .300.

The Yankees were hoping to coax one more season out of Mantle, if nothing else for his gate appeal at a time the club had sunk to its lowest ebb, attendance-wise, since 1945. Mantle, at $100,000, was still the highest paid player in baseball, but he hated what he'd become—a pitiable, broken-down shell of the five-tool superstar who had once been the best all-around player in the game.

Then, just as spring training was about to begin, there was a players' strike, and Mantle and all the Yankee veterans stayed out of camp. As evidence of his own uncertain status, especially after two years away from the game, no pressure was exerted on Murcer to also stay away, so there he was, on opening day of camp, whistling line drive after line drive in the batting cage. Upon closer inspection from the Yankee brain trust, it was obvious Murcer had put on some 15 pounds while in the service of his country, all in his chest and shoulders. The skinny teenage shortstop now had the look of a power hitter about him.

After a couple of weeks, the strike—the source of which was a dispute over the players' pension fund—was settled and all the Yankee veterans returned to camp. With one notable exception. The night of the settlement, Mantle whisked into Fort Lauderdale and met privately with Houk and Yankee president Mike Burke where, it was concluded, he would retire. An era had ended, but as Burke watched with increased interest as the bulked-up new kid from Oklahoma kept hitting all those spring training line drives, he could foresee the dawning of a new one. Pete Sheehy, the venerable clubhouse man whose tenure had extended back to the days of Babe Ruth and Lou Gehrig, must have thought the same thing. Sheehy was always extremely selective in assigning uniform numbers, placing subtle, unspoken esteem on the lower ones. That spring he gave Bobby Murcer No. 1, which had not been worn since Richardson retired in 1966. And when the team got back to New York for the start of the season, Murcer found the locker assigned to him by Sheehy was the one just vacated by Mantle.

"I figured it would make the kid happy," Sheehy explained. "I know

Mickey liked him. They were both from Oklahoma. What the heck? Somebody had to use it. Might as well be Murcer."

Unfortunately, the new, bigger and stronger Murcer was a far less agile and fluid shortstop.

The team opened the season in Washington and Murcer and Jerry Kenney, the other hotshot rookie, hit back-to-back homers in the Yankees' 8–4 success against the Senators. He hit a homer in his second game, too, and batted .393 that first week of the season. In the home opener, also against Washington, he hit a homer, a double and a single and drove in four runs—and then homered again the next day. Five homers in his first nine games. Say hello to the new Yankee superstar; the new fans' darling; the new Mantle.

Soon after, though, Murcer went into an 0-for-20 slump. On April 24, he'd gone six days without a hit when he broke out of it in resounding fashion with a single and two homers in Cleveland, giving him seven homers in 14 games along with a lusty .325 average. Mike Burke's brain was now swimming with ideas as to how to promote his new young star. "He has the chemistry and ability to make it big, real big," Burke said of Murcer. "We didn't have to do a thing. It's written in the newspapers. It's on the TV. The fans saw it. They want to be able to tell their friends: 'I saw Bobby Murcer breaking in!'"

But then the Yankees went into a disastrous tailspin, losing 15 out of 18 from late April until mid-May. Murcer, the new star, felt the pressure, especially when the focus of the slump came on his play at shortstop. In a weekend series in Oakland he made two errors in each of the first two games as the Yankee losing skid reached 10 out of 11. The next night in Seattle, the Yankees watched helplessly as the expansion Seattle Pilots scored seven runs in the first to wipe out the 2–0 lead Murcer had provided them with a homer in the top of the inning. Later in that game, after getting buzzed by a fastball to the head from Pilots pitcher Marty Pattin, Murcer bowled over Seattle shortstop Ray Oyler at second base, touching off a wild melee. Both he and Houk were tossed out of the game, but their banishment to the clubhouse provided the Yankee manager with the opportunity to discuss with his struggling shortstop an idea he'd been mulling over in his mind for a few days.

"The joke was they couldn't sell any seats behind first base and they were losing a lot of money so they had to move me to the outfield," Murcer said, chuckling. "At first, they put me at third base and as I was taking ground balls there in Sicks Stadium, that glorified Triple A ballpark in Seattle, some fan yelled out: 'Look out! He's got it again!' I ran in after I made the throw and Ralph tapped me on the shoulder and said: 'Young man, when you come to the ballpark tomorrow night, I want you to take some fly balls in the outfield. See how it feels. If you don't like it, let me know.' I said: 'I don't get it, Skip. What do you mean?' and Ralph said only half-joking, I'm sure: 'Son, I just want to get you as far out there where I hope they never hit you a ball.'"

Houk, characteristically, downplayed the position change of his new star player. "This was actually something we considered doing in spring training," he told the media. "We had to do something because we didn't want it to start affecting Bobby's hitting."

Murcer played a couple of games in right, then shifted over to center when Houk moved Kenney to shortstop.

"Now the comparisons with Mickey really started," Murcer related. "Both from Oklahoma . . . both signed as shortstops . . . both moved to center field . . . and people used to ask me all the time: 'How do you feel being compared to Mickey Mantle?' My answer then is the same as it is now: 'It doesn't bother me being compared to Mickey. What bothers me is how *Mickey* felt having me compared to him.'"

We both laughed at Murcer's self-effacing joke. "At the same time, I can honestly say it *never* bothered me," he continued. "I never gave it one iota of a thought. People thought it bothered me more than anything else in the world. *How could you live under that comparison/legacy type thing?* Maybe it was because I was so young. I'm sure that had a lot to do with it. But in my mind, Mickey was my guy. How was I ever going to be as good as him in the first place? I didn't have the mentality to put myself in that arena."

"What about the mere notion of playing center field in Yankee Stadium?" I asked him. "I mean, you had to know that was the most hallowed piece of real estate in baseball, with Mickey immediately before you there, and, before him, DiMaggio?"

"I just thought that was the way it was supposed to be," Murcer replied, matter-of-factly. "I guess it was the same thing as when I turned down the extra $10,000 from the Dodgers to sign with Greenwade. I figured I was gonna make it up in the World Series. What can I say? I was naive. But once I started playing out there, Mickey embraced me whenever he came around, and that made it easier. On the other hand, Joe was always a little standoffish whenever I'd see him, at Old-Timers' Day ceremonies—I think because he felt I hadn't proved myself."

As it was, Murcer's switch to center field coincided with the gradual, overall transition of the Yankees as a team. The amateur draft, which was instituted to enable the perennial have-not teams to compete on equal terms for talent with the wealthier teams, actually worked to the Yankees' advantage in the first few years of its existence. This was, of course, because the Yankees had abruptly deteriorated into one of the worst teams in baseball; and their low finish in the standings from '65 to '69 afforded them a higher selection place in the draft. Following their last-place finish in 1966, they had the overall first pick in '67 and took a left-handed power hitting high school outfielder from Atlanta named Ron Blomberg, who would reach the majors by 1971. The following year, picking fourth overall, they took Kent State catcher Thurman Munson with their No. 1 selection. Munson would need only two years of minor league apprenticeship before taking over as the Yankees' No. 1 catcher and, later, became the cornerstone player in their championship renaissance.

"I remember when Thurman first came up," Murcer said, "and thinking what a cocky kid he was. When you see a guy like that who's pretty sure of himself, you kind of wait and see if he's going to self-destruct or become a great player. I was the one player left over from the days of the big guys, the one who got the buildup, and, so, Thurman and I gravitated to each other fairly quickly."

Munson's first full season, 1970, the Yankees improved from fifth to second, Munson hit .302 and won American League Rookie of the Year honors. In a June 24 doubleheader at Yankee Stadium against Cleveland, Murcer homered in four consecutive at bats. The following season was the best of Murcer's career. He hit .331 with 25 doubles, 25 homers, 94 runs scored and 94 driven in. Munson tailed off with the bat (.251), but led American League catchers in fielding (.981) and tied a Yankee record for catchers with only one error. A decade after Mantle and Roger Maris became intrinsically linked through their home run heroics the Yankees had a new (albeit, poor man's) tandem of "M&M Boys." As such, they were featured on the cover of the 1974 Yankee yearbook.

Murcer had another standout season in '72, reaching a career high in homers with 33, leading the league in runs with 102 and earning his one Gold Glove for defensive excellence. Munson rebounded to hit .280 that year and Blomberg hit 14 homers in his first full season as the Yankee first baseman. But the '72 Yankees finished fourth and, even worse, attendance at Yankee Stadium dropped under one million for the first time since World War II. When they finished fourth again in '73, and fell under .500 for the first time since '69, Houk resigned as manager. Murcer, who'd hit .300 again (actually .304) in '73, with 22 homers and a team-leading 95 RBI, could not foresee the impact Houk's departure would have on him. Nor could he imagine how the Yankee Stadium renovation project—which was to begin in 1974— would be the ruination of his career.

The new Yankee manager (after an aborted effort by new owner George Steinbrenner to sign Dick Williams, who had won back-to-back '72–'73 world championships with the Oakland A's) was Bill Virdon. The bespectacled, soft-spoken Virdon was a stern and humorless taskmaster—as the Yankee players discovered early on in spring training when, after each daily workout, he put them through arduous base-running drills that left them panting and complaining they were in boot camp. Virdon had been a premier defensive center fielder with the Pittsburgh Pirates in the '60s, and this, no doubt, prompted his special interest in Murcer.

From the moment he walked onto the field at Shea Stadium—which was to be the Yankees home for the next two seasons—Murcer detested the place. It was cold, windy and noisy beyond belief with the incessant jet traffic overhead, and devoid of any charm from his viewpoint. And that was *before* he came to realize he was inexplicably unable to hit the ball into the stands there. His left-handed batting stroke had been tailor-made for Yankee Stadium's inviting (344 feet) right field porch. By comparison, Shea's right field power alley was approximately 30 feet further away. After averaging just over 25 homers his previous five seasons, he dropped off to a mere 10 in '74 and didn't hit his first at Shea until the next-to-last week of the season. As the year wore on, Murcer developed a mental block hitting at Shea, his frustration level mounting with each succeeding fly ball of his being hauled in on the warning track. He was over-swinging and getting totally out of sync.

And there was more, equally unexpected adversity, about to be heaped on him by Virdon.

Late in spring training that year, in a transaction that attracted scant attention, the Yankees purchased outfielder Elliott Maddox from the Texas Rangers. A right-handed hitter who'd hit only two home runs in 724 at bats over the previous three seasons, there didn't even seem to be any certainty Maddox would make the team, and if he did, it figured to be only as a backup player. At least that's what everybody assumed. Virdon, however, had different ideas about Maddox. For one thing, he loved his defensive skills. In Virdon's mind, the Yankees didn't have the kind of conventional power hitters that had been the staples of their championship past. Thus, in order to contend, he believed it would have to be with pitching and defense. When the Yankees went into a prolonged tailspin in May, losing 13 out of 16, Virdon had his opening. He already felt Murcer had lost a step in center field—his Gold Glove in '72 and league-leading assist totals in

'70 and '73 notwithstanding—and he wanted to get Maddox into the lineup. So when Murcer came to the ballpark on May 28 and saw "RF" inscribed next to his name on the lineup card, he did a double take—followed by another double take when he saw Maddox's name in the lineup with "CF" next to it.

"Virdon penciled me in to right field without ever even talking to me about it," Murcer said, "so I went to his office and I asked him very calmly: 'I see you've got me playing right field tonight. Why right and not center?' He said: 'Right now, I just think Elliott's a better center fielder.' I was stunned. I thought I had enough prestige on the team for the manager to at least talk to me before he made the move. To be honest, I thought it was a very unprofessional thing for a manager to do. That was a pretty major move, the way I saw it. It wasn't like going from third base to the outfield, because I'd already established myself in center field. And it came at a time when there was a whole lot of publicity about my home runs being down, so I was pretty shattered inside."

It was a thoroughly frustrating season—literally—from start to finish for Murcer, who spent the last two days of it as a spectator while the Yankees lost out in the American League East on the final weekend. They had been 60-61 and in fourth place as late as August 20, but Virdon refused to concede. "We can still win this thing," he said. "All we have to do is win 30 of our last 41 games and we'll win. That will give us 90 victories and enough to win the division."

They won 29. Part of Virdon's optimism was the fact that the Yankees had already begun a late-season surge. From August 1 to September 15, they went 29-15 and actually climbed into first place as the Red Sox, who had held the division lead for most of the season, went into a fast fade. And even after being swept by the eventual division champion Baltimore Orioles in a three-game series in New York, Virdon's team hung in, winning eight of the next nine games to close to within one game of first place with two to go. While his power stroke may have deserted him, Murcer remained the Yankees' most productive hitter with a team-leading 88 RBI going into that season-ending series against the Milwaukee Brewers. But on the plane ride from Cleveland to Milwaukee after a giddy three-game sweep of the Indians, things got a bit rambunctious and two of the Yankee reserve players, catcher Rick Dempsey and utilityman Bill Sudakis, began needling each other to the point where, with each succeeding beer, it got more and more personal. The hostilities between Dempsey and Sudakis became further heated on the bus trip from Milwaukee's Mitchell Field to the Pfister Hotel where the Yankees were staying and, as the players began checking in, the two suddenly became engaged in fisticuffs. As Yankees traveling secretary Bill Kane later described the scene: "It was wild—like an old fashioned Western furniture fight— with guys jumping over couches, tables and lamps crashing to the floor, as everyone rushed to break it up."

Unfortunately, in the fight's aftermath, the only thing broken, other than a couple of lamps, was Murcer's finger.

"What had happened," Murcer said, "was that we got delayed in Cleveland because of severe thunderstorms and by the time we got on the plane, everybody had had a few pops and was feeling no pain. It festered on the bus and by the time we got to the hotel they were scuffling. I tried to jump in and break it up but somehow I got knocked to the floor and in all the commotion someone stepped on my hand and broke my finger. The next day, my finger was all swollen and I couldn't play. We lost that Saturday game to the Brewers, while the Orioles won in Detroit to clinch it."

And, little did Murcer know, it would be another four and a half years before he'd play another game for the Yankees.

The arrival of Steinbrenner in 1973 signaled a whole new Yankee management team, one that didn't look at Bobby Murcer as the indispensable franchise player Burke had marketed from that breakthrough '69 season. And while, at the press conference announcing CBS's sale of the team, Steinbrenner insisted he would be too busy with his shipbuilding business in Cleveland to be a hands-on owner, GM Lee MacPhail instinctively knew otherwise and departed at the end of the '73 season to become American League president. Burke left even sooner. As the point man for CBS in the sale, Burke envisioned himself staying on as club president and running the team for Steinbrenner. But once he learned Gabe Paul, the general manager of the Cleveland Indians, had been *Steinbrenner's* point man in the deal and was, in fact, being brought in as a top-level executive in the operation, Burke saw the handwriting on the wall and resigned as president. It didn't matter either that, prior to the '74 season, Steinbrenner made Murcer the highest-paid Yankee in history with a contract for $120,000. What soon became abundantly clear was that Steinbrenner's intention for the Yankees was to purge them of everything and everyone identified with the failed CBS/Burke regime. Upon signing Murcer to the record contract, Steinbrenner warned: "I tried to convey to Bobby just what we are trying to do here and what I expect his role to be in accomplishing our objective."

Between the dramatic drop-off in home runs and the switch by Virdon from prestigious center field to right, Murcer's role on the Yankees became diminished in Steinbrenner's eyes. The owner was also far more consumed with his suspension from baseball by Commissioner Bowie Kuhn for having been convicted of making illegal contributions to Richard Nixon's presidential campaign, and Paul had been entrusted with the operation of the team.

On the morning of October 21, 1974, Murcer was sound asleep in his Oklahoma City home when the ring of the telephone awakened him, shortly after eight o'clock. On the other end of the line was Paul, who, after apologizing for waking him up, matter-of-factly informed Murcer he'd been traded to the San Francisco Giants for Bobby Bonds, a onetime budding superstar in his own right.

"I thought I was having a nightmare, I really did," Murcer said. "I was half-asleep. I later found out just before he made the call Gabe had called in Marty Appel, the Yankee PR man, and said, somewhat gleefully I guess: 'I want you to hear *this!*'"

Murcer cleared his throat. It wasn't the first time I'd heard him recount the story, but I knew that no matter how many times he'd told it through the years, it was never easy for him to talk about it. His life, he maintained, was never the same after that day.

"Gabe and I had always had a little bit of a personality conflict," Murcer continued. "I was not a pro–Gabe Paul person, because he was totally opposite in philosophy from Mr. Steinbrenner, who was on suspension at that time. Gabe was only interested in a team looking good and keeping the budget down. He was satisfied with mediocrity.

"The impact of that trade never left me simply because, in my mind, there was no other organization in baseball than the New York Yankees. There still isn't. Anybody who had an opportunity to play with the New York Yankees should thank their lucky stars. But you would only know that if you've been here."

Over the long term, the blockbuster one-for-one trade of franchise players proved to be far more beneficial to the Yankees—albeit indirectly. Like Murcer, Bonds was coming off a decidedly subpar '74 season in which his home run and RBI counts had dropped from 39 and 96 to career lows of 21 and 71. There were also unfounded rumors he had a drinking problem and didn't take care of himself—which were doubtless contributing factors in his becoming a baseball vagabond after 1975, getting traded six more times in his career. With the Yankees in '75, Bonds was everything they could have hoped for, putting together the fourth 30-homer, 30-steal season of his career (and first by a Yankee). It might have been an MVP-caliber season had it not been for a serious knee injury he suffered attempting to make a diving, game-saving catch against the Chicago White Sox in Comiskey Park, on June 7. At the time, Bonds was leading the American League in homers (15) and RBI (45). But playing hurt the remainder of the season, his overall production suffered, as did the Yankees, who fell out of first place later in the month and ended up third, 83-77.

The following December, Bonds's brief Yankee career ended when Paul traded him to the California Angels for center fielder Mickey Rivers and right-handed pitcher Ed Figueroa. It turned out to be one of the best in a series of inspired Paul trades that transformed the Yankees into a team that won three consecutive American League pennants and two world championships over the next three seasons. Rivers, a diminutive speed merchant whose 43 stolen bases in '76 were the most by a Yankee since 1944, gave the team a bona fide lead-off man and offensive catalyst. Figueroa, meanwhile, was the Yankees' winningest pitcher during that '76–'78 championship run, with 19, 16 and 20 victories.

So in a belated way, the Yankees' trading of Bobby Murcer proved to be instrumental in restoring them to the superiority they had known prior to his arrival in 1966. Murcer, however, could only watch from afar with envy. He was miserable in San Francisco, with Candlestick Park's bone-chilling winds even more inhibiting for him than the intolerable conditions and clime at Shea. He wasn't there more than a few months when he begged Giants owner Bob Lurie to trade him. But while he still had trouble hitting home runs, Murcer had an otherwise solid season (.298, 91 RBI) for the Giants, and Lurie felt he couldn't justify turning around and trading the man he'd gotten for Bobby Bonds. However, his thinking changed when arbitrator Peter Seitz's December 1975 ruling that players were not bound to the reserve clause in their contracts signaled the dawning of free agency in baseball. Knowing he had no chance of persuading Murcer to sign a new contract with the Giants, Lurie managed to send him to the Chicago Cubs in February of 1977 for third baseman Bill Madlock, who was coming off back-to-back batting titles.

Alas, Chicago wasn't Murcer's kind of town either, nor were the "Friendly Confines" of Wrigley Field all that friendly to him. He did maintain his home run stroke, hitting 27 in 1977. But in '78, his skills appeared to deteriorate dramatically. He struggled through the season, his scant nine homers and 64 RBI the worst of his career. He maintained the wind blew in all season, but even when the wind blows out at Wrigley, it can be much more favorable for right-handed hitters, sweeping in from Lake Michigan from right to left field.

Murcer also feuded with Cubs manager Herman Franks, who accused him of not putting out, and Cubs GM Bob Kennedy labeled his outfielding as "Triple A"—a bitingly harsh indictment of a player who was making $320,000 per year. It didn't matter either that Murcer had been named Cubs captain the year before. He wanted out and Chicago wanted him out. A headline in the *Chicago Tribune* just prior to the start of the '79 season said it all: "There are 320,000 reasons why Bobby Murcer will play."

"I had a no-trade contract," Murcer recalled, "and, finally, this one morning [June 26, 1979] Kennedy came to me and said: 'Look, I know you have a no-trade contract, but we've had some interest from the Yankees about you. How would you feel about that? I'm not saying we'll make a trade, but I need to know whether you'd give approval.' I said: 'Well, Bob, uh, that'll be all right with me.' They had me traded by noon and I was with the Yankees in Toronto that night."

The cost to the Yankees was a minor league pitcher named Paul Semall, who never saw the daylight of Wrigley Field—which was okay by the Cubs. They just wanted to unload the salary.

Murcer was 33 now and the Yankee team he joined, though world champions the previous two seasons, bore an all-too-familiar resemblance to the one he'd left four and a half years earlier. They had dropped out of the pennant race early—really on April 19, just 12 games into the season—when Goose Gossage, their overpowering and dominating relief ace who had led the American League with 27 saves the year before, suffered a sprained thumb ligament in a clubhouse shower room scuffle with teammate Cliff Johnson. During Gossage's time on the disabled list, from April 21 to July 12, the Yankees were 41-35. Meanwhile, the eventual AL East champion Baltimore Orioles pulled away from the pack by going 39-15 in May and June.

In Murcer's first game back with the Yankees, he singled twice in their 11–2 romp over the Toronto Blue Jays, but the season was pretty much lost. By the time Gossage returned two weeks later, the Yankees were languishing in fourth place, eight games behind the division-leading Orioles. And then, on August 2, Thurman Munson, who'd remained Murcer's closest friend on the team, was killed in a fiery crash of his private jet at the Akron-Canton, Ohio, airport.

"The series before it happened," Murcer recalled, "we were in Chicago playing the White Sox. I still had my apartment there in Arlington Heights, and after the Tuesday game, Thurman, Lou [Piniella] and I all went back there. Thurman had been after Lou and me to fly from Chicago to Canton with him on Wednesday, spend the off-day on Thursday in Canton with our wives, then fly with him from Canton to New York the next day. But I told him I couldn't do that. I'd heard from Reggie and Nettles—who had both flown with him—about his plane and I just didn't want to do it. I finally went to bed about two o'clock, leaving Thurman and Lou in my kitchen talking baseball. I still can hear them, arguing into the night as to who was the best pinch hitter and how you pinch-hit and their philosophies of hitting. They just wore me out. But that's my last memory of Thurman before the tragedy."

The next day, after the Yankees completed the series against the White Sox with a 9–1 win, Murcer and his wife, Kay, drove Munson to the small suburban airport where his Cessna was waiting. At Munson's behest, they got into the cockpit of the plane and sat with him there on the runway for about 20 minutes as he talked about flying and how much of an outlet it was for him. His primary reason for buying the plane was so he could get back to Canton more often to be with his family during the season. As the Murcers got out of the plane, Munson asked them to wait down at the end of the runway and watch him take off.

"So we positioned ourselves at the end of the runway in our car in this tiny airport," Murcer said, ". . . and then he took off and I'm watching this big old powerful jet go roaring over our heads and I thought to myself: 'I cannot believe Thurman is up there all by himself in that powerful machine, flying that crazy plane.'"

As Munson's plane disappeared into the night sky over Chicago, it was the last time Murcer ever saw his friend. Late in the afternoon of the next day, Murcer got a phone call from a friend in New York who had just heard on the radio Munson had been killed in a crash of his private plane while practicing takeoffs and landings at the Canton airport.

"I was just blown away," Murcer said. "I immediately called the house in Canton and got Diana, Thurman's wife, on the phone, but she was in shock. Kay and I flew to Canton that night and stayed at the house with Diana and the kids."

In what may well have been the most emotional baseball night in the history of Yankee Stadium, the Yankee players, numbed by the death of their captain, arrived at the ballpark for their game against the first-place Orioles only to find Munson's locker, on Steinbrenner's orders, cleaned out of all his belongings with the sole exception of his chest protector and shin guards. His nameplate above had been replaced with a simple No. 15. It remains the same to this day. The capacity crowd stood solemnly as Cardinal Terrence Cooke eulogized Munson as "a good family man who was blessed with skill and talent." Then, at the conclusion of the National Anthem, the throng remained standing and politely applauded for a full 10 minutes as the Yankee players stood at attention at their positions, openly sobbing, the sole exception being the catcher's box, which was empty. One other element amid the haunting dramatics of the night was the attendance figure that flashed on the scoreboard in the seventh inning: 51,151.

Three days later, at the 90-minute funeral at the Canton Civic Center, Murcer delivered the heartfelt and touching eulogy, his voice choking as, again, Munson's aggrieved Yankee teammates sat in the church staring, still disbelieving, at the casket in front of them.

The life of a soul on earth lasts beyond his departure . . . you will always feel that life touching yours; that voice speaking to you.

He lives on in your life and in the lives of all others that knew him.

And live he did . . . he lived . . . he led . . . he loved. Whatever he was to each one of us . . . catcher . . . captain . . . competitor . . . husband . . . father . . . friend . . . he should be remembered as a man who valued and followed the basic principles of life.

He lived . . . he led . . . and he loved. He lived blessed with his beautiful wife, Diana, his daughters, Tracy and Kelly, and his son, Michael.

He led . . . this team of Yankees to three divisional titles and two world championships.

He loved . . . the game . . . his fans . . . his friends . . . and, most of all, his family.

He is lost, but not gone. He will be missed, but not forgotten.

As Lou Gehrig led the Yankees as the captain of the '30s, our Thurman Munson captained the Yankees of the '70s.

Someone . . . someday . . . shall earn that right to lead this team again. For that is how Thurm—Tugboat, as I called him— would want it. And that is how one day it will be. No greater honor could be bestowed upon one man than to be the successor to this man, Thurman Munson, who wore the pinstripes with number 15 on the field . . . number 15 for the records . . . number 15 now for the Hall in Cooperstown.

But in living, loving and legend, history will record Thurman Munson as No. 1.

Immediately after the burial at Sunset Hills Cemetery five miles from downtown Canton, the Yankees took a chartered flight back to New York to complete the four-game series against the Orioles. Steinbrenner had been quoted as saying if the charter didn't make it back in time for the game: "So be it. We'll forfeit." And in a pregame interview with ABC's Howard Cosell, he said: "I meant that about the forfeit. The kids won't recover."

Again, Yankee Stadium was heavy with grief, the flags still at half-staff and hundreds of banners in tribute to Munson draped from the railings and facades. In one of their last conversations, as they reflected on the state of the team on the way to the airport in Chicago, Murcer said to Munson: "Look, if I get my stuff together, will you?" And Munson replied: "You better believe it!"

For that one night against the Orioles, Murcer fulfilled his promise to Munson, driving in all five runs of the Yankees' 5–4 victory with a three-run homer off Dennis Martinez in the seventh inning and a two-run single off Tippy Martinez in the ninth. The homer was Murcer's first as a Yankee since he'd left in 1973, and the crowd of 36,314 stood applauding for a full two minutes after he'd circled the bases and raised his arm skyward. He had not intended to play that night, his body and mind drained from the events in Canton, but he thought better of it, especially after Piniella asked out of the lineup for the same reason.

"We were just kind of oblivious to what was going on," Murcer said. "I had thought about not playing, but I knew Thurman would have wanted me to play. I can just picture him sitting there and saying: 'What are you crazy?' When we got back to the Stadium, I lay down in the clubhouse and slept for a couple of hours until around 4:45 when Billy [Martin] woke me up. He said: 'I'm not gonna play you tonight 'cause you're worn out, and I said: 'Billy, I have to play. I don't know if I'm tired or not. I just know I have to play.' In retrospect, I guess what's surprising is that Billy left me in to face Tippy Martinez, a real tough lefty, when we were trailing by a run in the ninth. I never used that bat again. I gave it to Diana.

"I don't remember a whole lot about that game or the days leading up to it. It was a blur. I do remember, though, after I hit the home run, Lou grabbed me and hugged me in the dugout. That was a very emotional time for Lou and me. The three of us had been together at my house only a few days earlier and now one of us was dead. I think that'll always be one of the hardest things for me to accept—Thurman never got a chance to sit back with us and say, 'Hey, remember the time . . .'"

He would remain with the Yankees nearly four more seasons, but Murcer never had a night, before or after, to compare to that one at Yankee Stadium. Although Steinbrenner had done him an immense favor bringing him home in 1979, Murcer was viewed as a platoon player now, and this was hard for him to accept. On one hand, he was thrilled to be a Yankee again. On the other, he was upset and increasingly frustrated by his part-time status. In 1980, he feuded openly with then Yankee manager Dick Howser, who used him primarily in a platoon situation with Piniella, in left field and at designated hitter. That he was able to club 13 homers and drive in 57 runs in just 297 at bats further fueled his public griping at Howser. It certainly didn't become him, and the sportswriters—who had sung his praises as the Bronx darling during all the lean seasons and saluted his return the year before—turned on him.

Responding to a Murcer pop-off at Howser in Anaheim in June, Mike Lupica, in the *Daily News,* wrote: "[Murcer] would grumble to one player about not playing, then stop himself short of controversy. He would mutter to another reporter. The grumbling and muttering was like the dull roar of distant thunder. You could see a storm was coming. The storm hit Anaheim the other night. Bobby Murcer took some shots at Dick Howser. He hinted there were some players dissatisfied on the Yankees. He said anyone could manage the Yankees. . . . The Yankee clubhouse is different this season. The atmosphere is clean. Veterans like Murcer should know better than to bring back the old air pollution."

It was as if there was this inner torment in Murcer, which he could no longer contain. Okay, so he hadn't fulfilled the promise of being the next Mickey Mantle. But he hadn't fulfilled his *own* promise either, and that was what he couldn't fathom. He couldn't understand why, just when he was getting it all together, the gods of baseball deemed Yankee Stadium in need of a facelift, and he had to leave the comforts of his own customized playground for a place so abhorrent and poorly suited for his talents. And there were all the other forces that had conspired against him—Virdon, Paul, the ill winds of Candlestick and Wrigley, and now, after they'd all gotten done with diminishing his career, this Howser.

"It killed me to be a part-time player," Murcer admitted now. "Howser started it, and I really don't know why, to this day, except for the fact that I was 34 years old and I guess they assumed I was too old to be a regular anymore. The worst part of all was finally getting to a World Series and having to watch it from the bench."

What had really eaten away at him was being a TV spectator, back home in Oklahoma City, when his pals, Munson, Piniella, Graig Nettles and Sparky Lyle, were performing in those '76–'78 World Series. There, but for the glee of Gabe Paul, could have been he. But in the strike-splintered 1981 season, the Yankees, by virtue of their first-place standing on June 12 when the players began their 50-day walkout, qualified for the postseason, and Murcer had his first and only October.

The 1981 season was the height of Steinbrenner's manic behavior as Yankee owner, during which he changed managers and general managers like pairs of socks, and on September 6, with the team having won seven of its last nine games, he fired Gene Michael as manager and replaced him with Bob Lemon. In 1978, Lemon had come "out of the bullpen" to relieve Martin as Yankee manager and guided the team to a remarkable comeback world championship. And it looked as if history was going to repeat itself in '81, as the Lemon-managed Yankees disposed of the upstart Milwaukee Brewers in a five-game Division Series and went on to sweep the Oakland A's in the American League Championship Series.

In the World Series against the Los Angeles Dodgers, however, Steinbrenner's antics—he got beaten up in an elevator fight in the Yankee hotel in Los Angeles, supposedly defending the Yankees' honor against two rowdy Dodger fans; and ordered the benching of Reggie Jackson—took its toll on the team and Lemon in particular. After winning the first two games in New York, the Yankees were trailing 5–4 into the eighth inning of Game 3 when the first two batters, Aurelio Rodriguez and Larry Milbourne, reached on singles. With the pitcher, Rudy May, due up, Lemon looked down the bench. It was clearly a sacrifice situation, but rather than waste a player, Lemon could just as well have had May bunt.

Instead, he sought out a pinch hitter, hollering: "Where's my bunter?" Nobody moved, and Lemon repeated his call for a bunter. Finally, when still nobody answered, he screamed: "Where the hell is Murcer?"

Murcer, sitting at the end of the bench, was dumbfounded. *Was Lemon serious? Was he really asking me to go up there and bunt? Is this how he was going to use the one guy on the bench who could hit the ball out of the ballpark?* Murcer, who had led American League pinch hitters with three homers (including an Opening Day grand slam) and 12 RBI in '81, couldn't recall the last time he'd been asked to bunt, and his unfamiliarity showed as he popped the ball into the air, just outside the foul line midway between home and third. Dodger third baseman Ron Cey made a diving catch of it and then recovered to throw over to Steve Garvey at first, doubling off Milbourne. Not only did that all but end the last Yankee threat in that game, they went on to lose the next three as well and did not appear in another World Series for 15 years. As for Murcer, his line for his one World Series was no hits in three pinch-hit at bats.

"The highlight of my World Series career," Murcer said with a laugh. "I'm still trying to figure that one out. Years afterward, Lou never let me hear the end of it. He'd yell at me from across restaurants: 'Where's my *bunter?'* I got just two other chances to pinch-hit in that Series, the last one when Lem sent me up to hit for Tommy John in the fourth inning of the last game at Yankee Stadium. The score was tied 1–1, and T.J., I know, was really hot about being taken out in that situation. It was kind of a quick hook, but Lem was desperate and I guess he decided that was when he was gonna take his one big shot. At least he let me hit away, and I took Burt Hooton to the warning track in right."

After that deflating and confounding World Series defeat, Steinbrenner vowed to remake the Yankees with youth and speed. In particular, he decided it was time to phase out Murcer and Piniella and assigned veteran scout Birdie Tebbetts to scour the National League for outfielders who could hit for high average and steal bases. Tebbetts zeroed in on the Cincinnati Reds and recommended to Steinbrenner two of their outfielders, Ken Griffey, who was later acquired in a trade, and Davey Collins, who was signed as a free agent. But as he was often wont to do, Steinbrenner hedged his bets as spring training approached and, in a bit of characteristic sentimentality on his part, he abruptly re-signed Piniella and Murcer to three-year $1.1 million contracts.

"I guess you could say that was my 'golden parachute,'" Murcer said, laughing again. "I had already sold my house in Franklin Lakes, New Jersey. The Yankees really didn't have a place for me, so I became the highest-paid pinch hitter in the history of the game. George had always said he was sorry for allowing Gabe to trade me and maybe this was his way of making it up to me. I only know I was forever grateful to him. Like I told the guys in my BAT address, I was one of the lucky ones."

Murcer's career finally came to an end June 20, 1983, when he announced his retirement and was replaced on the Yankee roster by an up-and-coming outfielder–first baseman, Don Mattingly. From the "highest-paid pinch hitter in history" he was now going to be, at least temporarily, the highest-paid broadcaster in baseball. Steinbrenner was obligated to pay him approximately $360,000 per year for the next two seasons and as Murcer said in recalling it: "The world could come to an end, but baseball contracts are still guaranteed."

On August 7, they held Bobby Murcer Day before another packed house at Yankee Stadium. After being showered with gifts and accolades from his teammates, past and present, as well as a videotaped salute from Mantle on the scoreboard screen, Murcer stepped to the microphone and said: "If I had to choose between the Hall of Fame or being honored here, I would choose this. I consider the Yankees the greatest sports franchise in the world; Yankee Stadium the greatest stadium in the world; and Yankee fans the greatest fans in the world. When they come out to honor a player, it's something special."

"You said in your speech on Bobby Murcer Day that you considered that a bigger honor than even the Hall of Fame," I said to him, "and yet, as the years have passed, Yankee fans seem to put you in the same exalted place as most of their Hall of Famers."

"It's a very heartwarming feeling to have people respect me and even think of me in that revered territory," Murcer said. "It's special for me because I've had such a passion for New York City. Over 40 years, I probably spent more time in New York than Oklahoma City. It never scared me one bit."

If nothing else, his lifetime numbers—.277, 252 homers, 1,043 RBI for 1,908 games—place him in the Hall of Very Good. On the Yankees' all-time top 20 lists, he shows up only once, his 175 homers having ranked 16th as of 2002. And yet, the perception of him as one of the great Yankees has lingered.

"Those two years I missed in the army . . . the four years I missed not being with the Yankees . . . and then when I came back it was like I'd lost some of my seniority," he said. "I was there for all the transitional years and just when we were getting ready to go to the top, I was gone and that hurt. If I hadn't been traded and stayed healthy, I could have contributed as long as I'd wanted to."

So he didn't come close to becoming another Mantle, and maybe his stats suggest he doesn't deserve to be held in quite the same esteem as all the other Yankee deities in Monument Park. Yet, in Bobby Murcer's case, the stats do not come close to defining what he was to the Yankees and their fans as the bridge to two championship eras. They cheered him like no other Yankee had ever been cheered the night he single-handedly won that game for his fallen friend and teammate, Thurman Munson. As far as they were concerned he was a part of that team Munson had led to the two straight world championships. And every Old-Timers' Day his introduction still draws among the lustiest of ovations. It is as if they wanted him to know they shared his pain at being deprived of fulfilling his Yankee destiny. And they had not forgotten that long-ago time when he was the best they had.

THE BOSS'S BOY

LOU PINIELLA

According to the 2000 census figures, the population of Tampa, Florida, and its metropolitan area is 2.4 million, or slightly more than double what it was in 1970 when Malio Iavarone opened up his restaurant and bistro on Dale Mabry Boulevard, the main thoroughfare that runs north and south through this Gulf Coast city. It was partly a private club back then, but through the years, as Tampa took on more and more of a big league identity with its landing of professional franchises in football, hockey and baseball, Malio's evolved into the prime gathering place for the area's sporting elite.

The hundreds of personally inscribed pictures of sports figures that blanket the wall along the entrance hallway and in the area of the more private booths just off the main dining room offer irrefutable proof of Malio being the *man* in Tampa. Or at least the man with whom the town's other more nationally renowned celebrities all want to schmooze. Only two of them, however, have been accorded their own private rooms in the place, and that's what separates George Steinbrenner and Lou Piniella from the rest of Tampa's sports cognoscenti, if, alas, not from themselves.

As it so happened, on the day I had arranged to meet with Piniella at Malio's, Steinbrenner was sitting in a booth adjacent to the Steinbrenner and Piniella rooms, having lunch with a group of men, one of whom was Eddie Robinson, the legendary football coach at Grambling University. The man they first started calling The Boss in New York more than a quarter-century earlier appeared startled to see me wandering past his booth.

"What are *you* doing here?" he asked. "Aren't you a little early for spring training?"

Steinbrenner, a native of Cleveland, arrived in Tampa in 1973, the same year he and a group of investors bought the New York Yankees from CBS for $8.8 million. Through the years, he gradually moved the Yankees' base of operations to Tampa, beginning with the minor league facilities in the mid-'80s and culminating in the state-of-the-art spring training complex and stadium he got the city to construct for him in 1996, about five miles north on Dale Mabry from Malio's, right across the highway from the NFL Tampa Bay Buccaneers' stadium.

He was right, this was early January and not only were there six weeks to go before his Yankees would begin spring training, the same went for the Seattle Mariners, whom Piniella had managed since 1993. The Mariners, however, trained in Peoria, Arizona, which caused a bit of a hardship for Piniella in that it took him away from home an additional seven weeks in a baseball season that already extended from April to late October.

Indeed, working all this time, 3,000 miles across the country in the great northwest, was not something Piniella envisioned when he sold the house in New Jersey he'd lived in for the 15 years he'd been with the Yankees as a player, coach, manager and general manager, and moved back home to Tampa. All the time Piniella was with the Yankees, they trained in Fort Lauderdale, which, if nothing else, was just a short trek across the state for his wife and family. But how convenient, he often thought, if he could have spent the entire spring right here at home. Instead, he had come home two straight Octobers, having lost to the Yankees in the playoffs, and all he saw were those huge NY logos emblazoned on all those buildings on North Dale Mabry, a painful reminder of what might have been.

"Believe it or not, George," I said, "I'm not down here to spy on you. I'm down here to see your favorite son, Lou."

"Lou?" he said. "Do you believe that guy was in here—in my place a week ago—with all his Mariners people, and they were entertaining some free agent player? Right here!"

He pointed to the Piniella room, as his party of friends in the booth smiled thinly, not sure if his sense of outrage was sincere or merely "George-jest."

"Well," I said, "if you were Lou where else in this town would you take a player you're recruiting for your ball club? The Yankee complex?"

Steinbrenner laughed. "Yeah, I guess you're right," he said, adding: "This is the only time of year Lou is ever around home here anyway. It's always fun running into him. You know how I feel about him."

It's fine now, I thought, some 13 years removed from when Steinbrenner fired Piniella as Yankee manager for the second time. Time heals all wounds they say, and even Piniella would admit he was a better manager now and a much calmer and controlled person than he was then. There are some things, however, that never change about a person and in Piniella's case it was the competitor within. Just because he no longer engaged in the childish, base-throwing, hat-kicking temper rages at umpires that had made his reputation as one of baseball's all-time red-asses, didn't mean there wasn't still that same burning desire to win, especially, it seemed, when it came to Steinbrenner and the Yankees.

A couple of weeks before, Steinbrenner had completed his off-season shopping spree, having bagged in the free agent market Jason

Giambi, the Oakland Athletics' muscular hitting machine and 2000 American League MVP; Steve Karsay, a versatile and talented late-inning relief pitcher with roots in Queens, and Rondell White, a gifted but much-injured right-handed hitting outfielder. White, in particular, had been a target of Piniella's Mariners, who had a glaring need for a power bat in left field. But, in the end, the Yankees moved more quickly and with more money and got their man.

Malio himself had shown me to a booth, three down from Steinbrenner's, and had brought a platter of stone crabs while we waited for Piniella, who, for all of his latent maturity, could still always be counted on to be at least an hour late for an appointment. And as if on cue for our 1 P.M. meeting, Piniella arrived a few minutes after two, by which time Steinbrenner and his party had departed.

"You just missed George," Malio said.

"The Boss," Piniella growled, bearing a mock frown. "He's had some winter, hasn't he? The *Yankees!* Is there *anybody* they didn't get that they wanted? We wanted White and they just swooped in and grabbed him . . . Sorry I'm late. I got caught up in shopping and forgot what time it was. What I need now is a nice martini."

Malio signaled to his restaurant manager, Christine Holloway, to bring Piniella his drink. The two of them had been friends for more than 30 years, having grown up together in Tampa, Malio attending Hillsborough High School and Piniella, the Catholic, Jesuit High. Before Piniella had arrived for our meeting, Malio confided that things tended to get a little tense in his restaurant back in the late '80s after Steinbrenner fired Piniella for the second time and the two would frequently be in the place at the same time. "Lou will always be my friend, we're like brothers," Malio said, "and George is my friend, too. When he's in one of his moods, I just stay away from him."

"George was saying how you guys were wining and dining some other free agent in here a couple of weeks ago," I said to Piniella.

"That Steinbrenner," Piniella said, now laughing. "He's something else. We were here, Pat Gillick, our general manager, Lee Pelekoudas, his assistant, Bob Engle, one of our other top guys, and myself, and we're having lunch with Roger Cedeno, another free agent outfielder. Wouldn't you know, The Boss comes in and does a double take when he sees us all sitting there. He says something about how he can't believe we're in here doing business in his place.

"He looks at Cedeno and he says: 'When you're done here, if you want some real money come back and see me. These people aren't gonna pay you anything.' He was laughing when he said it, but then a little while later he walks back and he's carrying a couple of pizzas with him and he says: 'This is what it's come to. I can't afford to eat here anymore. I've spent all my money and look at me now: I've got to resort to take-out pizza.'"

Piniella rolled with laughter again and lit up a cigarette as Holloway set his martini down in front of him.

Actually, it had been almost exactly three years earlier when The Boss had assembled his Yankee brain trust in the Steinbrenner room to finalize negotiations on one of the biggest trades in club history—pitchers David Wells and Graeme Lloyd and infielder Homer Bush to the Toronto Blue Jays for future Hall of Famer Roger Clemens. It was mentioned in all the stories across the country that Malio's was where The Boss polled his troops on the deal and hashed out the final details before making the call to Toronto.

"George had me install a private phone line for him in his room," Malio noted.

"You'll notice," said Piniella, "I don't have a phone line in *my* room."

Nor nearly the space. The two rooms are in fact one very large private dining room, which Malio had partitioned a few years ago to create two smaller rooms. Steinbrenner's, however, takes up about three-quarters of the space. One assumes he wouldn't have it any other way, even though Piniella's room is mostly ceremonial—a testimonial from his pal Malio—and rarely used by him for anything other than perhaps a private dinner party.

He is one of the finest athletes ever to come out of Tampa, and there've been plenty of them before and after him—Rick Casares, the great Chicago Bears running back; Al Lopez, the Hall of Fame catcher and manager; Steve Garvey, Wade Boggs, Tony LaRussa, Dwight Gooden, Fred McGriff, Tino Martinez, Luis Gonzalez. Piniella excelled in both baseball and basketball at Jesuit High and went to the University of Tampa on a basketball scholarship. Throughout high school, however, he had drawn most attention from baseball scouts, particularly Spud Chandler, the old Yankee pitcher and 1943 American League Most Valuable Player, who was then working for the Cleveland Indians.

"I was offered bonus money of over $50,000 from both the Phillies and the Tigers after I graduated high school," Piniella related, "but my parents wanted me to go to college. I played baseball and basketball my freshman year at Tampa and after taking my final exams, I came home and Spud was sitting in his car right there in my driveway and he says: 'Do you want to play pro ball?' And I said: 'Yeah, I really do.' The amazing thing was, because nobody else thought I was gonna sign, the Indians were the only team to offer me a contract at that time and I signed for half of what I'd been offered the year before, including the rest of my scholarship at Tampa. I didn't know anything about what Spud had done as a pitcher with the Yankees, but he was very convincing."

Chandler, it turned out, was just the first in a long line of former Yankees to play a significant role in Piniella's career—before he ever became a Yankee—and, looking back at it years later, he came to believe that there must have been some hidden destiny there. Upon signing a contract with Chandler that June day in 1962, Piniella was assigned by the Indians to their rookie league team in Selma, Alabama, where he hit .270 in 70 games. The following December, however, he was left off the Indians' 40-man roster and subsequently drafted by the Washington Senators, who sent him to Peninsula in the Class A Carolina League. And though he hit .310 with 16 homers and 77 RBI in 143 games, his stint in the Senator organization was likewise short-lived.

"I had made $650 a month playing for Selma," Piniella recalled, "and when I got drafted by the Senators—I was the first player picked in the major league draft that winter—I thought I'd get a handsome raise. That's where I encountered more Yankee ties. George Selkirk, who'd been an outfielder with the Yankees in the '30s and '40s, was the Senators' general manager and he sent me a contract for the same $650 a month. I wrote him a sort of feisty letter and got an equally feisty letter in return. So I re-signed for the $650 and had the real nice year in the Carolina League.

"The following year the Vietnam War was beginning to heat up, and the Senators got me into a National Guard unit in Washington, D.C. I missed about half the summer. While I was in the army, doing my reserve duty, I was traded to the Baltimore Orioles."

What had soured the Senators on Piniella was a serious off-the-field injury he'd incurred late in the '63 season. In what he would only say was a "flight of fancy during a party we held late in the season," he tore up his left forearm crashing through a glass door. They were ready to call him up to the big club, too. Instead Piniella wound up in a hospital with 40 stitches. That winter, the Senators sent him to the instructional league, but the strength in his arm had been sapped by all the torn muscle and tendon damage and he could barely swing a bat.

"So I came out of the army late in 1964 and reported to the Orioles' farm team in Aberdeen, North Dakota, which was managed by Cal Ripken Sr.," Piniella said. "We had quite a team there. Jim Palmer was there . . . Mark Belanger was my roommate . . . and the next year I went to spring training with them in Miami where I met my next Yankee connection—Hank Bauer, who was the Oriole manager. I had a few problems with Hank, too. He didn't like my carousing too much.

"One night he caught me out after curfew. I was at the bar and the bartender came over and said: 'A nice gentleman over there just bought you another Jack Daniel's and water.' I looked over and there's Bauer. He yelled to me from across the room: 'Enjoy it, because tomorrow you're gonna pay for it!' The next day, I got to the ballpark and he said:

'Son, you don't need your bat or your glove today. I just want you to start circling the field.'"

He roared with laughter again, then asked the waitress if she could bring him a pack of Marlboro Lights.

By now, Piniella had been a professional baseball player for three years and had already been with three organizations. It also became quickly apparent his relationship with the Orioles was going to be a strained one. The general manager of the Orioles, Lee MacPhail—who had previously been the farm director for the Yankees—told Piniella when he acquired him that if he showed he had his strength back in the brief time left to play that season at Aberdeen he'd be brought to the big leagues.

"MacPhail made good on his promise and I joined the Orioles that September," Piniella said. "My first at bat was against the Angels and a pitcher named Fred Newman. I grounded out to second base and when I came back to the dugout, our pitcher that day, Robin Roberts, said: 'Son, I could have done that!' The next spring the Orioles sent me to their minor league camp in Bainbridge, Georgia, and I rolled in there about two in the morning. They had these barracks and I'm just lying down on my bunk and this guy comes by and shines this light in my eye. I was a little discourteous to him . . . I said something . . . and he said: 'Who in the hell do you think you are, coming down here from the major league camp, showing up in the middle of the night when everybody's already been working out!' That was my introduction to Earl Weaver. After he got done ranting at me, he said: 'Tomorrow you won't need your glove or your bat!' They got me again!"

That summer, Piniella played for Weaver in Elmira, New York, and, for the first time, struggled with the bat, hitting only .249.

"That was the year I got introduced to the slider," he said. "Plus, Earl and I didn't get along too well. At one point, he came to me and said: 'Son, you're never gonna get to the majors. You're too much of a red-ass.' I said to him: 'Earl, you're a fine one to talk!' At the end of the year they traded me back to Cleveland."

"By now, didn't you start to wonder why you kept getting traded?" I asked.

"I wasn't smart enough to figure it out then," he said, "but I am smart enough to figure it out now that I've been in management so long. I had a bad temper and a little bit of an arrogant attitude. I was respectful, but I probably thought I was better than I was. In a lot of ways, that season in Elmira and getting traded again was a wake-up call for me. Up until then, all through Little League, PONY League, high school and college and the pros I'd never known failure. Going back to the Cleveland organization was the best thing that ever happened to me because it got me together with Johnny Lipon."

Despite his budding bad boy reputation and the subpar year he'd had at Elmira in '65, the Indians invited Piniella to the major league camp the following spring, primarily because they wanted to convert him to a catcher. That experiment was short-lived, however—Piniella said it took only one session catching the hard-throwing but often erratic Sudden Sam McDowell to convince him catching was not for him—and he was sent out on the first roster cut to the Indians' Triple A team, the Portland Beavers of the Pacific Coast League. The Beavers were managed by Lipon, a baseball lifer who'd been a backup shortstop in the big leagues from 1942 to 1954 and then a minor league manager at all levels for the next two decades.

"Lipon told me: 'With your hitting style'—I was a straight pull hitter—'you're going to have to start making changes. You have to start hitting the ball up the middle and to right and left center and forget pulling,'" Piniella related. "He said he was willing to live with that as long as I worked on it. Then he got me an old Nellie Fox bat with the thick handle and made me choke up on it and every day this man would come out early to the ballpark and throw batting practice to me with the stipulation that I didn't pull the ball. That's when I started developing into a major league ballplayer and Johnny Lipon had more influence on me than any other person. He forced me to change and, more importantly, he *allowed* me to change at the

Triple A level. I was forever thankful to that man. I told him, too."

Still, promotion to the big leagues was slow in coming. Despite steady improvement into a consistent .300 hitter, Piniella spent the next three seasons at Portland and contemplated quitting.

"Baseball was going to expand for the 1969 season," he said, "and I made up my mind if I can't get to the big leagues with that, then I just wasn't good enough. I got drafted in the third round by the new Seattle team after the '68 season and went with them to Tempe, Arizona, for spring training where my roommate was Mike Ferraro, who'd been drafted out of the Yankee system. Years later, he'd be one of my coaches with the Yankees, but you can see where this whole Yankee connection was kinda weird. Plus, the general manager at Cleveland, who'd originally signed me, then traded me, then got me back was Gabe Paul, who wound up going to the Yankees and trading for me again!"

Like all his previous professional big league stops, the expansion Seattle Pilots proved to be a brief venue for Piniella. It seemed they had a shortage of left-handed hitters and the day before the '69 season was to begin, they traded Piniella to the Kansas City Royals for a left-handed hitting outfielder named Steve Whitaker.

"Another ex-Yankee," Piniella mused, "and then when I joined the Royals, the manager there was Joe Gordon, yet *another* ex-Yankee, who'd been an MVP for them in 1942. You tell me if I wasn't destined to be a Yankee? I really enjoyed playing for Joe. He gave me my first real chance in the big leagues. I was his Opening Day lead-off hitter and center fielder and went 4-for-5! I wound up winning Rookie of the Year—the oldest American League Rookie of the Year ever. I'd still have that distinction if it weren't for my two Japanese kids in Seattle [reliever Kazuhiro Sasaki and right fielder Ichiro Suzuki, who won back-to-back Rookie of the Year honors in 2000 and 2001]. They saved me."

Piniella hit .282 with 11 homers and 68 RBI in '69 and improved those numbers to .301-11-88 the following year. He spent five seasons in Kansas City, but after a drop-off from .312 to .250 in 1973, the Royals traded him to the Yankees for veteran relief pitcher Lindy

McDaniel. This proved to be the first in a series of successful trades executed by Paul (who had moved from the Indians to the Yankees after being instrumental in helping Steinbrenner purchase the team from CBS) that transformed the Yankees into champions again. In subsequent seasons, Paul acquired first baseman Chris Chambliss and reliever Dick Tidrow from the Indians; center fielder Mickey Rivers and right-handed pitcher Ed Figueroa from the California Angels; second baseman Willie Randolph from the Pittsburgh Pirates, and shortstop Bucky Dent from the Chicago White Sox—all of whom played pivotal roles in the Yankees' 1976–78 championship teams. Wily old Gabe, who was also the front man in the free agent signings of Catfish Hunter and Reggie Jackson, surely had a Midas touch when he was running the Yankees for Steinbrenner in those early years. At the same time, though, he never forgot the lessons of frugality when negotiating players' salaries that he'd learned from previous terms as GM of the revenue-challenged Indians and Cincinnati Reds.

"I found that out right away," Piniella said. "The 1974 season was, I think, the first year of salary arbitration and, even though I'd hit only .250, when I got traded to the Yankees I felt I should have a cost-of-living increase going to New York, which was a lot more expensive to live in than Kansas City. We couldn't get a deal set with Gabe so I filed for $57,500 and the Yankees countered with the same $52,500 I'd made the year before. That season they were renovating Yankee Stadium and the Yankees were playing at Shea and they had all their offices out there in trailers when my attorney and I went to New York to talk to Gabe.

"There was a little Chinese restaurant right next to Shea Stadium, which is where Gabe met us. We had a nice lunch, but we didn't resolve anything and we were ready to go to arbitration that afternoon. Then, just before we were ready to leave, they brought us a dish of fortune cookies. I opened mine up and the message inside said: 'Be satisfied with what you get.'"

He laughed some more and drained the rest of his martini.

"That's a true story! Don't tell me that damn message wasn't planted there by Gabe! So we settled for $55,000 and I became a Yankee."

He was a Yankee maybe, but he hadn't yet met the new owner. And even though they were both now Tampa residents, they didn't know each other. Their first meeting was the day Piniella arrived at spring training in late February of 1974, oblivious to the Yankee code of grooming. His hair was near shoulder length and he had a couple of days' growth of facial hair when he reported for duty at the Yankee clubhouse in Fort Lauderdale that morning.

"I went to the clubhouse man, Nick Priore, and asked for my uniform and he said to me: 'You have to go see Mr. Steinbrenner first,'" Piniella said. "So I had to go see The Boss, over in his trailer, before I got my uniform. I walked in there and George says to me I have to get my hair cut and everything trimmed a little bit. I told him: 'I don't see why I have to do this. What has this got to do with baseball and how I play?' Then I said: 'Our Lord and Savior Jesus Christ had long hair.'"

"That must have been interesting," I said. "What was his response?"

"He said to me: 'Son, I want you to come with me,' and we walked around to this little lake that was out beyond the outfield wall at the complex," Piniella related. "When we got there, he said: 'If you can walk across that pond, you can wear your hair any way you want!' So I got my hair cut and then I *officially* became a Yankee."

And thus began the happiest years of Piniella's life. It was the most special of teams, he said, able to bond—and win—together in spite of all of Steinbrenner's manic meddling and constant injections of turmoil into the status quo. Piniella was the one they all got along with, mostly because he was so easygoing and fun-loving off the field. Whether or not it was his Spanish blood, he, especially, seemed blind to race and all its accompanying prejudices. At the same time, his notorious Spanish temper and obsessions for swinging a bat in front of the clubhouse mirror made him such easy prey for his teammates' good-natured barbs. The acerbic and irreverent bus ride banter between Piniella and Catfish Hunter, especially, became the stuff of legend through the years.

On one trip in 1979, as the team was pulling into Kansas City after a late-night flight from New York, the two of them engaged in one of the all-time classic rank sessions. It began with Catfish demeaning Piniella for having been replaced in the Royals' outfield by a singles hitter named Jim Wohlford, who hit a total of 21 homers in 15 years in the major leagues.

"Here we are," Catfish announced, as the Yankee bus crossed over the bridge that led into Kansas City, "the city where Jim Wooah-ford . . . *Jim fucking Wooahford* . . . beat Lou out of a job! Can you believe that?"

"That's okay, Catfish," Piniella shot back. "I can't wait till we get back to New York. When are they having another day for you, anyway? How many more toasters and sets of golf clubs do we have to give you to get you out of here? The next time we go to Boston and you pitch there, they're gonna have to close down Lansdowne Street and declare it a hard hat area because of all the damn home runs! As it is, from now on when you pitch in the Stadium, I've got to sit in the right field seats with a crab net to catch all those balls hit into the seats."

The memory of it turned Piniella somber for a moment. The two most respected players on those '70s Yankee championship teams were Hunter and Thurman Munson, and now both of them were gone, cut down in the prime of their lives; Munson in a crash of his private jet in 1979, and Catfish in 1999, the victim of amyotrophic lateral sclerosis, the same muscle-deteriorating disease that had killed the Yankee great Lou Gehrig. Munson had already been the team leader when Piniella came over to the Yankees from the Royals in 1974, while Hunter, who had been the pitching ace of the Oakland Athletics championship teams of 1972–74, brought his own quiet, veteran leadership and savvy when he signed with the Yankees as a celebrated free agent on New Year's Eve 1974.

The true measure of Munson's and Hunter's respect was that Steinbrenner never dared to engage them in verbal warfare as he was wont to do so often with his players in those days. When Munson died in '79 and Hunter retired the same year, it was as if The Boss had been unchained and no Yankee was safe from his rages and retributions. And it was around the time of Hunter's death in 1999 that Piniella's friends noticed a difference in him in that his characteristic ragings had become tempered by a new spirituality.

"Catfish," Piniella said softly, "was as good a teammate as anyone could ever play with, and a good friend, too. It was so tragic the way he died, and you know, it's amazing, my father-in-law suffered the same fate a year or so later. As for Thurman, he epitomized what the term competitor meant. Just a tough, tough, cranky competitor. Productive. Played hurt, with stitches, knees always bothering him . . . whatever. It was clearly his team when I got there. What good people on those teams. Nettles at third base, another really tough competitor, and then they got Willie from Pittsburgh to play second. The whole thing, you could see, was starting to fall into place."

In 1974, Piniella's first year with the Yankees, they went down to the final weekend of the season before losing out to the Baltimore Orioles by two games. Perhaps because he was under investigation by the Justice Department for making illegal campaign contributions to President Nixon, Steinbrenner, who would later be convicted of the charges and suspended from baseball for a year, had not yet emerged as the tyrant for which he would become legendary. And so the Yankees, and particularly Piniella, were mercifully spared his wrath in the aftermath of that calamitous lost weekend in Milwaukee.

Under first-year manager Bill Virdon, they had actually led the American League East in early September, only to suffer a three-game sweep against the Orioles at Shea Stadium in the middle of the month to fall back and never regain the lead. The Orioles, who were now managed by Piniella's old nemesis, Earl Weaver, staged a remarkable stretch drive, winning 28 of their last 34 games, 15 of them by one run, to overtake the Yankees. With two games to go, however, the Yankees were still mathematically alive as they pulled into Milwaukee for the season-ending series against the Brewers.

That slim chance, however, went up in flames before they ever got on the field. On the team bus from the airport, an argument broke out between teammates Bill Sudakis and Rick Dempsey that escalated into a full-blown fight when they reached the hotel. Bobby Murcer, who'd become the Yankees' right fielder after Virdon moved him out of center (where he'd been a fixture since 1969), sought to break it up and, in the process, suffered a broken finger.

With Murcer unable to play the next day, Piniella was assigned to play right for the first time all season. The Yankees were winning 2–0 going into the eighth inning behind a stalwart pitching effort from George "Doc" Medich when the Brewers threatened with a one-out triple by Bob Hansen. The next batter, Don Money, hit a slicing fly ball to right-center that Murcer probably would have caught, albeit with some difficulty. Piniella, however, couldn't get a read on the ball, and switched directions in trying to follow it. Elliott Maddox, rushing over from center, then made a desperate, diving effort to catch it, but missed as the ball skirted between them for another triple. The next batter, Sixto Lezcano, tied the game with a sac fly and the Brewers went on to win it in the 10th, to officially eliminate the Yankees.

"That was the infamous dropped ball to which Weaver later said 'I knew Piniella would somehow screw it up for them,'" Piniella said, laughing some more."He told me later: 'That's why when you went to the 1972 All-Star Game I told you not to bring a glove!' He used me as a pinch hitter. That damn Weaver! The next year, we had a lot of injuries and Bill Virdon got fired in August. I've got to say, though, Virdon made me a good outfielder. For whatever quality outfielder I turned out to be, he's responsible. He took it as a personal challenge to work with me on my outfield defense in spring training, both years he was the manager.

"Virdon was a real taskmaster. After every spring training workout, he'd have us run bases around the infield and he'd stand there and give you the thumbs-up to go in or the thumbs-down to take another lap. Well, no matter how fast I'd run, he'd always give me the down. I did this for about 4, 5 times. So, one day, I ran behind Duke Sims and when

Virdon was giving Duke the up I got right on the other side of him so Virdon couldn't give the down to me! Wouldn't you know, he came into the clubhouse to get me, but I was already in the shower."

After that '74 season, Piniella played almost as much right field as he did in left for the rest of his career. The fielding skills he learned from Virdon all came to fruition that sun-splashed October 2, 1978, afternoon in Fenway Park in the playoff game against the Red Sox. The Yankees were clinging to a 5–4 lead in the ninth inning, thanks mostly to Dent's three-run homer in the seventh, when Rick Burleson drew a one-out walk and Jerry Remy hit a slicing liner to right that was almost identical to the one Piniella had botched in Milwaukee four years earlier. Blinded by the sun, Piniella put his glove up and did all he could just to keep the ball in front of him, as Virdon had taught him. Upon retrieving it on one hop, and recovering with amazing quickness to fire the ball on a line to third base, he was able to hold Burleson at second—which proved to be a critical play when Jim Rice followed with a fly-out to right that would have easily scored a runner from third. Yankee closer Goose Gossage then retired Red Sox icon Carl Yastrzemski on a pop-up to third to end the game.

Years later, Don Zimmer, who was the losing Red Sox manager, said another play Piniella made in right field that day was the one he considered to be even more pivotal in the Yankee win. In the sixth inning, with Boston leading 2–0, the Red Sox had runners at first and second with two outs against Ron Guidry when the left-handed hitting Fred Lynn hit a fly ball into the right field corner. From his vantage point in the dugout, Zimmer was certain the ball would go for an extra-base hit that would add to the lead, only to be stunned to see Piniella run over and make the catch.

"I couldn't believe Piniella was in position to make that catch," Zimmer said. "Afterward, I asked him how he got over there like that and he explained to me that he saw Guidry was getting tired and felt Lynn would be able to pull the ball. So he moved a few feet closer to the right field line. To me, that's just smart outfield play. That was the turning point of the game as far as I'm concerned."

"When you look at my whole career, basically it was always associated with hitting," Piniella said, "but when you want to look at a defining moment of my career, it was probably those two defensive plays in the playoff game. I remember after the game, Mike Lupica of the *Daily News* asked me how I was able to make that play and I told him: 'When you play on a world championship team, *somebody's* gonna make that play and that's the truth. When you play on a world championship team, people make plays, whether it's me or whoever. It was the same thing in the '78 World Series when Nettles made those four sensational plays at third base when Guidry was pitching Game 3. That turned the whole Series around."

The change of Yankee managers from Virdon to Billy Martin in August of 1975 touched off one of the most tumultuous periods in Yankee history. With each passing day after his suspension was lifted, March 1, 1976, for "good behavior," Steinbrenner's ego was inflating commensurate to the team's rising attendance and increased exposure on the back pages of the New York tabloids. The fiery Martin merely reinforced that and, then, after the Yankees' return to the World Series in 1976 for the first time in 12 years, Steinbrenner threw a torch into what was already a highly combustible mix of himself and Martin by signing Reggie Jackson. The Yankees had been swept by the Cincinnati Reds in the '76 series and Steinbrenner was determined to spend whatever it took to give them baseball supremacy. In Jackson, the premier slugger on the free agent market who had led the American League in homers in two of the previous four seasons, he saw not only a missing link cleanup hitter but also an irresistible gate attraction.

"Reggie came over there and he was used to being the top guy in the clubhouse and rightfully so, but we already had a top guy and that was Thurman," Piniella said. "At the same time, Billy wasn't too fond of Reggie being on the team as a free agent so there was friction almost from day one. Nevertheless, we played through all of it and won. It was a team in which all the components didn't get along all that well, but when the game started, everyone was competitive and put all that behind them."

The growing hostility between Jackson and Martin reached the breaking point in Boston on June 18. It was the Saturday afternoon national TV game of the week and, after Jackson seemingly loped after a ball in right field that fell in for a hit, Martin sent Paul Blair out to replace him in the middle of the inning. When Reggie got to the dugout, angry words were exchanged with Martin and, in full view of the TV cameras, they had to be restrained from coming to blows with each other.

A primary source of contention between the two was Martin's avowed refusal to bat Reggie in his accustomed cleanup spot. Now, the die had been cast and the rumblings grew louder with each passing day that Steinbrenner was going to fire Martin because of his inability to get along with the Yankees' newest star. A couple of weeks after the Fenway Park incident, things came to a head in Milwaukee when Piniella, Munson and a couple of other players asked for a meeting with Steinbrenner in his suite at the Pfister Hotel, where the team was staying.

"Primarily," Piniella said, "we went to George about getting Billy to hit Reggie fourth. It wasn't something we did behind Billy's back—in fact he came in to the meeting shortly after we had gotten there—and we all sat down as a group and convinced Billy to hit this guy fourth. We were a very confident team and, believe it or not, we had a great relationship with the owner then. Was he liked by everyone? No. But everyone appreciated the fact that he wanted to win, that he was competitive as hell and that he'd do anything in his power to make the team succeed, including writing checks—which he did a lot of. That's what I remember. What a great situation that was between the owner giving us the resources and the professional bunch of athletes we had on that team."

As he talked, he instinctively rubbed the '77 world championship ring on his finger. It is the only ring he wears, despite having won another one in '78 and a third one as manager of the world champion Cincinnati Reds in 1990.

"I've always worn this ring," he said, "I guess because it was my first one. The first one is always the most special and that '77 season, in which we won 40 of our last 50 games to kind of storm to the pennant the way we did, and then Reggie hitting those three home runs in the last game of the Series against the Dodgers . . ."

He paused and continued rubbing his ring as if reliving that electric Bronx night in his mind.

The following season, in which the Yankees repeated as world champions only after making up a 14-game mid-July deficit on the Red Sox, Martin, who had continued to clash repeatedly with Jackson and Steinbrenner, resigned under fire, July 24. Piniella had his confrontations with Steinbrenner, too, although, as the rest of the players all recognized, theirs was a relationship based on affection. Because they both lived in Tampa and would frequently run into each other at the various sports banquets, as well as in places like Malio's and the race track, Steinbrenner felt a closeness to Piniella that he didn't have with the rest of his players. As the years went by, he would frequently be quoted as saying: "Everybody knows, Lou is like a son to me."

Of course, such comments merely emboldened Piniella those times when Steinbrenner would take to pouting over losses and scolding his team.

After the Yankees lost two straight games to the Milwaukee Brewers that evened the best-of-five divisional playoff series in 1981, Steinbrenner elected to address the troops in the clubhouse before the deciding Game 5. In his best General George Patton "when the going gets tough, the tough get going" manner, Steinbrenner told his players how he'd learned to be tough by working on the docks in Cleveland as a youth where the family had its shipbuilding business.

"I told George afterward, it was a great speech," Piniella said, "but then I added: 'Of course you and I know the only time you were ever down on the docks was to gas up your daddy's 100-foot yacht!' He laughed. We had a good relationship and he knew I liked to kid around with him a lot."

In a similar incident, Steinbrenner was infuriated when the Yankees lost the final game of the 1978 season to the Cleveland Indians, thus forcing the one-game playoff with the Red Sox in Boston for the division title. On the chartered flight up to Boston, Steinbrenner was sitting by himself in the front of the plane, fuming silently. Once the plane reached its cruising altitude, Piniella got out of his seat and walked up to the owner and startled him by saying for everyone in earshot to hear: "What are *you* so pissed off about, Boss? You're the luckiest guy in the whole world. Not only are you gonna go back home to win another world championship, you're gonna get another gate out of this!"

There were other times, however, when the verbal jousting between the two wasn't just kidding around. In the spring of 1982, for instance, Piniella had just been given a new three-year $1 million contract by Steinbrenner—a sort of golden parachute to a favorite Yankee player who, at 39, had been considering retirement. It was a nice gesture on Steinbrenner's part, but there was one small catch: a weight clause, which required Piniella to report to camp under 200 pounds. Steinbrenner had even gone to the lengths of sending his longtime aide, the former Heisman Trophy–winning running back from Ohio State, Hopalong Cassady, to Piniella's home in Tampa to work out with the veteran outfielder.

It was a noble idea on Steinbrenner's part, but it wound up turning into a farce as Piniella, seeing the obstacle course Cassady had set up for him at a local track, made a wager with the old football star that he, Cassady, couldn't complete it in a stipulated time. Cassady took him up on it and for the next few days, Piniella would sit in the stands with a stopwatch, drinking coffee and reading the newspaper, while Cassady huffed and puffed his way around the track. As he shook his head, indicating to Cassady that he still hadn't made the time, all Piniella could think of were those constant thumbs-down gestures he'd gotten from Virdon eight years earlier.

By the time Piniella reported to Fort Lauderdale that spring, he was in no better shape than he'd been any previous year and was, in fact, 10 pounds over the prescribed limit. A furious Steinbrenner announced Piniella was being fined $1,000 a day—as per the terms of the contract—until he got down to 200 pounds. The Yankee manager that year, Bob Lemon, was ordered to play Piniella a full nine innings in all games, and the Yankee version of the battle of the bulge was on.

Midway through the spring, as the fines mounted and Piniella became increasingly irritated by his added workload, he reached the breaking point. Prior to a Yankee exhibition game against the Montreal Expos in West Palm Beach, Piniella called the beat reporters together and began a blistering tirade at Steinbrenner. Pacing up and down along the first base line, he declared: "I'm sick and tired of being treated like Little Orphan Annie here. I am utterly disgusted with George Steinbrenner and his policies. I was invited here early and end up getting fined $1,000 a day. I should have stayed home and saved myself $7,000! I've been around baseball 20 years and I'm suddenly being treated like a 19-year-old and I find that insulting. I'm not happy with the damn fines. I'm like Smith-Barney. I've worked hard for my money."

Steinbrenner, clearly relishing having gotten to Piniella, was quick to respond. "Sometimes Lou Piniella has to be treated like a 19-year-old," he said. "Everybody in Tampa will tell you that. I've got it in black and white. He knew what he was signing. If I'm a man and my employer is paying me $350,000—which is more than the president of the United States is making—I'd sure as hell take seven pounds off and honor that contract!"

Like most Steinbrenner/Yankee tempests, this one died down shortly thereafter and, eventually, Piniella's fines were rescinded by The Boss. For Steinbrenner, it had been worth every penny of it in that it had gotten the Yankees the back page of the New York tabloids two straight days in the middle of the NCAA basketball tournament.

"I know a lot of people thought George and I staged that one," Piniella said, "but it was real. It did make for good stuff for the writers, though. Today, though, I tell my players: 'Do what I *say*, not what I *did!*' You've got to remember. I had *fun* playing baseball. We joked around a lot and that was the environment we had with that team, and when we were winning it was great. It was just a great group of characters—Sparky [Lyle], Nettles, Willie, [Mickey] Rivers, Catfish, Thurman, Goose [Gossage], Roy White, Reggie, Gator [Ron Guidry], Chris Chambliss, the "Snatcher."

By 1979, however, the cast of characters had begun changing. Lyle was traded to Texas in a multiplayer deal after the '78 season that netted a future pitching star in Dave Righetti. Following Munson's death and Hunter's retirement in '79, Chambliss was dealt to Toronto for catcher Rick Cerone; Rivers was sent to Texas for another flamboyant outfielder, Oscar Gamble; and all the while Steinbrenner was changing managers like underwear. After the particularly tumultuous 1983 season—in which Martin, in his third term as manager, was suspended twice for run-ins with umpires and Steinbrenner was fined $50,000 and suspended for a week for his own transgressions against the umps—Gossage and Nettles departed for the San Diego Padres. By 1984, Piniella, Guidry and Randolph were the only ones left from the '76–'78 championship clubs and, in the interim, there had been 10 manager changes, including Martin three times and Lemon and Gene Michael twice each.

Piniella was 41 by then and relegated mostly to pinch-hitting duties. He could still hit, as evidenced by the .302 average he compiled that last season in 86 at bats. But he knew the time had come for him, and that the Yankees wanted to give his spot on the roster to a younger outfielder. He retired on June 17 of that '84 season with a career .291 average and 102 homers for 16 years in the big leagues and was immediately named by Steinbrenner to be the Yankees' hitting coach. As transitions from player to nonplayer go, this could not have been easier or more pleasurable. Not only was Piniella going to be teaching his passion, hitting, he was going to be working for Yogi Berra, whom Steinbrenner had made manager in 1984.

However, sixteen games into the 1985 season, those tranquil notions were dashed when Steinbrenner fired Berra and replaced him with Martin, further announcing that he wanted Martin to groom Piniella to be a manager. Having already been fired twice by Steinbrenner, Martin was sufficiently insecure and so his relationship with Piniella was strained from the outset. He regarded Piniella as a threat, rather than an aide, while Lou was more uncomfortable than he'd been in his entire career, including that year in Elmira with Weaver.

The height of angst (not to mention absurdity) between the two was when Martin was hospitalized July 28 in Texas with a collapsed lung and Piniella took over as acting manager. The Yankees had moved on to Cleveland for a five-game series against the Indians and, before the first game, Piniella was informed that Martin planned to manage the team by telephone from his hospital bed in Texas. The Indians' switchboard operators were instructed to patch Martin's calls through to the Yankee dugout during the course of the game.

From his command post back in Tampa, Steinbrenner thought, if nothing else, this was going to make for great theater and assure the Yankees more back-page publicity. He was right on both counts, although it wasn't quite what he'd hoped for. It seemed the Indians' mischievous team president, Peter Bavasi, had gotten wind of the dial-a-manager scheme and instructed his operators to forward Martin's calls to the *Indians'* dugout.

After repeatedly having to get his calls transferred back to the Yankee dugout the first couple of games, Martin apparently checked out of the hospital the third day and checked into a bar. According to Yankee catcher Butch Wynegar, who had been instructed to take the calls on the dugout phone and relay Martin's instructions to Piniella, "there was loud music when Billy called and I could hardly hear him." And later during that game, Piniella himself took one of the calls and became exasperated when a clearly inebriated Martin slurred over the phone line to him: "Why don't the players like me?"

"It was a mess," Piniella said, "and when all the stories got in the papers about Billy managing by phone, pranksters started calling in and getting their calls transferred to our dugout. I was in an uncomfortable position to begin with, but this made a circus out of it."

When the team got home to New York and Martin reassumed command, Piniella missed the first game. He was home mulling quitting as coach and had to be convinced by Steinbrenner to come back—after which he made a point to tell reporters he was no longer interested in managing; that the experience in Cleveland had really soured him on it. Nevertheless, when the season ended, Martin was fired and after a two-month charade in which Steinbrenner kept insisting GM Clyde King would be solely responsible for choosing the successor, Piniella was named manager.

"The reason George picked me to be the manager was because I got along with everybody," Piniella asserted. "We had a lot of factions in that clubhouse but I got along with every one of them. I'm forever grateful to him for giving me the opportunity, but, at the same time, the reason I had to leave there was because I would have always been perceived as George's boy, and I had to go out and do it someplace else."

Under the circumstances, he did pretty well, guiding the Yankees home second, five and a half games behind the Red Sox in 1986 with a 90-72 record, despite a pitching staff that had an ERA of 4.11—the first time in 36 years a Yankee staff had yielded more than four runs per game. Between his own inexperience and the ever present specter of Martin (who, despite his third firing, was celebrated by Steinbrenner on August 10 by having his No. 1 uniform retired), Piniella could have found the job to be daunting. For the most part, however, Steinbrenner left him alone to find his way as a manager, perhaps feeling that Piniella had been his creation.

The '87 season was a whole different story, though. After a promising first three and a half months, in which Piniella had the team in first place by three games at the All-Star break, everything went asunder and it was clear his honeymoon with Steinbrenner was over. Dave Winfield, who hit .295 with 20 homers before the break, slumped to just .250 with seven homers after it. Gary Ward, the other leading run producer in the first half with 61 RBI, hit just .218 with 17 RBI the rest of the season. And Rickey Henderson, counted on to be the team's top-of-the-order catalyst, was sidelined 55 games with a hamstring injury in June, July and August. Only Don Mattingly, who hit .327 with 115 RBI, had a consistent offensive season, and even he missed 18 games in June with a back injury.

Again, too, the pitching failed Piniella in '87, hitting the wall in August by going 11-17 with a 5.02 ERA. It was in the midst of a 2-8 road trip in August that tensions between Steinbrenner and Piniella boiled over into an ugly war of words. It had actually started late Sunday afternoon of August 2, before the team left Yankee Stadium for the plane trip to Cleveland. After the game that day, Steinbrenner and Piniella had gotten into a heated argument over a roster move. Steinbrenner had wanted to send left-handed reliever Pat Clements to Columbus, while Piniella strongly objected. The next night, after the Yankees lost 2–0 in Cleveland, Steinbrenner called the press box and instructed his public relations director, Harvey Greene, "Tell Lou to be in the hotel room for a phone call from me at 2 P.M. tomorrow."

Piniella figured this was a typical Steinbrenner anger impulse; that The Boss would forget all about calling him the next day. So instead, he went out for a long lunch with Bobby Murcer and two of Steinbrenner's limited partners in the Yankees, Mickey Friedman and Eddie Rosenthal. But Steinbrenner *did* call and when Piniella wasn't in his room, The Boss privately seethed. That night the Yankees lost 15–4 to the Indians, a game in which backup catcher Mark Salas committed three passed balls, and the next day when Piniella called GM Woody Woodward to discuss bringing up a new catcher, he was informed that nobody in the organization was allowed to talk to him.

Two days later, in Detroit, Piniella assembled reporters in the clubhouse and told them how he'd been trying to bring up a catcher but was told the general manager wasn't allowed to talk to him. That, in turn, prompted Steinbrenner to release through Greene a rambling two-page statement in which he excoriated Piniella for not being in his room to take his phone call. Then, out of the blue, he totally undermined Piniella with his players by claiming that in their prior conversations Lou had called Salas "a bum" and accused Henderson of "jaking it" with his hamstring injury.

When the Yankees got home a few days later, Steinbrenner and Piniella had what was termed a "clear-the-air" session at the Stadium, but it hardly cleared the air. Rather, Piniella's position became even more untenable when Steinbrenner told Phil Pepe of the *Daily News* that he may have "acted too hastily" in naming Piniella manager without any prior experience, adding that it was a mistake but that he was prepared to stick with Lou for the remainder of the season. In the meantime, Steinbrenner had a letter of insubordination placed in Piniella's file.

It was therefore no surprise that, after the Yankees faded to fourth place, 89-73, using a club-record 48 players in the process, Steinbrenner fired Piniella and replaced him with Martin for 1988. At the same time, he announced Piniella would be going upstairs to become general manager. Mind you, this was the period in which Steinbrenner was at his manic worst, and Billy IV turned out to be more abbreviated than Billy I, II or III. In early May of '88, a drunken Martin was beaten up by bouncers in a Texas strip joint called Lace and later that month was suspended for three games for throwing dirt all over umpire Dale Scott. Finally, on June 23, Steinbrenner put Martin out of his misery by firing him once again and instead merely transferred the misery to Piniella, who, in a delusional moment, agreed to take the job again, actually believing it would be different this time.

It wasn't, of course. The Yankees, beset by an aging and injury-riddled pitching staff and subpar years by Mattingly and Henderson, played only .500 ball for Piniella the rest of the year and finished fifth, three and a half games behind Boston. After the season, he and Steinbrenner mutually agreed the Yankees should get a new manager. This time Steinbrenner, having recycled Martin, Piniella, Michael and Lemon multiple times, went outside the organization and hired Dallas Green. Piniella spent the 1989 season in the Yankee TV booth, then severed ties with the organization once and for all by agreeing to become manager of the Cincinnati Reds.

"I had to get out of there and prove my worth in baseball as a manager," Piniella said, "and I didn't want there to be a Lou III, IV or V."

Liberation from Steinbrenner brought instant gratification for Piniella. Under his guidance, the '90 Reds went wire-to-wire in winning the National League West, then dispatched the Pittsburgh Pirates in six games in the NL Championship Series, before capping a near perfect season by sweeping the favored Oakland Athletics in the World Series. Steinbrenner was appearing as the guest host on *Saturday Night Live* when the Reds were finishing off the A's in Game 4 of the Series and, presumably, wasn't watching when his protégé and prodigal son was being doused with champagne in accepting the World Series trophy. Later, in the relative quiet of his office, Piniella was asked by one of the lingering reporters if he could sum up his feelings about winning a world championship.

"I have only one thing I want to say," he replied. "George, I can manage!"

It was a proclamation from the son who had spent the better part of his development years seeking approval from his surrogate baseball father. He would stay two more years in Cincinnati before resigning when his contract expired, having grown weary of the Reds' eccentric owner, Marge Schott, rubbing tufts of dog hair on him for good luck, as well as the increasingly penurious direction the organization seemed to be taking. A month later, after a lot of soul-searching with his wife, Anita, Piniella decided to accept a three-year offer from the Seattle Mariners to become their manager. Throughout their three years in Cincinnati, the Piniellas had kept their home in New Jersey, subconsciously in Anita's mind anyway, in anticipation of Lou going back to the Yankees as a proven manager to Steinbrenner. Now, he couldn't be any further away from New York or The Boss.

Nevertheless, they would have many epic confrontations in the years to come, Piniella's Mariners versus Steinbrenner's Yankees.

The first would be the American League Division Series of 1995 when the wild card Yankees, after winning the first two games at Yankee

Stadium (including a marathon 15-inning Game 2), went out to Seattle and got swept, resulting in Steinbrenner parting ways with yet another manager, in this case Buck Showalter. Piniella would later say coming back from 0–2 to beat the Yankees in that series was almost as sweet as winning it all with the Reds in 1990. It was, he said, a further affirmation to Steinbrenner that he could manage.

The ALCS of 2000 and 2001 would not be nearly so sweet as, on both occasions, Piniella's Mariners were simply out-pitched by Joe Torre's Yankees. In 2001, he found himself up against not only his old team, but also the city that had embraced him as one of its own through those 15 seasons from 1974 to 1989; that now had been brought to its knees from the events of September 11. Having lost the first two games in Seattle, the Mariners ran into a maelstrom of emotion in New York. Following a 14–3 trouncing in Game 3, the Yankees dusted themselves off and put the Mariners away with wins the next two nights. The Yankee Stadium crowd seemed to unleash all the city's pent-up joy and retribution upon the Mariners and afterward, even the defeated Piniella admitted getting caught up in it.

"I played here and I know these fans and I have to say I really felt good for them tonight," he said at the postgame press conference. "I know that sounds funny from a guy who's getting his ass kicked in this series, but you can't help but feel that way after all this city's been through."

Then again, everyone who'd been around Piniella those last couple of years agreed he'd become a much mellower Lou, and every so often he'd even reveal a spiritual side. For that, he said, the credit had to go to Anita, who, when he'd incurred some major financial difficulties because of a series of bad business investments, helped him work everything out while convincing him how otherwise blessed he'd been with his family and his baseball career.

"My wife," Piniella said, "has been a rock for me. She's put up with me and all my impatience and tantrums for 35 years and she did a great job raising our three kids while I was away so much. She's taught me how to manage myself better. Oh, I still hate to lose, but now I don't let the anger of losing fester. I look back on the way I acted and I feel embarrassed."

Listening to him talk about Anita as the calming influence on his life brought to mind an incident in 1986 when he was managing the Yankees and became embroiled in one of his typical animated temper tantrums over a perceived blown call by the home plate umpire. After finally being ejected from the game when the umpire had had enough of his antics, Piniella stormed all around the home plate area, repeatedly kicking his cap, which he'd earlier flung at the umpire's feet. It happened to be Anita's 40th birthday and she was watching the game on TV when a reporter called her and asked her what she thought of her husband's performance.

"It's my 40th birthday today," she said, "and I just found out I'm married to a four-year-old."

"Yeah, that was me," Piniella said. "I think that's why, later on, I locked horns with Paul O'Neill so much when I had him as a player in Cincinnati and when I managed against him with Seattle."

"You were a lot alike," I offered, "especially with your tempers and your obsession with hitting."

"That was the thing," Piniella said. "I have the utmost respect for Paul. I like the guy. I *really* do. But every time I'd see him argue over a called strike or throw his bat in disgust, he reminded me of my past."

The stone crabs had been devoured and now Malio had brought over a bottle of red wine he wanted Piniella and me to sample. The lunch crowd had long since cleared out, leaving just the three of us in the place, along with a couple of busboys, who were resetting tables in the dining room.

"Come, bring your wine, we'll go back to George's and Lou's rooms so they can clean up here," Malio said.

"You know," said Piniella, ignoring his pal, "it gets harder every year coming home after the Yankees have won another championship. This last one, when I got home after losing to the Yankees in the playoffs for the second straight year, really got to me. I was so upset, I took my '77 ring off my finger and flung it across the bedroom. I told Anita to put it away somewhere; that I was sick and tired of losing to the damn Yankees and I didn't want to wear it anymore."

"But you're wearing it again," I noted.

"Yeah," he sighed, "nothing could ever take away from the pride I had of being a Yankee and being a part of those great championship Yankee teams. Plus, even though we couldn't beat them in either 2000 or 2001, I know I've proved to George that I can manage. It's true, he's been like a father to me. Believe it or not, I've still got that letter of insubordination. It's the only thing I took with me after I left."

He smiled and took a sip of his wine. We got up from the table and began heading back to the empty Steinbrenner and Piniella rooms. Glancing at Steinbrenner's name plaque on the wall, next to his, Piniella turned wistful.

"Here we are," he said, "side by side. It should have been that way. Like I said, I think he knew that all along I could manage, but he just didn't have all the patience for me. That'll always be my one regret—that I didn't get the opportunity to win in New York."

MR. OCTOBER'S LEGACY

REGGIE JACKSON

*"The only reason I don't like playing in the World
Series is because I can't watch myself play."*

A muggy dampness hung in the air around the batting cages
beneath the grandstand at Legends Field in Tampa where
Reggie Jackson was hollering words of advice and
encouragement in both English and Spanish to 28-year-old Panamanian
outfielder Ruben Rivera, who, in another 24 hours, would be handed
his unconditional release from the New York Yankees. It was late
morning and Rivera, who had admitted to Yankee officials he'd stolen a
game glove and, allegedly, a bat from teammate Derek Jeter's locker
and sold them to a memorabilia dealer a few days earlier, was taking
extra batting practice under the sole supervision of Jackson.

From the time he'd first come up to the Yankees in the spring of

1995 as the most highly acclaimed organization prospect since Mickey Mantle, Rivera had become a special project of Jackson, the Hall of Fame slugger who returned to the Yankee fold in 1993 after a long estrangement from principal owner George Steinbrenner, to serve as a "special advisor" and spring training batting instructor. It was part of the pact Jackson made with Steinbrenner after Reggie had announced he would go into the Hall as a Yankee, even though he'd spent only five of his 21 major league seasons in pinstripes.

After the right-hand-hitting Rivera had completed nearly a half-hour of swatting the machine's pitches, Jackson, who'd been exhorting him to concentrate on hitting the ball to right and center field, called him over to the side of the cage, draped his arms over his shoulders and engaged in what was clearly a very private conversation. Rivera nodded occasionally as Jackson spoke softly to him, their faces only inches apart. It lasted for a couple of minutes until Jackson gave Rivera a brief hug and said, audibly enough to be heard from the other side of the cage: "Just stay cool. We'll talk later."

Upon spotting me standing in the tunnel outside the cage ropes, Jackson nodded. He was in his instructor's garb, a navy Yankee parka and home pinstripe pants. The rest of the Yankees were all working out on the main field in the stadium and the three practice fields that immediately adjoin it. Rivera, I later learned, was told he couldn't take part in the regular workout until the front office determined what action to take for his offense.

"Tough day today," Jackson said to me. "I really like that kid. I wish I could help him, but I think it's too late. Maybe if I'd have known about it sooner . . . but then some things there's nothing you can do. What's really a shame is we really need him. He's the best outfielder we got."

We walked down the tunnel to the Yankee clubhouse, which was mostly empty. Although there were still about 15 minutes before the workout would be over, Jackson had agreed to begin talking to me about what it meant to him to have been a Yankee—and with the passage of time, being an integral part of the Yankee lore. First, however, he wanted to unburden himself of something he'd been trying to talk to Steinbrenner about—to no avail—for a couple of years.

"I know you want to talk about '77 and all the other stuff and we'll get to that," he assured me. "But there's a sadness I'm feeling right now and it's much, much bigger than what happened to Reggie in '77 with Billy. Or what happened in '81 with George. Or what happened with Charlie Finley in Oakland. Where in all those instances they went out of their way to hold back my progress; to put up some sort of obstacle to stop me from being successful. In the big picture, it's nothin'. It built character. It made me who I am today. It cost me some home runs and RBIs. It changed my life, of course, but overall, I'd say, for the good.

"The only negative I dwell on that I wish could be is that I've never gotten a chance to really give to the game; to give to the kids in the game the knowledge I have about winning. I never have really been included and that is the only thing that I'm sorry about. I really wanted to be involved directly in the decision-making process of this ball club, as well as giving to the game and the players, and I never have been given the opportunity to do that. I've been given flashes, bits and pieces of it, through Joe Torre, but it never really came to pass."

He was, of course, a sun unto his own galaxy long before he ever became a Yankee.

Reginald Martinez Jackson was born May 18, 1946, in Wyncote, Pennsylvania, a predominantly white, Jewish suburb of Philadelphia. Jackson was of African-American, Spanish, Indian and Irish descent. His father, Martinez, was a tailor and dry cleaner by trade and a bootlegger on the side who made corn liquor in the basement of his shop in the two-family house at 149 Greenwood Avenue. The family lived above the dry cleaning store, but when Jackson was six years old, his parents separated and his mother, Clara, left forever, taking her other three children from a previous marriage with her. The scars of his parents' breakup remain to this day. In his 1984 autobiography, with Mike Lupica of the *New York Daily News,* Jackson wrote that his propensity for dating white women and his inability to make a total commitment to any woman was probably the product of his never having really had a mother. On the other hand, he clearly idolized Martinez, even though the old man was unable to attend his graduation from Cheltenham Township High School because of a prior engagement—a six-month stint in the Norristown prison for bootlegging.

Jackson often credited his father with having taught him values and the importance of getting an education. Martinez recognized early on his son's athletic ability, but saw it as a means of getting a scholarship to college rather than a professional career. Young Reggie worked in the dry cleaner store doing odd jobs for his father, who paid him a dollar-a-week allowance. The story Jackson loved telling was about the day his father gave him a quarter and asked him to go down the street to the drugstore and bring back a pint of Neapolitan ice cream. Upon arriving at the drugstore and being told they were out of Neapolitan, Jackson had to think fast. Knowing his father craved Neapolitan, he ran across the street to the gas station, where he knew the proprietor, and asked to borrow 50 cents. He then went back to the drugstore and bought a pint each of vanilla, chocolate and strawberry—his own makeshift Neapolitan—and proudly brought them home to his father. Even though it cost Martinez an extra 50 cents for his favorite ice cream, he let Reggie know he was impressed with his son's enterprising way of getting the job done.

Martinez was still incarcerated the day in late August of 1964 when Jackson and a friend got into his Pontiac and left Wyncote, pretty much for good, for the drive cross-country to Tempe, Arizona, where he had a scholarship to play football for Arizona State and its famed taskmaster coach, Frank Kush. Jackson later said Kush's grueling "survival of the fittest" practices steeled him for the world outside the life of professional athletics and helped reinstill in him the values his father had tried to teach him back in Wyncote.

All the while, however, Jackson had his mind set on playing baseball. On a bet with two of his classmates who were on the baseball team, he got himself a tryout one afternoon after football practice and wowed the coach, Bobby Winkles, with one prodigious drive after another over the stadium fence. Winkles wasn't easily wowed either. His baseball program was even more renowned than Kush's football teams at ASU. Winkles's teams were 524-173 (.752) in his 13 years there, including College World Series titles in 1965, '67 and '69.

In Jackson's sophomore year at Arizona State, he set a school record with 15 homers in 52 games, and in one game against the University of Arizona he became only the second college player to hit a ball completely out of Phoenix Municipal Stadium. The Sun Devils went 41-11 in 1966 and at the end of the season, the Kansas City Athletics, with the second overall pick in the amateur draft, selected Jackson. The year before, the A's, with the No. 1 overall pick, had taken another Arizona State product, center fielder Rick Monday, and signed him for a bonus of $104,000. Their initial offer to Jackson was $50,000, which he rejected. When they upped the ante to $75,000, plus college tuition for two more years for a total package of $85,000, Winkles advised Jackson to take it. The New York Mets, meanwhile, took a high school catcher named Steve Chilcott with the No. 1 pick in the '66 draft, purportedly because Mets board chairman M. Donald Grant had let it be known he was leery of Jackson's background, particularly the fact that he was dating a white girl. (In fact, Jackson's fiancée at the time, Jennie Campos, was Hispanic, but the Mets apparently didn't bother to scout *her*.) In any case, Chilcott hurt his shoulder in the minor leagues and never made it, while Jackson went on to hit 563 homers in the majors, not including the record three he hit in Game 6 of the 1977 World Series.

"I wonder what ever happened to Steve Chilcott?" Jackson said wistfully. "It would've been interesting, wouldn't it? If the Mets had taken me?"

Jackson was seated in a booth in Damon's, the restaurant in Steinbrenner's Bay Harbor Hotel in Tampa, and as he said it, he threw his head back, stretched his arms and closed his eyes. We had agreed to continue our conversation a day later over breakfast, away from the spring training complex, where Jackson felt more comfortable talking about himself.

His career with the Athletics, in Kansas City and Oakland (where they moved in 1968), was both prolific and stormy. He needed barely a year and a half of minor league apprenticeship before making his debut with the A's in late '67. Two years later, he hit 47 homers and knocked in 118 runs to establish himself, at age 23, as one of the premier power hitters in the game. With Jackson as their big man, the A's quickly emerged as a force as the '60s gave way to the '70s, winning three consecutive world championships in 1972–74. In '73, Jackson was named American League Most Valuable Player when he led the league in homers (32) and RBI (117) and two years later, his final season with the A's, he tied for the league lead in homers (36) again. On June 3, 1974, Jackson was featured on the cover of *Time* magazine while being proclaimed in the text of the story as "the best player on the best team in sports."

Yet, with all his easy and intoxicating success, there was almost constant turmoil and conflict.

In 1972, asserting his authority as union player rep with the A's, Jackson got into a clubhouse scrap with teammate Mike Epstein over Epstein leaving an excessive amount of passes for a game. When Epstein told Jackson it was none of his business, Reggie retorted: "I'm making it my business," and crossed out a name Epstein had left on the pass list. Epstein, in turn, threw a punch at Jackson and the two wrestled each other to the floor and kept flailing away until A's manager Dick Williams charged out of his office and broke it up. Another time, in 1974, Jackson again asserted himself with a teammate, openly criticizing A's outfielder Billy North (who was bothered by a pulled groin muscle at the time) for not running hard to first base on a groundout. North, stung, told Jackson: "You're not Number 5 [A's manager Alvin Dark]. I only take orders from Number 5." When Jackson said he didn't want to get into an argument over the issue, North said bluntly: "You can do better than that and not bother to talk to me anymore. We're not friends. You dig it?" But a couple of weeks later, in Detroit, the simmering feud between the two erupted into a wild clubhouse brawl when North reportedly kept uttering cutting remarks at Jackson, and Reggie finally jumped him. Several A's players sustained cuts and bruises attempting to break it up and catcher Ray Fosse, who suffered a slipped cervical disc and pinched nerve, missed half the season. The next day, A's owner Charlie Finley cast most of the blame for the brouhaha on Jackson.

Whether it was the hard bargain Jackson drove for his $85,000 bonus or merely the natural clash of egos between a flamboyant owner and equally flamboyant star player, Finley and Jackson were engaged in a cold war—mostly over money—the entire eight seasons Reggie played for the A's. In '68 and '69, Jackson staged spring training holdouts for better contracts and early in the '69 season, Finley ordered then manager John McNamara to bench him against left-handed pitchers. The advent of free agency in December of 1975 proved to be Finley's demise, as the cantankerous, tightfisted A's owner simply couldn't—or wouldn't—pay the salaries his players could now get on the open market. In Jackson's case, Finley didn't bother waiting until Reggie took his leave as a free agent at the end of the 1976 season. That spring, their annual contract dispute was especially rancorous with Finley finally automatically renewing Jackson for a 20 percent pay cut to $112,000.

The die was cast. Finley, in effect, was filing for divorce from the man who had hit 254 homers for him over eight seasons and played a principal role in five division winners and three world championship teams for Oakland. A few days before the '76 season opened, Finley made it official by trading Jackson and pitcher Ken Holtzman to the Baltimore Orioles for outfielder Don Baylor and pitcher Mike Torrez. It was essentially a "rent-a-player" deal for both clubs as Finley made it clear he had no intention of keeping Baylor beyond the '76 season and Jackson told the world of his intention to test the free agent market after the season. And there was no question of his preeminence in that market.

After putting together one of his best all-around seasons with the Orioles in '76—.277, 27 homers, 91 RBI and a career-high 28 stolen bases—Jackson went home to California and waited for his phone to start ringing.

"It was an exciting time for me," Jackson said. "I'd be lying if I said it wasn't. To be wanted like that. I was hoping to be a Dodger and I also gave strong consideration, believe it or not, to the Padres. I always liked San Diego and it was closer to home for me. But the Dodgers didn't make an offer until it was too late—after I'd already agreed to a deal with the Yankees—and the Padres couldn't afford me. The Dodgers had Al Campanis, their GM, and Maury Wills court me and I told them: 'I wish you guys had come into this thing sooner. I've already made a deal with Steinbrenner and shaken his hand.'

"The team that really surprised me—and which offered me the most—was the Expos, who were owned by Charles Bronfman, the Seagram heir. They had Dick Williams, who was their manager then, and John McHale, the GM, follow me around, but the driving force was the Bronfmans. They offered me $1 million a year for five years. Then, right after I met with them, I went to New York. I remember there had been conversation in the newspapers in which Thurman Munson said, 'If we're gonna go after [Bert] Campaneris and Joe Rudi, the guy from Oakland to get is Reggie Jackson.' Later on, after I signed, came all that deal about George having given Thurman a verbal agreement that he'd always be the highest-paid Yankee."

"Did George live up to that?" I asked. Jackson shook his head and smiled.

"So, getting back to the recruiting process, how did George ultimately win you over?"

"Well, for one thing," he said, "when I came to town I had a woman companion with me and they gave me a room in the Americana Hotel that only had a single bed! After we got that straightened out, George picked me up the next day. It was cold and we walked around the streets of Manhattan a little bit and all these guys in the cabs and trucks were yelling stuff at us. 'Hey, Reggie! Come to New York!' 'Sign him, George!' It was pretty wild. George was showing me off to the city. While we were walking, George made me an offer—$2.1 million for five years—and I thought to myself: 'Wow. He's not even close!' There's no way.

"We had lunch at '21' with the Fisher brothers, Larry and Zack, who were very wealthy real estate developers, another real estate guy named Tony Rolfe, who was assigned to find me an apartment, and George's pal, Bill Fugazy, the limo guy. I remember saying to the maître d': 'You're required to wear a tie in this place and there's not even any carpets on the floor!'

[He laughed softly.]

"I guess it was a day or so later when George upped his offer to $2.6 for five and finally $2.96. The final offer included a Rolls-Royce, which I had asked for and George gave me."

It would be a long while before Reggie Jackson would ever have a happier day as a New York Yankee.

At the gala press conference to announce his signing, in the Versailles Terrace of the Americana Hotel, November 29, Jackson lavished praise on Steinbrenner, saying: "He took it on his own to hunt me down. He's a lot like me. He's a little crazy and he's a hustler. It was like trying to hustle a girl in a bar. I got the feeling I was his personal project to go with the Yankees." He went on to say he hoped and expected to provide what the Yankees needed to win it all in 1977. Conspicuously absent among all his statements that day was any mention of Yankee manager Billy Martin.

Throughout the winter, there were periodic comments from Jackson about how he expected to have an impact on the Yankees. Meanwhile, whether he realized it or not, there was a growing resentment building among the Yankee players who felt their accomplishment of going to the World Series in '76 was being shortchanged by the team's new star. When he arrived at Fort Lauderdale the following spring, Jackson got a decidedly chilly reception in the Yankee clubhouse. For an uneasy 15 minutes or so, nobody acknowledged his presence. Finally, Catfish Hunter, his old A's teammate, came over to his locker and shook his hand. As Moss Klein, the beat writer from the *Newark Star-Ledger*, remembered it: "It was kind of like Pee Wee Reese going over to Jackie Robinson and putting his arm around him that time in 1947. Everybody on the team respected Catfish, but nobody else dared to make the gesture of acceptance to Reggie."

And regardless of his supposed urgings to Steinbrenner to sign Jackson, the reserved, often grumpy Munson had some reservations about this egotistical, hot-dogging outsider. Munson was, after all, the Yankee captain—the first Yankee captain since Lou Gehrig—and while he fervently wanted Steinbrenner to do what was necessary to take the team to that next level after being swept by the Big Red Machine Cincinnati Reds in the '76 World Series, he didn't want anyone coming in trying to usurp his acknowledged role as team leader. It took barely six weeks into the 1977 season for Munson's and the rest of the Yankees' worst fears about Jackson to be realized.

On May 23, the June issue of *Sport Magazine* hit the newsstands with the featured article in which Jackson was quoted as saying of his role with the Yankees: "You know, this team . . . it all flows from me. I've got to keep it all going. I'm the straw that stirs the drink. It all comes back to me. Maybe I should say me and Munson . . . but he really doesn't enter into it. He's being so damned insecure about the whole thing. Munson thinks he can be the straw, but he can only stir it bad."

Jackson immediately insisted the author of the article, Robert Ward, had grossly misquoted him. And in his autobiography he said the "straw that stirs the drink" quote was an off-the-cuff remark he made while holding a swizzle stick as the two of them sat at the Banana Boat Bar in Fort Lauderdale. He vehemently denied ever disparaging Munson.

"Years later," Jackson related now, "I heard from a longtime writer that Ward had admitted manufacturing the quote. That was the first time I felt reprieve because I remember what I said. I guess the great comment came from Thurman through Fran Healy, who brought us together in hopes of patching things over. Healy was my closest friend on the team, but Thurman liked me and was really supportive later on. I told Healy I was misquoted; that it was all bullshit, and Thurman said to me: 'Misquoted? For three fucking pages?'"

At that, Jackson laughed out loud, prompting the two men in the booth behind him to turn their heads.

"The whole thing about it," he continued, "was that I really didn't want to do the story to begin with. I finally agreed and we went to the Banana Boat because I knew that was the bar where Mickey and Whitey used to hang out in Fort Lauderdale. So I ordered a piña colada and as I'm talking to this guy, holding my stirrer, I said: 'I'm kinda like the final ingredient here. I'm not the guy. They've got all these guys.' And he says, pointing to my stirrer: 'You mean like the straw that stirs the drink?' I said: 'Yeah, I guess that sounds okay. I'll be the final ingredient.'"

According to Jackson, it was around the same time that first spring as a Yankee he had serious misgivings about his decision to sign with them.

"I wasn't there two weeks and I heard these jokes about Ken Holtzman, my teammate with the A's who was now with the Yankees, being a Jew," Jackson related. "When I was standing around the bat rack and getting a bat to go hit, I said to myself: 'I wonder if they know I'm standing here?' The fact that they didn't consider I was black . . . the way they were talking about Holtzman as a Jew . . . and I wondered: 'What the hell are they saying about *me?*' I felt very alone and awkward that day, even though there were other blacks on the team. From that day on, I wanted to leave the Yankees. I talked to Gabe Paul, the GM, about it, and asked to be traded."

"Gabe was Jewish," I said. "What did *he* say?"

"He told me: 'Reggie, you have to look at the whole doughnut, not just the hole in the doughnut.'"

"That was a favorite Gabe-ism," I countered.

There was, of course, no way the Yankees were going to trade

Jackson. He was Steinbrenner's new marquee player and, however inaccurate his quotes may have been in *Sport Magazine*, by his sheer, overriding talent he was the straw that stirred the drink. But as he was soon to find out, his stirring bruised egos, not the least of which was that of Billy Martin. Martin wore No. 1 and thought of himself in the same manner. A once prodigal Yankee son—he'd been traded away as a player in 1957 because Weiss felt he was a bad influence on Mickey Mantle and Whitey Ford—he was brought back as manager by Steinbrenner in August of 1975 and, the following year, directed the Yankees to the World Series for the first time since 1964. Though Martin, too, was left smarting from the humiliating sweep the Yankees suffered at the hands of the Reds in '76, he was not among those urging Steinbrenner to sign Reggie Jackson. He told Steinbrenner to try to sign second baseman Bobby Grich (whom he envisioned as a shortstop) or Rudi, but the Yankee Boss was focused on only Reggie.

Martin didn't want any more stars on this Yankee team, least of all one who had a penchant for speaking his mind and stirring it up. And when his recommendations of Grich and Rudi were ignored and he was totally left out of the loop by Steinbrenner on the Jackson pursuit, Martin began to feel diminished. So from day one, Martin viewed Jackson with a wary eye, and tensions between them were instant and lasting. In Martin's mind, Steinbrenner had now decreed Reggie to be No. 1 and that was something Billy found too hard to swallow. Much of the Yankees' success in 1976 had been attributed to Martin's aggressive—hit-and-run, squeeze, base-stealing—managing style, and now Steinbrenner deemed power to be the Yankees' primary weapon.

It didn't help that Jackson hurt his arm in spring training and had trouble throwing the ball; and that he got off to a slow start, both at bat and in the field. By the end of May, in the aftermath of the *Sport Magazine* flap, Jackson was hitting .250 with eight homers, 23 RBI and 39 strikeouts in 42 games. Worse, from Jackson's standpoint, was Martin's refusal to bat him cleanup. A No. 4 hitter for nearly his entire career, Jackson found himself in the No. 5 slot at the start of the '77 season and didn't get to hit cleanup until the 21st game of the season. That lasted only nine games, and it was not until early August that Martin finally relented. Jackson hit cleanup from August 10 through the rest of the season, batting .288 with 13 homers and 49 RBI during that 51-game stretch.

Meanwhile, the simmering feud between Martin and Jackson came to a head on June 18 in Boston. Jackson, previously acknowledged as an above-average outfielder, had experienced some problems with fly balls during the course of the first two months of the season. On this day in Fenway Park, he appeared to misjudge a bloop fly to shallow right by Jim Rice and then was slow in getting over to it as it dropped in for a base hit. From his vantage point in the dugout, Martin thought Jackson loafed on the play. His response was to send reserve outfielder Paul Blair out to right to replace Jackson—right then—in the middle of the inning.

Jackson, dumbfounded as he trotted in toward the dugout, publicly humiliated, removed his glasses as if readying himself to have a piece of Martin, who was on the top step of the dugout yelling at him. As Martin and Jackson began shouting at each other and getting closer and closer—in full view of the national TV cameras—Yankee coaches Yogi Berra, Dick Howser and Elston Howard rushed to separate them. After the commotion subsided and order was restored, Howard reassumed his seat in the dugout and was heard to say: "Man, I've been around this team a long time, but this team is too much! I've never seen shit like this day in and day out!"

The next day, Steinbrenner came to Boston with rumors rampant of Martin's impending dismissal, and Phil Pepe wrote in the *Daily News*: "Was this the straw that breaks the camel's back?" Whether Jackson was guilty of not hustling on Rice's pop fly was no longer the issue. Martin's losing control was. Steinbrenner and Paul met with Martin that Sunday, but nothing was resolved, and when the team moved on to Detroit, it looked more and more certain Martin was going to be fired. Behind the scenes, however, Jackson met with Steinbrenner and pleaded with him not to fire Martin. Jackson knew if the popular manager was fired, it would create a fan backlash and he, Jackson, would bear the brunt of it. Steinbrenner finally agreed and Martin was spared.

Ironically, the following year when Martin and Jackson had their next big public tempest, Martin *did* eventually get fired, even though he had been in the right this time and Reggie was clearly in the wrong. Depleted by injuries, the '78 Yankees fell way behind the division-leading Red Sox as pressures mounted on Martin and Jackson, who was battling a personal slump. Once again, Martin removed Jackson from the cleanup spot, and took him out of right field as well.

Then, on July 17, in the 10th inning of an eventual 9–7, 11-inning loss to the Kansas City Royals, Martin ordered Jackson to sacrifice against reliever Al Hrabosky with Munson on first. Jackson, clearly affronted, gave no indication of acknowledging the order, which prompted third base coach Dick Howser to come down the line to make sure he'd gotten the sign. After a halfhearted bunt attempt on Jackson's part, Martin took the sign off only to become infuriated when Jackson attempted another bunt and struck out.

Again, Martin had to be restrained from coming to blows with Jackson, but this time Steinbrenner had no choice but to back his manager. The next day, it was announced Jackson was being suspended by the Yankees for five games for insubordination. He returned to the club the following Sunday in Chicago, by which time the Yankees had won all five games in his absence. Martin was therefore the least happy person to see Jackson back. This was especially so when Martin peered out of his office in the visiting team clubhouse at Comiskey Park and saw Jackson surrounded by reporters, presumably telling his side of the story, and making no effort to join his teammates on the field for pregame hitting and fielding drills. Afterward, while waiting to board the Yankees' flight home, Martin brooded over Jackson at one of the O'Hare Airport bars and worked himself into an inebriated state.

He had been gradually unraveling anyway as the Yankees slid to as many as 14 games behind the Red Sox, and even the winning streak hadn't assuaged him. He detested Jackson and was convinced Steinbrenner privately sided with the insubordinate superstar. As he left the bar and was walking through the airport on the way to the plane, Martin vented his anger with two of his least favorite Yankee beat men, Murray Chass of the *New York Times* and Henry Hecht of the *Post*, spouting: "The two of them [Steinbrenner and Jackson] deserve each other. One's a born liar and the other's convicted."

The latter was a reference to Steinbrenner's conviction—and suspension from baseball—for making illegal campaign contributions to Richard Nixon in 1968. Needless to say, this *was* the straw that broke the camel's back. The next day in Kansas City, Martin tearfully resigned as Yankee manager, saying: "I owe it to my health and my mental well-being."

In the often bizarre world of George Steinbrenner, however, the best way to win favor with The Boss is to be fired by him. Steinbrenner had beaten Martin to the ground and now he sought to build him back up again. Five days later, on Old-Timers' Day at Yankee Stadium, Steinbrenner announced that Martin would be returning as Yankee manager in 1980.

Shortly after the Old-Timers' Day announcement, Yankee publicity director Mickey Morabito, in an effort to oblige all the beat writers who'd been unsuccessfully trying to reach Martin for an interview, set up an informal lunch at Alex and Henry's restaurant in the Bronx. An hour into the lunch, Morabito realized what a terrible mistake he'd made. As Martin began throwing down drinks, he was unable to restrain himself from again venting his feelings about Jackson.

"I never looked at Jackson as a superstar," he said, "because he'd never shown me he was a superstar. I look at him as one of 25 players. I never put him above Chris Chambliss, Thurman Munson, Willie Randolph, Mickey Rivers, Roy White . . . there were times I even thought of Chicken [Fred] Stanley over him!"

When the session finally ended late in the afternoon, Morabito went back to his office at Yankee Stadium and began packing some of his personal belongings into a carton while contemplating where his next employment would be once the papers hit the stands the next day and Steinbrenner found out about this press conference for Martin he'd set up. Needless to say, there was no one in the city of New York more relieved than Morabito when, instead, the newspapers went on strike. Martin's blast at Jackson only appeared in the suburban papers, which Steinbrenner never saw.

"I never really knew Billy Martin," Jackson said, looking down at his plate of egg whites, "and the way he lived his life I guess I'm kinda glad I didn't know him. This guy was a drinker. This guy was vindictive. He openly used the 'n' word. I never really understood why he didn't like me. I mean the players went to him two-thirds of the way through the '77 season and said: 'Why don't you let this guy hit cleanup?' One day he said he thought Fred Stanley was a better player than Reggie Jackson. What was that all about? He did his best to make me into a bad outfielder."

"The incident in Boston was probably the impetus of that," I interjected.

"After that, we had a meeting at the top of the Sheraton Towers in Boston with Gabe Paul," Jackson continued. "Billy came into the meeting late, was drunk and when he looked at me as I was telling my side of the story, he said: 'Get up, boy, I'm gonna kick the shit out of you!'"

"What did Gabe say to that?" I asked. "He must have been panicked."

"Gabe said: 'Sit down, Billy, before you lose your job.' I said to Gabe: 'You're a Jew, Gabe, how do you think I should react to that?' and Gabe said: 'Reggie, I understand.'"

"Was the Boston incident the most embarrassed you've ever been in baseball?" I asked.

"I don't know," he said. "Charlie Finley threatened to send me back to the minor leagues in 1970 after I'd held out and gotten off to a bad start after hitting 47 homers the year before. I've been humiliated, believe me. Johnny McNamara, the manager, told me

Charlie had ordered him not to play me. And then there was the time here, in 1978, when Billy would only play me against left-handed starters, hoping I would fail."

He squinted his eyes and put his fork down, pausing in thought for a brief moment.

"You know," he said, "it was such an ugly situation with Billy and me that I've tried to discard it from my mind. I don't like talking about him anymore. If you don't have anything good to say about someone . . . if you have these bitter feelings that you make 'em come back out . . . Nobody's ever gonna tell a story to make themselves look bad and if I go on with this, I'm just gonna make myself look good, to make Billy look bad, and I don't really have a big interest in that. Everybody knows how we felt toward each other. As a Christian, I should forget, but I won't ever forget. Billy's gone now and I have a good relationship with his son. There's no need to trample on his grave."

There was only one time when the two of them expressed genuine affection for each other—after the last game of the 1977 World Series. It had been such a torturous season for both of them, but despite everything—the *Sport Magazine* story, the Boston incident, the cleanup controversy, Steinbrenner's constant threats to fire Martin—it had somehow all ended in mutual triumph. Martin had managed to walk Steinbrenner's tightrope without falling off, while guiding the Yankees to their first world championship in 15 years. And Jackson, with a team-leading 110 RBI and a virtuoso performance in the World Series in which he hit .450 with five homers, eight RBI and 10 runs scored, had indeed been the straw that stirred the drink. The euphoric scene in Martin's Yankee Stadium office after Jackson's record-tying three homers in the clinching Game 6 was one for the Yankee ages. There they were, the three of them—Steinbrenner, Martin and Jackson—showering each other with champagne while professing their eternal love to each other.

"There was no question everybody had made it tough for me that year," Jackson said, "and I proved to myself and them that George had made the right decision to sign me. Other than that, I don't care to remember a whole lot about that scene in Billy's office, other than to say, yeah, we were all high in our own way over what had just happened."

"What about the game—the ending—itself?" I asked. "Hitting three home runs to tie Babe Ruth's record?"

"That's different," Jackson said. "I remember especially standing around the batting cage and Dick Young—who was the guru of sportswriters—was watching Dick Howser throw BP to me, and if I had 50 swings, I hit 35, 40 into the stands, all in one spot, which was the old 470-foot mark up in the bleachers there, within a hundred foot radius. I got a standing ovation when I walked out of BP and all the Dodgers were watching. Young said to me: 'You're locked in, Reggie. Maybe you ought to save some for the game.'"

He did, three of them, with three swings. The Yankees had missed a chance to wrap up the Series in Los Angeles by losing Game 5, 10-4, and the Dodgers jumped out to a 2–0 lead in Game 6 on Steve Garvey's two-run triple in the first off Mike Torrez. The Yankees responded with two runs in the second, only to have the Dodgers regain the lead on a solo homer by Reggie Smith in the third.

Then in the fourth, after Munson singled to left, Jackson hit the first pitch from Dodger starter Burt Hooton into the right field stands to put the Yankees ahead 4–3. A sac fly by Piniella later in the inning made it a 5–3 game. Buoyed by this quick show of return support, Torrez settled into a groove and shut the Dodgers out the rest of the way. In the meantime, Jackson single-handedly cemented the game for the Yankees by clouting the first pitch he saw from reliever Elias Sosa for another two-run homer in the fifth and climaxing the night with another—this one massive—first-pitch homer off knuckleballer Charlie Hough into the vacant center field bleacher area in the eighth. The three home runs in one game tied Babe Ruth's World Series record set in both 1926 and '28 and his five home runs for the Series was a record unto himself. It was the night Reggie Jackson earned his indelible nickname "Mr. October."

"Of the three pitchers I faced that night, the only one who made me nervous was Sosa," Jackson recalled, "because I'd never faced him. I remember calling upstairs to Gene Michael and asking him: 'What does this guy throw?' Michael said: 'Fastballs in. He's got a good fastball.' Well, Sosa threw it right where Michael said he was gonna throw it. I just worried it wasn't gonna stay high enough to clear the fence. Then when they brought Hough in for the eighth, I couldn't believe it. I used to kill Wilbur Wood, Eddie Fisher, [Hoyt] Wilhelm, all those knuckleballers. I remember the time in Milwaukee, in '68, when they brought Wilhelm in— the White Sox used to play some home games there—and the announcer said: 'Hoyt Wilhelm is closing on the all-time record for games pitched, 907, set by Denton True "Cy" Young.' And the first fucking pitch he threw, I hit over the bleachers in right . . . heh, heh, heh.

"So I looked around and saw Charlie Hough coming into this game and I couldn't believe what was happening. What I thought, as he was coming in, was that they were going to realize how well I hit knuckleballers and they would take him out. But he was announced, so he had to face one hitter. I prayed he'd throw me a knuckler—which he did, only it didn't knuckle, and I crushed it, really crushed it, nearly 500 feet into the black. Only the second man ever to hit one there in the new Yankee Stadium."

"You must have felt like you were having an out-of-body experience. Three homers in three swings of the bat?"

"What I felt," said Jackson, "was vindicated. All the stuff I'd been through with Billy . . . none of it mattered anymore at that moment. I can't imagine ever feeling as good as I felt, taking that turn around the bases."

"Mr. October," I said.

"I'm not sure exactly when that started," he said. "It was Thurman, I guess, who really started it. We were in Detroit during the '77 season and I'd hit two home runs in the game and somebody went up to him to interview him and he said: 'Go talk to Mr. October over there'—in reference, I guess, to the way I'd hit in my two World Series with the

A's. But even before that, when I hit .310 against the Mets in the '73 Series, Joe Garagiola called me 'October's child.'"

Jackson's second season with the Yankees, while not as spectacular and explosive as the first, was eminently more reassuring for him, especially after Martin resigned under fire as manager in late July and was replaced by the easygoing Bob Lemon. Sometime before he signed with the Yankees, Jackson was quoted as saying: "If I ever played in New York, they'd name a candy bar after me." In the aftermath of his record-making '77 Series, that's exactly what they did and on Yankees' home Opening Day 1978, the Reggie Bar made a momentous (if dubious) debut. The Standard Brands Candy Company, which created it, gave out free bars to all the fans at Yankee Stadium as part of an Opening Day promotion, but when Jackson hit a three-run homer in the first inning off Chicago White Sox knuckleballer Wilbur Wood, the Reggie Bars began raining down on the field, as the fans, picking off where they'd left off after his three-homer climax to the World Series the previous autumn, chanted "Reggie! Reggie! Reggie!" The homer had come on a 2-0 pitch, making it four homers in four consecutive swings for Jackson at Yankee Stadium, the latter two off his favorite patsies, knuckleball pitchers.

When the Yankees made their remarkable comeback from 14 games behind the Red Sox to win the AL East in a playoff and then dispatch the Dodgers in six games in the World Series, Lemon was hailed for bringing a needed calm to a team in turmoil. Lemon, characteristically, deflected all the credit, saying: "I just let them play and tried to stay out of their way and not screw it up. If you're looking for one reason why we were able to do what we did, give credit to the newspaper strike."

"Bob Lemon told me when he took over the ball club: 'I know what you can do with the bat. You're gonna be playing every day. I'm gonna hit you fourth. Don't worry about it,'" Jackson said.

Jackson played a primary role in the Yankees' '78 comeback drive and led the team in RBI (97) for the second straight season while tying with Graig Nettles for the team leadership in homers (27). He also led the team in slugging (.477), and while Bucky Dent's three-run homer is always remembered as the key blow in the Yankees' playoff victory over the Red Sox at Fenway Park, it was actually Jackson's solo shot off Boston reliever Bob Stanley in the eighth that provided the Yankees with their 5–4 margin of victory. In his entire '78 postseason—the Red Sox playoff game, the American League Championship Series against the Kansas City Royals and the World Series against the Dodgers, Jackson hit .400 with five homers and 15 RBI in 11 games. His one humbling moment that entire October—his epic, seven-minute battle with Dodgers hard-throwing rookie right-hander Bob Welch in the ninth inning of Game 2 of the World Series—was also one of the few times he incurred the wrath of the normally unflappable Lemon.

Welch had been summoned into the game by Dodger manager Tommy Lasorda, after Dent opened the ninth with a single for the Yankees and Paul Blair drew a walk one out later. With Dodgers leading 4–1, Welch got Munson to fly to right, then turned his attention to Jackson with the Dodger Stadium crowd's wary anticipation of Reggie tying the game with another of his patented October home runs. A haze had settled in as twilight neared, and Welch had only one intention in his effort to get Jackson out. He was going to throw him nothing but fastballs—to his weakness—up and in. Time and again, Welch fired high and hard and time and again Jackson swung, missing on 1-1, fouling two more off on 1-2, watching a waste pitch away to even it at 2-2, then fouling another off. Welch threw another ball to run the count full, then threw four more fastballs in approximately the same place, all of which Jackson fouled off. Finally, on the 13th pitch, Dent broke from second, causing Jackson to lose his concentration for a fatal instant as he swung and missed. Game over. Mighty Reggie had struck out. As he came back to the dugout, he flung his helmet in fury, cursing the fact that Lemon had sent the runners even though there were two outs. Lemon, who was mad enough at having lost the game, wasn't about to be held accountable by Jackson for the way it ended. In a rare display of public anger, Lemon shouted at Jackson to shut his mouth and even made an overture to take him on physically if that's what he wanted. The Yankee players and coaches quickly got between them and tempers cooled, even if the immediate atmosphere from the high-intensity battle with Welch was still charged.

"That was the single most intense confrontation I ever had with a pitcher," Jackson said. "It was pure power versus power. I was wrong to react the way I did afterward, but I was frustrated. I never put more into one at bat than I did in that one, and I lost. I still get a charge watching it on the old films."

Unlike the mythic Casey, though, Jackson got his revenge. In the seventh inning of the clinching Game 6, he faced Welch again and, this time, blasted the first pitch he saw for a mammoth two-run homer, high into the Dodger Stadium right field stands.

"I felt like I'd hit it off those mountains out there," Jackson said. "Right before I went up, Thurman said to me: 'Payback time, Jack.'"

By now, the initial alienation between Jackson and his Yankee teammates—Munson especially—had all but dissipated. Whatever cynicism they may have felt about his bravado and "magnitude of me" ego, he'd managed to nullify by backing it up. However grudgingly, they had to agree he *had* taken them that extra mile to the top of the baseball universe. He'd been everything as advertised, especially the October part of it. And, so, when Munson was killed at 3:02 P.M. on August 2, 1979, in the crash of his private twin-engine Cessna while practicing takeoffs and landings at the Canton, Ohio, airport, there was no one around the Yankees more deeply affected than Jackson.

"I'd love to know where Thurman's place would be today," Jackson said, his voice taking on an almost reverential tone at the mention of his once-rival-turned-close-friend. "Just as I've since mended my relationship with Graig Nettles [with whom he engaged in a celebrated fistfight at the Yankees' victory party in Oakland after the 1981 ALCS against the A's], I'm sure that my relationship with Thurman would be one that would be very strong. Even as early as '77, when things were really tough for me with Billy, Thurman began to befriend me. He'd talk to me in the on-deck circle—we had a lot of conversations there about opposing pitchers and how we were going to approach them. And Thurman was one of the ones who went to George about talking Billy into letting me hit cleanup again.

"In '79, we were in Seattle and Nettles and I both had friends in Southern California, and Thurman asked us if we wanted a ride to Orange County in his jet. He had his instructor pilot with him and another guy and we flew back with him. On the flight, both Nettles and I noticed there was something wrong with the door and something wrong with the altimeter, which told you how high you were flying. I remember when we got into Orange County, there was a low fog ceiling and when we went to land, we were too low and had to make another shot at it. When we landed, Thurman said there was something wrong with the airplane and had to call some people in Wichita and get it fixed.

"A couple of weeks later, we were sitting around the clubhouse in Chicago—we had an off-day the next day before beginning a home stand in New York—I had to go to Connecticut for an electronics company I was doing some business with at the time—and Thurman asked me if I'd like to go to Canton with him and spend the day with him and his family. He said something to the effect 'I'm really glad we're friends and that we've gotten past all that other stuff' and 'maybe you might want to go with me tomorrow. I'm gonna practice flying in the afternoon and you can come with me.' I told him that sounded pretty cool, but that I had this other commitment in Connecticut. I really didn't want to go because I remembered that last flight.

"When it was announced, I was in the office of the company in Connecticut and the radio was on. I hear the guy say: 'We'll be back in a minute with the death of a great Yankee.' At the time, I thought like it was *me*. I was just so startled, shocked, like I was in a dream, looking down. It was so hot that day—that's the other thing I remember. I called my agent, Matt Merola, and we both talked for a few minutes, kind of stunned. He knew Thurman had asked me to go to Canton with him."

I asked Jackson if he thought Munson's death changed the

dynamics on the team insofar as the leadership torch passing to him.

"Not really," he said. "I never thought of it as my team. I may have thought of myself as the star of the team, but never as it being my team. I never felt as if I had everybody there as a Reggie supporter. I remember the team at times pitting myself against Mickey Rivers in kind of a jestful way, but really it was negative; where I thought a lot of players took advantage of Mickey and made fun of him. They didn't laugh with him; they laughed at him, and I was very hurt by that. I remember, too, a lot of black players didn't like me. Early on, I had trouble with Chambliss, Carlos May, Blair, Jimmy Wynn. They were not supporters, probably out of their loyalty to Billy. At least I think so. Willie Randolph, though, was a great friend and supporter. Willie was his own person, as he is today. Roy White, Guidry, Holtzman, Ed Figueroa, Catfish . . . they were all behind me. I'd say it was pretty much a split clubhouse in terms of Reggie Jackson up until 1979–80 when things eventually got turned around because I was there and I'd performed."

While it may never have been his team, as he maintained, the fact was, after Munson's death and the second firing of Martin following the '79 season, Jackson was the unquestioned driving force on the Yankees. Under Dick Howser (who'd been lured back from coaching baseball at his alma mater, Florida State, to replace Martin as manager in 1980), Jackson flourished, putting together the best season of his career. He hit .300 for the only time, tied for the AL lead in homers with 41 and knocked in 111 runs. Unfortunately for him, the Yankees' loss to the Royals in the ALCS—a three-game sweep after they'd won 103 games over the regular season—prompted Steinbrenner to fire Howser. And with Howser went Jackson's last support system with the Yankees.

"I loved Dick Howser," he said, "and his wife, Nancy. Dick had a great attitude toward everything. He was a good leader—a little man in stature but strong-willed and big in leadership skills. He had a great sense of humor, too. He could make you laugh and get your mind off things. He didn't have a projection of self-importance. I really wanted to have a good year for him and I did. You know when he was a coach for Martin, he did all the administrative work. He made out the lineup cards and stuff when Billy would be in there sleeping off a hangover and, from the era I was from, I always thought that there was a double standard there. Imagine if Billy was black and he came in there with a hangover or was asleep on the couch while we were all out there, practicing. I say that because it was a big deal that I was a black star in New York. I used to talk to my father about it and he'd say: 'Just do your job and don't bother with that stuff.'

"When I was a kid in Philadelphia, you adjusted to being second-class, because that was a part of life. I wasn't allowed to play with a lot of my white friends . . . couldn't go into the neighborhood pool in Glenside . . . could *never* go to the country club or golf course. You just grew up with that and you never thought too much about it or else you'd get bitter. I think of Elston Howard, the first black Yankee, who was a coach when I got there. He was from an era before mine—a more accepting era—and in their eyes he was an okay colored person. As a coach, he was a very steadying presence around the Yankees. But I think the way I conducted myself was more an influence on him than he was on me because he looked at me, sometimes in amazement at the things I would say or do because you just weren't supposed to do those things as a colored man."

Shortly after Steinbrenner fired Howser and replaced him with Gene Michael (who had been the general manager in 1980), he signed Dave Winfield, the most coveted prize of the free agent class that winter, to a revolutionary 10-year, $23 million contract. Jackson could sense the winds of change around the Yankees. His own five-year contract was to expire after the '81 season and Steinbrenner had made only tacit initiatives about an extension. It was plain to see The Boss was grooming a new, younger, more versatile star to carry the Yankees through the '80s. What Jackson did not know was that, at one of Steinbrenner's private player evaluation meetings late in the '81 season, batting coach Charlie Lau had reportedly said Reggie's bat speed had slowed and that it would be a mistake, in his opinion, to re-sign him after '81.

Thus was the premise which Steinbrenner went by in 1981 in terms of how he viewed the superstar player he'd courted so fervently and wined and dined at '21' only five years earlier. Of course, Jackson's subpar performance in '81 gave further credence to Lau's alleged appraisal.

And Jackson's relationship with Steinbrenner became strained from the outset of the '81 season when he reported late for spring training and the Yankee owner abruptly cut off negotiations on a new contract. After that, Jackson moped openly; his confidence—always his most indomitable attribute—deflated. Periodically, he'd summon to his locker writers he'd always considered his allies and vent about the cold treatment he was getting from Steinbrenner. He desperately wanted to stay and finish his career as a Yankee, he said, but, like the jilted lover, it was obvious Steinbrenner didn't want him anymore. When the players went on strike, June 12, Jackson was hitting a pathetic .199 with six homers, and though he rallied in September to get his average up to .237, with 15 homers which tied Nettles for the club lead, his worst chagrin was yet to come. After hitting a game-tying two-run homer in the Game 5 Division Series finale against the Milwaukee Brewers (which the Yankees went on to win 7–3), Jackson pulled a calf muscle in Game 2 of the ALCS against the Athletics and missed the rest of the series. His scuffle with Nettles during the victory party only further diminished him in Steinbrenner's eyes, and though his calf injury had healed by the third game of the World Series, he was stunned when told he would not be playing. In what had to be the lowest ebb of Reggie Jackson's career, Steinbrenner had decided the Yankees were better off with Jerry Mumphrey in their World Series lineup than Mr. October.

After the Yankees lost that Game 3, 5–4, Steinbrenner relented and told Lemon (who was in his second stint as manager) he could return Jackson to the lineup. In Game 4 it was Mr. October reincarnated, as Jackson reached base safely five times with a homer, two singles and two walks. It wasn't enough, however, to overcome an 8–7 Dodger victory that evened the Series. The Dodgers won again the next night, then wrapped the Series up with a 9–2 drubbing of the Yankees in Game 6 back in New York. Much like the 1960 Yankees had felt after losing in seven games to a clearly inferior (in their eyes) Pittsburgh Pirates team, the '81 Yankees could not fathom how this World Series had possibly slipped away from them. Most agreed, however, the turning point was when Steinbrenner began micromanaging by ordering Lemon to keep Jackson on the bench after they'd won the first two games. They were even more embarrassed when, at the conclusion of the final game, Steinbrenner had his public relations director, Irv Kaze, issue a public apology to the fans.

"To this day, I don't know why they sat me down," Jackson said, sighing. "All I know is, it took 'em, what, 15 years to win another World Series? They did everything they could that year to bring me down. They'd made up their minds I couldn't play anymore and they benched me, DH-ed me, had me undergo physicals. They had my eyes checked, my teeth checked, my head checked . . . everything they could to humiliate me."

The final humiliation was the Yankees never even making him an offer to stay. But he did have one last grand hurrah at Yankee Stadium the following April. In his first game back, now as a member of the visiting California Angels, he spoiled Michael's debut as Steinbrenner's latest recycled manager by hitting a home run of pure Jacksonian proportions, high and majestic, off the facade of the upper deck in right. Even his old pal, Ron Guidry, the victim of the homer, couldn't conceal his admiration for Jackson afterward. "I had to keep myself from laughing," he said. "It was about really the only fun I had in the game." In terms of spontaneous combustion and sheer storybook theatrics, it was a moment for the Yankee Stadium ages that ranked right up there with anything Babe Ruth or any of the other Yankee immortals had ever done. And the fans reacted accordingly, first chanting "Reg-gie! Reg-gie! Reg-gie" until he obliged them with a curtain call, then segueing into an even more pronounced "Steinbrenner sucks! Steinbrenner sucks! Steinbrenner sucks!"

"That was one of the bigger Reggie nights," Jackson conceded, grinning. "I can't put it ahead of Game 6 '77—nothing can ever top that for me—but as far as personal vindication and the adulation from the fans, it was right up there."

In retrospect, it is hard to believe he was a Yankee for only five seasons, given all the dramatic moments he crammed into that brief period. Ruth was a Yankee for 15 years; Lou Gehrig for 17; Joe DiMaggio for 13; Mickey Mantle for 18. And yet, Jackson's Yankee legacy—the eight homers in just 15 games over three World Series, the Reggie Bar Opening Day homer, the '78 playoff game homer, and even the homer off Guidry in that first game back at the Stadium—had managed to put him on the same lofty pedestal as the rest of them. He may not have been the greatest of Yankees, but in his brief time in pinstripes, nobody stirred the drink and provided more indelible Yankee Stadium memories than he did.

I wondered where he saw his place in Yankee history. I knew he was justifiably proud of all he'd accomplished for them from 1977 to 1981, but I also knew he would never be so presumptuous as to suggest he'd been bigger than the deities in Monument Park—Ruth, Gehrig, DiMaggio, Mantle, or, for different, more sentimental reasons, even a folk hero like Yogi Berra.

"I've been fortunate to have been a part of the fabric of this game; to have been cheered the way I was, to have been thanked by the people for what you gave them, as I was," Jackson said. "There's no truer statement than what a guy like Gehrig said about how lucky you are. You go to the front of the line; get special treatment when you don't deserve it. Just because I was a baseball player and got a chance to show people that I stood for something—which most people don't get a chance to do. To look back on all the negatives and have bad memories and reflecting back on this organization and George . . . that's not where I want to be. I wish I could be more a part of it all now, but I don't know if that will ever be.

"This game is 100-plus years old and there's been 1,000-plus stories, but the story that was built in '77 is mine and it's a good story. That's my handprint, my footprint. I believe the controversial part of me will always come out in a negative way and that's fair, in comparison to the other great Yankees, Ruth, Gehrig, DiMaggio, Mantle, Berra, who did things in a purposeful way. To say that Reggie sometimes was self-serving . . . that he didn't always do things the way they should have been done, and that he was difficult, that's a fair statement, too. But all in all, I think they'll say he was a great player for us, and a winner. I wasn't the perfect Yankee, I know that, but I'm extremely proud of all I accomplished there in those five years . . . and the fact that, no matter what, I'll always be October."

DOWN ON THE FARM WITH DONNIE BASEBALL

DON MATTINGLY

T he sun was just beginning its ascent over the South Bronx, and
a small crowd of fans hovered behind the barricades in the
October morning's chill as the New York Yankee team bus
pulled alongside the parking lot in front of Yankee Stadium. It was the
culmination of the longest trip—certainly in terms of personal
anguish—anyone on the bus could ever imagine taking; a trip that had
begun over 3,000 miles away on the other side of the continent, some
nine hours earlier, when the Seattle Mariners, completing a comeback
from an 0–2 deficit in games, defeated the Yankees 6–5 in an
excruciating 11 innings, to clinch the best-of-five 1995 American
League Division Series.

No one in the Yankee party could yet believe it had come to this.
Hadn't it been just five days earlier, in this very same locale, when they'd
boarded the bus, as thousands of fans stood cheering them in the

pouring rain, still exhilirated by Jim Leyritz's 15th-inning home run that had taken the Yankees to the brink of their first American League Championship Series in 14 years? But now it was over, and with the last fans of the season imploring them for autographs from off in the distance, they gathered in the parking lot to say their goodbyes to each other. Most of the wives, their mascara smeared beyond redemption, were still crying, while their vanquished husbands, with faces like zombies, exchanged hugs and uttered false promises of seeing each other again next spring.

Apart from this scene, Don Mattingly simply wanted to find his car. With his wife, Kim, clinging to him as he desperately weaved his way around the crowd to his '87 Mustang in the back of the lot, Mattingly had only one thing on his mind: *Let me get the hell out of here.* He had said all his goodbyes on the gut-wrenching overnight plane ride and everyone knew, in his case, they were *real* goodbyes. As one member of the Yankee traveling party told me later: "Every time you turned around on the plane, Donnie was sitting in another seat. He worked his way up and down the aisle, making sure he didn't miss anybody. It was what you might expect. He was the captain."

Mattingly navigated his car out of the lot and executed a right turn onto the access road that leads out onto the Major Deegan Expressway. He did not acknowledge the fans behind the barricade waving to him, nor did he pause, even for a fleeting moment, to look back at the Stadium that had been his home away from home for 13 New York summers. Traffic on the Deegan at this waking hour was sparse and the Mattinglys were across the George Washington Bridge and in their house in Tenafly, New Jersey, in barely 15 minutes. They would spend the next three days in solemn, numbing seclusion there, sending out for food, talking on the telephone only to Kim's parents back home in Indiana, who were looking after their three sons, Taylor, Preston and Jordan. Finally, after what he'd considered to be a sufficient mourning period for the death of a season he knew had been his last, Mattingly turned to Kim and said softly: "C'mon, honey. Let's go home."

With that, they put their arms around each other, walked out the front door into the Jersey sunlight, got into a waiting limo and headed to the airport for their flight to Indiana, leaving New York, the Yankees and baseball—as they had known it—behind them forever.

For the next 15 months, Mattingly remained incommunicado to the world outside his private domain—a sprawling, 7,000-square-foot home on two acres of gated property, and a 43-acre horse farm, a mile down the road, on the outskirts of Evansville, Indiana. It was here, in Evansville, where he and Kim had grown up, met each other in high school, fallen in love and gotten married; and here where they always knew they would make their life together beyond baseball.

They just didn't know it would be this soon.

Even when he finally ended his self-imposed seclusion and returned to Yankee Stadium on January 23, 1997, to officially announce his retirement, Mattingly made it clear he was not interested in returning to the organization in any sort of long-term capacity. His job now, he asserted, was being a full-time father to his three boys, and overseeing the ranch, which he'd built for Kim and her burgeoning business of breeding show horses.

It was hard to imagine Don Mattingly totally divorcing himself from baseball and yet, aside from his three- to four-week pilgrimages each March to the Yankees' spring training headquarters as a special batting instructor (which he did not begin until 2000), he rarely strayed from the farm. He was, he insisted, "just a dad and horse farmer" when I proposed paying a visit to him in Evansville to see for myself this magical place that has so consumed him, as baseball once did.

Since there was still only limited jet service to the Evansville airport, I had elected to fly into Louisville and drive the rest of the way, which was about a 130-mile straight shot west on Interstate 64. Mattingly had given me a phone number to call when I got close—which I did, upon approaching his house and seeing that the iron gates to the driveway were closed.

"Just keep on driving down the road," he said. "I'm at the ranch.

You can't miss it. You'll see the big wooden posts and the sign 'Diamond 5 Farms.'"

A cold and steady spring rain had begun falling as I drove the car between the huge wooden posts and followed the winding gravel road up a gradual hill, past a lake on the left, to the large white barn where Mattingly was waiting, along with his youngest son, Jordan, and a helper whom he introduced as Greg; Mattingly was wearing a heavy dark blue windbreaker, a retro San Francisco Seals baseball cap, and a pair of very scruffy old shoes that, presumably, were a prerequisite for walking among the horse stalls.

"I forgot to tell you to bring some old shoes," he said. "That's okay, though. I've got a pair you can wear. They're the baseball shoes they gave me in spring training this year."

As I put them on, I couldn't help but think to myself: "Never let anyone tell me I couldn't walk in Donnie Baseball's shoes." They were a tad too big, but when I saw where he was leading me, I was grateful to have them. The barn was actually connected to an indoor arena with a sawdust and mud floor where the horses are put through their daily workouts. The four of us navigated our way around a large pile of hay to a stall which housed a newborn horse with spindly legs about five feet tall and what, I figured (wrongly), was the parent horse.

"Our newest baby," Mattingly said proudly. "She's about 12 days old. That's the recipient mare with her. It just carried the baby. She's got nothing to do with the genes."

Mattingly then proceeded to explain to me the breeding process in which a mare is inseminated with the embryo of another show horse and merely carries the egg until birth. The brood mare stays with the colt for four to six months afterward when they are gradually weaned away. My curiosity was drawn to a plaque on the door to the stall that was inscribed: "Oh My's Living Legend."

"That was Kim's first show horse," Mattingly explained. "Beautiful horse. She died of an aneurysm in this stall 10 days after giving birth. We try to put a history in all these stalls."

Kim, it turned out, was in South Africa this weekend, attending the show horse world championships, although as Mattingly said with a chuckle: "She just needed a vacation." In any case, it was clear he had no interest in leaving his Indiana home for South Africa, especially if it meant putting the supreme test to his chronically cranky back by taking a 23-hour plane trip.

It was the same—probably congenital—back condition, which had flared anew in the prime of his career when he was the acknowledged best player in the game, robbing him of his power and ultimately sending him into his premature retirement at age 34. He steadfastly refused to blame the back condition for his dramatic decline after the 1989 season, and even to this day he would not concede a recent operation—in which doctors had extracted a piece of disc that had become tangled in the nerves—could have made any difference.

"I feel better than I've felt in years," Mattingly said, "and I can't believe it's been only a little more than a week since I had the operation. I came home from spring training and it had gotten so bad I could no longer stand the pain. We called George and they flew me to New York and set me up with one of the best back surgeons in the country."

"What if you'd have gotten the operation back in 1989?" I asked.

"It wouldn't have changed anything," he said with a shrug. "It's something that was there from the time I was a kid and it's always gonna be there. In this case, it was starting to affect my legs. They never like to operate, but it got so I couldn't deal with the pain any longer. I still have to take it easy, watch my weight and not overdo anything. When it first flared up in '87, it was a spasm. The funny thing was, right after that I went on that home run streak."

He had missed 18 games earlier in 1987 because of the back, prompting the first scare stories from the New York tabloids about his career being in jeopardy, and on July 8, the day the streak began, he had only eight homers. He hit a pair of two-run shots against the Minnesota Twins at Yankee Stadium that day, then added four more in the next four home games against the Chicago White Sox. The streak was interrupted by the All-Star break, after which the Yankees went to Texas where Mattingly homered twice more in his sixth straight game, against the Rangers, to tie the American League record. One of the homers that first night in Texas was a grand slam off knuckleballer Charlie Hough and the other a two-run shot off Mitch Williams, who would later attain baseball infamy by giving up the World Series-winning homer to the Toronto Blue Jays' Joe Carter in 1993. Afterward, however, Mattingly was surprisingly downcast about his six RBI night—the reason being, he explained, his seventh-inning muff of a ground ball to first.

"I made an error," he said, deflecting all the attention being given to his tying the AL consecutive game homer record. "Tonight wasn't a good game."

Of course, by this time, reporters had become accustomed to Mattingly downplaying his personal accomplishments. From the time he'd arrived in the big leagues at the tail end of the 1982 season, he'd been this self-effacing Indiana country boy, clearly uncomfortable with answering questions. And even after he became the Yankee captain (in which the unwritten part of the job requirement is to serve as the team spokesman after games), he seldom provided reporters with anything approaching a Hall of Fame quote. In addition, they knew how much pride he took in his defense, and, so, the streak did not become a media frenzy until the next night when Mattingly hit a mammoth drive into the right field seats off Texas left-hander Paul Kilgus to propel the Yankees to an 8–4 victory.

He had taken sole possession of the AL record and now, suddenly, his sights were set on the major league record of eight straight games with a homer, set in May of 1956 by Pittsburgh Pirates first baseman Dale Long. In the visitors' clubhouse after that Friday night game, the clubhouse man left a bottle of Freixenet sparkling wine on ice in front of Mattingly's locker. There was no avoiding the attention to the streak, although Mattingly could not offer anything other than: "I haven't hit a home run trying to hit one. They just seem to be happening. I don't know why."

The next night, after grounding out to first in the first inning against Texas right-hander Jose Guzman, Mattingly caught up with a 2-0 fastball on the outside corner and drove it over the wall in left-center in the fourth to tie Long.

"See, that's why I don't see how an operation would have made any difference back then," Mattingly was saying now. "It was there. It was always there. I'd had a spasm that put me on the [disabled] list and yet I was still able to hit all those home runs. How could I have done that if my back was so bad?"

"How did you?" I asked.

"It was the strangest thing," he said. "I hadn't been hitting real good before my back went out and when I came back, I was talking to [Bobby] Murcer, who told me: 'Just relax up there. Get quiet.' And that's what I did. It was like I was just sitting there, real comfortable, quiet . . . in my own world. Probably before I'd been jumping at the ball, and Murcer, who knew how I was supposed to look, was able to spot that. There's a certain amount of mechanics to hitting, but it's also a matter of getting that *feeling* back, which is what happened. I don't know if I was ever more locked in than during that streak. But even though I was hitting those home runs, I was iffy. I was always kinda fighting it. It wasn't pain as much as it was a constant ache that never let you get loose.

"In the '90s, especially, it became a battle. I wasn't ever able to get loose and then I tried to make changes and really screwed myself up. But you can't complain, because nobody wants to hear it."

While Jordan and Greg began tending to the hay pile, tossing forkfuls into the stalls for the horses' lunch, Mattingly led me to an office room at the rear of the arena. There was no way to avoid tracking hay and mud onto the office's clean wooden floor and I heard Mattingly mutter something to himself about making sure to clean the place up again before Kim got home.

"There isn't a day I wake up here and not have something to do," he said. "I want to live over here at the farm full-time after the kids grow up."

I remembered from when he was playing, there were numerous stories about the batting cage, complete with pitching machine, he'd erected off the garage in his house so he could hit all winter long.

"What about hitting?" I asked. "Do you still find yourself getting into the cage on occasion?"

"Nah," he said. "I really can't hit anymore. The only time I use the cage is when I work with the kids. We've kinda closed that cage down."

There was a knock on the door and Mattingly got up to let in a 60-ish, ruddy-faced man whom he introduced as his father-in-law, Dennis Sexton. Sexton, a former defensive back at the University of Mississippi, had been one of Mattingly's first baseball coaches in legion ball.

"Yeah, and after the games, I was always having to chase Donnie off my front lawn," Sexton laughed. "He kept coming around trying to make time with my daughter. That was a long time before he made the big money."

But Sexton was pretty sure the skinny left-handed outfielder-pitcher was going to have a big future in baseball. All of Evansville was, if only because no one could remember seeing a more perfect or lethal batting stroke. His high school coach at Memorial, Quentin Merkel, remembered first seeing him, at age 14, and marveling: "He hit *every* pitch hard. Didn't matter where it was—inside, outside, high, low—he was right *on* it! I never saw a high school kid before or after who could hit the ball so consistently. I'd go out every spring hoping I'd see someone hit the ball the way he did—to find a boy on your team like that is a *gift.* "

And when he was 18, Mattingly was featured as one of the "Faces in the Crowd" in the July 16, 1979, issue of *Sports Illustrated.* Next to his picture, it was noted how he'd batted .500 and .522 over the previous two seasons to lead Reitz Memorial High to a 59-1 record, while his 140 RBI in four years equaled the highest total ever for scholastic baseball. Interestingly, also featured in the "Faces" that same week was an amateur Missouri state golfing champion named Payne Stewart.

According to legend—advanced primarily by the man himself—

Yankee owner George Steinbrenner was on an airplane reading *Sports Illustrated* when he spotted the Mattingly item in the "Faces in the Crowd" and instructed his scouting and player development chiefs to "look into this kid and make sure we don't miss him in the draft." If that really did happen, as Steinbrenner had often claimed, his baseball people apparently didn't pay much heed to him. They got Mattingly, all right, but waited until the 19th round of the draft.

"I was disappointed," Mattingly remembered. "I really thought I was gonna go in one of the first 3 to 4 rounds. I'd hit nearly .600 in high school and I had so much confidence. But I couldn't run, I didn't hit for power then, and my arm strength was nothing special, so I could understand it. The year I signed, they took a first baseman, Todd Demeter, with their No. 1 pick and put me right into the outfield, which was a good thing. I developed more arm strength. I believed in myself, though. I dreamed of playing in the big leagues. Each level I went to, I had success. After I signed, my goal was never to spend two seasons at any level of minor league ball."

He never did, either.

After breaking in with Oneonta in the New York–Penn rookie league in 1979 and hitting .349 in 53 games, he advanced to Greensboro in the Class A South Atlantic League and won the batting title in 1980 with a .358 average. The next year, at Class AA Nashville in the Southern League, he caught the eye of Yankee officials, even more so, it turned out, than switch-hitting center fielder Willie McGee, who was in his second season at that level and hit .322 to Mattingly's .316.

"That was the year of the strike, and the Yankees sent all their coaches around the minor leagues to look at their prospects," Mattingly related. "Yogi was one of the guys who came to Nashville and I guess he liked what he saw of me. I later heard he told the front office that I could hit major league pitching now. The funny thing is, McGee and I had the same year, but over the winter they traded him to the Cardinals and the next year he was in the big leagues while I was at Columbus."

It so happened that was one of the worst trades in Yankee history. They had a glut of outfield prospects at the time—Mattingly included—and as the story goes, they arranged to "loan" McGee to the Cardinals for a year while they sorted them all out. He was traded for a retread left-handed reliever named Bob Sykes with the provision the Yankees would get him back at the end of the '82 season. Except, two weeks into the season, McGee was in St. Louis and wound up the Cardinals' everyday center fielder, hitting .296. When Cardinal owner Gussie Busch was told by his front office execs McGee had been on loan from the Yankees and was supposed to be returned to them, he sniffed: "That's tough. No way we're sending him back. We'll be killed by the press! Do what you've gotta do to make it up to them, but no way are they getting McGee back." It was then arranged for the Yankees to get a top shortstop prospect from the Cardinals, Bobby Meacham (who was blocked in St. Louis anyway by Ozzie Smith), along with outfielder Stan Javier, in exchange for three non-prospect minor leaguers.

Meacham played six seasons with the Yankees, one of them, 1985, as their regular shortstop, while Javier was shipped to the Oakland Athletics as part of the big December '84 trade for Rickey Henderson. As for McGee, he would go on to play 17 more seasons in the big leagues, retiring in 2000 with 2,254 hits and a career .295 average.

"I couldn't believe it when they traded McGee," Mattingly said. "All I knew was, when I got to Nashville and saw I could hit with him, I *knew* I could play. There wasn't anybody I saw in that league I didn't feel I couldn't hit."

One of my everlasting memories of him had always been that first spring training in Fort Lauderdale in 1982. Yogi Berra had already put the word out to the Yankee beat reporters about this left-handed hitter he'd seen at Nashville during the strike.

"Watch him," Berra said, "he's gonna be a good one. Soon, too."

When Berra spoke, which wasn't often, reporters listened, and, as such, this 21-year-old outfielder–first baseman with barely three years of minor league apprenticeship was accorded an undue amount of attention that spring, despite the surplus of proven quality hitters—Dave Winfield, Ken Griffey, Lou Piniella, Murcer, Oscar Gamble—seemingly in his path to a place in either the Yankee outfield or first base.

Every morning, Kim would pull into the parking lot in their beat-up and well-traveled Chevy Monte Carlo, Mattingly in the passenger seat and their cocker spaniel, Honey, hanging out the back seat window. They would kiss and Mattingly would hop out, duffel bag in hand, and go to work.

"You two looked like something out of the *Beverly Hillbillies,*" I said. "Two country kids with nothing but a dream."

"Yeah, I guess that's not far wrong," he replied, laughing. "But you know, Kim and I spent my whole minor league career together, living in $125-a-month apartments with no screens and struggling just to get by. I'll always think of them as good times, and in a lot of ways, I'm glad we didn't meet after I started making money."

At the end of the spring, they sent him to Columbus—Triple A— and, for the first time, Mattingly felt challenged. At the halfway point of the season, his average was hovering in the .260s with no homers. He knew he was never going to get to the next level this way, but he hadn't lost his confidence.

"It took me a little time to get rollin' at Columbus," he said. "Triple A, I found, was a big adjustment. Instead of guys challenging you with their best stuff, like I'd had in all the lower minor leagues, there were a lot of veteran pitchers who'd been in the majors and threw a lot of slop. Gradually, I got used to seeing more breaking pitches and I said to myself: 'If I get 300 at bats, I'll get hot somewhere in that stretch and then I'm gonna roll.' In the second half of the year, I got 58 of my 75 RBIs and all 10 of my home runs."

The "no vacancy" situation with the Yankees wasn't much different when he reported to Fort Lauderdale the following spring. As always, Steinbrenner had seen to it the Yankees were fully stocked with quality, veteran hitters. Winfield was a fixture in right field; Griffey was now ensconced at first base with Roy Smalley, yet another high-salaried veteran, vying for playing time there; Piniella and Murcer were still around, and over the winter, Steinbrenner had brought in two expensive free agent sluggers, Don Baylor and Steve Kemp, to further solidify the lineup. The manager, Billy Martin, admitted to being impressed with Mattingly's hitting potential, especially after watching the slope-shouldered Stan Musial look-alike hold his own at all three outfield positions and first base while hitting the ball consistently hard in the Grapefruit League and winning the James P. Dawson Award as the outstanding rookie in the Yankee camp. Martin just didn't know what to do with him.

"He makes the team," Martin finally said at the end of the '83 camp. "I'll figure out how to get him into the lineup."

Because of an injury to Griffey, Mattingly found himself in the Opening Day lineup, at first base, against the Detroit Tigers, before a packed-house Stadium crowd of over 55,000. The Kid from Evansville had arrived, but by day's end, he knew it was short-lived. For when they talk about Don Mattingly's career as one of the finest-fielding, hardest-hitting first basemen in the history of the game, they will not include his debut. The Yankees were clobbered 13–2 that day, and Mattingly had no small part in the humiliation. One ground ball to first went right through his legs; another tied him up trying for a double play before he was able to cleanly field it. He also mishandled two less-than-perfect throws from third baseman Graig Nettles.

Much as Martin might have liked what he saw in Mattingly, patience—as with his Boss, Steinbrenner—was not one of Martin's virtues. For the rest of the month, Mattingly found himself sitting on the bench until finally being told, after seven games and only 12 at bats, he was being sent back to Columbus. It was a blow, especially after his private vow of never spending more than one year at any minor league level, but as he said: "I was only 21 years old, and I really needed to play—somewhere."

That "somewhere" didn't necessarily mean in the Yankee system, either.

"To be honest," Mattingly said, "I was figuring they'd probably trade me."

According to Bill Bergesch, who was Steinbrenner's GM at the time, the Yankee high command all agreed this was one prospect who was a keeper. "The Giants, I know, called us and asked about Mattingly," Bergesch recalled, "but we'd talked it over with George, and even though we were overloaded at the time with veteran hitters, *everybody* was in love with Mattingly's bat and we told any club that called us we would not discuss him."

Apparently, five years later, trade discussions with the Giants involving Mattingly were a little more serious. By then, Al Rosen, who'd been Steinbrenner's GM in the late '70s, had taken over as president of the Giants. Sometime after the '88 season, Rosen and Steinbrenner had discussions about a trade that would exchange Mattingly for the Giants' lefty-hitting first baseman, Will Clark.

"We expanded it with other players," Rosen recalled, "but it never really got close to being a firm deal. George had concerns about Clark's elbow and I had concerns about Mattingly's back. George and I were always having dialogue about players. I don't recall what happened— maybe we both just had second thoughts after thinking it over. The genesis of deals is that, as time goes by, you rethink your positions."

As for '83, Mattingly responded to steady play at Columbus with a hot bat, and was up to .340 after 43 games with still no call from above. Now, he was getting frustrated, and in his first public show of the self-confidence that would mark his career in New York, he announced to Columbus reporters after the June 15 trading deadline passed: "I want to make a statement every time I play, and I'm going to do it until I get my shot—with someone. But what I would most like to prove is that you don't have to be a free agent to play for the Yankees."

Five days later, Bobby Murcer announced his retirement from the Yankees and Griffey went on the disabled list with a twisted knee. Martin had his opening again. Mattingly was recalled and installed at first base. In addition, Kemp, who couldn't adapt his batting stroke to

Yankee Stadium, had been felled by a shoulder injury in early April after an outfield collision with Willie Randolph and Jerry Mumphrey, and never was able to regain the form that had earned him a five-year $5.45 million contract from Steinbrenner. Martin was down on Kemp anyway and when the lefty-swinging outfielder continued to struggle with the bat as the season wore on, it opened up the opportunity to play Mattingly in the outfield as well. In all, Mattingly played 42 games at first and 48 games in the outfield his rookie season, batting a respectable .283.

The next year, two things happened that would dramatically affect Mattingly's career: Over the winter, Berra replaced Martin as manager, and, on June 17, 1984, Piniella announced his retirement and became the full-time Yankee batting coach.

"I learned to be a power hitter from Lou," Mattingly said. "My body was starting to mature from weight lifting and Lou taught me about weight shifting and how to incorporate it into my swing. I started pulling the ball. At the same time, Yogi just let me play. He'd told me that spring I was gonna be his swing man, going back and forth from the outfield to first base, but he started me at first and wound up leaving me there."

It was really a no-brainer. Mattingly, who had decided to go to winter ball in Puerto Rico after the '83 season and play exclusively first base, dazzled Berra with his defensive play while, at the same time, reaffirming the manager's 1981 assessment of his hitting ability. In the minors, Yankee roving hitting instructor Mickey Vernon, a two-time batting champion with the old Washington Senators, had told Mattingly: "Don't change anything about your short, compact swing. Just get the big part of the bat on the ball—you can play in the big leagues right now with that swing and you don't need home runs to do it." Piniella made only minor changes in Mattingly's swing, but in terms of ultimate results, they were significant. And so, in the comfort zone of Berra as his manager and Piniella as his ever-encouraging mentor and alter ego, he came of age that '84 season, hitting 23 homers and driving in 110 runs—both career highs to that point—and winning the

American League batting title .343 to .340, in a compelling down-to-the-last-day race with Dave Winfield.

With the Tigers having blown away the American League East field by getting off to a record 35-5 start, the Mattingly-Winfield batting race became the only race in the Bronx that summer, but passions in New York ran just as high as if the Yankees were battling for a pennant. No Yankee had won a batting title since Mickey Mantle's Triple Crown year, 1956, and this race between teammates had all the elements of David vs. Goliath. Only it was Mattingly playing the role of David, to Winfield's Goliath.

At 6-foot-6, 230 pounds, Winfield, a three-sport star at the University of Minnesota, was a magnificent physical specimen with what scouts call all-encompassing skills. He could hit for both average and power, run, throw and field. Before signing what was then the richest contract in baseball history—a 10-year, $23 million free agent deal with the Yankees in 1980—Winfield had played eight seasons with the San Diego Padres, going straight to the big leagues from college, where he'd had the distinction of also being drafted by the Atlanta Hawks of the National Basketball Association, the Utah Stars of the American Basketball Association and the Minnesota Vikings of the National Football League. He was, in short, the embodiment of *The Natural*, the popular motion picture of that summer.

As the Mattingly-Winfield batting race wore on, it evoked memories of the Roger Maris–Mickey Mantle home run race of 1961, with reports of the Yankee players taking sides, along with the fans. In this case, the reports had some validity, if only because Mattingly was perceived as a "grind-it-out" blue-collar player by his teammates, while Winfield, who often arrived at the Stadium wearing three-piece suits and carrying a briefcase, was more an entity unto himself. Between the lines, nobody played the game harder, but as soon as it was over, Winfield was always one of the first players out of the clubhouse. Distant as he may have been, however, Winfield was keenly aware of the heavy sentiment toward Mattingly and he was wounded by it. During a road trip in Detroit in August of that season, I remembered being taken aback when, in a rare display of public anger, Winfield had vented his feelings to me about the batting race and charged that players and reporters alike were making it a racial thing. "They're pitting player against player, teammate against teammate," he seethed. "It's becoming a black-white thing and it's splitting the clubhouse in half!"

"Was that *your* impression?" I asked Mattingly now.

"To be honest," he replied, "it didn't get that complicated for me. I was still a young kid and '84 was really my first full year, and it was easy for me because I was still just trying to establish myself. I wasn't worried about winning the batting title. I was hitting around .330 and having a great year. I had nothing to lose. I was gonna let it all hang out and if I finished second, I finished second. I wanted to win, but I figured I was a winner that year no matter what.

"I didn't feel like it became a race thing or anything, but I did feel like he was definitely the underdog, even though I was supposed to be the underdog. It was natural for people to feel that way. I was the young kid coming up, first full year, making the minimum, and he'd been the free agent who got the big contract, a superstar for a long period. Everybody was rooting for the young kid. It's just natural. People always root for the guy who's not supposed to win, like Gonzaga against North Carolina or Duke. Dave was under a lot of pressure because of that—plus all the friction that was going on between him and Steinbrenner. I didn't have to deal with any of that. I didn't know about all the political stuff going on and, so, it was easy for me and, I'm sure, a whole lot tougher for him.

"I told a lot of people that later. He really treated me great during that whole race. He did not make me feel uncomfortable. He could have made me uncomfortable as a young player, but instead he treated me with nothing but respect the whole way through and I learned a lot and gained a lot of respect for him because of it."

The final day of the '84 season, a day that would come to define Mattingly's career, Yankee Stadium was three-quarters filled—30,602—

despite the fact the team they were playing, Detroit, had clinched the division title almost three weeks earlier. For the Yankee fans deprived of an October for three years now, this was nevertheless the supreme season-ending drama—*mano against mano*—with Winfield, the favorite, holding a two-point lead, .341 to .339, over the kid challenger.

Tiger manager Sparky Anderson obviously had a sense of theater, too. He chose as his starting pitcher that day a rookie right-hander named Randy O'Neal, whom he would not even include on his postseason roster. It was as if he was saying to Mattingly and Winfield: "Take your cuts, boys, and may the best man win!"

In the end, it was no contest. Mattingly singled off O'Neal in the first, doubled in both the third and fourth and capped off a stunning 4-for-5 performance by singling off Tiger closer and AL MVP Willie Hernandez in the eighth, to finish at .343. Winfield, on the other hand, managed just one hit in four tries to drop a point to .340.

"I went in thinking it's awfully hard to pick up two points on your average in one day that late in the season, so I was pretty relaxed," Mattingly said. "I thought: 'If I can just get that first one, maybe, after that, I might get hot. So I got that little jam shot on my first at bat and then hit a couple bullets after that. The last one, Hernandez threw me one of those tough sliders of his, up and in—he was one tough, damn lefty—and I got out in front of it and hit a bouncer between first and second."

"It must have been a great feeling of satisfaction," I suggested.

"Oh yeah," he said. "I was only 23 years old and I remembered how my oldest brother, Jerry, was only 23 when he was killed in a construction site accident, and all I could think was how lucky I was. I think I appreciated everything that happened to me a little bit more after that. My number, 23, always had a lot of special meaning, too."

Between the batting title and the way the Yankees had played as a team over the second half of '84—posting the best record in baseball, 54-34, after the All-Star break—Mattingly went home to Indiana that winter with a good feeling about everything. He felt he'd made it, and now he was ready to become a part of that storied Yankee tradition of winning championships. When, over the winter, the Yankees executed a blockbuster trade with the Oakland Athletics for baseball's future all-time stolen base king and premier lead-off hitter, Rickey Henderson, he was even more certain of a ring in his very near future.

For his first year and a half, he'd been mostly sheltered from the continual in-house Yankee politics that generated out of the owner's box. He was the kid trying to earn his keep on a team stacked with veteran All-Stars. Now *he* was the All-Star and, improbable as it might have seemed to him, he was a player they had all begun to look up to. From an individual standpoint, he would not disappoint them, but he could not control the turmoil and instability that would plague his Yankee teams the rest of his career, denying him the only glory in baseball he ever wanted—a World Series.

It began in earnest April 28, 1985, the day Yogi Berra was fired as manager by Steinbrenner, just 16 games into the season.

"You were very close to Yogi," I said to him. "He was your first champion in the organization. That had to be one of the worst days of your life."

"It was pretty bad," he said, getting up to stretch. "We were gonna be a good club that year, you could see it, but we were really kinda banged up early. Rickey hadn't played yet and Winny was hurt, too, a leg problem or something. We were—what?—6-10? That's not a big deal. So, yeah, it was pretty disappointing. But I guess that was just part of the learning curve for me, looking back. As a player, you always have loyalty to the guy you're playing for. I'll never forget coming into that locker room, in Chicago, after it happened. Baylor flipped over a table. I was really upset. The rest of it is kind of a blur.

"It was so early. We were just one good week from getting over .500 and going on a roll. We wound up having a great year. It might have been the best team I played on. Shoot, we won 97 games that year and don't even get into the playoffs! You know what I remember most about '85? We beat the crap out of the Royals early on and they wound up world champions."

He opened the door that led to the arena and spotted Greg off in the distance, waving to him.

"C'mon," Mattingly said, "time to walk the horses."

I got the feeling, even all these years later, it was uncomfortable for him to talk about those lost Yankee seasons. It was part of the reason he'd retreated to Indiana—to a life apart from baseball. He had done all he could; accomplished so much in so short a period of time, and it hadn't been enough. Here, at least, he was fulfilled.

His face brightened as we approached the stall and Greg led the new foal and her surrogate mother out into the arena. Mattingly took the reins of the brood mare and Greg took the baby and together they led them on a spirited jaunt around the arena. Jordan, meanwhile, was jubilantly driving a golf cart (painted with Yankee pinstripes and Mattingly's No. 23) back and forth from the barn area. So this was it, I thought: Donnie Baseball, down-home horse farmer and full-time dad. Who needed New York?

After about 20 minutes, Mattingly and Greg shepherded the horses back into the stall and Jordan heaved a couple of more forkfuls of hay over the gate for them. It was time for lunch—ours—and Mattingly suggested we go back to the house first to clean up. I followed him out of the farm, down the road and through the electrically controlled iron gate at the foot of his driveway. He was driving a huge black Chevy Suburban, which he parked alongside the house. We had barely gotten out of our cars when the back door opened and Taylor, his oldest son, came out, followed by a quartet of overly exuberant greyhounds.

"Don't mind them," Mattingly assured me, "they don't bite. They just want to get to know you. Kim and I rescued a couple of 'em from the local dog track."

"Horses, dogs, anything else I should be aware of?" I asked.

"There's a couple of cats, too," Mattingly said. "But they stay in the garage, out of harm's way. They know the dogs will kill them."

After the dogs had their quick romp around the backyard, we all went into the house. Mattingly disappeared to change his clothes and instructed Taylor to give me a tour. As Yogi would say, the house was "nothing but rooms" and seemed to go on forever.

"Mom and Dad kept building on more rooms when we were all born," Taylor explained. "It *is* pretty spread out, isn't it? I guess you probably want to see Dad's room."

He led me up the stairs and down the hallway to a large T-shaped office. Along the wall facing the entrance was a long glass-enclosed case in which a couple dozen trophies and other artifacts were displayed, most prominent of which was Mattingly's 1985 Most Valuable Player award.

Not since Mantle in 1956 had any Yankee had a season like that one in terms of sheer dominance and total hitting. To whatever skeptics there were left who might have wondered what he could do for an encore, after winning the batting title in only his second season in the bigs, Mattingly answered: everything else. He hit .324 with 35 homers and led the American League in RBI (145), doubles (48) and total bases (370). The gap of 21 RBI between Mattingly's 145 and Baltimore's Eddie Murray's 124 was the largest between 1-2 finishers in the American League in 32 years. He was also second in the league in hits (211) and slugging (.567). His RBI count was the most by a Yankee since Joe DiMaggio's 155 in 1948, his hits the most by a Yankee since Red Rolfe's 213 in 1939. He struck out only 41 times that season, the first player to lead the league in RBI and fan so few times since Ted Kluszewski of the Cincinnati Reds had 141 RBI and only 35 strikeouts in 1954. He also won the first of his nine Gold Gloves while extending his streak of 153 games without an error at first base.

As I gazed at the MVP plaque, recalling in my mind the way Mattingly had simply overwhelmed everyone in baseball that season, emerging as the best player in the game—at 24, no less, and in only his third year—he reappeared behind us on the stairs.

"The MVP award certainly appears to be in a place of honor," I said.

"It was a magical year for me," Mattingly admitted. "I mean, 145 RBIs, 35 bombs? Where was *this* coming from?"

It was also an enlightening year for him. As a kid growing up in Indiana, he really didn't know anything about the Yankees and their tradition. (In a candid interview once in 1984, he even admitted, as a kid, thinking Babe Ruth was a comic book character.) But after three years in pinstripes, he'd become increasingly familiar with all the great Yankee names and now, after this monumental season, he found himself being linked with them. The 48 doubles was especially intriguing to him since Lou Gehrig, the Yankee legend to whom people (however prematurely) had begun comparing him, held the club record with 52, set way back in 1927. The fact was, Gehrig and Mattingly *did* have a lot of similarities. They were both superb-fielding, power-hitting, left-handed first basemen with quiet, unassuming demeanors. Gehrig, however, was a Yankee deity and Mattingly, in only his third season, was embarrassed to hear himself talked about as the second coming of the Iron Horse.

Still, that doubles record was something he did not believe to be unattainable for him.

"I remember late in the '86 season, my brother Randy came up to New York to visit with me," Mattingly said, "and I always looked up to Randy, all through junior high and high school football. He was my oldest brother, and we were out bar-hopping after a night game and we ended up at Elaine's. Seems like we always ended up there. It was late and he'd probably had too many beers, but he said: 'You know, it's just time. You made a run at Gehrig last year. It's time for him to go down!' It was funny. I'd never thought about it much, but after he said that, he made me want to do it. For the first time, I thought it was okay for me to go after Gehrig."

Like the '84 batting race with Winfield, Mattingly's assault on Gehrig came down to the final day of the '86 season and was tinged with all sorts of added drama irrespective of any pennant race. For one thing, Mattingly was also locked in a nip-and-tuck battle with the Red Sox's Wade Boggs for the batting title as the Yankees converged on Fenway Park for an otherwise meaningless season-ending four-game series against the already crowned division champs.

Boggs, however, was sidelined by a hamstring injury, meaning Mattingly was going to have to go it alone. He went into the series trailing Boggs .348 to .357 and needing two doubles to break Gehrig's record.

On Friday night, Mattingly collected two hits in four at bats, a fifth-inning double and a seventh-inning single, giving him 232 hits for the season to break Hall-of-Famer Earle Combs's 1927 Yankee club record. The double, a sharp one-hopper that glanced off the glove of Don Baylor at first, tied Gehrig and raised Mattingly's average to .350. But without Boggs, the batting race was devoid of much of its passion and the New York tabloids responded predictably with headlines screaming "Chickened Out!" (a clever double reference to Boggs's meal of choice before every game).

In the doubleheader on Saturday, Mattingly went 4-for-l0, with three singles in the first game and a homer in the second, his 30th. His batting average at the end of the day stood at .351, meaning he would have to go 6-for-6 on Sunday to overtake Boggs.

"It's difficult," Mattingly said at the time, "but there's no concession from me. I don't know what that word means."

Nobody had to tell him that only one Yankee in history—the very unlegendary Myril Hoag, on June 6, 1934—had ever gone 6-for-6 in a game.

Although he didn't come close, he managed to leave the Fenway Park crowd in awe. Lou Piniella, the Yankee manager, inserted him in the lead-off spot in order to give him every opportunity, and in his first at bat, Mattingly drew gasps by hitting a homer. Then in the fourth, he lined a 1-0 pitch off the Green Monster wall in left that went for a double—his record 53rd— as two more Yankee runs scored. That proved to be his final hit of the season, but as he would later admit, it was one of the biggest ones of his career, if only because it had fulfilled a promise to his brother.

Ordinarily, a four-game sweep of the Red Sox at Fenway Park would be cause for jubilation in Yankeeland, but this one was empty, other than perhaps convincing Steinbrenner that Piniella deserved another year as manager. At least, Mattingly could take pride at having knocked two more of their legends out of the record book while personally taking the fight right down to the finish. Bob Tewksbury, a rookie pitcher on that '86 Yankee team, perhaps summed up best what Mattingly had become when he said to *Sports Illustrated*'s Peter Gammons: "I guess everyone now looks at him the way we, his teammates, have for a long time—with a degree of awe, almost reverence. I love to sit in the dugout and just watch his eyes."

And you could certainly make the case Mattingly's 1986 season was just as dominant—and MVP worthy—as '85. He played in every game, hit a career-high .352, smacked 31 homers and drove in 113 runs. His 238 hits, 53 doubles, 388 total bases and .573 slugging percentage all led the league, and he again led all first basemen in fielding while winning a second straight Gold Glove.

But once again, the Yankees finished second and out of playoffs, this time five and a half games behind the Red Sox, and in the MVP balloting Mattingly finished a distant second to Boston's Roger Clemens, the dominant pitcher in baseball that year with a 24-4 record and league-leading 2.48 ERA. After the voting was announced, there was a predictable hue and cry in New York.

"I spoke my case back then," Mattingly said. "I felt everyday players should get MVP consideration over pitchers. That 1986 season, I put the whole package together, average, power, RBIs, and it was probably my best year. I always felt I should hit .350 and higher. I really did. And that was the only year I ever did, and I did it with all the power."

"The season ending as it did, with Boggs sitting out the batting race, and you getting Gehrig's record, was all a little strange," I said. "It was like you were playing in the Twilight Zone—a game unto yourself."

"I always felt you needed to compete with yourself to get the best of yourself," Mattingly said. "A lot was made of my rivalry with Boggs, because Winny and I beat him out in '84 and he beat me out in '85 and '86. I loved that Boston rivalry, but even though Boggs and I both loved hitting for high average—in his case scary averages—I didn't look at it as me against him. The guys I was competing against when we played Boston were [Roger] Clemens, [Bruce] Hurst and [John] Tudor. For me, the *pitchers* were the rivalry. I wasn't thinking about Boggs, Rice and Evans."

After a third-place finish in '84, and a pair of seconds in '85 and '86, the Yankees fell to fourth in '87, prompting Steinbrenner to shift Piniella to GM and bring Billy Martin back for a fifth time. The constant upheaval in the manager's chair and the front office, however, had begun to take its toll on the organization. Too many ill-advised free agent signings, combined with mostly barren drafts, doomed the Yankees to some of the worst finishes in their history as the '80s turned into the '90s. Mattingly never wanted to admit it to himself, but his dream of playing in a World Series was becoming more and more unrealistic.

"It seemed like we hit the wall an awful lot in August, pitching-wise," Mattingly said, in reference to his five prime seasons, '83–'87. "We always brought in offense—like Texas today. We'd trade one hitter for another, we'd sign 2, 3 free agent hitters, but, after Gator [Ron Guidry] in the '70s, we never got those dominant kind of pitchers, either through our system or in the market. Instead, after Gator got hurt, we were trying to win asking Tommy John and Phil Niekro to make 30 quality starts at 42 years old. Nothing against them. They were gamers and great pitchers in their prime, but they should have been No. 4 or No. 5 starters with us and we were asking them to be No. 1 or 2. We just didn't have good enough pitching. It was as simple as that. If you don't have the pitching, you're not gonna win. It wasn't until Stick [Gene Michael] was GM and started going out and getting pitching, like Jimmy Key, [David] Cone and [David] Wells that they started winning again."

Left unsaid was the fact that, by then, it was too late for him.

We had moved on past the trophy case to Mattingly's desk around the corner. Behind it was a bookcase atop which rested eight Gold Gloves, all in a row.

"I like Gold Gloves," Mattingly said. "They're a recognition from your peers and I always took the most pride in my defense."

I expected to see dozens of pictures of Mattingly and his teammates displayed throughout the room, but there was only one. Alongside the Gold Gloves, conspicuous by itself, was a small 8-by-10 black-and-white framed photo of Yogi Berra. Somehow, I wasn't surprised.

It was already close to 2 P.M. and Taylor was anxious to get some lunch. The brief house tour completed, we piled into the Suburban and headed out to the highway that led to the north side of Evansville where Mattingly had grown up. I had asked him if we could swing by the Little League field where he'd first caught the eye of Quentin Merkel, the man who, to this day, he maintained, taught him more about baseball than anyone else.

It is called Garvin Park, home of the North Little League, and it sits on top of a hill in the shadow of Bosse Field, a restored 87-year-old minor league park that seats about 15,000. As we approached Garvin Park, Taylor pointed out a sign that had been painted on the fence in front of it: "Evansville Youth Baseball—Home of Don Mattingly."

"I'm glad my kids never had to play here," Mattingly said with a trace of disdain, "so they could just be themselves and not have to hear all that crap about their dad. Other than that sign, though, nothing much has changed about the place. I'd ride my bike here, crying 'cause my mom wouldn't let me go to practice until I got my chores and my homework done."

Bosse Field was of much more interest to him. Constructed in 1915 in order to house a minor league team for Evansville in the Class B Central League, it survived numerous defections through the years. For the longest time, it was the home of the Evansville Evas of the historic Three-I League, for which such baseball greats as Warren Spahn, Hank Greenberg and Chuck Klein served part of their minor league apprenticeship. Tommy Bridges, the Detroit Tigers ace curveballer in the '30s and '40s, led the Three-I League in strikeouts for Evansville in 1927. These were the legends Mattingly had heard about as a kid and were part of the reason he joined forces with a group of local baseball enthusiasts in raising money to restore the park and keep the school board from tearing it down after the Evansville

Triplets of the Triple A American Association were sold and moved to Nashville in 1984.

"It's a neat old stadium," Mattingly said as he stopped the car alongside the outfield wall. "I worked there in the summers, cleaning up and stuff. I got 50 cents a ball and we'd go out onto the field in the day and take big league gloves and play. I'll bet you didn't know they filmed a lot of *A League of Their Own* here. My brothers and I grew up going to games in this stadium. We saw a lot of guys go from the Triplets to the big leagues—Jerry Manuel, the White Sox manager; Lance Parrish, Kirk Gibson, Bob Molinaro, Cotton Nash, the great Kentucky basketball player. Ole Les Moss managed here. Jimmy Leyland, too . . . it would've been a shame if they'd torn it down. We've got an independent league team here now."

"It's a long way from Yankee Stadium," I said.

"Yeah, it'll always be a small-town stadium, but we had our own legends."

"What did you think when you started to meet all the Yankee legends—DiMaggio, Mantle, Yogi, etc.?" I asked.

"Oh, man," Mattingly said, "it was awesome. It's *still* awesome just thinking that I'm a part of all that now."

"Aside from Gehrig's doubles record and Combs's hits record, which you broke, you had to be awed at all the Yankee records—Ruth's and Maris's homers, DiMaggio's 56-game hitting streak . . ."

"Let me tell you about the first time I met Joe D.," Mattingly interrupted. "It was an Old-Timer's Day in 1984. I was on a 20-game hitting streak and he was across the room on the other side of the clubhouse surrounded by a bunch of reporters. I really wanted to talk to him about hitting, but I didn't want to bother him. A while later, I'm walking down the tunnel to the field and I feel this hand on my shoulder. It was Joe D. and he's got this smile on his face and he says to me: 'Why do you want to fuck with me, kid?' We both laughed, but then I went out and took an 0-for-4. The funny thing about it is, I saw him later that year, in Anaheim, when I had another 20-game streak going and I went

0-for-4 *that* day, too! What can I say? Joe was a *jinx* for me. I wonder if he knew that?"

Mattingly laughed as he accelerated the car and drove around the back of Bosse Field onto a road that led out of the park area. He continued on through town, over some railroad tracks and past what appeared to be a row of old factory buildings. Eventually, we crossed into a more suburban area and when we came to Van Husen Street, he made a right turn, slowing the car down.

"Over there on the right," he said, pointing to a small, white Cape Cod house, "that's where my mom and dad live."

His father, a retired postman, had raised five children in this house and, according to Mattingly, never let on to them they were just getting by. Don and his brothers played football, basketball and baseball and were never asked to get jobs to augment the family income. After Mattingly made it big, he tried to talk his father into getting a house in Florida.

"But he wouldn't move," Mattingly said. "You know how it is with folks who have lived in the same house all their life. They're happy there and they don't want anything more."

He drove on, back through town and into an industrial park area where, tucked away on the side of a plain brick building, was a tiny store front pizza joint with a sign in the window that said: "The Slice."

"Best pizza anywhere around here," Mattingly said. "The closest you'll find to New York."

There were only two other people in the place, plus a kid who looked to be not much older than Taylor, feverishly preparing a pizza in the oven area behind the counter. We waited nearly five minutes at the counter before he was able to take our order, and Mattingly grabbed a couple of Cokes out of the wall refrigerator.

"It'll be worth the wait," he assured me.

"We were talking about those last, frustrating seasons, when everything really fell apart," I said.

"I try not to think about those," Mattingly said. "It was a tough time for the team and for me."

The back finally blew out on him in 1990, the year after he'd joined Ruth, Gehrig, Combs, DiMaggio and Bill Dickey as the only Yankees to attain six straight .300 seasons. He doesn't remember exactly how or when it went. He just knows it became a terrible chore just to get himself loose, and there was nothing he did that could dull the steady ache he felt. The torque, the power, the ability to crush the ball in any direction in the ballpark had all been sapped from him. He missed 54 games in '90, and struggled through his worst season, hitting a piddling .256 with only five homers and 42 RBI. The following year was better— .291, 17 HR, 86 RBI—but still a far cry from the kind of numbers he was used to putting up when he was sound. In '94, the Yankees were in first place, at 70-43, the second-best record in baseball, when the players went on strike, August 12, and the season was subsequently cancelled. It may well have been Mattingly's best shot for a ring. We'll never know.

At last in '95, he finally got his October—and made the most of it.

The season itself was fraught with adversity and pitching woes, not unlike any of Mattingly's previous Yankee seasons. Jimmy Key, the team's best pitcher in '93 and '94, blew out his shoulder and underwent rotator cuff surgery. Melido Perez and Scott Kamieniecki, who'd combined for 17 wins in the strike-shortened '94 season, were disabled for considerable periods of time and contributed little. Even Black Jack McDowell, the No. 1 starter acquired from the White Sox in the off-season, got off slowly and didn't really round into form until August. The offense, punctuated by Mattingly's paltry seven homers and 49 RBI, wasn't much better. Yet, somehow, the Yankees managed to win enough games (79-65 in the strike-shortened season) to qualify for the American League wild card and a berth in the divisional series against the Seattle Mariners, winners of the AL West.

When they won the first two games in New York, the latter in a riveting 15 innings, decided at one o'clock in the morning on Jim Leyritz's homer in the pouring rain, it was as if all the lean years of Mattingly's tenure had been—or were certainly about to be—washed away in this glorious downpour. All they needed was one out of three in Seattle.

Game 3, in which McDowell (who hadn't pitched in over two weeks because of a back injury) matched up with Seattle's intimidating 6-foot-10 left-handed ace, Randy Johnson, was close through five innings. Then in the sixth, McDowell tired and was relieved after loading the bases. Yankee manager Buck Showalter brought in lefty Steve Howe (who'd had a 7.70 ERA in September) to face lefty-swinging Tino Martinez. Martinez promptly singled home a run and Seattle went on to score three more runs in the inning to go ahead 6–1 en route to a 7–4 win.

After that loss, there was considerable speculation as to whether Showalter would go for the kill in Game 4 by starting his best pitcher, Cone. Instead, however, he chose Kamieniecki, a decision he would come to rue. The Yankees had staked Kamieniecki to a 5–0 lead by the third, only to have him cough most of it up on a three-run homer by Edgar Martinez in Seattle's half of the third. The struggling Kamieniecki needed 101 pitches to get through five innings, by which time the Mariners had tied the score at 5–5. As would be vividly illustrated the next day, Showalter had lost faith in his bullpen, perhaps with good reason. After going ahead 6–5 with a run off Sterling Hitchcock in the sixth, the Mariners broke the game open with five in the eighth.

To that point, Mattingly had carried the Yankee offense in Game 4 with four hits, including two doubles and two RBI. But in the pivotal eighth, a defensive gaffe on his part helped set the stage for a game-breaking grand slam homer by Edgar Martinez. With a runner on first, the Mariners diminutive second baseman Joey Cora laid down a bunt to the first base side which Mattingly fielded. Instead of flipping the ball to Yankee pitcher John Wetteland covering the bag, however, Mattingly attempted to tag Cora, who scampered around him and beat him to the bag. Wetteland next hit Ken Griffey Jr. with a pitch before surrendering Martinez's slam.

It also had been a wild throw by Mattingly that allowed the Mariners to tie the game in the fifth, and afterward he was disconsolate. "When I was a kid, I dreamed of being a hero in a game like this," he said. "I just made bad decisions on throwing the ball. I'm disappointed with both decisions I made."

In Game 5, the last baseball game of Don Mattingly's career, David Cone took the ball for the Yankees—and kept it for 147 pitches as the resolute Showalter refused to trust his bullpen with the precarious 4–2 lead in the eighth. Again, it had been Mattingly who spurred the Yankee offense with a two-run, opposite-field double that broke a 2–2 tie in the sixth.

But in the eighth, Cone had clearly begun to labor. He was tagged for a solo homer by Griffey—Junior's fifth of the series—to close the score to 4–3 and then, after the Mariners loaded the bases, he walked pinch-hitter Doug Strange to force home the tying run. As Showalter began his trudge out of the dugout, signaling for Mariano Rivera, the then-rookie, Cone literally collapsed on the mound from exhaustion. It was perhaps symbolic of what the entire Yankee team, Mattingly especially, was experiencing.

The game went into extra innings and Piniella, who was now managing the Mariners, mirrored Showalter insofar as a lack of faith in his regular bullpen operatives. With no outs and Yankees at first and second in the ninth, he called on Johnson, paying no mind to the 116 pitches the Big Unit had thrown only 48 hours earlier. Johnson would pitch out of that jam by striking out Wade Boggs and getting Bernie Williams and Paul O'Neill on harmless pop-outs, and he struck out the side in the 10th. But in the 11th, a walk to Mike Stanley, a sacrifice bunt and an RBI single by Randy Velarde off Johnson gave the Yankees the lead again and suddenly they were three outs away from redemption and advancement to the ALCS.

They never got even one.

Once again it was the pesky Cora, who undid them by beating out another bunt to lead off the inning. Griffey followed with a single, but with Jack McDowell, his first-game starter who had relieved Rivera, obviously tiring, Showalter made no move to bring in his closer, Wetteland, who was standing in the bullpen, his arms at his sides, and a look of disbelief on his face. The final act was McDowell hanging a split-fingered fastball to Edgar Martinez and the Yankee nemesis ripping it into the left field corner as Cora and Griffey raced home for the 6–5 Seattle victory.

For Mattingly, the line on his one and only postseason series was a .417 batting average, four doubles, a homer and six RBI. At least he had the satisfaction of knowing he'd made the most of it. At least he knew he could play with the best of them in October, too.

"The last month of that season, I seemed to find my swing again," Mattingly said between bites of his pizza. "I was constantly getting out in front of the ball and then, in BP I noticed [Darryl] Strawberry and [Ruben] Sierra, guys we'd gotten during the season, lifting their front foot before they swung. So I started trying it and 'bam!' I hit the ball right on the nose. It took a few more BP sessions before I was comfortable enough to try it in the game. But then one day, I said to myself: 'I'm kicking today.' I tried it off [Charles] Nagy, who was an off-speed pitcher I figured would give me trouble, and got two knocks. I started really working on it from that point on and found I was hitting a lot easier than I had been before, and I was driving the ball again.

"The playoffs were a whole different thing as far as your concentration level and guys like Mo [Mariano Rivera], Bernie and [Andy] Pettitte got their feet wet there. I feel pretty good about what we'd built. We left Joe a pretty good foundation when he came in there in '96 and started that run."

We finished our pizza and got into the Suburban and headed back across town to Mattingly's house. As he drove, I said to him: "It must have been pretty hard watching that '96 World Series on TV."

"It was," he said, "but it was even harder on Kim. She wouldn't watch that last game. I watched, because these were all my friends, and I wanted to see them win. But once the game was over, and they'd beaten the Braves, I turned the TV off. I couldn't watch the celebration. I was happy for those guys, but the timing . . . you know . . . really sucked."

"Did you have a lot of second thoughts about quitting when you did—especially after that great last series against the Mariners?"

"Not really. I could have been part of that ride, but I'd have been selling out. Even though I really couldn't do the things I did early in my career, I still felt in my heart I could compete in the same way. Playing hard every day, giving everything you got. If I'd have kept playing, it wouldn't have been that, because I knew I wanted to be home. I was at a point where I wanted to see my kids grow up and as a player, you start cheating yourself, you start cheating the people, and I just wasn't gonna do that."

He left on the table a .307 batting average, 222 homers, 1,099 RBI, 2,153 hits and 442 doubles for 1,785 games over 14 seasons. Maybe if it had all been spread out a little more, instead of so much bunched into 1984–87, he'd have looked better in the eyes of the Hall of Fame voters. Kirby Puckett, who played 12 years in the same era, had very similar numbers—.318, 207 homers, 1,085 RBI, 2,304 hits, 414 doubles in 1,783 games—was elected to the Hall in his first year of eligibility on the ballot, in 2001, with 443 votes. Mattingly finished a distant ninth that year with 149 votes. But Puckett never had a bad season and also had the benefit of two World Series to Mattingly's none—during which his star shone brightest, as he led the Minnesota Twins to world championships in 1987 and '91. His composite World Series batting average was .308 with two homers and seven RBI for 14 games.

"I knew when I retired it was gonna be rough for me," Mattingly said. "Another five years, if I'd have gotten to 3,000 hits, I might have looked a lot different. But you can't get into that kind of thinking. In or out, the Hall of Fame doesn't change how I think about things, or how people feel about you as a player. I followed my heart, and your family is more important than anything. I feel like a Hall of Famer, to be honest. I'm not saying I should be in. I just feel that when I was playing I could play with anyone. I never felt overmatched. I loved playing and the hardest part was to walk away when I did. But another contract and I wouldn't have known my oldest son. I couldn't live with that."

We arrived back at the house again and Mattingly guided the Suburban through the gate and up the long driveway. The rain had tapered off to more of a cold mist. As we got out of the car, Jordan and Mattingly's middle son, Preston, could be seen playing with the greyhounds in the lighted den. My day trip to the Mattingly ranch and family compound in the middle of America's heartland had come to an end. I sensed it had been therapeutic for him, reliving those bittersweet final days of the '95 season and reaffirming in his own mind his decision to leave when he did.

"I remember one time, during just a regular old season game in the '90s, I looked up in the stands and there was this sign that said: 'Don Mattingly—The Chosen One' and I thought to myself: 'What does that mean, anyway? What am I chosen for?'" Mattingly related as we stood there in the driveway, ignoring the mist. "Now that it's done, maybe it means I was chosen to be the guy right in the middle of it all who doesn't get his shot at it."

He laughed as he said it, and I could see he'd come to terms with being robbed of so much—the World Series championships that came in bunches in the years immediately following his retirement; the Hall of Fame—because his body had betrayed his will. Another reason he'd stayed away, especially in '96, was because he wanted to allow his first base successor, Tino Martinez, to make as seamless a transition as possible. In the early going of '96, however, Martinez slumped, and the Yankee fans, remembering Mattingly's gallant last stand the previous October, booed Martinez and chanted "Don-nie Base-ball!" after each Tino strikeout. At one point, Mattingly phoned Martinez and offered him words of encouragement—which Tino later acknowledged helped him relax and regain his batting stroke.

"You can look at it a lot of ways," he said. "I got to play for the greatest organization in professional sports; just a great experience that's allowed me to do all kinds of things. But sometimes in life you just don't get what you want. You can work hard for it; you can try your hardest, do everything you think you need to do to get there, and sometimes you still don't get there. Sometimes you're not supposed to get there.

"Looking back it at now, it's not a struggle, not even '96 now. 'Cause I remember when I was 22 I always said I wanted to be able to look in that mirror when it's all over and not have to think, 'I wish I'd done this. I wish I'd worked harder. And even my decision not to play anymore—it wasn't because I didn't think I could play anymore, or that I didn't love the game anymore. The reason was because I wanted to be with my kids. It was pretty simple. It was the way I felt then and it's the way I still feel. I can look back now with no regrets about not playing, and that's a good feeling. I'm at peace with all of it."

We shook hands and Mattingly wished me a safe trip back to New York, in all the rain that was moving east. As I made my way down the driveway, through the rearview mirror I watched him walk into the house, his arm on Taylor's shoulder. For 13 New York summers, he had lived out his dream, and for at least four of them he'd been the best there was in the game. His name, Donnie Baseball, was as synonymous with the Yankees as the Babe, the Iron Horse, the Yankee Clipper and The Mick. Even if he didn't share a World Series ring or a plaque in Cooperstown with them, his place in Yankee history was secure, and I figured that mattered to him. Just not as much as *this* place did now.

TWILIGHT OF THE WARRIOR

PAUL O'NEILL

Oh the days dwindle down to a precious few . . .
September, November
And these few precious days, I'll spend with you . . .

T he 2001 baseball season was in its precious days, although in the wake of the September 11 terror attack in New York, precious days had taken on a whole different meaning. From purely a baseball standpoint, it was a typical September for Joe Torre's Yankees. They had long since put the Boston Red Sox to bed for the winter and wrapped up their fourth straight American League East division title. Now they were in the process of healing their nagging injuries, which, in the context of the city's and the nation's healing process, seemed quite insignificant.

Nevertheless, the baseball season was to go on, as the country was to go on. As Torre said: "We can only do what we do, and that's to play baseball, and do our best to help heal the nation's grief—if nothing else by providing entertainment." So began the annual pilgrimage into October for Torre's team. They had been there every year he'd been their manager, since 1996, only once, in 1997, not going the distance to the World Series. Unlike other years, however, this time they would carry the banner of a terrorist-ravaged but unbowed New York City and its heroic firefighters, police and rescue workers, symbols of the nation's pride. As such, they felt the strange allegiance of the entire country.

On this day, Paul O'Neill was sitting in front of his locker at the far end of the Yankee clubhouse, glumly looking down at the cast encompassing his left foot. It was the third straight September O'Neill had been incapacitated by a persistent injury threatening to curtail his activity in the postseason. (The year before, he'd injured his ribs and lower back running into the outfield wall, chasing a foul ball in a meaningless game on the final weekend of the season, and he didn't seem to fully recover until the World Series when he went 9-for-19 with two doubles, two triples and a pair of RBI in playing a key role in the Yankees' five-game triumph over the Mets.)

This time it was a stress fracture of the fourth metatarsal bone, which the doctors had said would keep him sidelined right up until the end of the month.

O'Neill had long since issued a moratorium on any discussion of this being his last season, even though he'd made it fairly clear he'd come to terms in his own mind about that. Early on, in spring training, he'd talked wistfully about wanting to spend more time at home in Cincinnati watching his kids grow up, while stopping just short of using the word "retirement."

He hated being interviewed, especially if it meant having to talk about himself. At the same time, though, he hated being hurt even more. He was 38 years old, his batting average hovering at an unseemly (for him) .267, with no time left to get it to a respectable level. Despite the fact he'd hit 21 homers and become the oldest player in baseball history to hit 20 homers and steal 20 bases in a season, it was a poor way to be going out. So if talking about his teammates and all they'd accomplished together in his nine years as a Yankee would take his mind off his present plight, well, he'd grudgingly give up a little of his idle time. Consider it therapy, I told him, to which he responded with a stony frown.

"All I know is, I can't run right now," O'Neill grumbled. "I can't do anything in this damn cast. At least they're saying I'll be ready for the playoffs. So, yeah, I guess I've got some time."

He became a Yankee November 3, 1992, coming over from his hometown team, the Cincinnati Reds, in a trade for fellow outfielder Roberto Kelly, who, to that point, had been regarded as the Yankees' best all-around player. That Kelly, a 28-year-old Panamanian who possessed the rare dual attributes of power and speed, had not attained superstar status in four seasons as the Yankees' regular center fielder was a bit of a puzzlement to the Yankee brass. At the time, Gene Michael was serving as Yankee general manager and chief executive while George Steinbrenner was again on suspension (this time for consorting with—and paying $40,000 to—an admitted gambler named Howard Spira in an effort to uncover discrediting information on Dave Winfield and the Yankee right fielder's charitable foundation). Michael was not nearly so enamored of Kelly as a center fielder as was the rest of the Yankee hierarchy. He also felt Kelly wasn't selective enough at the plate and surmised this would probably always be the case with him.

A year earlier, Michael had gotten a phone call from his old pal Lou Piniella, who was managing the Reds. Although O'Neill had been one of Piniella's most productive hitters, hitting 16 homers in the Reds' 1990 world championship season and improving on that to 28 homers and 91 RBI the following year, the relationship between these two strong-willed perfectionists had become extremely contentious. Piniella had attempted to get the 6-4, 215-pound O'Neill to pull the ball more in an effort to make him into a 40-plus-homer man. Piniella would disparagingly call him "Big O'Neill" in chiding him to better take advantage of his size and strength. O'Neill had tried, but the change in his hitting style increasingly frustrated him, and his strikeouts rose accordingly, from 65 and 64 in '88 and '89 to 103 and 107 in '90 and '91. (After leaving the Reds for the Yankees, he would surpass 100 strikeouts only one more time the rest of his career.)

"The year before we made the deal for O'Neill, Lou called me and proposed doing O'Neill for Kelly," said Michael. "At the time, I didn't think we should be so quick to give up on Kelly, but then, a year later, [Reds GM] Jim Bowden called me and proposed it again. By then, Lou had left Cincinnati to go to Seattle, and I had decided Kelly just wasn't the center fielder we hoped he'd be. Plus, Bernie Williams was coming along and was ready to step in there. We also were too right-handed in our lineup, with only [Don] Mattingly an everyday left-handed batter. So with all that in mind, along with the fact that I felt O'Neill's style of hitting would benefit by Yankee Stadium, I made the deal—against the wishes of most of our people who didn't want to trade Kelly. Because of that, I told Bowden I had to get back another player besides O'Neill. Originally we were supposed to get Eric Owens, a utility guy who went on to have a decent career and who would have been a good player for us. Instead, we ended up getting another guy (outfielder–first baseman Joe DeBerry), who never made it, and I blame myself for Owens somehow getting dropped from the deal. I should have never let that happen, although I'm pretty satisfied with the way it worked out."

In O'Neill's nine seasons with the Yankees, he hit .300 six times (including a strike-shortened .359 "batting title" in 1994), and drove in 100 or more runs from 1997 to 2000, despite never hitting more than 24 homers. In addition, he proved to be a superb right fielder. Kelly, on the other hand, became a baseball journeyman after his trade from the Yankees. The Reds traded him to the Atlanta Braves in 1994, and he would go on to play for five other teams, mostly as a fourth outfielder, before retiring after the 2001 season.

Just the same, the trade was greeted with more skepticism than anything else in New York. The majority of Yankee fans, especially all the talk radio yahoos, did not share Michael's assessment of Kelly's diminished center-fielding skills, and O'Neill, because of his well-publicized tiffs with Piniella, was perceived as a temperamental platoon player who couldn't hit left-handed pitching. There was also a question as to whether this intense Ohio-bred player who'd enjoyed the small-town shelter of Cincinnati for six years could handle the media scrutiny and related pressure that came with playing in New York.

"From my standpoint, I was excited about being traded over here," O'Neill was saying now. "When I got here, the pinstripes still had all the history and nostalgia for me, and even though they'd been down for a few years, Donnie was here. All you ever heard about the Yankees was Don Mattingly, and so, when I got traded here, I said to myself: 'Wow. I'm leaving home, I don't know what to expect in New York, but I'm going to get a chance to play with Don Mattingly.'"

With Jimmy Key, the unflappable control master, emerging as the new Yankee ace, winning 18 games, Boggs rebounding from his worst (.259) season to hit .302 and O'Neill raising his average from .246 the year before to .311, the Showalter-led Yankees made a dramatic improvement in 1993, finishing second, 88-74, seven games behind the eventual world champion Toronto Blue Jays in the AL East. The next year they were in first place by six and a half games, at 70-43, when the players went on strike August 12 and the season was eventually canceled.

"We were on the way in '94 with the best record in the American League," O'Neill said, "and that was sad, especially for Donnie because that might have been his best chance to get to the World Series. We never did get there for him, but I got more out of being his teammate than I did with just about everything else in my time as a Yankee. His work ethic, the way he approached every game, his all-consuming will to win. Believe me, even though he wasn't *physically* a part of all those championships we won, he was a major part of them because of what we all got from him.

"That was the first thing everyone said when we won the wild card in '95; that Donnie was finally going to get his October. It's not like he just scraped through it. He had a great playoff, and it was awesome to see and awesome to be a part of. Then you think about how we lost. We go out to Seattle two games up and lose all three there after we had a lead in all of them. It just goes to show the importance of the bullpen. I guess the other thing I took away from that series with Seattle was the way Mariano [Rivera] pitched. He'd come up to us as a starter that year, and then wound up in the bullpen, and you could see he was giving guys a lot of trouble. It didn't take him 3, 4 years to figure out how he was going to be successful. He did it in a matter of months."

What will also be most remembered about that series was Showalter's loss of confidence in Yankee closer John Wetteland, who gave up an eighth-inning, tie-breaking grand slam homer to the Mariners' lethal designated hitter Edgar Martinez to lose Game 4. The next day Showalter allowed David Cone to throw 147 pitches before ultimately relieving rookie Mariano Rivera and then, not with Wetteland but rather with another starting pitcher, Jack McDowell, after the Mariners tied the score in the eighth inning. And he stayed with McDowell even after the Yankees took a lead in the 11th.

"I think Buck had given up on Wetteland the night before," O'Neill said, pausing in thought. ". . . We lost that final game on the last play [a two-run double by Martinez off McDowell] . . . and I remember my wife was pregnant and I still remember the outfit she had on. And I'll always remember how long that flight home from Seattle was. I remember going to breakfast the next morning and it was as if we'd just walked off that field. It was so final. So over. There was not another series. To lose in the playoffs, after you've played so long that year just to get there . . . and you're so close to the final thing and then it's over . . . that quick."

O'Neill hit .333 with three homers and six RBI in the losing cause against Seattle which, if nothing else, had to be of some personal gratification coming as it did against Piniella, who was now managing the Mariners. Mattingly's Yankee swan song was a .417 average and six

RBI for the series and Rivera, in his preview of the greatness to come from him, pitched five and a third scoreless innings of relief over three of the five games, striking out eight and walking just one. After losing the 1995 Division Series, Mattingly retired and Showalter left as manager, following a contract dispute with Steinbrenner. Again, the field of candidates was rather limited in terms of managers with major league experience who'd had prior success and who had marquee value in New York. The latter was of special importance to Steinbrenner, whose suspension had been lifted in March of '93 and who was now running the team in full force again. The only available candidate who came close to meeting any of those criteria was the Brooklyn-born Torre, who had played for and managed the crosstown Mets and, 13 years earlier, had won a division title as manager of the Atlanta Braves.

Steinbrenner's senior front office advisor, Arthur Richman, strongly recommended Torre to him, and Michael, likewise, felt Torre, because of his experience and New York background, was the only viable candidate. (Richman had previously worked in the Mets' front office for nearly 25 years and knew Torre as a player and manager for the Yankees' crosstown rivals in the late '70s.) Initially, Torre was approached by the Yankee brain trust about the general manager's job from which Michael had stepped down after Steinbrenner's return. Torre declined to interview for the GM job, but enthusiastically accepted the invitation to become manager when called again a few days later. He had just come off five and a half seasons as manager of the St. Louis Cardinals, during which he finished an undistinguished third three times and second once. So his hiring was greeted with less-than-ardent reviews from the New York media. Indeed, on the eve of the press conference to introduce him as the new Yankee manager, Torre was welcomed home to New York by a headline in the *New York Daily News* that blared: "Clueless Joe."

"What was it about Torre that brought the whole thing together?" I asked O'Neill.

"Any time you bring in a new manager there's always gonna be a little grace period, obviously," O'Neill said. "But looking back, he was the most perfect manager they could have hired. You had the ups and downs of that '96 season, plus the media, plus New York City, and then you had Joe Torre, who had the ability to bring it all down, into perspective, and take the field and play a baseball game. He was a guy who was unfazed by all of that and was the perfect fit for us. He was what we needed in a manager and a leader."

When the Yankees assembled for spring training in Tampa (where they'd moved after 34 years in Fort Lauderdale) in 1996, there was a lot more different about the club than just Torre. Tino Martinez had been acquired in a big December 7 trade with Seattle to replace Mattingly at first base. Setup reliever Jeff Nelson, who would go on to play a major role over the next five seasons for the Yankees, also came over in that trade in which promising left-handed starter Sterling Hitchcock and third base prospect Russ Davis went to the Mariners, who were in the midst of a payroll-cutting mode. In addition, catcher Mike Stanley, who had given the Yankees four more than serviceable seasons after being picked up by Michael off the Texas Rangers' scrap heap in January of 1992, was let go as a free agent and replaced by Joe Girardi, a trade acquisition from the Colorado Rockies.

Although former Houston Astros general manager Bob Watson had been hired to replace Michael, the Yankee front office was pretty much being run by committee with Michael's input still carrying the most weight, and Steinbrenner, of course, always having the final vote. Watson was most instrumental in the Girardi deal and the signing of free agent second baseman Mariano Duncan, who went on to have a career season in '96, hitting .340 in 109 games. Michael, because of his relationship with Piniella, had been the point man on the Martinez deal, while most people around the Yankees agreed it had been Steinbrenner who made the decision to let McDowell go as a free agent and replace him in the starting rotation with left-hander Kenny Rogers (whose reputation for having a fragile psyche made him suspect in the eyes of the Yankees' front office baseball operatives, especially at four years,

$20 million). Steinbrenner also took it upon himself to acquire outfielder Tim Raines (who contributed 9 homers and 33 RBI in 59 games in '96 as well as bringing an intangible leadership presence in the clubhouse) in a trade with the Chicago White Sox, and to sign ex-Met and Tampa native Dwight Gooden, despite the 31-year-old right-hander's drug and injury-troubled past.

But perhaps the most significant personnel change of all for the '96 Yankees officially took place March 24 in spring training when veteran shortstop Tony Fernandez broke his elbow diving for a ground ball and was lost for the season. Despite Torre's proclamation in December of '95 that Derek Jeter would be the Yankees' starting shortstop in '96, Steinbrenner's senior aides knew how impatient The Boss was with rookies. Accordingly, behind the scenes, it was decided there at least should be an unofficial competition between Jeter and Fernandez for the starting job, and in staff meetings that spring, a couple of Steinbrenner's senior aides, hedging their bets, expressed reservations to The Boss about the 6-3, 195-pound Jeter's footwork at shortstop.

It all became moot, of course, when Fernandez went down. The job was Jeter's and the quietly confident 21-year-old, barely three years out of Kalamazoo (Michigan) Central High School, never looked back—especially after a spectacular, over-the-head catch of a blooper hit by Indian shortstop Omar Vizquel in the seventh inning on Opening Day in Cleveland. The Yankees were leading by only 2–0 at the time and, with Cleveland's pesky lead-off hitter Kenny Lofton on deck, Torre noted afterward: "The game might've been on the line right there if Derek doesn't make that catch." Jeter also homered in his first at bat that day and went on to hit .314 for the season—the first Yankee shortstop since Gil McDougald in 1956 to hit over .300—and was named American League Rookie of the Year.

"I remember saying—actually a lot of us saying—Derek was the best all around player we ever played with," O'Neill said. "I played with a lot of great players. Mattingly played well, especially in big games and big situations. But from day one—that day in Cleveland—you just knew

Derek was going to become this great player. The confidence he had. There's just so many ways he helps you win a game. He saw us lose in '95, when they brought him up in September and let him stay with the club in the postseason, but when he came back the next spring, even though he had some throwing problems, it was like he'd been with us for 10 years. His personality was suited for handling all the media attention in New York."

Following the lead of their neophyte shortstop, the Yankees overtook the Baltimore Orioles for first place with a sweep of a two-game series at the end of April and remained on top the rest of the season to win their first division title since 1981. But in deftly guiding the Yankees to the American League East title, Torre was forced to do some major maneuvering with his starting pitching rotation as his two titular aces, Cone and Key, were felled by injuries, and Rogers struggled mightily, reinforcing his critics' warnings about his inability to handle the pressure-cooker environment of New York.

On May 10, Cone underwent surgery to remove an aneurysm from his right shoulder and did not return to the rotation until September 2 in Oakland where he turned in a dramatic and heartening performance, holding the Athletics hitless on 85 pitches for seven innings before Rivera came on and yielded the only hit in the Yankees' 5–0 win. Key, who had missed most of the '95 season with rotator cuff surgery after winning 35 games the previous two seasons, went on the disabled list again on May 15 with a stiff shoulder, but came back to beat Oakland 5–1 at the end of the month to enable the Yankees to break a first-place tie with Baltimore. While nursing his aching shoulder, he managed to win 12 games and two more in the postseason, including the 3-2 Game 6 World Series clincher over the Atlanta Braves, which wound up being his last game as a Yankee.

Meanwhile, filling the starting pitching void in '96 most unexpectedly was Steinbrenner's personal reclamation project, Gooden, the erstwhile Mets superstar right-hander who had been suspended from baseball the final six weeks of '94 and all of '95 for repeated violations of baseball's drug policy. Gooden earned the No. 5 starter's job out of spring training and on May 14 put his own dramatic imprint on the Yankees' championship '96 season by hurling a 2–0 no-hitter against Piniella's Mariners. He would go on to win six straight decisions from early June until mid-July until experiencing a dead arm in August, which curtailed his effectiveness the rest of the season. He finished up at 11-7, but was left off the postseason roster when Cone came back.

Flush with his success in the Gooden reincarnation, Steinbrenner sought to follow up with another reclamation project of a fallen Mets superstar. On July 4, it was announced the Yankees were purchasing the contract of Darryl Strawberry (who had been with them at the tail end of '95 before being released) from the St. Paul Saints of the independent Northern League. Strawberry, too, had sabotaged his once promising career with drug and alcohol abuse, and had also served time in prison for income tax evasion. Nevertheless, Steinbrenner deemed him a prodigal worth saving and the 34-year-old Strawberry rewarded The Boss's faith by slugging 11 homers in 63 games the rest of '96, and adding four more in the postseason. (The sad footnote to Strawberry's career was his relapse into drugs in the spring of 2000 and his subsequent arrest and reincarceration in a Florida jail. His final career stats: .259 average, 335 homers, 1000 RBI, 2 releases and 3 suspensions over 17 seasons.)

In the '96 Division Series, the Yankees lost the first game to the Texas Rangers, then swept the next three. They followed a similar script in both the American League Championship Series against the Orioles and the World Series against the Braves, winning all their games on the road. The World Series, especially, was vindication for Torre and Wetteland. Following the first of their two losses to the Braves at Yankee Stadium to start the World Series (an embarrassing 12–1 blowout), Steinbrenner, perhaps reminded of the "Clueless Joe" headline that had trumpeted his manager's hiring 11 months earlier, trudged into Torre's office and began venting about the plight of his team. After giving his boss a few minutes to air his frustrations, Torre said calmly: "Look, George, I understand how you feel. We didn't play very well tonight, and I'll tell you what, we may not win tomorrow night either. But I guarantee you we're going down to Atlanta and win all three games there. Atlanta's my town. And then we'll come back here and finish them off."

Steinbrenner was dumbfounded at Torre's uncharacteristic bravado. But considering all Torre had been through that season—his brother Rocco, a New York City police officer, had died of a heart attack in June and his other brother, Frank, was awaiting a heart donation at Columbia Presbyterian Hospital—it was understandable why he maybe didn't view this as much life-and-death as Steinbrenner. Besides, his bold prediction turned out to be right on the mark.

After losing Game 2 the Yankees went to Atlanta and won Game 3, 5–2, as Cone out-dueled the Braves' Cy Young award–winning lefty Tom Glavine. The riveting Game 4, in which the Series turned dramatically in the Yankees' favor, was one for the ages. Seizing opportunity against a wobbly and ineffective Kenny Rogers (who was kayoed in the third inning), the Braves jumped out to a 6–0 lead after five innings and were poised to go up 3–1 in games. But in the sixth, the Yankees began to solve Braves starter Denny Neagle and cut the deficit to 6–3 on three singles, a walk and an error.

Two innings later, they tied the score in electrifying fashion off Braves closer Mark Wohlers, whom Atlanta manager Bobby Cox had summoned one inning earlier than had been his custom during the regular season, in an effort to go for the kill. Wohlers was immediately greeted by singles by Charlie Hayes and Strawberry. Then, after Duncan grounded into a force-out of Strawberry at second, Wohlers inexplicably eschewed his patented 100-mile-per-hour fastball and threw a hanging slider to Jim Leyritz, who slammed it over the left field wall to even matters at 6–6. The game continued for two more suspense-tingling innings before being decided when Boggs, Torre's last pinch hitter on the bench, drew a bases-loaded walk in the 10th and the Braves committed an error to allow another run to score.

Game 5 was equally tense, the Yankees fulfilling Torre's prophecy with a 1–0 win in which Andy Pettitte got the best of John Smoltz. The game's lone run was scored in the fourth when Braves outfielders Marquis Grissom and Jermaine Dye couldn't get together on Hayes's lead-off fly ball to right-center. The ball glanced off Grissom's glove and Hayes wound up at second. He came around to score on a double by Cecil Fielder.

In truth, however, the turning point of the game was the last play when O'Neill made a saving catch of pinch hitter Luis Polonia's long drive to right-center field. In the wake of a lead-off double by the Braves' Chipper Jones (who went to third on a groundout), Torre replaced Pettitte with Wetteland and brought the infield in. Wetteland succeeded in getting Javy Lopez to hit a hard, one-hop grounder right to Hayes at third, forcing Jones to hold. Now Torre had Wetteland intentionally walk the left-handed hitting Ryan Klesko, prompting Cox to send up Polonia, another lefty, to bat for Dye.

The heavy and sultry air at Fulton County Stadium was thick with tension as Polonia engaged in a fierce battle with Wetteland, fouling off six straight pitches, before measuring a fastball and stroking it toward right-center. O'Neill had been hobbled by a sore left hamstring which the doctors had said would need five weeks of rest. But at this point, Torre and he agreed as long as he could swing the bat and make the routine plays in right field they would run the risk of him blowing it out completely. As Polonia's ball took flight, it was clear this was not going to be a routine play and Torre and the rest of the Yankee bench stiffened in silence while looking warily out at the wobbly O'Neill in right. The sense of disaster was not lost on O'Neill either, although he had no time to think about the consequences of not getting to the ball. Instead, he began his gimping pursuit, chasing the ball unevenly to his right as the 51,881 fans held their collective breath, anticipating a game-winning hit. He looked like an old man chasing a pulling-away bus, and the dread of just about everyone watching from the Yankee dugout was that he wasn't going to make it. Yet somehow, he did.

Two pitches earlier, Yankee outfield coach Jose Cardenal had moved O'Neill about eight feet further to his right, figuring that Polonia, a slap hitter, wasn't apt to pull the ball, especially off Wetteland. So as soon as Polonia finally hit the ball fair, O'Neill had gotten a head start and as it began its descent, he made a desperate lunge, extending his right arm as far as he could, to make the catch and end the game.

"My heart was pounding when I saw the ball keep going and going," O'Neill said. "All I could think was 'Oh my God, can I get to it?' Later, Tino came over to me and told me the guy from first base would have scored, too, if I hadn't got to it, and they'd have won the game. That made me feel kinda sick, thinking about that."

As for Wetteland, he picked up the saves in all three games in Atlanta and, in final retribution for the Showalter slight the year before, was on the mound for the final triumphant out (and a fourth straight save) in Game 6 at Yankee Stadium two nights later.

"I think we realized in '96 when we saw all those people at the parade in the Canyon of Heroes—I think all of us were just blown away by that—just how many people around the New York metropolitan area are this involved," O'Neill said. "It really hit home to us that, by winning, everybody gets his just due; gets to be a part of it. That's what that team was all about. It didn't matter who led the team in hitting or RBIs. You win the World Series and you know that everybody did enough. Everybody's name is on that ring. Don't get me wrong, I know everybody wants to win. But to have a great year like we did, and then to celebrate and drink champagne on that last day with the guys who you went through it all year with . . . there's nothin' else, and after '96 we came to expect that.

"After those first two losses at Yankee Stadium, being in the World Series for the first time, I think there was a little question in everybody's brain: 'We've gotten this far, but can we win this thing?' But after that first win in Atlanta, all of sudden the mindset changed. If there was one thing we'd been able to do all year was, when we got teams down, we finished them. The Braves had us down. They didn't finish it. You get into a big game, you're so used to winning big games, you expect to win them. You need a break or some kind of way to score runs, you expect it to happen. When players start thinking that way, they become tough to beat. Looking back, I don't recall Joe having any meetings after those first two games in New York. We didn't need any rah-rah speeches and run through the doorway. We instinctively knew how to win games and what it takes."

He gently rubbed his cast and gazed blankly around the room as his teammates finished dressing and began strolling out to the field for the pregame workout. "The only time I remember having any kind of speech like that was before Game 5 of the [2000] Division Series in Oakland," he continued. "We'd had a chance to finish it in New York. We had Rocket [Roger Clemens] on the mound and, on paper, all was great. Then, all of a sudden, we were on a flight back across the country to play a Game 5. So before the game, it went right back to 'we're here to do one thing, and that's to win' and, in that moment, it all made sense. We had to go all the way out there, but so what? It had been a terrible night before, and it had been a terrible flight. But it wasn't that awful, and you win the series and a week later you're back in the World Series. You have to be able to see that."

It was because of all they accomplished in '96, what they had learned about themselves, O'Neill could never accept their failure to repeat in '97, even three years and three straight world championships afterward. If nothing else, though, 1997, he believed, merely hardened their resolve.

After getting off to a sluggish start (14-13 in April), the Yankees trailed the first-place Baltimore Orioles throughout May, June, July and August, and were dealt a severe blow on August 17 when Cone, the club leader in victories at the time, went down with a shoulder injury. He would make only two more starts—at the tail end of September. And there were more injuries: Strawberry was sidelined nearly the whole season with a bum knee; designated hitter Cecil Fielder missed two months with a thumb injury; Bernie Williams was on the disabled list twice with hamstring problems; and Raines missed considerable time with a hamstring injury. Although they managed to cut the Orioles' lead from nine and a half games to two in September, the Yankees were forced to settle for second place and the wild card entry to the postseason playoffs. For his part, O'Neill led the club in batting (.324) and finished seventh in the American League in RBI (117) and doubles (42).

It was the backdoor way of qualifying for October baseball—and not by Yankee standards as defending world champions. Nonetheless, there was an undercurrent of sentiment that, had it not been for all the injuries, they would have successfully defended their division title. Thus, they went into the playoffs quietly confident of making their way back to the World Series.

Instead, they never got out of the first round, eliminated by the Cleveland Indians after leading two games to one in the best-of-five Division Series. In Game 4 they took a 2–1 lead into the eighth inning and were five outs away from advancing to the ALCS when Rivera gave up an opposite-field, game-tying homer to Sandy Alomar Jr. Until then, Yankee relievers hadn't given up a run in the series—and the Indians took their lead from that in winning the game off Rivera's successor, Ramiro Mendoza, in the ninth on a single, a sacrifice and a grounder by Vizquel off the reliever's glove that rolled into left field. In the deciding fifth game, the Indians won 4–3 as three relievers, Mike Jackson, Paul Assenmacher and Jose Mesa, pitched four-hit shutout ball over the final three innings.

The final Yankee gasp was O'Neill's, which, looking back, should probably not have surprised anyone. "O'Neill was a player so intensely competitive, it's hard to imagine him ever making the last out in a big game," said Don Zimmer, Torre's bench coach and trusted sidekick. Zimmer, who also grew up in Cincinnati, was especially fond of O'Neill and loved needling him about his intense demeanor. "O'Neill is one of the most professional people I've ever known in baseball," Zimmer added. "I just feel sorry for him because he never had the fun in baseball he should have had. It hurt me to watch him put himself through what he did. He's about the only guy I know who could never understand that the best of the best in this game fail two thirds of the time. He could never accept making an out."

Little by little, the Yankees chipped away at Cleveland starter Jaret Wright's 4–0 lead in the decisive Game 5, finally cutting it to 4–3 on Boggs's pinch hit RBI single in the sixth inning. After failing to cash in on a pair of two-out base hits off Indian closer Jose Mesa in the eighth, the Yankees were down to their final out in the ninth in the person of O'Neill, who lashed a rising liner to right-center. For a moment, it looked as if it might be a game-tying homer, only to hit the very top of the wall and bounce back into play. O'Neill, running full tilt without any thought of the ball possibly going out, slid into second just ahead of the throw, for a double.

Watching from a private box on the club level of Jacobs Field, Steinbrenner turned to his son-in-law, Steve Swindal, and said: "That O'Neill has the heart of a lion. He's a real warrior." It was a term The Boss would repeat to reporters in the clubhouse later—after Bernie Williams flied out to left to end the game and the Yankees' season.

"I hate Game 5," the visibly drained and dejected O'Neill said at his locker afterward. "It doesn't seem fair. They got so many breaks. Of course, that's what we got last year. We had our chances, but now everyone here is going to look back and think of something they could have done."

"You never could accept that '97 loss, could you?" I said to O'Neill now.

"That one and '95," he said. "Like I said, there was a mind-set with that team. We *knew* what it took to win."

The strange irony, I offered, is that Mattingly will always be remembered for what he did in a losing effort against Seattle in '95, and the one hit for which O'Neill will most be remembered was that last-gasp double which earned him his "warrior" nickname.

"If I'm just remembered for being a part of what that team accomplished over those five or so years," O'Neill said with a shrug, "then that's good enough for me."

And, though dispirited by '97, the best for that team was yet to come.

The 1998 Yankees can justifiably lay claim to the "Best Team Ever" title after amassing an American League record 114 wins in winning the East Division title by 22 games over the Red Sox. They led the majors in runs (965, which was an average of six per game) and hit 207 homers, second most in their history to the 240 by the Roger Maris/Mickey Mantle '61 club. In addition, Yankee pitchers led the league in ERA (3.82), fewest walks, lowest opponents' batting average, shutouts, complete games and fewest hits allowed. A midseason exclamation point to all this was David Wells pitching a 4–0 perfect game against the Minnesota Twins on May 17. The only other perfect game in Yankee history had been Don Larsen's 2–0 masterpiece in the fifth game of the 1956 World Series against the Dodgers. The eerie coincidence between the two was that Larsen and Wells were both unapologetic free spirits who went to the same Point Loma High School in San Diego.

The Yankees continued their dominance in the '98 postseason, sweeping the Texas Rangers in three games in the Division Series, before avenging their '97 loss to the Indians by dispatching them in six games in the American League Championship Series. They then capped the spectacular season with a World Series sweep of the San Diego Padres.

The '99 season, while ending in similar triumph, was nevertheless tinged with tragedy and serious illness. On March 8, two weeks into spring training, came the word out of Hollywood, Florida, that Joe DiMaggio, the "greatest living Yankee," had passed away after a lengthy battle with lung cancer at age 84. Two days later, Torre stunned his team by announcing he had been diagnosed with prostate cancer that would require immediate surgery, followed by a lengthy absence from the team. The 68-year-old Zimmer, who was severely handicapped himself by a bad knee, was appointed interim manager for the rest of spring training and the first 36 games of the season. On June 19 the 40-year-old Raines went on the disabled list for the rest of the season after being diagnosed with lupus, a disease of the connective tissues that, while treatable, has no known cure. Then, on September 9, the Yankees were jolted by more tragedy with the news of the death of Hall of

Famer Catfish Hunter from amyotrophic lateral sclerosis (Lou Gehrig's disease) in Hertford, North Carolina. At Steinbrenner's urging, Hunter had visited the Yankee spring training camp in Tampa the previous March. Steinbrenner was right about the visit being uplifting and therapeutic for both the Yankees and Hunter, but shortly afterward the great pitcher's condition worsened rapidly. Finally, and most close to home, the fathers of three Yankees—Scott Brosius, Luis Sojo and O'Neill—all passed away during the course of the '99 season.

On the morning of the fourth and final game of the '99 World Series against the Braves, O'Neill's father, Chick, died in Lenox Hill Hospital in Manhattan at age 79 from heart disease. In his grief, O'Neill played the full nine innings in right field in the Yankees' 4–1 victory over Atlanta—their 12th straight World Series win going back to '96. As the Yankees celebrated their 25th world championship in the Yankee Stadium infield after the final out, O'Neill covered his eyes and wept uncontrollably. His dad, a onetime minor league pitcher in the Dodger chain, had been everything to him; the man who molded him as a ballplayer and a competitor.

"You think you're prepared for those things," O'Neill said in recalling that bittersweet night. "But you're never prepared. I'm grateful I had a chance to talk to my dad a couple of days before. He understood we were playing in the World Series and the last thing he would have wanted was for me not to play. Winning that 25th world championship was huge, but I had my father in my mind the whole game. There's not a day that goes by where somebody or something doesn't remind me of him. He was my hero."

In winning their third straight world championship in 2000, the Yankees held first place from July 7 on and managed to survive a horrendous late-season slump in which they lost 15 of 18 games from September 14 to 30 and were outscored 148–59 while nearly squandering the nine-game lead they'd had at the start of the month. Although puzzled by the near-total breakdown of his team's play, Torre remained confident there would be no hangover into the postseason—

and he was right. Still, getting to the World Series for the third straight year was no cakewalk. It took them the full five games to finally put away the Oakland A's in the Division Series and another six before knocking out the Mariners in the ALCS. The reward for that exhaustive process was a Subway Series against the Mets and the predictable accompanying media circus.

The Yankees won a riveting Game 1, 4–3 in 12 innings, tying it in the ninth off Mets closer Armando Benitez. It was O'Neill who started the tying rally by drawing a one-out walk. A pair of singles then loaded the bases for Chuck Knoblauch, who lofted a sacrifice fly to send the game into extra innings and history. No Met reached base after the ninth inning against the Yankee bullpen trio of Nelson, Rivera and Mike Stanton, while in the 12th, reserve infielder Jose Vizcaino, who was given a rare start by Torre because of his lifetime success (10-for-19) against Mets starter Al Leiter, climaxed a 4-for-6 night by singling home the winning run. In all, it took four hours and 51 minutes to complete the longest World Series game ever.

Game 2 touched off the wild hostilities between the two clubs, sending the media into a frenzy, the likes of which New York baseball fans hadn't witnessed since the Dodgers and Giants left town in 1957. In the center of it all was Roger Clemens, once a hated Yankee rival all those years as the preeminent pitcher in the American League with the Red Sox. Clemens, who had spurned Steinbrenner's advances after being written off and sent into the free agent market by the Red Sox after the 1996 season, wound up in pinstripes anyway, just prior to spring training of '99, when he was acquired in a blockbuster trade from the Toronto Blue Jays for David Wells. He was a modest 13-8 in 2000, and after hurling a brilliant and vintage one-hitter against the Mariners in the ALCS, drew the starting assignment for Game 2.

There had been considerable anticipation of Clemens's start, stemming back to a July 8 incident in which the hard-throwing "Rocket Man" had hit Mike Piazza in the head with a fastball during an interleague game between the two city rivals. In the days leading up to

Clemens's World Series start, the local TV stations and ESPN repeatedly showed the replay of the Clemens's skulling of Piazza, which further inflamed the passions of the New York baseball fans.

And when they finally faced off the tensions exploded in a way no one could have predicted. This time, Piazza hit a foul ball that shattered his bat, a large portion of which shot straight out to the mound at Clemens. Not realizing the ball was foul, Piazza began running to first at the same time Clemens, having retrieved the bat portion, heaved it across the first base foul line. The jagged piece of wood barely missed Piazza and, as the two glared at each other and exchanged angry words, both dugouts emptied. Order was quickly restored and Clemens was eventually fined $50,000 for his actions, but for the rest of the World Series, the media was consumed with Clemens, who, by the way, went on to pitch eight shutout innings in the Yankees' 6–5 Game 2 win, which was nearly blown by the bullpen.

Although the Mets did manage to end the Yankees' streak of 14 consecutive World Series wins by ambushing Orlando (El Duque) Hernandez with a pair of eighth-inning runs in a 4–2 Game 3 victory, Yankee pitching dominated the next two nights at Shea Stadium, 3–2 and 4–2, to prevent a Clemens-Piazza redux.

For O'Neill, the 2000 postseason had been a gradual recovery process from the hip pointer he'd suffered in September. He stumbled through the final month of the season; hit just .211 in the Division Series against the Athletics and .250 with five RBI against Seattle in the ALCS. His World Series against the Mets was one of his best—9-for-19, .474—after which he said: "Whether you like us or not, we're winners. Everybody was waiting for the collapse after the way we played in September. Everybody was waiting for us to lose."

The cast came off September 24, more than a week later than the doctors had initially projected, and still O'Neill was hurting. He took some balls in the outfield a couple of days later, reporting that he felt much better but was "by no means 100 percent." At the same time,

Torre expressed reservations about O'Neill being on the postseason roster, at least for the first round of playoffs. "Sure I'd like to be in there," O'Neill said evenly. "But there's no reason to go out there if I can't compete."

The extension of the regular season through the first week of October in order to make up the games postponed by the events of September 11 gave O'Neill the time he needed to get his foot well enough to play. He returned to the lineup October 3 against the Chicago White Sox, as the Yankees' designated hitter, not right fielder, and singled to right in his first at bat. In his third at bat, he slammed a two-run homer into the right-center field bleachers, providing the Yankees with their 2–1 margin of victory. It had been nearly six weeks since O'Neill had felt so good, although he chose not to test his foot by stepping out of the dugout and acknowledging the Yankee Stadium crowd of 14,695 imploring him to take a curtain call. Instead, he offered a sheepish wave of his helmet as if embarrassed by the crowd's reaction.

"It's just not me, stopping the game for 8,000 people," he said later.

After experiencing no further pain in his playing time against the Tampa Bay Devil Rays over the final weekend of the series, O'Neill pronounced himself ready for the playoffs. Torre agreed, but with the condition he not play in the field, at least for the first round against the Athletics.

At the outset, it appeared as if O'Neill's final postseason was going to be very brief.

Because of their superb trio of hard-throwing young starters, Tim Hudson, Mark Mulder and Barry Zito, the A's were actually slight favorites over the defending world champions for the Division Series, in part, too, because of the perception that the Yankees had lost some of their offensive might each succeeding year after the great '98 season. So when the A's won the first two games of the Division Series at Yankee Stadium, never trailing in either of them, the obituaries were being written in earnest. Even the Yankees' staunchest believers had doubts about their ability to win two games in Oakland and bring the series back home, although, as O'Neill revealed later, the players were not among them.

Game 3 in Oakland, in which Mike Mussina and Rivera out-dueled Zito 1–0, was, if nothing else, an omen that the Yankees hadn't lost their clutch touch. The lone run came in the fifth inning when Yankee catcher Jorge Posada, hitless in nine previous career at bats against Zito, hit an 0-1 fastball over the left-field wall. But if that was the deciding blow, the saving play—and the one largely credited with turning the series around—was supplied by Jeter two innings later. With the A's Jeremy Giambi on first base with two outs, Terrence Long hit a drive into the right field corner. Yankee right-fielder Shane Spencer fielded the ball cleanly, but in his haste to get it back to the infield overthrew the cutoff man. Giambi, who was running with the pitch, rounded third and, initially, looked certain to score standing up. But rushing in from his shortstop position to the no-man's-land between first base and the pitcher's mound where Spencer's relay had ended up, Jeter scooped the ball up and flipped it backhand to Posada, who applied the tag on the astonished Giambi. Afterward, Jeter matter-of-factly explained the play was something the Yankees had worked on in spring training—a statement A's third base coach Ron Washington found hard to swallow.

Before the game the next day, Washington sought out Zimmer to ask about Jeter's claim.

"Don't try to tell us you guys really practice that play in spring training," Washington said.

"Well, if you don't believe it, then don't ask me," Zimmer retorted.

"Honestly," Washington said, "why would you practice a play like that—where a guy misses the two cutoff men?"

Zimmer responded by explaining the play was actually the offshoot of a similarly botched cutoff during a routine spring training workout.

"I was a shortstop practically my whole career," Zimmer said, "and never once did I go near the first base line. But I'm saying to myself, on a play like this, the shortstop has nothing else to do. Why not have him serve as a kind of rover around the mound area where he can back up on any play?"

"Okay," said Washington, partly mollified. "I'll give you the fact that you guys actually worked on the play. But how do you explain the throw being in the absolute perfect place for the catcher to put the tag on the base runner?"

To that, a sly smile came over Zimmer's face. "Derek Jeter," he replied.

Later that day, the Yankees accomplished what few had thought possible a few days earlier. They pummeled the A's 9–2, with Bernie Williams driving in five of the runs, to force a deciding fifth game at Yankee Stadium. O'Neill, who had not played against Zito the previous day and had been the DH in the first two games, was in right field for the fourth game and went 1-for-3.

Sitting alone at his locker as his teammates were busily dressing for the trip home, O'Neill shook his head when I suggested to him that perhaps the reports of the Yankees' demise had been a tad premature.

"We haven't accomplished anything," he snapped, "other than coming out here and winning two ball games."

He was right, of course. There was still one to go and the Yankees, above all, had proven the home field advantage to be a myth in postseason. Still, as I hovered there, it was as if he suddenly felt a need to release some of his pent-up passion for winning.

"You know," he said, looking straight at me now, "there's a reason why we're so driven. We know what it is to lose. We've felt the heartbreak."

With that, he brushed past me and headed off to the shower. That was the first time I realized how much the loss to the Indians in '97 had affected him. He'd said what he said, made his point about the mettle of his team, and as I headed out of the clubhouse to the elevator that led upstairs to the press box, I, too, had no doubt of the outcome the next night in New York.

Clemens was nowhere near his best for Game 5, but neither was

Game 1 winner Mulder or the A's defense which committed three critical errors that led to runs. Both Clemens and Mulder were gone in the fifth, but the Yankee bullpen pitched shutout ball over the last four innings to seal the 5–3 victory.

Having cleared that significant hurdle, the Yankees now faced Piniella's Mariners, winners of an American League record 116 games during the regular season, for the right to advance to the World Series for the fourth straight year. They caught a break, however, when their old nemesis, the Indians, extended the Mariners the full five games in the Division Series and, in the process, put Piniella's pitching rotation in disarray.

Piniella was forced to open the ALCS in Seattle with his third-best starter, Aaron Sele, who surrendered a two-run homer to O'Neill in the fourth that sent the Yankees off to a 4–2 win behind the combined four-hit pitching of Pettitte and Rivera. Continuing their uncanny postseason success on the road, the Yankees beat Piniella's ace, Freddy Garcia, 3–2 in Game 2. Then, after absorbing a 14–3 clobbering in Game 3 at Yankee Stadium, the Yankees finished the Mariners off with victories the next two nights. In defeat, Piniella paid tribute to the New York fans, saying he had to feel good for them, "considering all they've been through since 9/11." Then, noting that O'Neill's parting shot at him had been a 5-for-12 (.417) series with two homers and three RBI, Piniella said: "I don't have anything against Paul. In truth, I really like the guy. I have nothing but the utmost respect for him as a player. If you really want to know the truth, the reason I was so hard on him was because, too many times, when he'd get the red-ass, he reminded me of me."

When the World Series opened in Arizona on the last weekend of October, O'Neill found himself on the bench. Sentiment aside, Torre had decided that, without the designated hitter, he had to go with his best percentage hitters against the Diamondbacks' formidable 1-2 pitching aces, Curt Schilling and Randy Johnson—and, on that count, O'Neill didn't make it. The stats showed he was 4-for-19 (.211) against Schilling lifetime, while David Justice, whom Torre had tabbed to play right field, was 10-for-28 with four homers and 12 RBI against the D'back righty.

"Joe believes David will have success," the disappointed O'Neill said. Then, forcing a smile, he added: "Obviously, I should've taken those at bats against Schilling more seriously."

With O'Neill on the bench, the Yankees lost both games in Arizona, Schilling limiting them to three hits and one run over seven innings and Johnson dominating them with a three-hit, 11-strikeout 4–0 shutout in Game 2. Justice went 0-for-3 against Schilling in Game 1, while Shane Spencer, Torre's right fielder for Game 2, managed one of the three Yankee singles off Johnson.

When the Yankees arrived at the Yankee Stadium clubhouse for Game 3, they found Yogi Berra waiting for them. Berra was not throwing out the ceremonial first pitch on this night—President George W. Bush had assumed that duty as a defiant gesture to the terrorists who would seek to inflict more death and destruction on New York City. But Torre considered Berra a good-luck charm and always wanted him around for big games. For his part, Berra liked getting to the ballpark early and hanging around the clubhouse, mingling with the players. Upon spotting Jeter at his locker, Berra approached him and said sternly: "You guys better win this thing. 'Cause if you don't, you gotta start all over."

Jeter laughed and nodded, as if to acknowledge the subtle message. Ever since he'd arrived on the scene in 1996, he'd marveled at Berra's 10 world championship rings, while half-kiddingly vowing to catch him. After the Yankees won their third World Series in a row the year before, Berra had reminded Jeter that *his* Yankee teams had won five in a row from 1949 to 1953.

Later that night, despite a still sputtering offense, the Yankees rediscovered their winning touch, edging the D'backs 2–1 on the three-hit pitching of Clemens and Rivera, thus setting the stage for two of the most memorable World Series games ever played.

Halloween night, they were down to their final out, trailing 4–2 in the ninth inning of Game 4 with Byung-Hyun Kim, the Diamondbacks' side-arming closer, seemingly about to lock it away. Kim, who had come on in the eighth and struck out the side in electrifying fashion, got Jeter on a groundout and struck Williams out to start the ninth. But then O'Neill—who Zimmer had always said could never be the final out—worked Kim to a full count before stroking an opposite-field base hit to left. That brought to the plate Tino Martinez, who, like O'Neill, was in his final days as a Yankee, though not by his own choice.

The worst-kept secret in baseball over the latter part of the 2001 season had been the Yankees' keen interest in Oakland's free-agent-to-be first baseman, Jason Giambi, the American League MVP in 2000 and runner-up to Seattle's sensational Japanese import Ichiro Suzuki in 2001. It didn't seem to matter to the Yankee brass that Martinez, off five solid 100-RBI seasons in six years with the team, was a huge fan favorite in New York and one of the most respected players in the clubhouse. His contract was up and the decision had long ago been made to adhere to the old Branch Rickey credo of getting rid of a player one year too soon rather than one year too late. The fans sensed Tino's imminent departure, too, and when he launched a line drive over the center field fence—his first hit of the Series—to tie the score in shocking fashion, the outpouring of appreciation and affection that flowed out of the stands was something to rival any of the great ovations at Yankee Stadium over the previous 75 years.

Thanks to O'Neill and Martinez, the two mainstays of this magical six-year Yankee run, they were back in business again. And in the 10th, the third principal performer of that run, Jeter, ended it with another two-out homer off Kim, who had turned into the Halloween night pumpkin. Just after Jeter connected, the scoreboard clock registered twelve midnight, and, an instant later, the scoreboard flashed: "Mr. November!"

Oh the days dwindle down, to a precious few . . . September, November . . .

There could never be another night like this at Yankee Stadium. Or could there?

Game 5 followed the same low-scoring script; the Diamondbacks striking for a pair of runs off Mussina in the fifth on solo homers by veteran center fielder Steve Finley and unsung reserve catcher Rod Barajas (who was filling in for injured Damian Miller), and taking that lead into the ninth. Once again Arizona manager Bob Brenly turned to his closer, Kim, to finish it and once again the 22-year-old Korean, after surrendering a lead-off double to Jorge Posada, was one out away from doing just that. Suddenly and in equally stunning fashion, it was Brosius, another of the old-guard Yankees whose contract was set to expire and who would not be back, who homered to left to tie the score. In every nook and cranny of Yankee Stadium—most notably the press box where most of the scribes, hardened to one miracle per decade, had already filed their columns and game stories—there was utter disbelief. As he watched Brosius's ball sail over the fence, Kim buried his head in his hands in despair. His infield teammates immediately surrounded him at the mound to console him.

For the second straight night, the game went into nail-biting extra innings. In the eleventh, the Diamondbacks threatened to break through on Rivera, loading the bases on singles by Danny Bautista and Erubiel Durazo, a sacrifice bunt and an intentional walk to Finley. But Rivera managed to extricate himself by getting Reggie Sanders on a liner to Soriano at second and Mark Grace on an infield force-out. In the 12th Brenly was forced to bring in Albie Lopez, his designated long man and mop-up reliever, and the Yankees seized the opportunity for victory as Chuck Knoblauch led off with a single, was sacrificed to second and brought home on a single by rookie Alfonso Soriano. Elias Sports Bureau research later revealed the Yankees to be the first team in postseason history to win two straight games when trailing after eight innings.

It had been an exhilarating and uplifting two straight nights for the Yankees and New York City, sobered quickly by the fact that the sudden death heroics had merely earned them a return trip to the desert and another go-round against the dual imposing presence of

Schilling and Johnson. And in Game 6, in which Pettitte came up empty and was battered from the game in the second inning, it was as if the Yankees had expended everything they had winning those games back in New York. They were clobbered 15-2, the Diamondbacks setting a World Series record with 22 hits. The 13-run loss was the worst ever inflicted on the Yankees in 293 postseason games and, for his part, Johnson was able to coast, turning the game over to the Arizona bullpen after seven innings.

In the Yankee clubhouse before Game 7, there was little conversation and none regarding the reality of this being the final game for so many of the team's core veterans, O'Neill, Martinez, Brosius and Knoblauch. "We had talked periodically about that during the last 6, 7 weeks of the season," O'Neill said, "but it was really kind of left unsaid. I knew I wasn't going to be back, but I'm not sure if the rest of them were so sure. We knew we had a job to do—a job we'd done so many times before—and I think that's all anybody was thinking about."

It became quickly apparent this game would be nothing like the previous night's travesty as Clemens and Schilling set out to keep matters orderly. Years earlier, while working out at a gym in Houston during the off-season, Schilling had suddenly been confronted by Clemens, who was also working out there. "You're an embarrassment to the pitching fraternity," Clemens told him. "Your work habits are a disgrace, you're wasting your talent and cheating the game." From that day forward, Schilling emulated Clemens, crediting him with turning his career around. Now here he was, facing off against his idol and mentor in the most important game of his career.

That did not stop him from predicting he would win the game in the postgame interview room the night before, and after six innings, it looked as if he was going to be right. The Yankees, who had managed only two runs and six hits off Schilling in his two previous Series starts, were trailing 1–0 going into the seventh when the old guard rose to the occasion one more time. Jeter and O'Neill started the inning with singles—the first Yankee hits off Schilling since the first—

and after Bernie Williams grounded into an infield force-out, Martinez singled home Jeter with the tying run. Schilling, who had tired and asked out of Game 4 after throwing 88 pitches, threw 90 pitches through the first seven innings and convinced Brenly to let him pitch the eighth. It was a decision they both would regret when the precocious Soriano led off the inning with a homer into the left field seats to put the Yankees up 2–1.

Once more, this was the prototype for all those Yankee championship victories since '96—keep it close with good starting pitching and get the lead to Rivera. Clemens, in out-pitching his admiring younger rival, struck out 10 over six and a third innings, and after Mike Stanton got the final two D'backs in the seventh, Torre turned the game over to Rivera for a six-out save. The eighth was vintage Rivera—three Diamondback strikeouts around a harmless single by Finley, and even when the veteran Mark Grace led off the ninth with a single to center, there was no undue concern on the Yankee bench.

In the pregame clubhouse meeting, it had been the normally quiet and reserved Rivera who'd surprised his teammates by saying aloud: "We're going to win, but no matter what happens, it's in God's hands."

Because of all this team had accomplished with four championships in the previous five years, Rivera was confident in its ability to get the job done. At the same time, though, he was a deeply religious man who understood that all things in life were subject to a higher being. In this case, it was his fielding above all else that betrayed him. With Brenly having ordered the sacrifice, Rivera quickly pounced on Miller's bunt, only to throw wild to second as pinch runner David Dellucci slid in safe. Now there were two on and nobody out. Another bunt by Jay Bell was turned into a force of Dellucci at third by Rivera and, momentarily, the din from the 47,589 Diamondback fans subsided.

When Tony Womack doubled into the right field corner to score pinch runner Midre Cummings with the tying run, it marked the first time Rivera had blown a postseason save since the homer to the Indians'

Sandy Alomar in '97. Moments later, Luis Gonzalez muscled a soft liner into left-center over the drawn-in Yankee infield and Rivera had lost the game as well. As the Diamondbacks celebrated on the infield, O'Neill, Rivera and Torre watched numbly from the Yankee dugout. They were physically, mentally and emotionally drained but somehow, they would say later, they didn't feel defeated. Unlike '97, they didn't feel there was anything more they could have done.

"We lost this World Series in an unbelievable manner," O'Neill would say to the media horde a few minutes later. "This World Series is going to be on Sports Classic next week, but this team should not be judged by Game 7, 2001. Too much has been accomplished by one group of people to have this be the only memory. We hustled. We battled. It's hard to get to this point of the season. You ask Boston. You ask Seattle. You ask Oakland. We were world champions with three outs to go and the best pitcher in the world, in my mind, going. There is utter disappointment, yes. But I was able to walk into this clubhouse with these guys for the last time, which is awesome. I can't be more blessed than I was. It's been a great nine years in this locker room."

Later that night, he would take the last plane ride home with them and while there would be tears, they would not be the same kind of tears as on the long flight back from Seattle in '95 or the equally melancholy short hop from Cleveland in '97. In his mind, they had all been warriors and, even in defeat, they had honor for the way they'd played the game. And *that* was what they'd be remembered for.

index

Sudakis, Bill, 299, 327
Sundra, Steve, 27-28
Suzuki, Ichiro, 322, 433

Tarnopol, Nat, 276-77
Taylor, Eddie, 199-200, 206
Tebbetts, Birdie, 115, 118, 259, 310
Terry, Ralph, 78, 174, 184
   in World Series, 75, 180-82, 231-32
Texas Rangers, 272, 297, 334, 378-79,
   396, 414, 417, 424
Thomas, Ira, 45-46
Thomson, Bobby, 69-70
Throneberry, Marv, 173-74
Tiant, Luis, 273-74
Tidrow, Dick, 211, 281, 323
Tittle, Y. A., 255-56
Topping, Dan, 111, 183-85, 192, 205,
   228, 290
   Berra and, 76-78, 80, 83, 185, 235
   Byrne and, 47, 52
   color barrier and, 149
   Houk and, 178, 183-84
Toronto Blue Jays, 208, 303, 317, 334,
   378, 411, 426
Torre, Joe, 35, 82, 84, 154, 179, 403,
   407-8, 413-19, 421-22, 424-26
   Berra and, 432
   cancer of, 424
   Jackson and, 345
   O'Neill and, 413-14, 419, 428, 431-32
   post-season and, 124, 340, 417-19,
   421, 426, 428, 431-32, 436-37
   Stottlemyre and, 198, 214
Torrez, Mike, 349, 360
Tresh, Tom, 203, 207, 234, 258
Triandos, Gus, 89, 148
Trimble, Joe, 99, 236
Turley, Bob, 54-55, 179-80
Turner, Jim, 97-98, 138

Vaughan, Arky, 32, 91
Veeck, Bill, 159-60, 283
Verdi, Frank, 278-79
Vernon, Mickey, 53, 386
Villante, Tom, 192-93
Virdon, Bill, 74-75, 160, 296-98, 326-29

Murcer and, 297-98, 300, 308, 327
Piniella and, 327-28, 332
Vizquel, Omar, 415, 422

Waldman, Suzyn, 82
Walker, Harry, 38, 263
Washington, Ron, 429-30
Washington Senators, 11, 52-53, 65,
   68, 101, 112, 127, 133-34, 152,
   159, 293, 386
   Byrne and, 48-50, 52
   farm teams of, 318-19
Weaver, Earl, 191, 195, 320, 326-27
Webb, Del, 111, 175, 178, 183-85, 192,
   205, 228, 290
Weiss, George, 54, 92, 104, 111, 184,
   209, 354
   Berra and, 63-64
   Byrne and, 45, 47, 51-52, 59
   Coleman and, 121-22
   color barrier and, 149-50
   Ford and, 136-37
   Houk and, 174
   Howard and, 150
   Rizzuto and, 17-18
Welch, Bob, 363-64
Wells, David, 317, 396, 424, 426
Wetteland, John, 401-2, 412, 417, 419-20
White, Bill, 161, 275
White, Ray, 6-9
White, Roy, 334, 357, 366
Wight, Bill, 89, 107
Williams, Bernie, 402-3, 410, 421,
   423, 430, 433, 436
Williams, Dick, 296, 348, 350
Williams, Don, 22-25
Williams, Mitch, 378
Williams, Pat, 23-24
Williams, Ted, 17, 31-32, 53-54, 72-73,
   86, 105, 113
Wills, Maury, 350
Winfield, Dave, 336, 367, 383-84, 409
   Mattingly and, 387-90, 393, 395
Wood, Wilbur, 361-62
Woodling, Gene, 91-92, 98, 102-3, 112, 135

Yastrzemski, Carl, 207, 328
Young, Dick, 153, 164, 190, 209-10, 360